ISLAM IN THE MODERN WORLD

ISLAM
IN THE
MODERN
WORLD
and Other Studies

Elie Kedourie

A NEW REPUBLIC BOOK

HOLT, RINEHART AND WINSTON
New York

First published in the United States in 1981 by
Holt, Rinehart and Winston, 383 Madison Avenue,
New York, New York 10017.
Published simultaneously in Canada by Holt, Rinehart
and Winston of Canada, Limited.

Library of Congress Cataloging in Publication Data
Kedourie, Elie.
Islam in the modern world and other studies.
Includes bibliographical references and index.
1. Near East — History — 20th century. I. Title.
DS62.4.K43   956′.04   80-17181
(Holt, Rinehart and Winston)
ISBN: 0-03-059213-5

First American Edition

First Printed in the United Kingdom by Mansell Publishing
1 3 5 7 9 10 8 6 4 2

Author's Note

This book complements two earlier works, *The Chatham House Version and Other Middle-Eastern Studies*, published in 1970, and *Arabic Political Memoirs and Other Studies*, published in 1974. Like the two other works, this one too presents various aspects of the fateful contact in modern times between the West and the Middle East. Certain themes are common to all three works: Great-Power policies in the region from the first world war onwards and the coming to be and spread of an ideological-nationalist and radical style of politics in the Arab world. But the present work sets out also to explore in detail a theme only touched upon in the earlier books, that of the fortunes of Islam in the Middle East under the stress and pressure of modernity, and the various ways in which it has tried to come to terms with, assimilate, or challenge the categories of modernity, particularly in those areas where politics and religion meet and intermingle.

The 17 chapters which make up this book have, with one exception, all been written in the past five years. Chapters 5 and 8 appear here for the first time. The other chapters, some in slightly different form, appeared as follows:

Chapter 1 in Bernard Lewis, ed., *The World of Islam*, Thames and Hudson, London, 1976; Chapter 2 in *The British Journal of Sociology*, London, Vol. VII, no. 3, September 1956; Chapter 3 in *The Policy Review*, Washington, Spring 1980; Chapter 4 in A. Udovitch, ed., *Critical Choices for Americans, Vol. X, The Middle East: Oil, Conflict and Hope*, Lexington Books, D.C. Heath and Company, Lexington, Massachusetts, 1976; Chapter 6 in *The Political Economy of the Middle East—Changes and Prospects since 1973*, Washington, 1980; Chapter 7 in *The Washington Review*, Washington, Vol. 1, no. 3, July 1978; Chapter 9 in *The Times Literary Supplement*, London, 30 November 1979; Chapter 10 in *Encounter*, London, August 1975; Chapter 11 in the *Times Literary Supplement*, London, 21 April 1978; Chapter 12 in the proceedings of a conference on the United States and the Middle East held at Tel Aviv University in 1978 and published by transaction books, Rutgers University Press, Trenton, N.J.; Chapter 13 in *Encounter*, London, May 1978;

Chapter 14 in *Commentary*, New York, July 1979; Chapter 15 in *Commentary*, New York, July 1977; Chapter 16 in *Middle Eastern Studies*, London, Vol. 13, no. 1, January 1977; and Chapter 17 in *The American Scholar*, Washington, Autumn 1979.

I am grateful to the respective editors and publishers for permission to reprint. Crown copyright records are reproduced by kind permission of the Controller, Her Majesty's Stationery Office.

I would like once again to thank the staff of the Public Record Office, London, of the Archives du Ministère des Affaires Etrangères, and of the Service Historique de l'Armée, Paris, for unfailingly efficient and helpful service.

I am particularly obliged to the Rockefeller Foundation for inviting me to the Villa Serbelloni, Bellagio, in the summer of 1978. The beauty and elegance of the surroundings and Dr. and Mrs. Olson's attentive and exemplary hospitality provided a magnificent setting and ideal conditions in which to study and to reflect. It was at the Villa Serbelloni that much of the work relating to Chapter 8 was done.

E.K.

The London School of Economics and Political Science,
March 1980

CONTENTS

ISLAM IN THE MODERN WORLD

1

ISLAM IN THE MODERN WORLD

The last two hundred years or so have not been kind either to Islam or to the Muslims. From the latter part of the 18th century their territories, whether in the centre or at the periphery, were simultaneously or successively under attack from non-Muslim Europeans. In Bengal, the British East India Company was becoming a fully fledged government, gradually branching out into the rest of the Indian sub-continent and supplanting the authority of the Mughal emperor of Delhi. Similarly the Dutch government, taking over the properties and rights of the Dutch East India Company in 1800, had decisively established its authority in Java by the fourth decade of the 19th century. In 1830, France invaded Algeria, and after almost two decades of war succeeded in conquering the country and opening it up to large-scale European colonization. During the same period, Russia too was steadily bringing into subjection ancient Muslim lands in the Caucasus and in Central Asia, and encouraging their settlement by large numbers of non-Muslims.

This process whereby large, immemorially Muslim territories came to be occupied or controlled by non-Muslims went on well into the 20th century. Between 1865 and 1873 Tsarist Russia extinguished the independence of the Central Asian amirate of Khokand and established a protectorate over the two other amirates of Khiva and Bukhara. France established a protectorate over Tunisia in 1881, and to all intents and purposes became its ruler. The British occupied Egypt in 1882, and remained its rulers, practically if not formally, until after World War I. The British occupation of Egypt led in due course to the establishment of an Anglo-Egyptian 'condominium' in the Sudan, in which the real power was unequivocally in the hands of the British. By the end of the 19th century, also, the Dutch had conquered the native kingdoms of Sumatra and established a rich and extensive empire in the islands of the Indonesian archipelago. And by the 1880s, the Muslim rulers of neighbouring Malaya came to acknowledge Britain as the protecting power. In the first decade or so of the 20th century, Italy invaded and conquered Tripolitania; and the French established a protectorate over the greater part of Morocco, while

the Spaniards, as their junior partners, exercised their protectorate over the rest of the Sharifian kingdom. As in Tunisia, in Morocco too the protecting powers established a network of their own officials who in effect governed the country.

European power affected Muslim states in other, indirect ways. By a natural development, the British empire in India led to British paramountcy in the Persian Gulf and to the control of Aden and Hadramawt. It also gave Britain a privileged position in southern Persia. Similarly, on the eve of World War I, the Ottoman empire had come to be divided into zones of influence between the European powers by means of informal, but nonetheless effective, understandings that allowed them to establish a preponderance of economic enterprise and, if they could, of political influence. As a direct result of this expansion, and of the concomitant weakening of Ottoman power and prestige, the Christian populations of the Balkans began to aspire to independence. These aspirations, supported more or less actively by one or other European power, led eventually to the independence of Greece, Serbia, Rumania and Bulgaria. All these territories contained sizable and old established Muslim populations whose position was undermined, and whose possessions and lives were, in many cases, imperilled or destroyed.

The long period of European dominance reached its apogee during and after World War I, in which its Young Turk rulers led the Ottoman empire to defeat and eventual destruction. The end of the war saw Mesopotamia and the Levant under Allied occupation, with British troops in Baghdad and Damascus—cities which had been Muslim time out of mind, and which no Christian had ever conquered. The aftermath of war, and the Bolshevik Revolution which it occasioned, led, in 1920, to the final extinction of Khiva and Bukhara as distinct entities, and the incorporation of their territories, in due course, within the USSR.

The term that is most frequently used to describe this European expansion into the Muslim world (and elsewhere) is imperialism. The term has now in fact become little more than a slogan or a catchword. Its origins, in any case, lie in European political and intellectual history, and it is only in the European context that it is at all intelligible. Muslims certainly would not have understood it or found it of much use in explaining their predicament. In their own traditional categories, the conflict with Europe, which issued in such a dismal series of political and military reverses, would have been seen as a clash between Islam and Christendom—as the latest phase of a conflict in which, over many centuries, two worlds, two militant faiths, had confronted and defied one another.

In this protracted confrontation, which dated from the beginnings of Islam, the Muslims had so far on the whole been conspicuously successful. Spain, it is true, had in the end been lost; but the other areas taken from the Christians became irreversibly Muslim, became indeed the heartlands of

Islam. The Grand Duchy of Moscow, again, had liberated itself from Tatar domination; but, on the other hand, the Ottoman empire succeeded in annexing extensive Christian territories in the Balkans and in Central Europe, and its armies could threaten Vienna as late as the 1680s. This long record of military success and assured domination had for Muslims a transcendental significance. It served to prove that Muhammad's message was true, that God prospered those who believed in Him and hearkened to His revelation. Political success vindicated Islam, and the course of world history proved the truth of the religion. Muslims fought to extend the bounds of Islam and humble the unbelievers; the fight was holy, and the reward of those who fell was eternal bliss. Such a belief, which the history of Islam itself seemed to establish beyond doubt, inspired in Muslims self-confidence and powerful feelings of superiority. Hence, the long series of defeats at the hands of Christian Europe could not but undermine the self-respect of the Muslims, and result in a far-reaching moral and intellectual crisis. For military defeat was defeat not only in a worldly sense; it also brought into doubt the truth of the Muslim revelation itself.

The loss of self-confidence, the failure of nerve which a long series of setbacks and defeats induced, took quite long to manifest itself. Even though there was great disproportion between European military and technical resources and those at the disposal of Muslim society, opposition to European encroachments was in many cases remarkably stout-hearted, resourceful and tenacious. The French landing in Algiers elicited native resistance which the conquerors found by no means easy to overcome. The best known of those who organized and led this resistance was the famous Abd al-Qadir, who originated from Oran in western Algeria. In the course of fighting the French between 1833 and 1847, when he was finally defeated and taken prisoner, Abd al-Qadir amassed a large following of tribes and came to control a large territory not only in the west, but also in the centre and in the east of the country. The French certainly regarded him as more than a mere guerrilla leader and more than once entered into agreements with him—agreements which in many ways resembled treaties between two sovereign states. Abd al-Qadir himself certainly looked upon his role as much more than that of a tribal leader. From the start he and his supporters considered the movement as the setting up (or restoration) of an Islamic polity of which Abd al-Qadir was the Imam who had received the suffrages (bay'a) of the faithful, whose duty was to uphold the faith, and protect the people of Islam. And Abd al-Qadir indeed attempted to set up a state which transcended tribal loyalties and rivalries, and to organize a modern army whose loyalty went to the Imam and to the (embryonic) state which he had set up. For this army, Abd al-Qadir drew up a code which laid down the different ranks of the troops, their respective uniforms and pay and the discipline to which they were subject. The code ended with a description of

Abd al-Qadir himself—an idealized picture, to be sure, but nonetheless significant in showing us precisely the ideal to which he himself looked up. The Imam, the code declared,

> cares not for this world, and withdraws from it as much as his avocations will permit. He despises wealth and riches. He lives with the greatest plainness and sobriety. He is always simply clad. He rises in the middle of the night to recommend his own soul and the soul of his followers to God. His chief pleasure is in praying to God with fasting, that his sins may be forgiven.
>
> He is incorruptible. He never takes anything out of the public funds for himself. All the presents which are brought to him he sends to the public treasury; for he serves the State, not himself. He neither eats, nor drinks, nor dresses, but so as religion ordains. When he administers justice, he hears complaints with the greatest patience. A smile is always on his face for the encouragement of those who approach him. His decisions are conformable to the words of the sacred book. He hates the man who does not act uprightly; but honours him who strictly observes the precepts and practises the duties of religion.
>
> From his boyhood he learned to mount the most fiery horse without a teacher. He never turns before an enemy; but awaits him firmly. In a retreat he fights like a common soldier, rallying his men by his words and example, and sharing all their dangers. Thus, brave, disinterested, and pious, when he preaches, his words bring tears into all eyes, and melt the hardest hearts. All who hear him become good Mussulmans.
>
> He explains the most difficult passages of the Qur'an and of the Hadeeth (Traditions) without referring to books or Ulemahs. The most learned Arabs and the greatest Talebs acknowledge him as their master and teacher. May God increase his nobleness of character, his wisdom, his learning, his understanding, his honour, glory, and success, a thousandfold.

It is immaterial whether Abd al-Qadir was in reality exactly as he is described in this passage. What is more interesting to note here is that this is a deliberate harking back to the simple piety, the uprightness, the egalitarianism and the valour that the faithful believed to characterize Islam under the Prophet and the well-guided caliphs. Abd al-Qadir and his followers indeed took very seriously the parallel between Muhammad's foundation of the Islamic polity and its restoration in Algeria by Abd al-Qadir. His son, in the voluminous biography which he devoted to his father, describes the occasion on which Abd al-Qadir was invested with office. It was Abd al-Qadir's own father who first proclaimed his allegiance to the new leader and gave him the title Nasir ad-Din, Champion of Religion. The ceremony, we are told, took place under a tree, and thus was significantly similar to that earlier one when, in the sixth year of the *hijra*, also under a tree, the Muslims pledged themselves to Muhammad and a Qur'anic verse (xlviii, 18) declared: 'God is pleased with the believers as they pledge themselves to you under the tree. He knows what is in their hearts and gives them peace, and rewards them with a forthcoming conquest.'

At the other end of the Muslim world, in Daghistan, an equally tenacious resistance to the Russian conquest of the Caucasus manifested itself in the movement knows as Muridism. The leaders of this movement were followers, *murids*, of the Naqshbandi religious brotherhood. They proclaimed the primacy of the *shari'a* and the duty incumbent on all Muslims to uphold it, by fighting the unbelievers and resisting their rule. The core of Muridism consisted of a select band of fighters who were organized as a religious brotherhood. This small band of warriors succeeded in over-awing many Daghistani tribes, and inducing or forcing them to join in a *jihad* against the Russian conquerors. The Murids succeeded in maintaining themselves from 1830 to 1859 against repeated assaults mounted by the Russians with all the military and technical resources available to a Great Power. It is of course true that the Murids were fighting a mountain war in terrain with which they were familiar, but the length and tenacity of their resistance remains nonetheless remarkable. There can be no doubt that this is to be attributed to the solidarity, cohesion and self-confidence which Islam produced and maintained. This religious impulse was sufficiently powerful to endow the movement with a rudimentary political structure in which the leaders of the Murids were recognized as Imams by their followers, this politico-religious office being held in succession by three leaders of whom the last, Shamil, became quite well known in the Europe of his day.

Resistance to European penetration took other, sometimes less sustained, but no less significant forms. The disturbance and the threat which this penetration represented would become manifest through the spread of millennial expectation focused and crystallized in the preaching of a leader who would claim to be the *mahdi* or *sahib as-sa'a*, the 'rightly guided one', the 'master of the hour'; he who in Muslim tradition was to inaugurate, by means of prodigies or superhuman acts, the everlasting reign of truth and justice. Thus, about 1838 there appeared in Algeria someone who claimed to be a descendant of Abd al-Qadir al-Jilani, the founder of the Qadiriyya religious brotherhood, and to be called Muhammad ibn Abdullah (i.e. to have the same name as the Prophet). He joined some tribes who were disaffected towards (the Algerian) Abd al-Qadir and began to preach against him. He declared that Abd al-Qadir was powerless to save the Muslims from the Europeans; that on the contrary he was their accomplice.

He claimed that he, Muhammad ibn Abdullah, was the awaited *mahdi* who would bring deliverance to the Muslims. Abd al-Qadir naturally resented this challenge to his authority.

He organized an expedition against the supporters of the so-called *mahdi*, defeated them and thus put an end to his preaching. A few years later, in 1845, when Abd al-Qadir was no longer at the apogee of his power, another *mahdi* appeared. He also was a member of a religious brotherhood, the Darqawa, and also called himself Muhammad ibn Abdullah. Prophecies attributed to a Moroccan saint were applied to this *mahdi*, commonly known as Bu Ma‘za, the Man with the Goat. According to these prophecies the man of the hour would eventually dominate all the Eastern countries, and all of Algeria would belong to him; but only after *banu 'l-asfar*, the yellow ones (i.e. the French), would have taken it: 'If you seize it now,' the prophecy went on, 'they will deprive you of your conquest; if, however, the French take this country first, the day will come when you will take it back from them.' The prophecy was not destined to be fulfilled in Bu Ma‘za's day, for the French defeated his followers and took him captive to France. Decades later, at the beginning of the 20th century, when Morocco was increasingly feeling the effects of European penetration, another member of the Darqawa appeared there to proclaim the millennial hope. Bu Hamara, the Man with the Donkey, who was active in Taza, to the east of Fez, between 1900 and 1909, preached against ‘Abd al-‘Aziz, the Sultan of Morocco. Bu Hamara accused the Sultan of following Western ways and delivering his country over to Christians. He claimed to be in reality a brother of the Sultan and thus a member of the Moroccan ruling house, a descendant of the Prophet. His followers proclaimed him Sultan, and Bu Hamara set up court at Taza as Mawlay Muhammad and proceeded to organize an army and to increase his standing by war as well as by propaganda. Emissaries of his among the Berber tribes quoted alleged sayings of the Prophet, declaring that he was the awaited *mahdi* who would regenerate Islam and expel the Christians from the Maghrib. His defiance of the Moroccan government came to an end when the Sultan's forces captured him and exhibited him in a public garden in Fez locked up in a cage.

Bu Hamara's movement was directed against a Muslim government, but his attack was justified by the allegation that this government was abandoning the Muslims into the hands of Christians. This reason, on the other hand, did not loom very large in the movement of the Sudanese *mahdi*, who in the modern history of Islam has come to be known as the Mahdi *par excellence*. The movement of the Sudanese Mahdi was directed against the Egyptian government headed by a descendant of Muhammad Ali Pasha who had invaded the Sudan in 1820, and against the Ottoman Sultan-caliph who was the nominal suzerain of Egypt. The Mahdi's movement, in other words, was directed primarily against a Muslim government. The Mahdi, Muhammad Ahmad ibn Abdullah, who claimed descent from the Prophet whose name he bore and who had belonged to a religious brotherhood that was an offshoot of the Qadiriyya, preached the restoration of the Islamic *umma* as it had been in the Prophet's time, and the ending of Egyptian rule, which he looked upon as alien and inimical to Islam. As is well known, having begun his movement in 1881, the Mahdi succeeded, with the help of a tribal army, in occupying El Obeid in 1883 and the capital, Khartoum, in 1885, and in setting up a state that survived under his companion and successor Abdullah ibn Muhammad until 1898, when an expedition led by Kitchener finally destroyed the Mahdist state. Though the government against which the Mahdi and his supporters rebelled was Muslim, it was—and had been for some decades—profoundly influenced by Western ideas, and drew heavily on Western administrative techniques, so that the Mahdi's rejection of an Islamic government was to a large extent still really the rejection of Europe.

But it was a rejection at one remove, rejection of ideas and methods that many Muslim governments in the 19th and 20th centuries adopted, whether enthusiastically, or only in sheer self-defense. And, along with direct or indirect European rule over Muslim territories, this spread of European ideas and techniques is the most significant and striking theme in the modern history of Islam.

In 1867, a well-known Muslim statesman, Khayr ad-Din at-Tunisi, who was to become Prime Minister of Tunisia and Grand Vizier in Constantinople, published an Arabic work which set out to acquaint his readers with European civilization and the political arrangements associated with it. The work was prefaced by a long introduction in which Khayr ad-Din examined existing Muslim institutions. This introduction was shortly afterwards translated into French and published under the title, *Réformes nécessaires aux états musulmans*. This title indicates clearly enough that Khayr ad-Din was critical of the Muslim polities of his day, and was convinced that they should be 'reformed'. The 'reforms' he had in mind were unmistakably inspired by the example of a Europe that was powerful and prosperous, and in which the citizen enjoyed freedom under the law. He quotes with approval the words of a 'leading European' to the effect that 'the torrent of European civilization' was overflowing the world and that non-European countries were 'in danger from this current unless they imitate it'. By the time Khayr ad-Din had published his book, this opinion was in fact common currency in Europe, as well as among the intellectual and official classes of the Muslim world. And as time went on, those who held it became much more numerous than those who shared the attitudes of Abd al-Qadir, Shamil, Bu Ma'za or the Mahdi. Nor is this surprising, for there was nothing unreasonable in believing that the Muslim world could attain the power and prosperity of Europe by the same methods that Europe had used, and that this could be done without endangering any of the essential values of Islam.

This was at the outset merely a simple uncritical assumption. In any case, those who had the power to initiate changes on the European model, namely the rulers, had neither need nor leisure to worry about the compatibility of such changes with Islam. By the end of the 18th century, it was amply clear that the military threat posed by the European powers was formidable. Survival meant the quick adoption of European military methods and techniques. The earliest one among Islamic rulers systematically to translate this conclusion into practice was the Ottoman Sultan Selim III (1789–1807). Shortly after his accession, Selim embarked on a determined effort to create modern arsenals and military technical schools. He also began organizing new military formations in which European instructors tried to instill in the recruits the drill and discipline which were by then practised in the armies of the great European states. These methods greatly impressed Selim and his advisers. As one of them wrote in a memorandum advocating the reforms, European troops 'keep in a compact body, pressing their feet together that their order of battle may not be broken; and their cannon being polished like one of Marcovich's watches they load twelve times in a minute and make the bullets rain like musket balls'.

Selim's reforms aroused fear and antagonism among the Janissaries and other traditional formations. Recourse to European methods and instructors was demeaning and irreligious. And a military formation so directly fashioned and controlled by the Sultan, who had stationed it in the environs of Constantinople, not only offended the prejudices of the Janissaries; it also threatened their position and their vested interests. For however infirm the Janissaries were now in the face of foreign enemies, they had become a formidable power in the state, enjoying privilege and profit, and by their readiness to mutiny checking the Sultan's power, and even on occasion deposing him. And, in fact, Selim's *nizam-i jadid,* or new order, so antagonized the Janissary heads and their supporters among the religious leaders that in May 1807 a revolt toppled the 'infidel Sultan' from the throne; and his successor, Mustafa IV, abolished Selim's innovations within a few days of his accession. Mustafa was himself deposed the following year, and replaced by his brother (and Selim's cousin) who reigned as Mahmud II until his death in 1839. The new Sultan resumed Selim's military reforms, but only after a very long interval. In the meantime another Muslim ruler, Muhammad Ali, Pasha of Egypt, tried (with what seemed a large measure of success) to fashion for himself a European-style army and navy with which to forward his very extensive ambitions.

Muhammad Ali, an Albanian from Kavalla, was an officer in the Ottoman force that was sent to Egypt in pursuance of an Anglo-Ottoman scheme to dislodge the French who, led by Bonaparte, had occupied Egypt, nominally an Ottoman province, in 1798. A man of great ability and ruthlessness, he managed to ruin his superiors and his rivals and by 1805 to be recognized by the Sultan as governor of the province. Ottoman Egypt in the 17th and 18th centuries was very much under the control of military grandees, the *mamluks*, who acted in virtual independence of Constantinople. When Muhammad Ali became Pasha of Egypt they were still a powerful force in the land, and able to act as a check on the Ottoman governor in the same way that the Janissaries acted as a check on the Sultan. In 1811 Muhammad Ali managed by treacherous means to massacre most of the *mamluks* and thus secure himself against any internal threat to his power. In 1815 he proceeded to train the forces at his disposal in European military methods. As in Selim's case, European innovations aroused opposition, and there was a mutiny that obliged Muhammad Ali to proceed cautiously. In any case, his ambitions required the recruitment of a large army. To have the necessary reservoir of power he invaded the Sudan in 1820–21 and enslaved large numbers of its inhabitants, whom he sent to Egypt to be incorporated in his armies. Experience, however, showed that slaves did not make good or willing soldiers, and on the advice of his European experts he began conscripting Egyptian *fellahs*. However, conscription had to proceed by violent means, and the peasants reacted with flight, self-mutilation and occasional resistance. Military reform may thus be seen to have meant a great increase in the demands made by the state on the subject, and to have *ipso facto* enhanced the power of the state to make such demands. Muhammad Ali, the modernizer, became literally the owner of Egypt. When he exterminated the *mamluks* he had also confiscated their lands to his own benefit. He also, on various plausible pretexts, confiscated the lands that benefactors had over the centuries put in trust for the upkeep of mosques and other charitable purposes. The beneficiaries of these trusts, writes the chronicler al-Jabarti (who was a contemporary of Muhammad Ali's),

> were greatly disturbed and many of them appealed to the sheikhs, who went off to speak to the pasha on this subject. They said to him that that would lead to the ruin of the mosques, whereupon he replied: 'Where are the flourishing mosques? If anyone is not satisfied with this arrangement let him raise his hands and I will restore the ruined mosques and provide them with the necessary means.' Their protests were of no avail and they returned to their homes.

Muhammad Ali laid his hand not only on the property of the *mamluks* and the charitable foundations. The title to all private property whatsoever became highly uncertain; and the owner was obliged to provide documents and title-deeds to the satisfaction of the Pasha's officials, whose interest and duty was precisely not to be easily satisfied: the more suspicious they were, the better they served the Pasha, and the greater the eagerness of the claimants to sweeten them with benevolences. Muhammad Ali also had a new cadastral survey made, in which his officials used a measuring unit smaller than that previously employed:

> When this was done [al-Jabarti tells us] they reckoned the land in the new *faddan*, showing an increase in area, and proceeded to tax it at the rate of 15, or 14, or 12, or 11, or 10 *riyals* per *faddan*, according to the nature of the region and the quality of the soil. The result was an enormous increase: thus the village which had formerly paid 1,000 *riyals* in taxes—a sum that had given rise to complaints on the part of [tax farmers] and peasants and had resulted in uncollectable arrears—was now assessed at between 10,000 and 100,000 *riyals*, more or less.

Muhammad Ali's centralized government machine was clearly more efficient than any of its ramshackled predecessors in extracting resources from the peasantry to cover his increased military expenditure. But terms like 'machine' and 'extraction' are here only metaphors. The reality to which they refer is simply that of compulsion by force or the threat of force. In his well-known work *The Manners and Customs of the Modern Egyptians,* Edward William Lane has a chapter on 'Government' which, he tells us, was written in 1834 and 1835 during 'the best period' of Muhammad Ali's reign. He includes in this chapter an episode involving the collection of taxes from a village that may serve to describe graphically what Muhammad Ali's extractive activities involved. Lane tells us that a tax-collector demanded 60 *riyals* from a peasant, who was unable to find this sum. So, the tax-collector confiscated the peasant's only possession, a cow, which he ordered to be slaughtered and divided into 60 portions, the butcher receiving the head as his fee. Sixty villagers were then called together, and ordered each to buy for a *riyal* a portion of the cow. The peasant, however, complained to the tax-collector's superior, who ordered all the parties, including the butcher and the 60 villagers, to appear before him. They all confirmed the peasant's story, and the butcher declared that had he refused to kill the cow, the tax-collector would have beaten him and destroyed his house. The Qadi was then sent for and the tax-collector's actions put before him. "He is [declared the Qadi] a cruel tyrant, who oppresses everyone under his authority. Is not a cow worth a hundred and twenty riyals or more? And he has sold this one for sixty riyals: This is tyranny towards the owner." The Defterdar then said to some of his soldiers, "Take the Nazir [i.e. the tax-collector], and strip him, and bind him." This done, he said to the butcher, "Butcher, dost thou not fear God? Thou hast killed the cow unjustly." The butcher again urged that he was obliged to obey the Nazir. "Then," said the Defterdar, "if I order thee to do a thing wilt thou do it?" "I will do it," answered the butcher. "Slaughter the Nazir," said the Defterdar. Immediately, several of the soldiers present seized the Nazir, and threw him down; and the butcher cut his throat, in the regular orthodox manner of killing animals for food. "Now, cut him up," said the Defterdar, "into sixty pieces." This was done: the people concerned in the affair, and many others, looking on; but none daring to speak. The 60 peasants who had bought the meat of the cow were then called forward, one after another, and each was made to take a piece of the flesh of the Nazir, and to pay for it two riyals; so that 120 riyals were obtained from these. They were then dismissed; but the butcher remained. The Kadee was asked what should be the reward of the butcher; and answered that he should be paid as he had been paid by the Nazir. The Defterdar therefore ordered that the head of the Nazir should be given to him; and the butcher went away with his worse than valueless burden, thanking God that he had not been more unfortunate, and scarcely believing himself to have so easily escaped until he arrived at his village. The money paid for the flesh of the Nazir was given to the owner of the cow.'

The unfortunate tax-collector, we may observe, was really victim not of his tyranny, which, in comparison with the oppression practised by his betters, was quite venial, but of his incompetence. Since Muhammad Ali had decreed that communities were collectively liable for the unpaid taxes of their members, the tax-collector had no need to sell cow's meat in order to secure the Pasha's due. In any case, we may note, whatever happened, the Pasha's interests were in no way harmed. In an agricultural country like Egypt the bulk of the taxes naturally fell on the countryside. As a peasant in Upper Egypt said: 'Muhammad Ali is jealous of the lice which eat up the fellah.' But it did not follow that the cities escaped the burden. On the contrary, all trades, however lowly, contributed their share. Even prostitutes had to pay a tax on their activities.

Muhammad Ali was not content merely to centralize and improve the collection of taxes. He gave himself the monopoly of trade in, and export of, most agricultural produce. Also, after a French textile engineer, Alexandre Jumel, had discovered towards 1820 a superior variety of cotton native to Egypt, the cultivation and export of this cotton became one of the Pasha's most lucrative sources of revenue. But cotton cultivation was not favoured by the fellah; it therefore entailed strict regulation of agricultural activities, and led to a great increase in the control exercised by the state over the life and livelihood of the peasantry. The perennial irrigation that went together with cotton cultivation also required that canals should be regularly cleaned and kept in good repair, and thus greatly increased the burden of the corvée on the peasant. In bad times, the burden of taxes and corvée led to a flight from the countryside that the Pasha found inconvenient. He therefore decreed that villagers who had left their villages over a period of ten years had to return or suffer the death penalty.

It is quite clear that Muhammad Ali was attempting to set up in Egypt a strictly centralized, 'planned' economy, the purpose of which was to extract from the inhabitants the maximum resources for use in the pursuit of political and military power. For it was not only agriculture that the Pasha minutely regulated; he arranged also to supply craftsmen with their raw materials and compelled them to sell all their products to him at a fixed price, which he resold at a great profit. He himself, or merchants he designated, enjoyed a monopoly in the export of manufactures. And lastly, in an effort to industrialize the country, he set up state factories which his own employees managed.

In the end, Muhammad Ali's centralized, all-embracing state proved short-lived. Eventually, his political schemes failed and his will flagged; again, he could not be literally all-seeing, and since the state he set up was rigorously centralized, no subordinate of his, whether prominent or humble, was willing to take upon himself decisions which could be for him a matter of life and death. The fate of the tax-collector is instructive not only in itself, but for its exemplary value in a state in which one man alone was free. Such a state of affairs, so Hegel said, characterizes the traditional Oriental despotism; but what we see in Muhammad Ali's state is something more potent and more fearful. It is that European 18th-century absolutism which its partisans called 'enlightened' and which, equipped with the 'social science' and the *Kameralwissenschaft* of the day, aspired to fashion society in the likeness of a machine, the cogs of which were the subjects, the operator of which was the ruler and the product of which was happiness rationally defined and scientifically apportioned by the government. And in fact we even see Muhammad Ali adopting the rhetoric of this 'enlightened absolutism'—if only for the benefit of his European visitors. Thus, to a British visitor who suggested that the fellahs be allowed a greater latitude in what to cultivate, Muhammad Ali replied: 'No! my peasantry are suffering from the disease of ignorance of their true interest, and I must act the part of the doctor. I must be severe when anything goes wrong.' These words show the Pasha of Egypt to be aware of the benefits not only of European scientific techniques, but also of the European rhetoric of 'enlightened' absolutism.

Muhammad Ali's record shows his professed tenderness for the 'true interest' of his subjects to be a cynical sham, and that his sole preoccupation was how to exploit them most efficiently. What distinguishes him from his predecessors is the greatly enlarged scope for intervention in social and economic activities which Europe suggested and justified, and the extreme centralization that European methods made possible. The point is made in a striking passage by a Russian observer writing in 1875 about the impact of Russian methods and ideas (and in this context Russian and European are synonymous) on Muslim Central Asia:

> As concerns the Mussulman despotism destroyed by Russian institutions [wrote N. Petrofsky], it would be difficult for us to

guarantee that these institutions seem less arbitrary and despotic to the natives than did their former Mussulman ones. Under Mussulman sway tyranny and arbitrary rule indeed existed, but this tyranny was far from being without limits, and was as much a product of the country as were all its other institutions, morals, and customs. It was native there and it was understood there . . . In consequence of their exclusively religious education of the same character as that of the whole mass of the population, and of the common character of their life, of their customs and of their habits, the Mussulman rulers confined their tyranny within certain well known and fixed limits, and their arbitrariness was considered as a necessary attribute of their power, without which the very existence of their rule would be inconceivable. On the other side, the people too looked on this arbitrariness with the eye of their ruler, seeing in him not a tyrant and a persecuting despot, but a lucky favourite of fortune, who had received the right to arbitrary and uncontrolled power . . . In a word, the native was at home with Mussulman tyranny.

We may supplement and confirm what Petrofsky has to say by a remarkable statement that comes from the other side of the Muslim world, from Morocco. Its author, Raisuli, was one of those tribal chieftains who were able to defy the Moroccan Sultan's decayed authority, and with tribal support carve out for themselves territorial enclaves which even the French and Spanish occupants of Morocco found difficult to subdue. At the end of his career (he died in 1925), when the Spaniards had been established for a decade and more in his part of Morocco, he expressed in a striking manner one reason why European methods were felt to be so irksome by traditional Muslim society:

> You give a man safety [he told a European interlocutor] but you take away hope. In the old days everything was possible. There was no limit to what a man might become. The slave might be a minister or a general, the scribe a Sultan. Now a man's life is safe, but for ever he is chained to his labour and his poverty.

In a discussion of the Russian impact upon Central Asia, Petrofsky goes on to make another point which is also of wide application:

> The natives [he wrote] were expected of themselves to understand the—for them—complicated organization of the Russian government, and to guess at the relations of the various branches of the administration which were quite new to them, and not easily intelligible . . . Naturally these institutions appear to the natives to be far more arbitrary and far more tyrannical than those under which they formerly lived under Mussulman rulers, not because

they are really arbitrary and tyrannical, but because, seeing their frequent change, the native is not able to understand and to explain to himself either the meaning of the frequent changes, or the existence of these institutions.

Exactly similar reasons account for the widespread hostility with which European reforms undertaken by Islamic rulers like Muhammad Ali were received by their subjects. There is, likewise, a significant similarity between Algerian resistance to the French, the Sudanese Mahdi to the Egyptian regime, and various towns and villages in the Levant who in 1834 rose against the Egyptian forces that had taken the area from the Ottomans a few years earlier.

In the modern history of the Islamic peoples, Muhammad Ali stands as an archetype, because he shows with extreme clarity how, not so much European conquests as European ideas and methods, affected these peoples. Of course, few if any Islamic rulers even attempted to do all that Muhammad Ali did to Egypt. But those who were convinced of the necessity of 'reform', i.e. of emulating European ways—and they became the majority among Muslim leaders—embarked on policies similar in some way or another to Muhammad Ali's which, whatever their ostensible aim, ended up by increasing enormously the power of the rulers over the ruled, widening the gap between them, and generating powerful tensions and strains in society. As we have seen, Selim's attempt to modernize the Ottoman army evoked a very powerful opposition, and it eventually led to his downfall. His cousin Mahmud II was naturally aware of the threat to himself that modernization policies represented, but as his actions showed, he was also clearly convinced of their necessity. He bided his time, and did not move until he had a force in Constantinople of which he could be sure, and until he secured support for his policies from religious and military leaders. In May 1826 Mahmud promulgated a rescript providing for the creation of a new force, to be drawn from the Janissary corps, to be given new weapons and training, and to be subject to new regulations in respect of discipline, pay and promotion. The Janissaries were unwilling to allow this new formation to be set up, and some three weeks after the Sultan's rescript, on 15 June, they rose in rebellion. He promptly abolished the Janissary order, and killed all the Janissaries he could catch. He also shortly afterwards abolished the other traditional military formations of the Ottoman army. The way was now open for the creation of a modern conscript army, fully under the control of the Sultan, administered and directed by officials and officers entirely dependent on his favour, and thus utterly obedient to his command. The history of the so-called Eastern Question before 1914 shows that in spite of continued 'reforms', the Ottoman army never really became a match for the European armies that were its potential opponents. In fact, ironically enough, it was in the very period when the Ottoman army, as well as other Ottoman institutions, was undergoing modernization, that the empire came to be known as the 'Sick Man of Europe'. But the modernization of the Ottoman army enabled Mahmud and his successors to establish the authority of Constantinople over provinces where nominally subordinate governors had to all intents and purposes become autonomous. Again, the very needs of the new army, financial and administrative, required the setting up of new centrally controlled departments which increased still further the power of the Sultan at the expense of his subjects. Such an expression is warranted, when we remember that like Muhammad Ali in Egypt, Mahmud laid his hand not only on the so-called 'military fiefs', which had been traditionally awarded to the 'feudal cavalry', but on the extensive resources of the *awqaf* or pious foundations on the pretext of improving and rationalizing their administration. The 'reform' that began with the army gradually but inexorably ended by involving everything in state and society. Some of the most serious of the proliferating consequences of 'reform' were prophetically described in 1830 by Captain Adolphus Slade, whom we may recognize as one of the most intelligent observers of the Ottoman empire in his day and later.

> Hitherto [Slade pointed out] the Osmanley has enjoyed by custom some of the dearest privileges of freemen, for which Christian nations have so long struggled. He paid nothing to the government beyond a moderate land-tax, although liable, it is true, to extortions, which might be classed with assessed taxes. He paid no tithes, the vacouf [i.e. pious foundations] sufficing for the maintenance of the ministers of Islamism. He travelled where he pleased without passports; no custom-house officer intruded his eyes and dirty fingers among his baggage; no police watched his motions, or listened for his words. His house was sacred. His sons were never taken from his side to be soldiers, unless war called them. His views of ambition were not restricted by the barriers of birth and wealth: from the lowest origin he might aspire without presumption to the rank of pasha; if he could read, to that of grand vizir; and this consciousness, instilled and supported by numberless precedents, ennobled his mind, and enabled him to enter on the duties of high office without embarrassment ... One more example, rather burlesque, however than correct. The Janizzaries of Constantinople somewhat resembled a chamber of deputies, for they often compelled their sovereign to change his ministers, and any talented, factious member among them, with the art of inflaming men's passions, was sure to obtain a good employment in order to appease him.

In Mahmud's new model state, on the other hand,

The few are strengthened against the many, the powerful armed against the weak. The sovereign, who before found his power (despotic in name) circumscribed, because with all the will, he had not the real art of oppressing, by the aid of science finds himself a giant—his mace exchanged for a sword. In scanning over the riches of civilization, spread out before him for acceptance, he contemptuously rejects those calculated to benefit his people, and chooses the modern scientific governing machine, result of ages of experiment, with its patent screws for extracting blood and treasure—conscription and taxation. He hires foreign engineers to work it, and awaits the promised result—absolute power. His subjects, who before had a thousand modes of avoiding tyranny, have not now a loop-hole to escape by: the operations of the uncorroding engine meet them at every turn, and, to increase their despair, its movement accelerates with use, and winds closer their chains.

But 'reform' acquired a momentum and dialectic of its own, and in due course those leaders who were convinced that Europe was the only model worth following, became equally convinced that 'reform', to be real and effective, had to mean more than the introduction of mere military techniques and administrative methods. We may perhaps gain a cursory but sufficient idea of the views of 'enlightened' Easterners if we look at the 'Discourse with a Governor-General or a Pasha' which Assaad Yacoob Kayat included in his phrase-book, *The Eastern Traveller's Interpreter*, the second edition of which appeared in London in 1846. In his discourse with the Pasha, Kayat's English traveller is made to instruct him as follows:

This is a fine country.
It wants good roads.
All prosperity to the nation comes from good laws.
Good government is the foundation.
Every one ought to be equal in the sight of the law.
Schools will do your country much good.
Printing-presses will promote many blessings.

And it must be said that the Pashas—or at any rate an influential party among them—were willing to be instructed. In his efforts at modernization, the Sultan was seconded by a number of high officials. Of these, the best known was Mustafa Rashid Pasha, who was outstanding in helping to transform the empire into a European-style *Rechtstaat* in accordance with the maxims propounded in Kayat's phrase-book. In these attempts, the Noble Rescript of the Rose Chamber of 1839 undoubtedly stands as a landmark. The Rescript was promulgated shortly after the death of

Mahmud II, who was succeeded as Sultan by his son Abd al-Majid. The empire was then seriously threatened by the Pasha of Egypt, whose armies had inflicted a crushing defeat on the Ottoman at Nezib (in southwestern Anatolia) in June 1839. In this emergency, the empire was very much dependent on Great Power support, and particularly on the support of Great Britain. The Rescript of the Rose Chamber expresses not only the genuine beliefs of the reformers but is also a response to the similar beliefs about the Ottoman empire (and the Islamic world in general) that were widely prevalent in the West. The Noble Rescript promised 'to seek by new institutions to give the provinces of the Ottoman empire the benefit of a good administration'. These new institutions related to:

1. The guarantees insuring to our subjects perfect security for life, honour and fortune.
2. A regular system of assessing and levying taxes.
3. An equally regular system for the levying of troops and the duration of their service.

Yet another landmark in this reform movement is also associated with a wartime emergency: the Imperial Rescript of 1856 that was promulgated in the aftermath of the Crimean War, and the architects of which were two disciples of Rashid Pasha, Āli Pasha and Fu'ad Pasha. The new Rescript affirmed and amplified the provisions of the earlier document and insisted particularly on the equality that was to be accorded to all the Sultan's subjects whether Muslim, Christian or Jewish. It 'confirmed and consolidated' the rights that the Noble Rescript had granted 'to all the subjects of my empire, without distinction of classes or of religion'. The Crimean War had ostensibly broken out over the Russian claim to exercise a protectorate over the Greek Orthodox subjects of the Sultan, and it was no doubt to close the door on further similar claims, but also because the architects of reform genuinely believed in the necessity of such measures, that the Rescript was particularly emphatic on the equality of treatment for all the Sultan's subjects, regardless of their religion.

Intermittently, throughout the 1840s, the declarations of the Noble Rescript were translated into laws, regulations and institutions, and the same was the case with the Imperial Rescript of 1856. The effects were not always—or even frequently—what might have been anticipated from these high-minded aspirations. Aimed at increasing the security, the liberty and the welfare of the subject, the new laws and institutions were in fact nothing less than a revolution in social, commercial and religious arrangements. The population did not take kindly to them, and they had therefore to be worked and enforced by the government. This, *ipso facto*, meant a further increase in the unchecked, centralized power of the government. This vicious circle meant in the end that government and the governed came to inhabit two distinct universes of discourse.

One feature in particular of the Ottoman legal and constitutional reforms seriously increased social tension and complicated the work of government. This was the provision, hinted at in 1839 and spelled out much more explicitly in 1856, whereby non-Muslims were to be treated by the state on an equality with Muslims. Such a policy could not but damage the cohesion of a state which, in the last resort, rested on Islamic feelings of pride and solidarity—feelings which, in the eyes of Muslims, were sanctioned alike by divine law and by the immemorial history of Islam. For a Muslim government to concede equality to non-Muslims seemed to the mass of its Muslim subjects a demoralizing humiliation. 'If the Jews and the Christians are our equals before the law,' asked an Ottoman official when the Noble Rescript of the Rose Chamber was publicly read in Cairo, 'what will become of us?' The Ottoman government was not alone in pursuing such a policy. When he invaded the Levant Muhammad Ali, too, for various reasons, chose to show favour to the Christians in this way, and indeed went much further than the Ottomans. This aspect of his policy was a potent reason for the revolt against Egyptian rule that broke out in 1834. Muslim feelings are captured in the words of a Damascene clerk who wrote that 'The government has become a Christian government, the rule of Islam is ended.' An official British observer, Richard Wood, described the Pasha's policies that evoked this bitter comment. Ibrahim (Muhammad Ali's son and commander of the Egyptian forces), wrote Wood in a letter of 1834,

> respected neither [the Muslims'] prejudices or their rights but proclaimed Toleration, Equality and equal taxation with the enjoyment of equal privileges throughout Syria. These severe steps towards the annihilation of Mahommedan superiority broke the spirits of the followers of the Prophet, and gave confidence and energy to the Christians, who, long accustomed to consider themselves doomed to perpetual servility, now fondly clung to the least spark of hope, but never accustomed to sway the sceptre, they knew not the advantage of using with moderation their power, nor could they foresee that their present elevation may be but transient. Abusing therefore of their exalted state, they despised their former Masters, who on the other hand dreaded that it was now their turn to be roasted in ovens as were the Christians at the time of the notorious Djezzar Pasha the Butcher [governor of Acre, 1775–1804] . . .

Wood went on:

> The Turks finding that their hopes of deliverance were frustrated, and that they were destined to be governed by Egyptians, and above all resenting what they termed the insolence of the Christians, many Towns revolted: among the foremost were Sidon,

Aleppo, Damascus, Nazareth; the present inhabitants of the country of Samaria, and the fellah Arabs of the Horan or Decapolis.

Less than three decades later, in 1860, the Levant, now once more under Ottoman rule, was again the scene of serious disturbances when Christian communities in Damascus and elsewhere were attacked and massacred. It is not to be doubted that this explosion was—among other things—an outcome of the Imperial Rescript of 1856, and the inter-communal tension its promises precipitated. Contemporary European observers, the majority of whom saw nothing but good in the reform policy, sarcastically remarked that the Rescript of 1856 'left nothing to be desired but its execution'. What is implicit in such a remark is that the reform was a mere paper reform, and that if only it had been implemented, the empire would have basked in peace and contentment. This was far from the truth. The very attempt to implement the promises of reform led to political and social tensions by undermining the self-confidence of Muslims, rulers and subjects alike, and raising the expectations of the non-Muslims. Unlike most observers, the sagacious Slade, in a work published two years before the Rescript of the Rose Chamber, anticipated exactly this outcome. Removal of the disabilities of the non-Muslims was

> not calculated to produce, as was fondly expected and is stoutly asserted by many, attachment to the Sultan's government, but, on the contrary, depression of the Mussulman interest, *on which alone his throne is based* ... Touched on theoretically, concession is a lady's fan; practically handled, it became a double-edged sword: it sets loose the fell tide of party rancour, which spurns an equal participation of rights, and it rouses the spirit of revenge, which scorns any justice, save the fullest measure—which is, to rule where ruled, to scoff at by whom scoffed. Arms thus given to the oppressed cannot be resumed: the confidence of the ruling sect cannot be regained.

Reform, then, meant change. But change did not necessarily mean unqualified or universal improvement. It did not make for visibly better government, and it did not serve to strengthen the state against foreign encroachments. On the contrary, the erosion of Muslim superiority, and the concomitant increase in the self-assertiveness of the non-Muslims, gave increased opportunities to foreign powers to intervene. Again, reform worked, in unforeseen ways, to the advantage of some groups and to the detriment of others; and it is of course impossible to say whether the advantage or detriment was the greater. Consider, for example, another piece of reform, the change in the land laws that was related to the abolition of 'feudal' tenures and tax-farming. A new, European-model land law was promulgated in 1858 which resulted in the transformation of customary tenures and of land in common or tribal ownership or use into state-registered, individually owned freeholds. This reform rode rough-shod over customary rights which, though not set down in official documents, yet had immemorially regulated agrarian relationships in large parts of the empire. The Land Code did not create a European-style small landed peasantry with a stake in the land. On the contrary, the small agriculturist, whether member of a settled village community or of a tribe which had never known individual ownership of land, found his customary rights and interests squeezed and destroyed by a law the operation of which was made even more vicious by the corruption and malpractices that a large, unwieldy, centralized bureaucracy naturally entailed. Was there, one wonders, any substantive difference between the conditions of the tribesman of southern Mesopotamia or the villager of the north Syrian plain whom the operation of a benevolent Land Code reduced to a kind of serf, and that of the Egyptian peasant who became Muhammad Ali's virtual property, or that of the Kazakh nomad whose tribal lands were expropriated in the latter half of the 19th century to the benefit of Russian settlers, or that of the Algerian Kabyles whose land was likewise expropriated to the benefit of French settlers? We must of course not forget that Russian and French settlement looked even more injurious; for the victims were Muslims and the expropriators Christian conquerors. But it is significant that the results of modernization by a Muslim state should be so similar to those produced by European conquests.

Another aspect of reform deserves examination. The Westernization of laws and the increase in the functions of government was accompanied by the setting up of provincial councils. These councils, composed of local notables elected by a complicated franchise, were deemed to represent the various communities of a province. To start with, as Rashid Pasha set them up, they were given judicial as well as administrative functions and were supposed to act as a check on the governor. As the historian H. W. V. Temperley observed, the council system 'was absolutely bad'. Councillors were under no real check by their constituents, and were thus hardly representative. The councillors, then, proved to be an oligarchy of quasi-officials who exploited to their own benefit the increasing intricacy of laws and administrative regulations, and whose mutual jealousies seldom advanced the public interest or the welfare of the ordinary subject. The evils of the council system were soon perceived, and both in 1852 and 1864 changes were made which diminished the powers of the councillors and, notably, removed judicial matters from their purview. But the councils never succeeded in becoming effective organs of local self-government or local representation.

One of the best works on the Ottoman empire written in English, Sir

Charles Eliot's *Turkey in Europe*, opens with an imaginary conversation between a European businessman and an Ottoman Pasha. At one point in their discussion the Pasha is led to speak in metaphors:

> This country [he exclaims] is a dish of soup and no one has any real intention except to eat it. We eat it in the good old-fashioned way with a big spoon. You bore little holes in the bottom of the soup-bowl and draw it off with pipes. Then you propose that the practice of eating soup with spoons should be abolished as uncivilised, because you know we have no gimlets and don't understand this trick of drinking through pipes.

To use the Pasha's arresting language, we may liken the European-inspired local councils to the scientific device whereby soup was sucked through the pipe, rather than eaten with an old-fashioned spoon. It is of course difficult, if not impossible, positively to say which was the more efficacious, but we may suspect at any rate that the more modern method caused in its victims the greater anguish, both because it was unfamiliar, and because a large number of small pipes had replaced the one big spoon. We may illustrate this by the reaction of the Tunisians to these reforms, similar to the Ottoman, which the Bey of Tunis (nominally a part of the empire) introduced at about the same time. Between 1857 and 1861 the Beys of Tunis introduced European-style laws, which aimed at ensuring security of the person, and equality in taxation and before the law. A centralized bureaucracy and a new network of tribunals were set up to carry out the reforms, and the edifice was crowned by a constitution promulgated in 1861. The constitution made provision for a grand council to which the ministers and the Bey himself were made ostensibly responsible. The council was made up of officials and notables, partly appointed and partly co-opted, and was supposed to be the authority of last resort in matters of taxation and in judicial affairs. These reforms proved to be a great burden for the subject. Under the old order, administrative matters were decided by the governor and judicial cases determined by the *qadi*, subject in both cases to an appeal to the Bey. Thus, as a French observer put it, the ordinary Tunisian had hitherto been 'eaten' by two men, and no more. With the coming of the new tribunals,

> he is eaten by all the members of these tribunals. He used to accept the decision of the local judge because it was a prompt decision, and only in grave issues would he appeal to the Sovereign. Today, the inhabitant of Gabes, which is 80 leagues from Tunis, who wants to appeal a judgment rendered by the local tribunal, has to go to Tunis. And even after a journey so costly for him, he does not enjoy the privilege of personally rehearsing his grievances before the bey. It

is yet another committee issuing from the supreme Council, a number of these detested mamluks transformed into a court of appeal, who will annul or confirm the first verdict.

The discontent that the Tunisian reforms aroused led to a tribal rebellion in 1864. The battle-cry of the rebels was: 'No more mamluks, no more *mejba* [a tax greatly increased by the council], no more constitution.' Among the demands made by the leaders of the rebellion was that the new tribunals should be abolished, and the Bey himself render justice according to the *shari'a*. The rebellion was eventually put down, but the constitution was suspended, never to be activated again.

Khayr ad-Din at-Tunisi, mentioned above, was one of those Tunisian officials who were, as has been seen, most persuaded of the necessity of European-style reforms, and he took a prominent part in carrying out the reforms of 1857–61. At one point, in fact, he became president of the grand council, the activities of which led to the rebellion of 1864. His work, *Réformes nécessaires aux états musulmans*, was written in the aftermath of this rebellion, and it contains a significant passage that seems to refer obliquely to the claims of the rebels. Khayr ad-Din enumerates four objections to reform advanced by those who believed that they were not suitable to Islamic society:

1. The Tanzimat [i.e. reforms] are contrary to the *shari'a*.
2. They are inappropriate since there is no disposition on the part of the *umma* [i.e. the Muslim community] to accept the civilization upon which they are based.
3. They will almost certainly lead to the loss of rights given the long time needed to settle lawsuits, and identical delays will be seen throughout the administrative system.
4. The increased government employment required for various administrations will require an increase in taxation.

But it was not only traditionally minded tribal chieftains in an outlying part of the Muslim world who were finding European reforms irksome in their application and doubtful in their results. Disappointment or disenchantment with reforms was to be seen also among those who were most exposed to European ideas. They too thought the new-fangled administrative arrangements were both oppressive and inefficient. But they did not exactly hark back to or yearn for a restoration of traditional Islam. If the reforms had failed this was because they were the shadow rather than the substance of European civilization. The secret of European power and prosperity lay not in machines or administrative organization. It lay rather in the political and social habits prevalent among Europeans—habits which made for initiative, inventiveness and enterprise. The essence of these habits may be summed up by the expression 'freedom under the law'. This could be secured only by limited, representative, constitutional government. Such government, it was argued, would be no more than a return to the pure tradition of early Islam, before it had been adulterated by despotism and superstition. Such an argument had little historical value since, whatever political doctrine might be drawn out of or extrapolated from the Qur'an, Islam almost from the beginning had known little else but autocratic rule, and was utterly unfamiliar with constitutional and representative government. Again, the administrative and military reforms had greatly increased the ruler's power, and weakened such defenses as had been traditionally available to the subject. And it is this greatly strengthened ruler, controlling a modernized army and a highly centralized administration, who was now bidden to transform himself into a constitutional monarch and allow his power to be regulated by a constitution and checked by the people's representatives.

There was of course little prospect of this coming to pass, and constitutional representative government could usually be established only by such action as would itself make more remote the successful operation of such a government. In 1876, when the Ottoman empire was in the throes of a military and financial crisis, a number of high officials conspired to depose the Sultan and establish a parliamentary government. They eventually put on the throne a young member of the Ottoman dynasty who seemed to agree with their views. And in fact, the new Sultan, 'Abd al-Hamid II, did, shortly after his accession, grant a constitution and a parliament. What this meant in effect was a transfer of power from the Sultan himself to the ministers and other members of the official classes who understood these innovations and exploited them to their advantage. This was in many ways analogous to the situation in Tunisia after 1861, and to that in the Ottoman provinces after the introduction of local councils which had served only to increase the power and perquisites of the local notables. 'Abd al-Hamid was naturally averse to any diminution of his power, and with shrewdness and good luck he succeeded in suspending both constitution and parliament after they had been operating for barely a year. His long reign, from 1876 to 1909, saw no abatement of the modernizing and centralizing tendencies that had become increasingly dominant in the 19th century.

One consequence of this was an increase in the number of officials and officers influenced by European ideas and who, precisely owing to their European-style education, were disaffected towards the regime. They were convinced that only its transformation into a state governed by a constitution and a parliament would save the empire from ruin. A conspiracy by junior officers, the 'Young Turks', succeeded, in July 1908, and forced 'Abd al-Hamid to restore the constitution of 1876. But parliamentary government in the Ottoman empire, and in its successor states after 1918, proved on the whole to be a mere façade: the reality was that of a centralized state endowed with a numerous and powerful bureaucracy run by an official class whose European-style education made it quite remote from the traditional-minded mass that it governed. In spite of ostensibly representative institutions, this official class was in reality little responsive to those whom it governed, because the latter were unfamiliar with elections and parliaments and because they were traditionally in awe of the rulers and, as the scope of government increased, progressively more dependent on it for their very livelihood. Political life consisted in rivalry and conflict between various groups within the official class; a conflict which, in the absence of constitutional checks and balances, was very often resolved by the military, who could not resist the temptation to take power into their own hands.

The European doctrines that so influenced their thinking led to exaggerated hopes about political action and what it could accomplish. This kind of expectation may be described as, among other things, secular and humanist: secular in stressing that the world has no supernatural dimension or providential destiny; and humanist in emphasizing that man is his own master and makes himself. Such a vision is, of course, far removed from the traditional Islamic outlook, and its impact, gradual as it was, was in the end both pervasive and far-reaching. We see it appear quite early in the contacts between European civilization and Islam. For instance, large parts of the Caucasus were conquered by Russia in the first three decades of the 19th century, and educated Muslims of this region came into intimate contact with European ideas and institutions. One of the best known of these was Mirza Fath'Ali Akhundzada (1812–78). Beginning with a traditional religious education, Akhundzada soon abandoned it for the study of Russian language and literature. In Tiflis, where he became a Russian official, he came in close touch with Russian intellectuals, some of whom were actually exiles in Transcaucasia because of their advanced political ideas. Akhundzada became known particularly as a playwright, and his plays contributed in the Azeri- and Persian-speaking world to the spread of a secular and sceptical attitude if not to Islam itself, then to the men of religion—divines, *qadis* and dervishes—who were portrayed as devious and corrupt, taking advantage of a credulous, respectful and superstitious public. Another comparable and significant figure in an out-of-the-way part of the Muslim world was the Bukhariot writer Ahmad Makhdum Donish (1827–97). The Khan of Bukhara was defeated by Russia and had to acquiesce in a Russian protectorate in 1868. It was then that he sent Donish as ambassador to St. Petersburg. Donish came back profoundly impressed with Russian culture, with the fact that women were unveiled, that books and periodicals were published in large quantities, that educated men were numerous, and the country, compared with Bukhara, prosperous. He became persuaded that these benefits were withheld from his fellow countrymen by the greed and corruption of the rulers and men of religion, and that the Bukhariots could take steps to end oppression, obscurantism and poverty. He did not mince his words:

The Emirs and the Vizirs [he wrote], the clergy and the aristocracy are all alike. You, reader, should find out what kind of man the Emir himself is, the sovereign of orthodox Muslims and your Sultan. Look around and you will see that he is a libertine and tyrant. His supreme Kazi is a glutton and hypocrite. Of the same kind are the Ra'is and the head of police. The latter is simply a perpetually drunk gambler and consort of brigands and thieves.

Donish also questioned the traditional Islamic beliefs. As one of his disciples wrote, the Muslim divines accused him of claiming to be able to predict the eclipse of the sun and the moon, which meant that he was impiously trying to put himself on a level with God, who alone can know the future.

The same disaffection towards Islamic institutions and practices may be seen among educated Indian Muslims who had come into contact with English thought and the British way of life. The famous writer Khwaja Altaf Husayn Hali (1837–1914), who has been described as the most distinguished poet of his generation, writes bitter words about the decadence of Indian Islam, and leaves his reader in no doubt about those responsible, namely the mystics and the theologians who have killed all initiative and spirit in the Muslims, and fostered intolerance and fear:

They speak only to inflame men's hatred, write only to wound men's hearts. God's sinful servants they despise; their Muslim brethren they brand as infidels. These are the paths of the learned divines, these the methods of our guides.

If a man goes to lay a problem before them, he will come away with a yet heavier burden on his soul. And if he is so unfortunate as to feel doubt about their answer, they will brand him unerringly as one of the damned. Indeed if he gives voice to some objection he will be fortunate to escape whole from their hands . . .

They offer him no guidance in morality, produce in him no purity of heart; but have multiplied external observances to such a degree that not for a single moment can he escape them. That religion which was the source of gentleness and goodness they have degraded into a code of rules for baths and ablutions.

The most colourful and best known of these modern figures who have depreciated Islam and demanded its replacement by some modern ideology was the Persian Shi'i who went under the name of Jamal ad-Din al-Afghani (1838–97). Afghani's activities extended to all the central lands of Islam: Persia, India, the Ottoman empire, Egypt; and he preached a secret doctrine of infidelity and scepticism. His teaching may be summed up in the words of a disciple, Muhammad Abduh, who, ironically, was to become Mufti of Egypt—one of the three highest religious dignitaries in the country.

In a letter to Afghani, Abduh wrote: 'We regulate our conduct according to your sound rule: we do not cut the head of religion except with the sword of religion.' Afghani's view of Islam comes out clearly in an exchange he had in Paris in 1883 with Ernest Renan. In a lecture at the Sorbonne Renan had attacked Islam as an engine of despotism, terror and persecution. In a commentary published in the *Journal des Débats,* Afghani agreed with Renan's estimate of Islam and expressed the hope that Islamic society 'will succeed some day in breaking its bonds and marching resolutely in the path of civilization, after the manner of Western society'.

The adventures and disappointments of the Muslim intellect in search of a valid amalgam between its native inheritance and 'the path of civilization, after the manner of Western society', as Afghani put it, have taken many forms. In politics, there was the quest for constitutionalism which, in the Ottoman empire and its successor states, paradoxically inaugurated a period—by no means over yet—of military *coups d'état* and unrepresentative military regimes. In the Russian empire and in the Central Asian khanates under Russian protection, there was a vigorous movement to reform Muslim education, to do away with the intellectual and social tyranny of the men of religion, and the political tyranny of the Khans. During the Russian Revolution of 1905 the modernizing leaders of the Tatars—those Muslims who had been under Russian rule since the 18th century and earlier—cast their lot with the Russian Kadets (Constitutional Democrats). The political program which they formulated at a congress of 1906 demanded legal equality for all the peoples of Russia, and equal access by Muslims to civil and military posts, the equality of all religions with the Orthodox faith and the institution of local self-government controlled by democratically elected councils. As events proved, this constitutionalist dream was incompatible with the Russian autocracy, and was far removed from the realities of Russian politics. What is noteworthy about it is that a congress speaking in the name of a Muslim community was ready to envisage a society in which Muslims would take their place on an equality with other faiths that Islam had hitherto considered inferior. With the Bolshevik Revolution a decade or so later, the life of politics seemed to hold a new promise of fulfillment to Russian Muslim intellectuals. Thus, one of Stalin's first Muslim collaborators in the Commissariat for Nationalities, Mullanur Vahitov (1885–1918), was certain, according to a Tatar author writing in the 1920s, that

> the influence of ancient Arab culture on the universal culture which would emerge as a result of world-wide socialist reconstruction would be immense. In his dreams he pictured this Islamic culture— whose impact extended from Arab lands to the sacred river, Ganges—as great, beautiful and profound in its content. He could not conceive of its possible disintegration or disappearance and

dreamed that in the future it would . . . illumine all humanity. Of this he was convinced.

Vahitov died before he could see how illusory such hopes were. It was otherwise with another Tatar, Sultan Galiev (1895–?1940), who served, between 1918 and 1923, as Stalin's colleague in the Commissariat of Nationalities. Sultan Galiev was a Marxist and a Communist, but in his eyes the class struggle was not so much one between capitalist and proletariat in an industrialized country as between Europeans and the Eastern world which they exploited, colonized and oppressed. And the liberation of humanity was to come from a liberated East of which the vanguard were the Communist Tatars in the Soviet Union. This was not only a deviation from orthodox Marxism, but a threat to the power of Moscow. Sultan Galiev was dismissed from his official post, and up to 1928 occupied himself in organizing political and doctrinal resistance among Soviet Muslims to the dominant, European, element in the Communist Party of the Soviet Union. For these activities he was arrested in 1929 and sentenced to a long term of imprisonment. He is said to have been released in 1939, but when exactly or how he died remains unknown.

The same disappointments or disasters overtook the modernizers of Central Asia in their attempts to engage in politics, and to ameliorate by political action the life of their people. The *Jadids* (i.e. modernizers) of Bukhara began to be active towards the end of the 19th and in the first decade of the 20th century. Starting with a desire to introduce modern education and thus, as they believed, do away at once with despotism and superstition, their horizon was suddenly widened by the Russian Revolution of 1917. Forming themselves as a Young Bukhariot party, they attempted to force the Khan to introduce in Bukhara the reforms they believed desirable, and in pursuit of their aim they finally collaborated with a Communist force which marched from Tashkent on Bukhara in 1920. The Khan was expelled and the Young Bukhariots proclaimed a seemingly independent Popular Republic. But the independence did not last long. It was terminated in 1924 when the ancient state of Bukhara (the independence of which had survived the Tsarist regime) became a Socialist Republic and was absorbed in the Soviet Union; it is now a part of the Uzbek Soviet Socialist Republic. The dreams and ambitions of the *Jadids* thus met with a failure that may be symbolized by the fate of their ideological mentor, Abd ar-Ra'uf Fitrat. Born sometime in the last decades of the 19th century, he was very active in educational and religious reform until World War I. In 1920 he took office as minister of education, and then of foreign affairs in the Popular Republic. When the Republic was suppressed he became a teacher in the University of Samarqand. In 1937 he was arrested, and his fate thereafter is unknown.

The Muslim modernizers in India who, like their counterparts in Russia, ended by becoming the leaders of their community were scarcely more lucky in their encounter with politics. Hali, whom we have quoted earlier, fervently believed that the welfare of the Muslims lay in adapting themselves to the modern world under the aegis of their British rulers:

> Your government has given you freedom. All the roads of advancement are wide open to you. From all sides comes the cry that, from prince to peasants, all men prosper. The rule of peace and prosperity is established in all lands, and caravans may travel in safety along every route.

It was a friend of Hali, the famous Sir Sayyid Ahmad Khan (1817–98), who laboured most successfully to bring home to his fellow Muslims a realization of the possibilities offered by Western science, and strove to convince them that if Muslims were to fulfill their destiny—which was to prosper, to be powerful and to make a mark in the world—they had better accept modern education which, he insisted, was fully compatible with Islam. So far as Sir Sayyid Ahmad Khan and the men of his generation could see, the future of India and its Muslims was bound up with British rule. Muslims were a minority in India and thus all the more looked to the British to safeguard their interests. But the subsequent rise of Hindu nationalism, the political mobilization of the Hindu masses by figures like Tilak or Gandhi, aroused increasing disquiet among the Muslim leaders. The ensuing prospects were considered by Muslim leaders, foremost among whom was Muhammad Ali Jinnah (1876–1948), as dangerous and even desperate. If Muslims were to preserve themselves and safeguard their identity, it followed that they had to establish a state of their own. There were, he argued, two distinct nations in India. Hinduism and Islam 'are not religions in the strict sense of the word, but are, in fact, different and distinct social orders. . . The Hindus and Muslims belong to two different religious philosophies, social customs, literatures. They neither intermarry nor interdine together and, indeed,' Jinnah affirmed, 'they belong to two different civilizations which are based mainly on conflicting ideas and conceptions.'

Jinnah was successful in obtaining such a state in Pakistan, which came into existence in 1947 when the British abandoned their empire in India. But Pakistan as the emanation of Indian Islam and its shield suffers from a double paradox. In the first place, Pakistan came into being as a result of the Muslims of India voting against a single state for the subcontinent. But Pakistan embraced nothing like the totality of the Indian Muslims; when it came into being Pakistan had about 65 million Muslims, while the new Hindu-dominated India contained no less than 35 million.

But the snares and disappointments of political action went even further. The whole *raison d'être* of Pakistan was Islam. This is what the 1956 constitution of Pakistan unequivocably shows. It ordains, in Part III, on 'Directive Principles of State Policy', that 'Steps shall be taken to enable the Muslims of Pakistan individually and collectively to order their lives in accordance with the Holy Qur'an and Sunnah.' But nothing in the history of Pakistan since its inception indicates that these statements have become more than mere words, and the rulers of Pakistan have discovered that to live 'in accordance with the Holy Qur'an and Sunnah' may not be compatible with the character of a modern state. Some six years after the birth of Pakistan, serious riots erupted in Lahore against the Ahmadis, a sect that orthodox Muslim divines consider heretical. These divines claimed that if Pakistan was an Islamic state, then it ought to maintain the distinction between Muslims and non-Muslims and deny Ahmadis (and by implication all non-Muslims) that equality of rights which modern civilized states recognize for all their citizens (and which the Pakistan constitution subsequently affirmed). The riots, in which *'ulama'* in Lahore took a leading part, were investigated by a court of enquiry which produced a notable report. This report (known as the Munir report) highlights the incompatibility between modern European-inspired constitutionalism and the Islamic notions of state which a state like Pakistan was supposed to put into practice. Pakistan, declared the report in a notable passage,

> is being taken by the common man, though it is not, as an Islamic State. This belief has been encouraged by the ceaseless clamour for Islam and Islamic State that is being heard from all quarters since the establishment of Pakistan. The phantom of an Islamic State has haunted the Musalman throughout the ages and is a result of the memory of the glorious past . . .

The modern Muslim, the report went on,

> finds himself standing on the crossroads, wrapped in the mantle of the past and with the dead weight of centuries on his back, frustrated and bewildered and hesitant to turn one corner or the other. The freshness and the simplicity of the faith, which gave determination to his mind and spring to his muscle, is now denied to him. He has neither the means nor the ability to conquer and there are no countries to conquer . . . He therefore finds himself in a state of helplessness, waiting for some one to come and help him out of this morass of uncertainty and confusion . . . Nothing but a bold re-orientation of Islam to separate the vital from the lifeless can preserve it as a World Idea and convert the Musalman into a citizen of the present and the future world from the archaic incongruity that he is today.

Almost a decade and a half after these words were written, we find Ayyub Khan, President of Pakistan from 1962 to 1969, complaining of the same incongruity and incoherence between the claims of Islam and those of the modern world. In a book published in 1967, Ayyub Khan remarked that

Islam visualizes life as a unity in which all activity is determined by the same principle. But, he went on to add, 'The picture of our society, as I saw it, did not conform to this. In practice, our life was broken up into two distinct spheres and in each sphere we followed a different set of principles.' It was a problem that the setting up of Pakistan did by no means solve for the Indian Muslims. Moreover, less than a quarter of a century after the foundation of Pakistan, it seemed that Islam did not constitute a tie sufficiently strong to keep the state together. In 1971 the Muslims of East Pakistan manifestly preferred to take advantage of an Indian military intervention to secede and form an independent state of their own.

It is apparent from Jinnah's language that he considered Islam more a 'civilization' and a 'social order' than a faith. In this of course he was not alone, for Westernized Muslims (and Jinnah was one of them) had long learned to transform Islam from an eternally true divine revelation independent of temporal changes and vicissitudes into a product and agent of historical change, or into a social cement. In other words, one was a Muslim not because Islam was true, but because it served, by means of the solidarity which it instilled, to keep together and thus endow with political power the societies in which Islam had hitherto held sway. This in fact is the political doctrine of Afghani, who, so we have seen, was a religious sceptic. A statement of his establishes with utter clarity the secular, humanist tendencies that he expressed and popularized:

> There are two kinds of philosophy in the world [he told a friend]. One of them is to the effect that there is nothing in the world which is ours, so we must remain content with a rag and a mouthful of food. The other is to the effect that everything in the world is beautiful and desirable, that it does and ought to belong to us. It is the second which should be our ideal, to be adopted as our motto.

To gain possession of the beautiful and desirable is, then, a feasible goal; it is the end of human activity, and specifically of political activity. Political activity harnesses the will of the multitude to the will of the political leader, who uses whatever captures the imagination of the mass. For the Muslim mass, the means is precisely Islam, and it is no surprise that Afghani favoured the preaching of an Islamic messianism promising the faithful earthly salvation and the establishment of a reign of prosperity and justice. Afghani, however, recognized that there were solidarity-producing beliefs other than religion. And these beliefs, along with this ambitious view of human abilities—namely to lay hold of all that is beautiful and desirable— became familiar and attractive to the Westernized leaders of Islamic society. Two such European creeds promising liberation and salvation here on earth are nationalism and socialism. Nationalism is the belief that the good life cannot be lived except within a politically autonomous 'nation', in which all members of the nation are brothers; while socialism is the conviction that injustice, poverty and unhappiness can be abolished through the abolition of private property. The excessive hopes placed in politics, the expectation that public prosperity and private bliss will alike flow from it, the religious aura with which political action and political leaders are endowed—such seems the clearest outcome of a century and a half of Westernization. An example may perhaps suffice to illustrate. In 1974 appeared a small volume of poetry by the Syrian poet Nizar Qabbani (b. 1923), entitled *Political Works*. Most of the poems denounced the political impotence of the Arabs as the result of a feeble and corrupt leadership. In one poem, the speaker confesses to having murdered an Imam, i.e. a man of religion, for having so long lulled the faithful with mere words:

> *In killing him I have killed*
> *All the weeds in the garden of Islam*
> *All who seek a living in the shop of Islam*
> *In killing him, honoured Sirs, I have killed*
> *All those who, for a thousand years,*
> *Have been fornicating with speech.*

In another poem addressed to the Palestinian organization *Fatah,* the poet declares:

> *Only bullets*
> *Not patience is the key to deliverance*

In yet another poem the Egyptian leader Nasser is commemorated shortly after his death with religious imagery the evocative power of which is here harnessed to the celebration of a secular political figure. Qabbani says:

> *We have filled the cups for you, O you with love of whom*
> *We have become drunk, as the Sufi is drunk with God*

And again:

> *You are the Mahdi for us. You are the Liberator*

The collection, however, ends with a poem celebrating the Egyptian crossing of the Suez Canal in October 1973. The poem is remarkable for the fusion between the public concerns of politics and the very private world of love, a fusion which is characteristic of the new outlook, at once unmistakably secular and fervently messianic, which seems to have captured the Westernized elite. The poem, entitled 'Observations in time of love and war', is addressed by the poet to his love. The lovers are together when they hear the news of the crossing:

> *Did you notice* [the poet asks]
> *How I overflowed all my banks*

How I covered you like the waters of rivers
Did you notice how I abandoned myself to you
As though I was seeing you for the first time.
Did you notice how we fused together
How we panted, how we sweated
How we became ashes, and how we were resuscitated
As though we were making love
For the first time . . .

The high sexual ecstasy which the poet here celebrates in so strident a fashion is brought about by the news of a successful military action. But politics (which embraces war) cannot sustain such fervour for very long: wars are sometimes lost, if also sometimes won, and in politics is no salvation. Disappointment with politics is sure to come. Will the failure of such inordinate hopes set up intolerable pressures and threaten frightful explosions? It is with such a question that an observer must end his survey of a Muslim world that has lost its classical poise, and is now highly strung and deeply disturbed.

2

ISLAM AND THE ORIENTALISTS

'The evolution of Muhammad's preaching,' says Professor Grunebaum in his book on Islam,[1] with its comparatively poor background of Arabian civilization into the cultural system of Islam with its claim to universal validity, forcefully colouring with its own and unmistakable patina every single object appropriated and every single thought accepted, is one of the most fascinating spectacles of history.' Taken in conjunction with an earlier work,[2] of which *Islam* may be considered a complement and a continuation, these essays achieve a precise, craftsmanlike and authoritative description of what constitutes the patina of Islam, and of the profile of Muslim society.

To understand the character of this society, we must understand its religion. Islam is not only the badge of Muslim society; it has remained, until the very recent past, the constitutive and regulative principle of Muslim life in its temporal as well as its spiritual concerns. The distinctive feature of Islam, as Grunebaum puts it, is that it is 'permeated by a sense of the autocracy of the Lord'. There are, it is true, verses in the Qur'an which seem to acknowledge the existence of free will in man, but as soon as a coherent and systematic body of theology began to exist, it was the other conception, also to be found in the Qur'an, of God's utter omnipotence, and the utter powerlessness of his creature, that assumed central importance among the orthodox Sunni majority. An earlier authority has indeed argued that this latter conception is the more fundamental, and that the verses which speak of free will were 'a campaigning expedient'.[3] However this may be, by the end of the third century of the Muslim era, when the main lines of orthodox Muslim theology, as they were accepted and transmitted down the centuries, became fixed, the omnipotence of God and the powerlessness of his creature had achieved final dogmatic acceptance. Between God and man an infinite gulf is fixed. It may not be bridged, and the very attempt to do so is blasphemous. God's power is unlimited and no one may question His decrees. Man must do what He enjoins and abstain from what He forbids. God has revealed His will through His prophets, and especially through

Muhammad, the seal of the prophets. Nothing can bind the will of God, and no fetter on His action can be imagined. What He promulgates today, He can abolish tomorrow: 'If God', says a theologian of the 9th century of the Muslim era, 'were to reverse His decision and to declare good what He had declared evil, and evil what He had declared good, nothing could stop this.' Orthodox Sunni Muslim theology, then, is strictly voluntarist, and its ethics rest on a nominalist foundation. The good is good not because it conforms to a Law of Nature or of Reason, but because God decrees it to be good. Law is absent not only from the moral life, but from the physical world as well. Orthodox Sunni Muslim theology is occasionalist: there are no causes and no effects, only the illusion of such. There is only one cause, God, the First Cause, and His will cannot be fettered by laws of causality. To quote D. B. Macdonald: 'There is no such thing as a secondary cause. When there is the appearance of such, it is only illusional. God is producing it as well as the ultimate appearance of effect. There is no nature belonging to things. Fire does not burn and a knife does not cut. God creates in a substance a being burned when the fire touches it and a being cut when the knife approaches it'. The occasionalism issues in a literal empiricism, making science as understood in Europe in modern times a doubtful and suspect activity. Grunebaum relates the other features of Muslim culture to the tenets of Muslim theology. The purpose of man's life is to worship God and obey His decrees. These he ascertains from Revelation. Knowledge therefore is worthwhile only as it deepens man's understanding of Revelation, and of Muhammad, the Agent of Revelation. The pious, Grunebaum points out, is to avoid any science that might endanger his faith. Thus a division takes place between praiseworthy knowledge, consisting of theology and ancillary subjects, and blameworthy knowledge, consisting of philosophical and scientific speculation which is useless either for this world or for the next. Philosophical speculation for its own sake is frowned upon, and orthodoxy rejects, from the early centuries of Islam, this particular aspect of Greek civilization. Indeed, what Islam borrows from alien civilizations is borrowed for its immediate usefulness: not the method of speculation, but its practical results. Since knowledge leads not to discovery, but only to a deeper insight into what has already been revealed, there can be no belief in 'progress', and 'change', Grunebaum says, 'has to be justified as the true interpretation of the divine ordinance finally arrived at, as the reversal from impious innovation to the purity of the beginnings, or else it must be ignored, denied, or fought'.

Just as Grunebaum tries to correlate theology and the Muslim attitude to science, so he tries to correlate theology and education, literature, and the ideal type of litterateur. Creation is the prerogative of God and therefore the 'the new faith was very careful to deny man any powers that might even by a purely verbal *quid pro quo* induce a misconception of man's innate gifts and hence of his position in relation to Allah'.

The educational ideal of Islam demands *polymathia*. The truth is already established, and the task of the student is to master what is already established; he 'is not expected to add to the store of inherited truth'. Similarly, poetical originality is discouraged. 'Throughout the great age of Arabic literature', remarks Grunebaum, 'the critics placed verbal perfection above poetical originality, and the public was well contented to hear the familiar motifs again and again if only they were couched in choice and carefully shaded language.' Grunebaum 'tentatively and somewhat hesitantly', it is true, sees a certain affinity between the occasionalism of Muslim theology and the fact that Arabic literature leaps from topic to topic and that it 'operates on a span of attention which is much shorter than that presupposed by Western literature'.

How, then, shall such a society, made coherent and guided in all its activities by a religious principle, attend to the problem of government, and how shall it regulate the exercise of power? The Muslim community is a community of believers ruled by the divine will, and divine will requires someone to enforce it against transgressors and unbelievers. 'Mohammed', it has been well said, 'ruled his community as divine commissioner.'[5] The orthodox Muslim state is not, Grunebaum points out, a welfare state; it is not, like the state in Greek thought, concerned with the happiness of its members. Its purpose is to enable the community of believers to worship God and obey His commands. L. Gardet, in the course of examining Muslim political thought, quotes a rector of al-Azhar who said in 1939: 'As for the celebrated maxim: Give unto Caesar what is Caesar's and unto God what is God's—it is in no way related to the principles of Islam.'[6] To obey the Prophet is to obey God and to disobey him is to disobey God. Similarly, obedience to the successor of the Prophet is mandatory, so long as he does not order what is contrary to Revelation. There can, then, be no scope for constitutionalism or theories of representation and consent. Early in its history, orthodox Islam decisively rejected the Kharidjite contention that government must be controlled by the general body of the believers. True, Muslim theology speaks of Consensus and Consultation. But Consensus is a principle of authority, a bulwark of tradition, to ensure that no innovation is accepted unless the learned of the community declare it to be in conformity with the Qur'an and the prophetic Tradition; and Consultation is not to be taken to mean representative government. 'Islamic constitutional law', writes Grunebaum, 'never limited the power of the ruler. Legal theory and accepted custom imposed certain bodily and mental qualifications on any candidate for the highest office, but no curtailment of executive absolutism was envisaged.' Equally, there can be no scope for Natural Law. The status of those who are part of the Muslim polity is regulated by Revelation. The rights and obligations of each class of inhabitants, believers, people of the Book, heathen, is determined by divine positive Law. The 'state' of this or that creature, writes Gardet, is not determined by what constitutes its essence, but is applied to it from the outside by God giving it a name and attributes. No rights are inherent in men as such; there is, for instance, no inherent right to freedom; freedom for the Muslim jurists is the legal status of not being enslaved to another. Grunebaum's words may sum up this brief discussion of the bases of political thought in Islam: 'Correctness as the basic purpose of life', he writes, 'makes for authoritarianism.'

Authority comes from God and must be exercised in the service of God. The exercise of power is necessary to the welfare of religion. Thus formulated, the theory assigns only one limit to authority, namely, that its exercise shall conform to Revelation: the ruler, the caliph, must command the performance of good actions and forbid the performance of evil. But who is to ensure that he will act in conformity with Revelation? The answer is, nobody here on earth. Two features of the theory vie with each other in making this the only possible answer. In the first place the theory has no place for constitutional checks and balances. In the second place, all power comes from God; if God sees fit to give power to a tyrannical, immoral, irreligious ruler, who shall dare to sit in judgment and gainsay His will? Quite early do we find this train of thought in the political theory of orthodox Islam. The Ummayads, the Murji'ites argued, were the rulers of the Muslims to whom fealty had been sworn; so long as they were not polytheists, it was the duty of Muslims to obey them, and to postpone until the last day all judgment of any misdeeds the Ummayads might commit. When, as came to be the case in Muslim history, there was a succession of tyrannical and unjust rulers, Ummayads, Abbasids and those who came after them, an imperceptible but fundamental transformation took place in Muslim political theory. Obedience to Muhammad as the head of the Muslim polity had been mandatory because it was part of the religious duty of the Muslim, and necessary to his salvation. Now obedience to the ruler was a necessity because rule—even the worst—is from God, and provides that modicum of security without which the believer is unable to attend to the devotions necessary to salvation. Any ruler is better than none. Rule and religion are twins. Religion is a foundation and rule a guardian: what has no foundation is destroyed, and what has no guardian is lost. Thus al-Ghazali, in an impressive—and what may be called a definitive—exposition of the duty of obedience to a ruler whose rule is effective. Rule and religion are twins: the assertion echoes down the Muslim centuries. Grunebaum declares the idea to be of Sassanian origin and to have gained currency in Abbasid times. He traces it in Ibn Qutaiba (d. 889 of the Christian era), in Ibn al-Mu'tazz (d. 908), in al-Bairuni (d. 1048). And al-Ghazali (d. 1111) builds round it his argument in *The Economy of Faith*.[7] The attitude persists into modern times. The Congress of the Caliphate meeting in Cairo in 1926 lays it down that a Muslim can legitimately become a caliph if he establishes his claim by conquest, even if he does not fulfill any of the other conditions required by the jurists.

The faithful resign themselves to the evil necessity of obeying rulers who transgress the divine law. The learned deplore and keep aloof. Their political science becomes a formal elaboration of the rules of conduct of the perfect Muslim ruler. And their 'narrow and worried' interpretation of the Muslim ideal 'would seem', writes Grunebaum, 'to bear most of the guilt of the corroding discord between fiction and reality that, in the later Middle Ages, pervades Muslim society more profoundly than it does, of necessity, any human organization'.

Actual politics is arbitrary, tainted with illegality, refractory to the operations of the intellect. No good man will endanger his salvation by participating in it. The attentions of government are to be avoided. Grunebaum quotes a saying attributed to the caliph al-Ma'mun: 'The best life has he who has an ample house, a beautiful wife, and sufficient means, who does not know us and whom we do not know.' Civic sense is absent, and municipal franchises unheard of. 'Power is fascinating and awesome but transient', and 'the prevailing attitude to power is scepticism . . . . ' The ruler is he who wields power, so long as he wields it. This is the balance of Muslim history as Grunebaum strikes it.

Such, in the main, are the lineaments of Muslim society and the operative principles of Muslim civilization. A powerful religious impulse and 14 centuries of history continuously interacting have combined to produce a culture the flavour of which is unmistakable. On this there is consensus among modern Orientalists. But a question arises. Could it have been, could it be otherwise? If one could disentangle the essential principles of Islam from the accidents of Muslim history, could one perhaps show that passive obedience, acquiescence in tyranny, and the justificatory virtue of force in government are not the inevitable consequences of Islam as a system of beliefs, but rather of extraneous influences powerfully impinging on Muslim society? Such a question is not, strictly speaking, historical. To answer it is to go beyond the delineation of the concrete and complex whole of beliefs, traditions, attitudes and actions which make a particular society what in the historian's eye it seems to be. To answer it is to assume that it is feasible to separate the sheep from the goats, to say of one factor present and active in a society, that it is an essential principle, and of another such factor, that it is an extraneous influence; and further perhaps, that influences once extraneous will always remain less significant than the essential principles. H.A.R. Gibb has argued that 'the nemesis of the over-rapid conquests of the Arabs—and the political tragedy of Islam—was that the Islamic ideology never found its proper and articulated expression in the political institutions of the Islamic states'.[8] The fact that the Muslim empire became so extensive so soon after the prophetic message meant, according to Gibb, that

Muslim society had no social institutions powerful enough to stand up to the military and political institutions, and the Ummayad caliphs soon began to show an interest in the Hellenic and Sassanid conceptions of universal empire and of absolute monarchy. This tendency became more powerful in Abbasid times. Gibb also had earlier spoken of a 'secretarial class' in the Abbasid court bent on introducing into Muslim society Persian traditions of rule and rigid class divisions.[9] The rapid extension of empire and the activities of the secretarial class meant that 'several of the principal elements of the Sassanian tradition were incorporated in the literature of the Arabic humanities, and acquired an established and permanent place in Islamic culture in the relation to the principles of government in spite of their conflict with its inner spirit'. And Gibb recurs to this point: '. . . the Abbasid caliphate,' he writes, 'so far from adapting its practice to the principles of the Islamic ideology, imposed on the official jurists of Islam the task of adapting their principles to its practice.' Gibb's argument, then, here seems to identify two opposites in Muslim history: the original Muslim principles of government, and the Sassanid corruptions thereof. In his *Mohammedanism*,[10] which replaces Margoliouth's volume in the Home University Library, Gibb seems also to endow *Araberthum*, as he designates the Arab idea, with the virtue of safeguarding Muslim orthodoxy. He goes so far as to speak of the 'Persian and Turkish veneer' which had overlaid the early Arabian principles of Islam; and he gives the impression that he believes, a little uncertainly perhaps, that the modern Arab nationalist movement and the reform of Islam are somehow connected. These views are not without precedent, especially in the writings of the Muslims themselves. In Abbasid times there was great mutual jealousy between the Arab and the non-Arab Muslims, and Arab writers emphasized the Arab character of true Islam and attacked the corruptions introduced by the foreigner. Even today, Arab Muslim writers argue that the fulfillment of Arab nationalism is the fulfillment of Islam.[11] But these views are not without difficulty. For even if we disregard the so-called Sassanid corruptions of Islam, we still have to take notice of the absence of constitutionalism in the ideal Muslim polity, of the unquestioned supremacy, under God, of the leader of the Muslim community, and of the occasionalism and voluntarism of Muslim theology; these may serve abundantly to explain the passive obedience, and the respect of the *fait accompli*, which give its unmistakable character to Muslim history. In any case, Gibb points out, by the fourth decade of Islam, the authority of the military power already overrode whatever restraints religion may have been capable of imposing. So that, we may perhaps conclude, these attempts to distinguish between Arab and Sassanid strands in Muslim history represent less an explanation of the Muslim past than a hope for the Arab future.

Modern European Orientalists have not always held these views. Margoliouth, in his Home University Library volume, has, it is interesting to note, a passage where he discusses the contribution of the different races to Islamic society. D.G. Hogarth, a perspicuous observer of Islam, wrote: 'Arab civilization owes a heavy obligation to the Greek, to the Persian, to the Jewish, but no heavier than are debited to all other greater civilizations. Every advanced human culture must be eclectic and its originality is reckoned by the measure in which it transforms and makes its own what it has seized.'[12] And Grunebaum remarks in *Medieval Islam* that 'Islam's originality consists exactly in the capacity of adapting the alien inspiration to its needs, of re-creating it in its own garb, and of rejecting the unadaptable', and that 'while very little of its conceptual and not too much of its emotional contribution is new or unique, its style of thought and range of feelings are without a real precedent'.[13] Grunebaum's, Hogarth's and Margoliouth's is surely the more catholic view.

Gardet puts the case, in an interesting manner, for a hopeful view of the future of Muslim politics. In the past, Byzantine and Sassanid influences, as well as historical contingencies, had made Muslim government tyrannical, lawless and oppressive. But there is no inherent logical reason, Gardet argues, why the voluntarist, authoritarian character of Muslim thought should always have these results. The Islamic ideology of which Gibb speaks consists of these ethical commands and prohibitions which may be summed up in Qur'anic injunction to the believer to command the good and prohibit evil. These commands and prohibitions are grounded not in Natural Law but in the Will of God. But these precepts, says Gardet, are in fact identical with those of which Natural Law affirms the objective and eternal validity. If historical contingencies have, in the past, led to the justification of passive obedience to arbitrary rule, may not different contingencies, in the future, lead to some other aspect of Muslim thought being emphasized? Just as Byzantine and Sassanid influence crystallized the tendency of Islam to emphasize the arbitrary nature of government as a manifestation of God's will, so Gardet hopes that the influence of European constitutionalism will lead Islam to emphasize the fact that the positive commands of God's will as they are authoritatively set out in the Qur'an enjoin the practice of justice, the respect of the rights of God and man, and the keeping of promises.[14]

Gardet's position is thus somewhat different from Gibb's. Whereas Gibb seems to look to Arabism for a restoration of the primeval and uncorrupt state of Islam, Gardet hopes for European influences to help in the work of rejuvenation. Gardet's hopes for the future raise the question of cultural contacts, of the effects of one civilization on another. Grunebaum discusses the matter in a chapter in *Islam* which deals with the ideas A.J. Toynbee has made popular. Grunebaum points out that Toynbee's theory of cultural borrowing cannot fit all areas and all periods. If we consider the spread of Hellenism in the Middle East, for instance, or the contributions which Byzantium, Persia and India made to Muslim civilization, we must disagree with Toynbee's theory, and conclude that cultural borrowing need not begin at a trifling level, that it does not compel ever-renewed borrowing, and that it need not be disruptive in all circumstances. But, of course, there is no gainsaying the fact that European influence in the Middle East has, in modern times, proved disruptive. Grunebaum attributes this chiefly to the political and military inferiority of the East today. Another, perhaps as potent, reason to which Grunebaum alludes lies in the character of what Europe has offered, and what the East has accepted. Nationalism has proved a great disruptive influence within Europe itself, and it is this doctrine which Muslim political thinkers have adopted and tried to interpret in Muslim terms. Nationalism is not tender towards constitutionalism and individual liberties, and by the very exclusiveness and arrogance which it fosters, prevents or powerfully impedes further borrowing from an alien culture. Here, then, are two reasons why Gardet's hopefulness may not be justified.

S.G. Haim has discussed the reasons why nationalist doctrine should have found an echo in Islam, and she finds the answer partly in the vivid sense of solidarity which the Muslim community has always inculcated in its members.[15] However tyrannical the Muslim state, and however aloof the learned classes of the community might hold themselves from the wielders of power, there was, as Grunebaum remarks, an overwhelming feeling for the oneness of the Muslim community, and a realization that any political sacrifice was justified to enable the community to continue under the law as far as possible. And the Muslim state was originally, after all, as Margoliouth pointed out, to be composed of soldier-priests. It is this solidarity, this identification of the individual with the state which nationalist ideology has mobilized. But in his *Modern Trends in Islam*[16] Gibb has argued that nationalism is 'clearly opposed' to Islam. This view is no doubt connected with the other view which he advances in his *Mohammedanism*: that with the gradual and increasing corruption of power there came to be 'two distinct societies living side by side and interacting to some extent but in their basic principles opposed to one another'. One may perhaps doubt whether this almost Augustinian opposition of the heavenly and the earthly cities has ever obtained widely in Islam: passivity, quietism, mistrust of power there certainly was, but along with this, a pride in the solidarity of Islam, and a closing of the ranks whenever unbelievers attempted to encroach on the Muslim estate. The Muslim community was both a heavenly and an earthly city.

Almost the only point where Grunebaum's views are at variance with the rest of his book is the passage where he asserts that in the Middle East today the middle classes are coming into their own—just as the *tiers état* did at the French Revolution, and that this is what makes significant the recent constitutional developments there. But constitutions introduced from Europe have not proved a success in the Middle East. What has proved a success, on the other hand, is the European technique of governmental control that was perfected during the 18th century, and the genesis of which M. Beloff has so well examined in his *Age of Absolutism*. This technique has enabled the rulers to extend and perfect their control over the subjects, and there is a good case for arguing that middle-class urban institutions of self-government, like trade and craft guilds which led a tolerated existence on the margin of official Muslim organization, have wilted and withered owing to the more searching and meticulous attention of government. In her inaugural lecture, Professor A.K.S. Lambton has well described how this process worked out in Persia.[17] In any case, we must be circumspect when talking of 'middle classes' in the context of Muslim history, and particularly so at present. Analogies from European history may lead us to think that the 'middle classes' have now wrested power from the 'feudal gentry' of Muslim society. But this analysis does not withstand a closer scrutiny. The rulers of the Middle East today have been, whether in Persia or the Ottoman empire or Egypt, members—humble ones, it is true— of the political and military institutions which the 'middle classes' are supposed to have captured. These men, imbued with nationalism and a radical contempt for traditions, were only able to capture the state and effect the momentous transformation which we now see, not because they were of the middle class, but because they belonged to the political and military institutions, and were able to use these institutions as levers for their disaffection. The passage of a quarter of a century since he published his book has only served to confirm that on this one point Grunebaum's great learning and capacious intelligence—which continue to instruct and delight his readers—has played him false.

3

RULE AND RELIGION IN IRAN

Watching the 1978-9 events in Iran, the world has stood wide-eyed and open-mouthed in astonishment. A regime seemingly solid and powerful crumbled into dust under the impact of preachings and denunciations directed from abroad by a divine who had been an obscure exile for the previous 15 years. The departure of the Shah was followed by the volatilization of his army, by a referendum instituting an Islamic republic, and then by one approving a constitution which gives supreme authority to the Ayatollah Khomeini who, since he set foot back in Iran in February 1979, has anyway been accepted without rival as the final arbiter in all public affairs.

How these remarkable events came to pass, why the imperial regime seemed paralyzed in dealing with urban demonstrations and riots, to what the Shah's curious passivity and hesitancy during the fateful autumn of 1978 is to be ascribed, what role exactly was played in these events by the United States and the United Kingdom, and what advice they gave their hapless friend—to all these questions, in the absence of reliable and detailed evidence, no satisfactory answer is yet possible. But it does seem possible, on the other hand, to establish what political doctrine Khomeini propounds, and on what ground he bases his claim to the exercise of supreme authority—a claim now formally ratified by what is claimed to be a majority of voters in the recent referendum. To establish this will throw some light on the intellectual crisis in contemporary Islam as it grapples with the problem of political order in the modern world, and attempts to fashion a theory of political obligation out of its own traditional concepts.

Khomeini's political doctrine is essentially simple.[1] It is that the world of Islam, Iran included, has for a long time now been the victim of Western aggression. This aggression has taken the form of imperialism, which is made necessary by, and in turn facilitates, capitalist exploitation. Imperialism and capitalism create moral corruption and thus, in addition,

---

'Persia' officially became 'Iran' in 1935.

constitute a deadly threat to Islam as a religion and as a way of life. This theme has recurred in Khomeini's discourse over the years. To take one example, he declares in his *Islamic Government* lectures: 'To achieve their unjust economic goals, the colonialists employed the help of their agents in our countries. As a result of this, there are hundreds of millions of starving people who lack the simplest health and educational means. On the other side there are individuals excessively wealthy and blatantly corrupt.' And again: 'How can we allow a handful of exploiters and foreigners who dominate by force of arms when they deprive hundreds of millions from enjoying in the slightest the good things and the pleasures which life bestows? The duty of the divines, as of all Muslims, is to put a stop to this oppression, and to strive for the happiness of millions of people and, by founding an Islamic government which will labour with a devoted zeal, to destroy and do away with tyrannical governments.'

About this doctrine it may be said, in the first place, that it constitutes the total reversal of a trend which had, outwardly at least, become increasingly dominant in the Muslim world from the beginning of the 19th century until the end of the second world war. Khomeini's doctrine, in other words, rejects Westernization as a way of safeguarding Islam and ensuring the welfare and prosperity of Muslims. But, in the second place, like the doctrine of Westernization, Khomeini's doctrine also draws on Western thought and categories. For it is not by accident that his doctrine bears a family resemblance to the Marxist-Hobsonian doctrines which, with the triumph of Bolshevism and the rise of the Soviet Union to Superpower status, have become the most popular and widespread doctrines in Asia and Africa. Nor is Khomeini the first or only proponent of these doctrines in the Muslim world. In the 1920s similar doctrines were put forward by Soviet Muslims such as Sultan Galiev who, taking a leaf out of Marxism, argued that the Muslims were among the truly proletarian nations in the world, the real victims of European capitalism. These views were firmly suppressed by the Soviet authorities and its authors liquidated. Again, in the decade immediately preceding Khomeini's sudden rise, the Libyan leader, Colonel Qadhafi, put forward his so-called third theory, in which the poor peoples of the south—Muslims included—were the down-trodden victims and the eventual heirs of the rich peoples of the north. To say that the origins of this doctrine, whatever its variants, are ultimately European is not to say that it has no points of contact or affinities with Islam. Its anti-Western stance chimes in with the traditional Islamic antagonism towards Christendom that centuries of conflict had generated. The doctrine, again, in denouncing capitalism and its vices and corruptions necessarily favours egalitarianism and collectivism as the balm with which to heal a diseased and moribund body politic. And in Islam, as it happens, there does exist a strong tendency to put the collectivity above the individual and to treat individual believers as equals. In traditional Islam these tendencies have not usually had political or economic consequences, but a doctrine that preaches the beneficence of such consequences will find an answering chord among the mass of the believers. This is particularly the case when the mass is discomforted and disoriented, and when its wonted train of life has been more or less violently disturbed. This will serve to explain why so many Iranian city-dwellers, most of them probably recent immigrants from the countryside living squalid and hopeless lives in an alien environment, are so ready to listen to Khomeini's good tidings, to come out in demonstrations and processions and generally manifest a vibrant collective enthusiasm. It will also explain the devotion shown by Egyptians to the similar teachings of the Muslim Brethren, and even perhaps the recent bizarre attempt by a large and determined group to seize the Grand Mosque housing the sacred stone, the Ka'ba, in Mecca. This group was led by a *mahdi* bearing (as is foretold in the prophecies) the same name as the Prophet, whose appearance on the first day of the new century (again as is foretold in the prophecies) will herald the restoration of justice to a world filled with injustice and oppression.

Khomeini's social and political doctrines may legitimately be described as radical. But this radicalism is not peculiar to Khomeini, or to Iran and Shi'ism. As has been seen, it has spread in various parts of the Muslim world, whether Sunni or Shi'ite. But there is more to Khomeini than political and social radicalism. For this Shi'ite divine also propounds a no less radical doctrine concerning political authority and its legitimate exercise.

Khomeini is a *mujtahid*, an eminent divine learned in the law of Islam. Had he been a Sunni and not a Shi'ite divine it would have been most improbable for him to have played the role he has lately played, let alone to have attained such prodigious success in playing it. Fairly early in the history of Islam it became clear that Sunni religious figures were firmly under the control of the rulers, and this has remained the case till the present day. It is otherwise in Shi'ism, and Khomeini's independence, his following, and even his success which seemed so unexpected, become intelligible in the context of Iranian Shi'ism.

Shi'ism has its origin in the political conflicts which rent the nascent Islamic community shortly after the Prophet's death. Shi'ites hold that Ali, the Prophet's cousin and son-in-law, and no one else, was Muhammad's legitimate heir, specifically designated as such by the Prophet in his own lifetime. It follows that others who claimed supreme authority in the Muslim community were illegitimate usurpers. Shi'ites also came to believe that only Ali's descendants were the legitimate rulers of the Muslim community. The Shi'ites who are now to be found in Iran (as well as in Iraq, the Lebanon and elsewhere) also believe that the twelfth descendant of Ali entered into a major occultation in the year 329 of the Hijra (i.e. 940 of the Christian era), that he is now alive but hidden, and that he will in due course re-appear to re-establish a state based on divine justice as revealed in the Qur'an. Hence these Shi'ites are known in the literature as Twelver Shi'ites.

For many centuries the Shi'ites led the life of a sect by and large without the benefit of a territorial base or political sovereignty. Indeed it was only from the beginning of the 16th century with the establishment of the Safavids (who ruled Persia from 1501 to 1722) that Twelver Shi'ism came to enjoy the benefit (and suffer the disadvantage) of being the officially established religion of Persia. It was during the long centuries of political powerlessness that the main lines and details of Shi'ite theology and jurisprudence were established and distinguished from the teachings of the other Islamic schools. This, of course, was the work of generations of eminent divines who, in a manner akin to that of the rabbis in post-exilic Judaism, preserved the identity and coherence of their community. These divines, then, enjoyed a standing and authority denied their Sunni analogues. This standing and authority can best be expressed in the terms of Twelver Shi'ite doctrine itself, which holds that at the major occultation of the twelfth Imam, i.e. head or leader, the divines were collectively designated as his general agents.

Prior to this major occultation, a minor occultation had occurred during which the Hidden Imam was deemed to communicate to his faithful through the intermediary of four agents. These received queries from the believers, transmitted them to the Imam and came back with his answers 'in his own handwriting'. The last communication to be made in this manner was that which the last of the four agents disclosed on his death bed. In this last message the agent was told of his own forthcoming death and was instructed that he should not designate anyone to fill his place, that the Imam would re-appear but only with God's permission and after a lengthy duration of global tyranny, and that in the meantime many would claim to have seen him, but such claims would be false. From the time, therefore, of this major occultation the Imam was incommunicado.

This doctrine of general agency meant in practice that the believers were to avoid appealing to the (usurped) authority of the ungodly rulers in whose territories they resided, and to regulate their communal and private affairs according to the rulings and judgments of their divines. The doctrine did not mean, and could not have meant or implied that these divines enjoyed the infallibility with which the Imam has come to be invested in Shi'ite theology. They could not enjoy any of his prerogatives, or even claim to transmit his orders and injunctions, since after the major occultation, the Imam was *ex hypothesi* incommunicado. Like any other mortal, divines were fallible, and like any other mortal they could become guilty of wrongdoing. What distinguished them from their fellow-believers was their greater knowledge of the law, a knowledge that imposed on them special duties and responsibilities.

The doctrine of the Hidden Imam was to have significant consequences for the political theory and the political attitudes of Twelver Shi'ism. In the course of time the Imam (as well as his 11 predecessors, beginning with Ali) came to be considered as much more than simply the legitimate ruler of the Muslim community. The Imam came to be seen as the spiritual guide leading men to the inner meaning of the universe, and akin to the *axis mundi* around whom the spheres of existence rotate. His significance came to be more soteriological and eschatological than political. In other words, the Imamate became more a topic for theology than for legal theory. The development of this Shi'ite mysticism has as its concomitant a depreciation of the political, and the inculcation of an attitude of patient expectation. This attitude, together with a belief in the esoteric significance of all appearance and all being are indeed what until very recently outside observers chiefly associated with Shi'ism. Nor would they have been mistaken. From early on a distinction was worked out in Shi'ism between Imamate, through which divine knowledge illuminates the world, and Caliphate, actual rule over men.

All this might have meant that Twelver Shi'ism would, unlike Sunni Islam, see a separation between the realm of religion and the realm of politics, the disappearance of that Caesaropapism that Islam fully shares with Byzantine Christianity, and the eventual development of a secular view of politics. Though the doctrinal prerequisites were there, such a development did not in fact take place. Why? It can perhaps be said that the Safavids, claiming descent from Ali, surrounded their rule with a religious aura that made it highly unlikely for a secular view of rule to emerge. Such an aura further enhanced the position of the monarch who had by then come to be traditionally revered as the shadow of God on earth. Though the idea of the ruler as the shadow of God on earth is pre-Islamic, by Safavid times it had become fully assimilated into traditional political attitudes. It provided an explanation and justification of the rule of a king who dispensed and guaranteed justice in society. This theory was distinct from the Shi'ite theory of the Imam as descendant of Ali and ruling by virtue of an unbroken line of designation from the Prophet onwards.

What attitude did the Shi'ite divines take towards the Safavids? They were at the outset greatly dependent on the rulers whose power was necessary to impose and protect Shi'ism as the official religion of the state. Though the later Safavids attracted the contempt of the divines through their impolicy, failures and dissolute mode of living, there is no evidence of any serious challenge to their rule based on doctrine. Nor was there any change in the general characteristics of the Shi'ite outlook, which continued to devalue politics and to focus its devotion on the Imam, the true king who was hidden, whose significance was spiritual and cosmic rather than mundane and earthly.

This political quietism and passivity continued to be a most salient, and at times the dominant, characteristic of Shi'ite religiosity in Persia. This was true not only of the population at large, but of those divines whose pre-eminence in learning and piety was such that it secured for them a peculiar primacy and authority recognized by their fellow-divines all over the Shi'ite world. The attitude to political power of those most eminent Ayatollahs was one of silence *(sokut)* or, if silence was to be departed from, then their duty, as they conceived it, was to advise and not to fight.

No dynasty following the Safavids could attempt to lay claim to descent from Ali, and could not therefore benefit from the religious aura that this descent conferred. Also, from the end of the 18th century onward the Persian state was continually and increasingly under pressure, both external and internal. European states, including Russia, which bordered on Persia, were becoming vastly more powerful than any Islamic state, and their interests—economic, political and military—could not but impinge in all kinds of ways on Persia. The downfall of the Safavids, again, inaugurated a long period of disorder. Eventually the Qajars emerged at the end of the century to establish a new dynasty that was to subsist until 1925 when Reza Khan put an end to it. During the Qajar period the Persian state did not enjoy the increased powers which centralization—the outcome of Westernizing reform—conferred on the Ottoman rulers or on Muhammad Ali of Egypt. At the same time the burden of a traditionally despotic state was felt to be increasingly onerous. A weak yet despotic government enhanced the power of the divines to act as shields and intercessors, standing between the government and the people. Their position was based not only on the respect and veneration shown to them by the people, but also on the fact that theirs were not official appointments, that they enjoyed financial independence which donations by the faithful made possible, that some of the most important centres of Shi'ite learning lay in Ottoman Mesopotamia, beyond the reach of Persian power. Also the educational and judicial functions that they, not the state, discharged further increased their importance.

Under the successors of the Safavids the monarch continued to be looked upon as the shadow of God on earth, and such discussion by the religious doctors of the relation between the ruler, and the Hidden Imam and his general agents the divines did not deny or impugn the legitimacy as such of an earthly ruler who acknowledged the lordship of the Hidden Imam, in governing the community of his fellow-believers. It would seem that there were even divines to be found who were ready to draw a distinction akin to the medieval Western distinction between the two swords, and to argue that rulers were delegated by the Imam to wield the sword, while divines were delegated by Him to preserve, transmit and promote knowledge of revelation and divine law. This distinction is not without analogy to the distinction between Imamate and Caliphate mentioned above.

Conditions in late-19th-century and early-20th-century Persia conspired to increase burdens and exactions on the non-official classes, and at the same time to bring the ruler, his court and administration into disrepute. One suspicion in particular came to be widely held and propagated, namely that misgovernment was a cause (and perhaps also a consequence) of increasing encroachments by foreigners—whether financial, commercial or political—and that these encroachments would end in complete domination of the Muslims by European unbelievers and the extinction of their independence. For many reasons, the religious classes felt particularly threatened by all these ominous developments, and eventually took the lead in opposing the oppression which the Shah and his servants were generally felt to be practising.

The two important events in which divines took the lead and revealed the extent of their popular following was the Tobacco Protest of 1891-2 and the Constitutional Revolution of 1905-6. In the first episode, the most eminent divine of the Shi'ite world, from his residence in Samarra in Ottoman Mesopotamia, denounced the monopoly of trade in tobacco which the Shah, in an attempt to augment his revenues had granted to a British syndicate, as opening the door to a dangerous foreign encroachment on the independence and the interests of the faithful. He proclaimed abstention from smoking as a religious duty so long as the monopoly was not rescinded. The ban was obeyed, and the Shah was compelled to cancel the monopoly.

The episode clearly showed the great power which the religious classes could draw from popular support. But it does not show that, in calling upon the believers to resist foreign encroachment, the divines were advancing a new theory which made the Shah's power unlawful per se, or *a fortiori* claimed that the divines were the only legitimate rulers in the community of believers. The same holds true of the events of 1905-06. These events, which eventually led to a constitution for Persia being granted by the Shah, also had their origin in popular grievances. These related to the profligacy of the Shah, the corruption and arbitrariness of his servants, and the encroaching influence of European powers and European officials to which such misgovernment and oppression led. The initial demands originally focused on the dismissal of foreign officials who had been imported to administer the customs, and on establishing a 'house of justice' where grievances could be heard and remedied. Here again, prominent divines took up and led the popular cause. But here, too, it cannot be said that a new theory of government, based on accepted traditional teachings, was put forward which might give sanction to the exercise of political power by divines, or might even dispute the legitimacy of the ruler. What in the end became a movement to obtain a constitution was based, in point of doctrine, on a hotch-potch of Western ideas hardly compatible with Twelver Shi'ite doctrines. Nor did the attacks on the Shah generally or systematically impugn monarchial legitimacy, but rather strove to cast doubt on the legitimacy of this particular Shah by portraying him as the agent and instrument of foreign domination, and by the insinuation that somehow or

other he was akin to, or descended from, those wrong-doing rulers who had
fought the Imam Ali and murdered his son, the Imam Husayn.

Just as Khomeini's substantive teachings, as has been seen, are
suffused with European assumptions and doctrines, so the arguments in
favour of a constitution advanced by divines in 1905-6 were also heavily
indebted to European sources. The most elaborate argument in favour of a
constitution written by a divine and claiming to demonstrate its contentions
by appeal to Islamic principles is broken-backed and flimsy, and in fact
derives, through the intermediary of an Arabic author, from a treatise on
tyranny by an 18th-century Italian progressive, Alfieri. The Constitution as
enacted, in fact, contains two utterly incompatible groups of ideas:
European and Islamic. On one hand, it is declared that sovereignty is a trust
confided by the people in the person of the Shah, that the powers of the realm
are derived from the people, and that all inhabitants of Persia enjoy equal
rights before the law. All these propositions, it is obvious, went against the
teachings of Twelver Shi'ism, just as did elections, which the Constitution
also enjoined. On the other hand, the Constitution enacted that Islam
according to the teachings of Twelver Shi'ism was the religion of the state,
and it made provision for the establishment of a board consisting of five
divines who were to examine all proposed legislation, and who had the
power to 'reject and repudiate, wholly or in part, any such proposal which is
at variance with the Sacred Laws of Islam, so that it shall not obtain the title
of legality'.

This last provision, which remained a dead letter, represents the
utmost that, in the favourable circumstances of 1905-6, the divines secured,
or perhaps even wished to secure, in order to register the central importance
of the faith in public life. But the strains between their principles and those
derived from Europe were too great to be resolved. The sticking point
proved to be the clause laying down equality of rights for all the inhabitants
of Persia. This could not be reconciled with divine law which decreed an
inferior status for non-Muslims. Only one of the prominent divines in
Teheran who had supported the agitation against the Shah declared himself
in favour. The others were henceforth alienated from the Constitutional
cause.

This cursory survey of Twelver Shi'ite political thought will serve
to underline how radical Khomeini's departure from it has been, how his
claim that divines should be rulers has introduced so novel an element in the
doctrine that it cannot but considerably increase the strains which the
attempt to come to terms with modernity has inevitably occasioned. As is
now well known, Ayatollah Khomeini, having fiercely denounced the Shah
for oppression and for delivering his country into the hands of the
Americans, and having called for the overthrow of the government, was
exiled from Iran in June 1963. He went to Turkey, and moved in 1965 to

Najaf (in Iraq), the most important Shi'ite shrine, where he was to remain until his departure for Paris in the autumn of 1978.

From Najaf, Khomeini continued to attack the Shah and his regime in the strongest and most uncompromising terms. He burned with conviction, and was as utterly sure of the justice of his cause as of its eventual triumph. As he told an audience of theology students in Najaf:

> It is fortunate that the Muslim peoples are with you and that the masses follow you and take your lead. You will grow stronger. All we need is the staff of Moses and the sword of [The Iman] Ali ibn Abu Talib and their mighty will. If we resolve to set up an Islamic rule, we will also get the staff of Moses and Ali ibn Abu Talib's sword.

This passage figures towards the end of a course of lectures on *Islamic Government* which the Ayatollah delivered in 1970, and which contains his vision of Islamic society and of the central role which the divines must occupy in it. The lectures are far from being mere rhetoric. They constitute a closely reasoned legal argument drawing upon Qur'anic verses, Traditions of the Prophet and the Imams, and on recognized Shi'ite authorities, the upshot of which is to establish the proposition that, during the absence of the Awaited Mahdi, the only legitimate ruler in the Muslim community is the pious and learned divine. Islamic government, he argues, can only be government according to the divine law. In his lifetime, the Prophet implemented the laws revealed to him: 'he punished, cut off the thief's hand, lashed and stoned and ruled justly'. Obedience to God meant obedience to the Prophet, and the same obedience was due to the Prophet's caliphs, i.e. successors, who were the Imam Ali and those subsequently designated to follow him. It is in general established that a government is necessary for the welfare of the believers—a government which would have the same powers as the Prophet and his (rightful) successors.

But, in the absence of the Hidden Imam, who is to carry on the government of the faithful? The answer for Khomeini is simple. During the absence of the Hidden Imam, those who wield authority over the faithful are the just and upright divines who are learned in the law and will execute it. How is this proved? Khomeini quotes a saying of the Prophet's asking God to have mercy on his successors ('caliphs' in Arabic). When he was asked who his caliphs were, the Prophet said: 'Those who will follow me, transmit my sayings and my doings and teach them to people when I am gone.' Here, by caliphs, it is clear, the Prophet meant the divines. But the word caliph used here by the Prophet, Khomeini's exegesis went, is exactly the same word that the Prophet used when designating Ali as his successor. Therefore this clearly means that the divines who are the subject of the Prophet's saying quoted above have, in the absence of the Imam, the same absolute authority to rule over the faithful as Ali had. Q.E.D. The divine, then, during the Imam's occultation is 'himself the Imam of the Muslims, their leader and their justiciar, he and no one else'. This doctrine is now enshrined in the new Constitution, and Khomeini obviously considers himself to be the pre-eminent divine of his age, and expects his position to be universally acknowledged.

It is evident that Khomeini's challenge to political authority is profoundly different in character from the earlier challenges of the divines during the Tobacco Protest and in the Constitutional Movement. His doctrine constitutes a radical departure from what, over the centuries, had been established as the outlook and ethos of Twelver Shi'ism. Khomeini effects this not, of course, by jettisoning Shi'ite teachings, but by so systematically and rigorously interpreting them as to make them unrecognizable in their new uncompromising rigidity. In so doing, he transforms Shi'ism from, on the whole, a passive and quietist religion into an activist and revolutionary one. If the Caesaropapism of the Safavids tried to subjugate the religious to the ruling institution, Khomeini's Caesaropapism in reverse tries to swallow rule and assimilate it wholly into religion, to make the exercise of political power strictly dependent on right belief, and to outlaw the ruler who does not punctiliously and exactly recite his catechism. This is a state of affairs which, barring short-lived phenomena like the rule of the Sudanese Mahdi, had never obtained in Islam. It puts us in mind of similar doctrines promoted in Europe in the era of the wars of religion: Calvin's teachings and John Knox's, or say that of the famous Huguenot pamphlet, the *Vindiciae contra Tyrannos*. Knowing what the outcome was of those vaulting aspirations, we cannot but entertain dark forebodings about this latest attempt to establish on earth the heavenly city. What this phenomenon reveals and portends is a profound disorder in the conditions of Muslim life today and a strain, acute and extreme, in Islamic political thought as it tries to come to terms with the new and unfamiliar situations. The strain may be exemplified by the conduct of Khomeini himself after his return to Iran. For if the doctrine which he propounded in his lectures of 1970 is the truth and the only truth, the referenda and elections to which he has resorted—predicated as they are on the sovereignty of the people and not of God—cannot but detract from, and diminish this truth. His audacious innovations leave the dilemmas facing the divines of 1905-6 unresolved and unsurmounted. And the dangers to Shi'ite Islam of Khomeini's adventure failing may turn out to be far from negligible.

4

RELIGION AND NATIONALISM IN THE ARAB WORLD

In their overwhelming majority, the Arabs are Muslim. This, of course, is no more than a truism to which it would be superfluous to draw attention, but for the fact that its consequences in Arab society and politics, fundamental and far-reaching as they undoubtedly are, have been widely neglected, or even utterly forgotten in the West. It is interesting to explain how this happened. It was during and after the first world war that the Arabs appeared once more on the stage of world politics. They appeared then as seceders from the Ottoman empire. This empire was the last great Muslim state in the world. When its rulers joined the war on the side of the Central Powers, they appealed to and tried to make use of Islamic loyalties. Success here would have put a formidable weapon in their hands to use against the British and the French who, in India, Egypt, the Sudan and North Africa, and elsewhere, ruled over large numbers of Muslims. It was, therefore, to the interest of the Allies to play down or to counteract the appeal to Islamic sentiments. One way of doing this was by encouraging dissidence and rebellion against the Ottomans by their own Muslim subjects. By establishing contact with, and encouraging the Sharif of Mecca to rise against his Ottoman suzerains, the British succeeded—or so they thought—in dividing Muslim ranks and in neutralizing the Ottoman call to a holy war against the infidel. Thus the rising of Husayn, the Sharif of Mecca, was represented by himself, and even more so by his British patrons, as an Arab national movement, a wholesome assertion of the claims of Arab nationality against the reactionary, pernicious and sinister attractions of Pan-Islamism.

The fear of Pan-Islamism on the part of Britain and France was nothing new. It dated, in fact, from the reign of Sultan 'Abd al-Hamid II (1876-1909). As the evidence shows, it was an idea widely and firmly held in Europe that 'Abd al-Hamid sat at the centre of an intricate web of intrigue and conspiracy with tentacles all over the world of Islam. The evidence also shows that such a conspiracy did not exist. What did exist was a very deep feeling of Islamic solidarity, a vivid sense of the Muslim world as a world on its own, standing over against the non-Muslim world. This feeling manifested itself now and again, whenever Muslims were in distress, or their existence or way of life threatened by non-Muslims. Examples abound. The Italian attack on the Ottoman province of Tripoli in 1911 evoked a widespread and active feeling of sympathy by Muslims for their fellow-Muslims who were the latest subject of European-Christian aggression. Another manifestation of the same Muslim feeling of solidarity is not so well known, but perhaps even more significant. In the same year as the Italian attack on Tripoli, a group of Muslims from Setif in eastern Algeria, and another from Tlemcen in western Algeria decided, separately, that they could not bear to live under non-Muslim rule. They abandoned their homes and immigrated to the Ottoman empire. The precise discontents which led to such a decision are not at issue here; what is remarkable is the character of the decision itself, namely that Muslims in difficulty sought a solution to their problems in taking up abode in the domain of Islam, however distant it was, and however uncertain their material prospects there.

This overriding feeling of Islamic solidarity somehow came increasingly to be depreciated and indeed forgotten during and after the first world war. Such oblivion, as has been said, suited the Allies. But there was more to it than a deliberate playing down of dangerous beliefs and attitudes. British officials in particular genuinely thought that Arab nationalism was opposed to, and would thus weaken, what they called Pan-Islamism. This was not the least reason for encouraging the Sharif's rebellion and spreading the gospel of a future independent Arab state. The notion that Arabism and Islam were opposites was spread by Arab nationalists. These, at the outset, were mostly officers who had deserted from the Ottoman army. Their training and education had Westernized them more or less profoundly; they were accustomed—like their young Turk fellow-officers—to the categories of contemporary European political discourse, and had adopted Western political ideals—first and foremost that of nationalism. In nationalism, as is well known, the primordial value is the nation, and not, say, class or religion. The Arab nationalists therefore sincerely proclaimed that their aim was to establish an Arab nation-state in which Muslims, Christians and Jews would enjoy equal citizenship. These nationalists were also aware that their Western patrons and protectors looked with fear and aversion on Islam as a political force, and they emphasized therefore all the more the opposition between Arabism and Islam.

It was between the wars that the theory of Arab nationalism was endowed with a body of theoretical literature, and began to make real headway in the schools and colleges whence the official classes—whether civilian or military—were recruited. As propounded then by its most influential theoretician, Sati' al-Husri, the doctrine of Arab nationalism clearly differentiated between loyalty to Arabism and loyalty to Islam, and it was in no doubt that the former ought to have the primacy over the latter. But this aspect of the doctrine did not occasion a great debate. The younger generations who were becoming enthusiastic Arab nationalists did not feel that there was anything in the circumstances of the Arab world that required a confrontation between Arabism and Islam: the struggle for Arab independence and unity—a struggle directed against European-Christian powers and against Zionism—was in no way weakened or harmed by Islam, or any Islamic figures or institutions. One can even go further and say that Islam actually gave great strength to Arab nationalism. This is because the Arab world is overwhelmingly Muslim, and Arab nationalist leaders, Muslims almost to a man, naturally attracted to themselves the powerful feelings of loyalty and solidarity towards their leaders which Islam has instilled in its followers. Whether these nationalist leaders practised their religion or were indifferent to it did not affect the issue. And the situation was the same all over the Arab world, in Iraq and the Levant as well as in the Maghrib.

On the level of practical politics, then, not only was there no oposition between Islam and Arabism, there was actual co-operation. But this co-operation was not formulated or incorporated in the doctrine of Arab nationalism until after the second world war. This development may be seen as a dialectical one, arising out of the very doctrine of Arab nationalism as originally formulated. The doctrine insisted, as has been seen, on the primacy of Arabism, on there being an historic Arab nation, now dismembered and subject to alien rule, but entitled—and destined— to full independence and unity. It was therefore necessary for the doctrine to seek out and describe the lineaments of this nation; the doctrine, in other words, had to rely heavily—as other nationalist doctrines have commonly done—on a Westernized historical mode of argument. But to define the Arab nation in terms of its history is—sooner rather than later—to come upon the fact that Islam originated among the Arabs, was revealed in Arabic to an Arab prophet. Great significance must be attached to this tremendous fact. The ideologies of Arabism drew in the main two consequences which, in spite of their difference of emphasis, yet produced a new theoretical amalgam in which Islam and Arabism became inseparable.

Thus, Ba'thist doctrine, as articulated by its most influential exponent, the Damascene Greek Orthodox Dr. Michel 'Aflaq, held that Muhammad the Prophet of Islam was also *ipso facto* the founder of the Arab nation, and was to be venerated as such by every Arab nationalist, whether Muslim or not. 'Aflaq developed the views in a lecture of 1943, in which he declared that Islam 'represented the ascent of Arabism towards unity, power, and progress.' In such a perspective, we may say, Islam is seen as the product and expression of the Arab national genius. Another theorist, the Baghdadi Muslim Dr. 'Abd al-Rahman al-Bazzaz argued somewhat differently. In an influential, not to say seminal, lecture of 1952, Bazzaz categorically stated that the apparent contradiction between Islam and Arab nationalism which is still present in the minds of many people is due to misunderstanding, misrepresentation and misinterpretation. He eloquently showed how Islam appeared in an Arab environment, was revealed to an Arab, and embodied the best Arab values. Islam was certainly a universal religion, but it is the religion of the Arabs *par excellence*. The position of the Arabs in Islam, he said, was like that of the Russians in the Communist world, i.e., it was a special and privileged position. There could in no way be a contradiction between Islam and Arabism: 'the Muslim Arab, when he exalts his heroes, partakes of two emotions, that of the pious Muslim and that of the proud nationalist.' We can even go further, and affirm that Islam and Arabism largely overlap; and where they do not, they are not in opposition. Moreover, Arabism exalts the original Arab values which obtained at the time of Muhammad, and in doing so it purifies Islam that had become tainted with foreign corruption, and restores its true essence.

Thus the ideology of Arab nationalism which was fashioned during and immediately after the second world war, and which holds the field today, in one way or another affirms a fundamental unbreakable link between Islam and Arabism. In doing this, it articulates the unspoken assumptions of Muslim Arab nationalists, and chimes in with their feelings and practical experiences. This articulation and codification into a doctrine in turn fortifies such feelings and justifies experience, so to speak, by philosophy. But there are other reasons why Islam has come to the fore today in the politics and the political discourse of the Arab world.

We may first mention the influence of the Muslim Brethren. This organization began in 1928 in a small way in Isma'iliyya—on the Suez Canal—where its founder Hasan al-Banna was a schoolteacher. To start with, the Brethren were not concerned with politics. Banna conceived it as his mission to reclaim to Islam and a self-respecting mode of life those Muslim multitudes who had been banished to the margin of society and become spiritually disoriented through the ravages of Westernization and Western forms of economic enterprise. In a very short while, the Brethren gathered a large and devoted following. But they did not long persist in showing a lack of interest in politics. If, as they believed, the ills of Egyptian society all stemmed from the abandonment of Islam, the cure for these ills, it followed, lay in the re-establishment of the original pure Islamic order. The very dialectic of their doctrine thus led the Muslim Brethren to become a political enterprise dedicated to changing the political and constitutional arrangements which then obtained in Egypt. The Brethren had a following not only among the unsophisticated, unlettered masses, but also among students, officials and junior officers, who were themselves highly discontented with the political corruption and maladministration which was rife in Egypt under the monarchy. It is significant that some of the Free Officers who carried out the *coup d'état* of 1952 were Muslim Brethren. Some ten years or so after its foundation, the movement was well on the way to becoming a formidable political power to be reckoned with in Egypt, and between 1945 and 1952 it is estimated that it had about half-a-million members and another half-million sympathizers.

The doctrine of the Muslim Brethren was in principle applicable not only to Egypt or the Arab countries, but to all the world of Islam. If they contributed to what is now the prevailing consensus about the connection between Islam and Arabism, this came about as a result of their stand on the Palestine question. From the establishment of the British Mandate in Palestine the strategy of the Palestine Arab leaders—who were of course Muslim in their great majority—was to denounce Zionism as a threat not only to Palestine, but also to Arabism and Islam. By thus widening the conflict they hoped—quite rationally—to strengthen their hand against the Zionists and their British sponsors. From the 1930s in fact, Palestine and the Zionist threat to which it was subjected became a leading preoccupation of the Pan-Arab leaders in Iraq and the Levant. The threat was to Palestine as part of the Arab nation, but of course it was equally and simultaneously a threat to Palestine as part of the domain of Islam.

The Palestine issue did not, in the 1930s, engage very much the attention of the Egyptian political leaders. This was to come later, when the Arab league was established in Cairo under Egyptian leadership and King Faruq aspired to the leadership of the Arab world. Even so, official Egypt remained cooler and less impassioned over Palestine than the Arab leaders of Iraq and the Levant, and in fact up to the very end of the British Mandate in May 1948 Egypt kept on insisting that it would not intervene. The Muslim Brethren, on the contrary, were from the 1930s steadfast champions of the Arabs of Palestine, and it was their writings, processions and speeches against the Zionist peril in 1945-48 that awoke the Egyptian mass to the merits of this Arab-Muslim cause and made them its fervent supporters. In addition it was the Muslim Brethren who took the initiative in organizing military help for the Palestinians, before the Egyptian army was ordered to intervene in the conflict. If Arabism became a popular cause in Egypt it was thus very much through the agency of the Brethren. In Egypt, therefore, Arabism and Islam were from the start very much associated with one another, both in theory and in practice: Palestine, which effectively involved Egypt in Arabism was simultaneously and inextricably both an Arab cause and a Muslim cause.

During Nasser's long dominance in Egypt the Brethren were generally under a cloud because they came into conflict with the *Ra'is* and because Nasser encouraged, for a variety of reasons, an official ideology of so-called Arab Socialism which deliberately eschewed appeal to Islamic sentiments, and the use of an Islamic vocabulary or Islamic concepts. But this official ideology remained merely official, something which everybody knew emanated from the government, and which was dead, which did not have the power to touch the feelings or move people to act. During Nasser's 18 years the Brethren were a proscribed body, but it is estimated that they had something like a quarter-of-a-million or 300,000 secret adherents. The figure seems by no means an exaggeration, for the Brethren appealed to that Islamic solidarity which is perhaps the most profound instinct of the people, and they thus constituted a hidden but powerful current.

Though the Brethren have still not been allowed to operate publicly as an organization, under Nasser's successor the Islamic theme in Egyptian public life has come very much to the surface. Sadat himself seems to have more religious fervour than his predecessor, and his regime seems to have no qualms about openly appealing to the traditional Islamic sentiments. Two apposite and striking examples may be given. In April 1972, Sadat gave an address in the mosque of Imam Husayn in Cairo on the anniversary of the Prophet's birthday. His theme was the fight against Israel, and the necessity to be patient and to stand fast against the enemy who will, inevitably, be defeated. Such a theme is by no means original. Arab leaders have devoted countless speeches to it over the years, but what is remarkable about Sadat's speech is that it is couched wholly in religious terms, and appeals entirely to the hallowed themes of Muhammad's life and career. America and Israel have forgotten, he says, that we are the bearers of Muhammad's message; they have forgotten that in spite of persecution Muhammad never surrendered; 'he fought bravely, he stood fast and resisted until the message of truth, the message of faith, the message of Islam was realized, and its standard was raised aloft at the end of twenty-three years.' Today 'we are bearers of the same creed, we are the bearers and trustees of the message. . . . We believe that God, exalted be He, is with us, we believe that right is on our side'. Sadat exhorted his listeners to be patient, as is enjoined on the believer, and when the time comes, to vindicate their honour in battle: to liberate not only their land, but also Jerusalem, the first *qibla* (i.e., the place towards which the Muslim turns at prayer) and the third *haram* (Holy Place). About Jerusalem there can be no bargaining: 'it is not the property of an individual, but the property of us all, of the Islamic *umma*.' Jerusalem will be retrieved 'from those of whom our Book has said that submissiveness and humility is their portion'. With these people there can be no direct negotiation, since in their relations with the Prophet at Medina they showed themselves to be 'vile, untrustworthy and treacherous'.

Another document is even more significant than this speech in exhibiting the political vocabulary and arguments by means of which the Egyptian regime seeks to establish a rapport with the people and involve them in its purposes. This is a small booklet entitled *Our Religious Faith is our Path to Victory*. This booklet was printed in a million copies in the summer of 1973 and distributed to all Egyptian soldiers, obviously in preparation for the coming war. In itself a booklet of this kind is nothing out of the ordinary. All armies find it essential to indoctrinate their soldiers, teach them the virtues of discipline and obedience, and the necessity of surmounting fear on the battlefield, as well as the allurements of enemy propaganda. What is remarkable about this Egyptian booklet is the manner in which it seeks to attain this end. It does this exclusively by quotations from the Qur'an and the Traditions of the Prophet, by recalling Muhammad's record and the early Islamic conquests. There is hardly any reference to Arabism as such, or to the Zionist or Israeli enemies. The cause is Islam, the example is the Prophet and his Companions, and the Jews are the enemies, the very same Jews that Muhammad had to fight. The relevant section here is entitled: 'Good Tidings of Victory over our Enemies the Jews.' The good tidings consist of citations from the Qur'an where the Jews are cursed for their transgression, denounced for their hostility to the believers and threatened with punishment here and thereafter. *Jihad* is recalled as a Muslim's duty the accomplishment of which is rewarded with Paradise, and the military virtues which *jihad* necessitates are extolled as peculiarly Islamic virtues which the Arabs have learned in 'the school of Islam'. Islam, the booklet says 'praises the believer who is strong, and considers him more useful and better in the sight of God than a believer who is [physically] weak'. Islam, again, exhorts the Muslim to be prepared to encounter his enemy: the Prophet is quoted as saying that 'Whoever learnt the Qur'an and then forgot it is not one of us, and whoever learnt shooting and forgot it is not one of us'; the Prophet, the booklet also recalls, approved the use of mosques as military training grounds.

In short, then, the cause for which the soldiers were to do battle is pre-eminently an Islamic cause, and the military virtues are pre-eminently Islamic virtues. The whole doctrine of the booklet may be summed up in the Qur'anic verse that God has made the Arabs as the best among nations (*umma wasatann*), which the booklet quotes and follows with the comment that God in his wisdom has designed Muhammad's *umma* to be an *umma* given to holy war, to be impregnable and not submissive or acquiescing in humiliation. Arabism and Islam are coeval or, rather, Islam is the soul of Arabism.

Such a view is now all the more influential because of a shift in the political centre of gravity in the Arab world. In the last decade or so, the income derived from the oil of the Arabian peninsula has greatly increased the weight of Saudi Arabia, and even of Kuwait and the United Arab Emirates, in Arab politics. The rulers of these countries, much less exposed to European influences and modes of thought, take for granted the equation of Islam and Arabism: for them, and indeed for their subjects, one would be meaningless without the other; Islamic pride blends completely here with the feeling of Arab tribal superiority. This enhancement of the importance of the Arabian Peninsula could not but influence the tone of Arab nationalist ideology, and reinforce the tendencies manifested in the writings of Bazzaz, the propaganda of the Muslim Brethren, and the political rhetoric favoured until recently by the Egyptian regime.

Yet other developments contribute to strengthen this current. One such is the character and influence of the Algerian regime. Owing to the circumstances in which Algeria attained independence in 1962, the regime enjoys particular prestige. Rightly or wrongly, the Algerian revolutionaries now in power are believed to have defeated France, a major military power, on the field of battle, and to have thus put an end to 130 years of European colonization and settlement which, up to 1954, seemed utterly solid and unassailable. During the first three years of independent Algeria, under Ben Bella, the ideology of the regime was European in its vocabulary and categories, a mixture of Marxism and nationalism which the writings of Frantz Fanon best exemplify. A great change came with the assumption of power by Boumedienne who, besides overthrowing Ben Bella, effected a radical break with the ideology by which the National Liberation Front [Front deLiberation Nationale (FLN)] had captured so many sympathies in France and elsewhere in the Western world.

Nothing indicates the change better than the fact that Fanon, so popular in the West, has been allowed to fall into oblivion in Algeria. The Algerian regime appeals precisely to that amalgam of Arabism and Islam which we have seen so prevalent elsewhere in the Arab world, and which strikes a sympathetic chord in a Muslim population for whom the French settler was indeed a greedy and oppressive conqueror but, above all, the Christian enemy who had tried—and failed—to humiliate Islam, if not to destroy it. These Islamic loyalties and reflexes, thus given a new lease on life, will operate in such a way as to anchor in the popular mind a traditional interpretation of current conflicts: the anti-imperialist struggle becomes an extension of the centuries-old struggle against Christendom, and the war against Zionism and Israel a continuation of the Prophet's war against the Jews of Medina.

Besides Boumedienne's Algeria, another Arab country, Libya, has recently come to play a prominent part in inter-Arab politics, and its influence has weighted the balance further in favour of existing tendencies. The *coup d'état* of September 1969 brought to power, in Qadhafi and his fellow-officers, a group fervently imbued with the ideals of Pan-Arabism, the glamourous champion of which during their formative years had been Nasser. But unlike their hero, the present rulers of Libya very strongly emphasize the Islamic roots of Arabism, and the inseparable connection between the two. So emphatically has Qadhafi, in particular, expressed himself about this that he has aroused general hilarity abroad. People have been amused by Qadhafi's intention to give what are generally considered outmoded and obscurantist Qur'anic prescriptions the force of law, by his seemingly naive admonitions to Jews and Christians to hearken to God's word as revealed to Muhammad, and by his impetuous, flamboyant and apparently childish attempts to bring about instant Arab unity.

It is true, of course, that Qur'anic prescriptions are not exactly adapted to the needs of the modern world, that there is very little chance of Christians and Jews meekly accepting the status to which Islam destines them, and that popular marches from Tripoli to Cairo are no more than a stunt. But it would be a great mistake to conclude from all this that Qadhafi is, therefore, only a figure of fun and of no consequence in the Arab world. For, after all, should it be forgotten that it was the Libyan revolutionary regime which, together with Algeria, first decisively routed the Western oil companies, thus starting the process which led to the present turmoil in the international oil market? Again, the exact detail of Qadhafi's proposals and suggestions does not really much matter; what will impress a great multitude of his fellow-Muslims and fellow-Arabs is their insistence on the abiding validity—and indeed superiority—of Islam, and the claim that, as a prominent member of the regime, Bashir Hawadi, put it, 'Arabism is a body and Islam is the living soul which moves this body.'

This statement was made in the course of a popular meeting which took place in Tripoli in October 1972. The meeting was organized in order to expound what Qadhafi has called his Third Theory. The theory claims to provide an alternative to Marxism and liberalism or capitalism, which are declared to be equally bankrupt. On examination, the Third Theory turns out to be based on Islam and Arabism and, in spite of a lame attempt to assert its universal value, to be really addressed to the Arabs, whose allegiance to Islam is taken to be part of the natural order of things. Thus, in a speech of October 1971, Qadhafi declared:

> The revolution of the Arab Libyan people represents something deep and well-rooted in the region. It is a new chapter in the evolution of the struggle of our Arab nation and of the Arab revolution. It affirms the established and individual character of the heritage of our nation, holds fast to Arabism and Islam, resurrects those values and principles which are most alive in them, and proclaims that the Arab nation is one nation having its place in the world and its role in the civilization of humanity.

At the meeting of October 1972, Hawadi affirmed: 'In our belief, the Arab personality must be founded on a total commitment to belief in God and in Islamic values.' And, at the same meeting Jallud, the prime minister, ended his speech by saying that, 'Arab unity, in so far as it constitutes a strength for the Arabs, is also a strength for Islam: this is something fundamental.'

This insistence on the intimate connection between Arabism and Islam must be considered as the most prominent feature of Arab nationalist ideology today, one which may well prove lasting and tenacious. Its effect on the Arab world cannot but be far-reaching. In appealing to and strengthening traditional Islamic sentiment, it will help reverse a trend which had been prominent in the Middle East since the 19th century, when Middle Eastern leaders like the Khedive Isma'il aspired to have their countries henceforth be a part of European civilization—in their eyes the only civilization properly so-called. This is scarcely now the case, and will be even less so when the effects of ideological indoctrination will have fully worked themselves through Arab society. A paradoxical situation will then arise. Though communication between the Arab world and the outside will be easier and speedier than ever, intellectual or spiritual intercourse will be more difficult, more hedged about with controls and restrictions than in the last 150 years, the Arab and the non-Arab world ending up by becoming, once more, like medieval Islam and Christendom, opaque and unintelligible to one another.

Nor are the reasons for such isolation far to seek. They are the outcome of those technical innovations borrowed from the scientific and industrial civilization of the West. Today, the state in most of the Arab world exercises strict centralized control over education, publishing and the press. Its hold over broadcasting and television is complete. It is, therefore, in a position to control what the young are taught and what citizens are told about public affairs in their own country and in the world at large. This comparatively new development has meant a prodigious reinforcement of the dominant political tradition in Islam, namely that of passive obedience to the ruler. But it does not follow from this, or from the undoubted fact— illustrated above—that Islam is, once again, politically to the fore both in theory and practice, that what we see is a simple reassertion of traditional values and attitudes. Tradition, rather, serves to clothe an ideology somewhat remote from the traditional worldview of the mass of Muslims. This ideology, which many Arab rulers obviously find attractive, has to do with 'socialism', 'social justice', and 'democracy'. Such notions are quite remote from, not to say alien to, the political tradition of Islam, as well as to the pre-occupations of the mass of traditionally minded Muslims. There is, thus, here a gap between the ideas and purposes of rulers and those of the ruled, which the traditional Islamic political vocabulary and rhetoric may possibly hide but cannot bridge.

The formulation of this ideology varies from regime to regime, but it may be conveniently summarized here by a sentence which occurs in the foreword of the work expounding Qadhafi's Third Theory, which has been recently published. 'Our religion,' the foreword asserts, 'is the religion of democracy and social justice for which the noble Qur'an has called since the appearance of Islam.' What meaning does such an assertion carry in the mind of Qadhafi and his associates? In the first place, it encapsulates a view of world history which—notwithstanding the claims for originality made on behalf of the Third Theory—has many points of similarity with the doctrines of the Tatar Sultan Galiev, the Chinese Li Ta-chao, and the Japanese Ikki Kita. Quoting the Algerian writer, the late Malek Bennabi, Qadhafi affirms

that the true division in the world is not between East and West or com-
munism and capitalism, but between North and South:

> There is no East and West; there is rather North and South: the
> North extends from Washington to Peking, the South from Tangiers
> to Djakarta; so that East and West can be considered as the two great
> camps allied against a third camp which is underdeveloped, or
> subjected by force. The Moslem world constitutes the centre of
> gravity of this camp . . . . the important thing is the existence of this
> doctrinal division in the world, this ideological map of the world.

Qadhafi, it is clear, operates with an amalgam of Marxism and
nationalism, in which the fundamental struggle takes place not between an
industrial proletariat and the capitalists oppressing it, but between poor
nations and the rich industrial nations who exploit them. It is this amalgam
which justifies the universalist claim of the Third Theory. It is clear,
furthermore, that the theory is activist in its thrust: struggle is emphasized,
and political legitimacy is associated with successful struggle against the
non-Muslim, capitalist or Communist exploiters. Thus, at the same meeting
of October 1972, where Qadhafi explained the fundamental division of the
world between North and South, another speaker affirmed that '*jihad* by the
sword by all means for the sake of God: this is what ought to govern our
relations with the other [i.e., outside] world in order to spread the message'.
The speaker went on to say that a limited truce might interrupt the *jihad* for a
time, but it must be resumed whenever the Muslims become strong. The
same speaker broached another activist, revolutionary theme when he said
that he who raises the banner of Arab unity, and struggles for its sake, is the
only legitimate Imam or ruler, 'and all the other Imams are illegitimate'.

Together with the identification of Islam with Arabism, this revolutionary activism is the most important characteristic of the dominant
ideology in the Arab world today. The activism is obviously directed against
the outside world: Qadhafi's opposition of North and South expresses
eloquently this particular thrust of the doctrine. But the activism has also an
inward direction which the claim that Islam represents democracy and
social justice, quoted above, may make clear. Such a statement represents
not so much a description as an aspiration. The aspiration is towards a
society in which poverty would have disappeared, and traditional political
and social hierarchies abolished. Clearly, such a vision has nothing to do
with traditional Islam as understood by its adherents, and is entirely derived
from a recent European model. This vision is not shared by the ruled and
this constitutes the gap mentioned above: where rulers and ruled used to
inhabit one common universe of discourse, they now inhabit two separate
ones.

What are the implications for the future of Arab politics of this
seemingly generous vision? The vision is a blueprint, but since it has almost

no contact with existing realities, the blueprint becomes an abstract doctrine. Political discourse ceases to be a way of dealing with emergencies in a customary and familiar manner, and becomes a series of logical-seeming imperatives to which all citizens must, at all costs, be committed.

Political indoctrination is the concomitant of this style of politics, and it has to be forwarded by means of an ideological rhetoric which cannot but obscure, and thus make more intractable, existing political problems. The doctrine or blueprint here in question goes under the name 'Arab Socialism' or 'Islamic Socialism.' These labels are meant to distinguish the doctrine from Marxism and similar European ideologies. The ground for the distinction is principally that the latter are founded on the idea of class struggle, whereas 'Arab' or 'Islamic' socialism is based on the solidarity and co-operation of all classes. But to make this co-operation and solidarity an actual fact requires large-scale intervention by governments in economic and social arrangements: property rights, business relations, intellectual activity must come under government control. This means a prodigious extension of that centralization and enhancement of power which is the most significant characteristic of the Middle-Eastern state in the 19th and 20th centuries. Economic, social and intellectual activities thus become gradually more politicized, and caught up in a tight mesh of administrative control and regulation. This state of affairs, while it certainly gives incomparably greater power to the rulers, by no means necessarily increases welfare, solidarity or co-operation. On the contrary, bureaucratic regulation may actually increase social tension, decrease welfare and make society at large altogether less prosperous and happy. In this way, the reality will contrast sharply with the claims and promises of the doctrine, and this may itself lead to political instability.

As has been said, the appeal to Islam will find a wide response among the traditionally minded masses. The 'socialism' which has somehow been yoked together with Islam and Arabism will not elicit from them the same response. Those who will be most attracted to it are the increasingly numerous products of the school and university systems who, by reason of their training, are recruited into the ruling institution as its younger members who, though less powerful, will still have access to the levers of military and political power. They will see that the reality does not conform to the doctrine, and will ascribe this to the corruption and backsliding of their elders. As the gap between the doctrine and the reality widens, the attraction of the ideology, and its critique of existing conditions, will grow. The mixture of socialism, Arabism and Islam is a powerful one, and so is its corollary, namely that justice and unity will not come about until Arab society is cleansed of reaction, privilege, capitalism and godlessness.

In order to carry out the purification, the younger members of the ruling institution, *purs et durs* as they are, will be tempted to resort to precisely those revolutionary methods sanctioned alike by the ideology and by the practice of their elders. If they are successful in their enterprise, they will set the ships of state—for a time at any rate—on the rigid course which ideological rectitude demands. This vicious circle is not likely to disappear because of the large sums which are now flowing into the Arab world from oil royalties. So much wealth which is, in any case, unevenly distributed through the region, and completely under the control of governments, is likely to exacerbate discontent and make for political instability: Iraqi oil revenues in the 1950s and Libyan prosperity in the 1960s did not prevent, perhaps even hastened, revolutionary upheaval. The circle of ideological discontent leading to *coup d'état,* leading to further discontent, can no doubt be broken, but this requires an efficient police apparatus itself immune to subversion, treachery or demoralization.

It may be asked what bearing the above analysis may have on the policymaker's preoccupations. The first consideration relates to prominence which Islam has acquired in Arab political discourse. If this tendency continues—and there is no reason to think otherwise—we must expect an increase in the impermeability of the Arab world to outside ideas, and increasing difficulty in communication. It may not be possible to show how this state of affairs will affect a specific negotiation, but its long-term indirect influence we might suspect to prove considerable. In the second place, the ideological style of politics, so rife in the Arab world, may give rise to illusions against which it is important to guard. Policymakers must be wary of ideology and its rhetoric. Its claim to be a report of present reality and a blueprint for future developments cannot be taken at face value. The caution ought to be superfluous, but recent experiences show that it is by no means so.

The attitude of US policymakers to so-called Nasserism in the decade of so after the *coup d'état* of July 1952 is a case in point. There seems to have been then a dangerous readiness to believe that, as the 'Free Officers' were saying, the ills of Egypt could be remedied only through a 'revolution'; that this 'revolution' would eventually create a new social structure which would promote economic development and prosperity, create a middle class, and hence establish democratic constitutional government; and that this would promote US interests in this region. In retrospect, one may clearly see that each chain in this line of reasoning was so weak as to be utterly worthless. But hindsight is not necessary to reach such a judgment. Even at the time, it would have been quite possible to be sceptical about large claims of this kind.

Policymakers, then, ought to be wary of confusing the interests of a government—foremost among which is self-preservation—and the claims and demands of its ideology; they ought to ask themselves whether the aims of an ideology can possibly be fulfilled, and whether the very attempt to fulfill them may not itself make these impossible to attain. Over and above everything else, policy ought not to be tied to large speculative views about long-term changes in politics, economy and society. British policy towards the Ottoman empire between the 1830s and 1914 started out by being based on the assumption that the preservation of the empire—which was a British interest—could be secured only through far-reaching 'reforms'. The 'reforms' were successful neither in themselves, nor in removing Ottoman military weakness which, if anything, became relatively worse. Then, during 'Abd al-Hamid's long reign, British attitudes to the empire became gradually more hostile, and no small part of this hostility derived from the belief that the Sultan was against 'reforms', and that he was a reactionary despot. After a brief burst of enthusiasm for the Young Turk *coup d'état*, British policymakers again dismissed the new rulers as hopelessly reactionary. There was a large element of misinformation and misunderstanding in these judgments but, even if there had not, they would still have been largely irrelevant to the issue whether British interests required or did not require a friendly Ottoman empire. In this particular case, the misjudgment on an issue which was anyway irrelevant may be shown to have led to an atmosphere such that the British took for granted Ottoman hostility in 1914, and what they did to avert it was too little and too late.

There is another episode in British relations with the Middle East which carries a lesson to policymakers who have to deal with an ideological style of politics. This is the encouragement of Arab unity during and after the second world war. Assuming that the current for Arab unity was powerful—which was by no means clear—it did not necessarily follow that to support it would automatically benefit British interests in the area— interests which were scattered and complex. The support which was, in fact, given led between, say, 1945 and 1952, to a new situation in which British interests were by no means safeguarded, but rather threatened in new and unexpected ways.

In sum, what is being argued for here is a crude empiricism in the belief that this is an area in which a long-term analysis of political trends would not, even if it were correct, yield any readily applicable policy prescriptions. The long-term prospect in these societies is one of intellectual isolation, if not downright hostility, while the ideological style of politics which has made such inroads makes for activism and instability. All that one may hope for is to exploit the instinct for survival of regimes which are narrowly based and insecure. This kind of policy can only be played by ear. Every morning one is dealt a new hand, and yesterday's match offers little guidance in today's challenge: agility is all. The conclusion is negative, but nonetheless of some value since, as the examples cited above show, its disregard has led in the past to disappointment and failure.

5

IBN SA'UD ON THE JEWS

In the autumn of 1937 Colonel H.R.P. Dickson, who had retired the previous year as British Political Agent in Kuwait, paid a visit to Riyad where he was cordially received by the ruler, King Abd al Aziz ibn Sa'ud, other members of the ruling house, and various prominent personalities in the royal entourage. In the course of his visit he had three private conversations with the King, and on his return to Kuwait he sent a full report of his conversations to the Government of India.

The first conversation took place in the Royal Palace on 25 October 1937. Ibn Sa'ud showed great affability, to illustrate which Dickson gave a sample of his 'polite references': 'O Dickson', he was quoted as saying, 'not only are you our friend, and the friend of the Arabs, but I see you come garbed as one of us and so are doubly welcome.' It is clear from this language that Dickson appeared in the royal presence dressed in Bedouin dress. He himself does not remark on this, seemingly taking for granted that this was the right and normal thing to do.

Nor did his attire arouse any comment at the Eastern Department of the Foreign Office to whom the India Office had sent a copy of Dickson's report. This is not surprising since the head of this Department, George Rendel, had earlier in the year himself visited Saudi Arabia as Ibn Sa'ud's official guest, and, upon arrival, he and his wife had donned Bedouin dress bestowed upon them by the King and did not discard it until the end of their visit. Dickson was a private, or at best a semi-official visitor, Rendel an official one; for him to go about in the dress of the country was tantamount to wearing his host's livery, thus signifying submission of some sort. As we also learn from his memoirs (*The Sword and the Olive*, 1957, pp. 106 and 113), the British Ambassador to Saudi Arabia, who was in the most formal sense His Britannic Majesty's representative, also wore Bedouin dress. In his memoirs Rendel has no comment to make on this remarkable state of affairs, clearly seeing nothing amiss in it. He is content admiringly to describe the garments which Ibn Sa'ud had bestowed upon him and his wife:

'these consisted of a heavy, very fine black-and-gold *abba* for my wife, and a *kefiyeh*, agal (or black camel-hair and gold head rope) and a brown *abba* for myself'. He also includes in his book a picture of himself and his wife so attired.

Europeans travelling in unsafe and lawless parts of the Middle East have as a matter of precaution donned local dress, but Saudi Arabia was not, in the '30s, an anarchic region, and it could not therefore have been for safety that visitors would wear Bedouin dress. Rather it must have been believed, in official circles, that proper respect for Ibn Sa'ud made it mandatory to be garbed like him when appearing in his presence. Deference of this kind seems to have been thought necessary nowhere else by representatives of the British empire. It is in striking contrast to the attitude indicated in *The Adventures of Hajji Baba of Ispahan* (1824), the author of which, James Morier, had been British Minister at Teheran. In chapter 77 the ceremony of receiving the British envoy at the Persian court is described, and we are told that 'on the article of dress, a most violent dispute arose: at first, it was intimated that proper dresses should be sent to him and his suite, which would cover their persons (now too indecently exposed) so effectually, that they might be fit to be seen by the King; but this proposal he rejected with derision. He said, that he would appear before the Shah of Persia in the very same dress he wore when before his own sovereign.' What Morier describes was and remained the only acceptable attitude to adopt on this issue.

It is not clear what brought about so total a change that Ibn Sa'ud came to be held in great awe in British official circles, his views accorded great respect, and his position in the Arab world believed to be very strong, even paramount. The consequences of this belief, which Rendel entertained very strongly, were apparent by the autumn of 1937. As is well known, disorders had broken out in Palestine in the spring of 1936, which the British Government found difficult to master. This situation, in turn, led Ibn Sa'ud and the Iraqis at first diffidently, and later with increasing confidence, to intercede on behalf of the Palestine Arabs and actually to offer to mediate between them and the Mandatory in Palestine. Rendel became strongly convinced that such mediation would be beneficial and his views in the end carried the day. The Arab rulers were allowed to appeal to the Palestine Arabs to cease their rebellion, and to hold out the inducement that Palestinian grievances would be championed by them in London. This event, which took place in the summer of 1936, was a decisive turning-point in the Palestine conflict.

So that by the autumn of 1937, when Dickson visited Riyad, Ibn Sa'ud had a legitimate *locus standi* to hold forth to his visitor on the subject of Palestine. This was indeed what his first conversation with Dickson dealt with. The Peel Commission had by then reported in favour of partitioning Palestine between Arabs and Jews—a scheme which aroused great

opposition among the Arabs, Ibn Sa'ud included. In this conversation
(reproduced from the Foreign Office files—F.O. 371/20822 E7201/
22/31—below) Ibn Sa'ud expresses his anxiety lest British support for
Zionism destroy a 'friendship of centuries, all for the sake of an accursed
and stiffnecked race which has always bitten the hand of everyone who has
helped it since the world began'. He disclaims any desire to take over
Palestine himself, expatiates on his influence in the Muslim world, promises
that he will 'definitely' not wage war against the English, but explains that
his people are pressing him to take action, and appeals to the British
government to deliver him from such pressures by ceasing to support the
Jews. But the most remarkable feature of his harangue—for this is how it can
best be described—is the extreme hatred towards the Jews which he voiced,
and the demagogic way in which he appealed to what he clearly believed was
the similar hatred which animated Christians:

> Our hatred for the Jews dates from God's condemnation of them for
> their persecution and rejection of Isa [Jesus Christ], and their sub-
> sequent rejection later of His chosen Prophet. It is beyond our
> understanding how your Government, representing the first Christian
> power in the world today, can wish to assist and reward these very
> same Jews who maltreated your Isa [Jesus].

What did Dickson make of Ibn Sa'ud's discourse? His assessment was that
there was no danger of Ibn Sa'ud being forced by his people to intervene in
Palestine, and that though he was 'indignant and distressed' at the partition
scheme in particular, he would make no anti-British move in Arabia, as
he was determined not to jeopardize his relations with the British government. Dickson ended by suggesting, however, that Ibn Sa'ud should be
generously rewarded for his 'neutrality' over Palestine—which he believed
would 'definitely' harm his prestige—by some sort of *quid pro quo*. Dickson
did not describe the sweetener he had in mind, but we may suspect that Ibn
Sa'ud calculated that by raising the issue of Palestine he would, at the least,
be able to press the British government to concede his territorial claims in
Eastern Arabia.

Events proved Dickson right, since Ibn Sa'ud made no anti-British
move, then or later, over Palestine. Rendel however disagreed with
Dickson's assessment. In a minute of 23 November 1937 (in E7201) he
declared that Dickson was 'unduly optimistic' in thinking that Ibn Sa'ud
would make no anti-British move over Palestine. Rendel himself was an
uncompromising opponent of the partition scheme and he succeeded finally
in having it abandoned by the Cabinet which had first welcomed it. Ibn
Sa'ud's speech to Dickson would have been invaluable grist to his mill, and
he was not keen that its rhetoric should be discounted. He would have very
much liked to circulate Dickson's report in order to send further shivers
down ministers' backs about the ferocity of Arab opposition to the partition

proposal, but as he regretfully minuted on 10 February 1938, it was 'not entirely suitable for general circulation' (F.O. 371/21873 E693/10/31). Whether sentiments similar to Ibn Sa'ud's would be so judged today is far from certain.

APPENDIX

Text of Foreign Office file 371/20822 E7201/22/31

His Majesty early on turned to the subject obviously close to his heart, namely the Palestine tangle, and for close on an hour and a half delivered himself as follows. He spoke for the most part in low earnest voice as though his words were not intended for his Counsellors sitting round and he continually kept placing his hand on my arm as though to emphasize his meaning.
(Here I shall use the King's words as near as possible using the first person plural for the most part).

'We are aware O Dickson that you are no longer a Government Official, but as you have held high and honourable post under His Majesty's Government for many years, we know also that you are trusted by your Government, and so not only do we make you doubly welcome, but we feel we can open our heart to you, and we are glad that you have been able to visit us in our capital.

'We are most anxious that the British Government should send us every eight months or so an experienced officer whom they trust, or equally well an ex-official like yourself, who can listen personally to what we have on our minds, and what troubles our hearts, for times are deeply serious and full of danger these days. We feel that personal contact of such a nature will be far more efficacious, than any amount of letter writing or telegraph representations. The latter though well enough in themselves must nearly always fail to convey the full meaning of our thoughts and anxieties, and if anything will tend rather to breed misunderstanding and misconception than remove same. But such person, if and when he is sent us must be thoroughly conversant with our language (Arabic), and must understand the wider meaning of our beautiful tongue which is so full of parable and expressive phrase. It is no use sending a man who has to listen to what we have to say through the medium of an interpreter. The person sent should know and understand our Arab psychology, be conversant if possible with our Arabian manners and customs, and above all should be acquainted with our Arab pride and our hopes, and have read something of God's Holy Word, as vouchsafed to us in our Blessed Qur'an.

'O Dickson when will your London Government realize that we Arabs by our very nature can be bought body and soul by an act of kindness, and vice versa become implacable enemies for all time of those who treat us harshly or deal unjustly with us.

'Today we and our subjects are deeply troubled over this Palestine question, and the cause of our disquiet and anxiety is the strange attitude of your British Government, and the still more strange hypnotic influence which the Jews, a race accursed by God according to His Holy Book, and destined to final destruction and eternal damnation hereafter, appear to wield over them and the English people generally.

'God's Holy Book (the Qur'an) contains God's own word and divine ordinance, and we commend to His Majesty's Government to read and carefully peruse that portion which deals with the Jews and especially what is to be their fate in the end. For God's words are unalterable and must be.

'We Arabs believe implicitly in God's revealed word and we know that God is faithful. We care for nothing else in this world but our belief in the One God, His Prophet and our Honour, everything else matters nothing at all, not even death, nor are we afraid of hardship, hunger, lack of this worlds goods etc, etc. and we are quite content to eat camel's meat and dates to the end of our days, provided we hold to the above three things.

'Our hatred for the Jews dates from God's condemnation of them for their persecution and rejection of Isa (Jesus Christ), and their subsequent rejection later of His chosen Prophet. It is beyond our understanding how your Government, representing the first Christian power in the world today, can wish to assist and reward these very same Jews who maltreated your Isa (Jesus).'

'We Arabs have been the traditional friends of Great Britain for many years, and I, Bin Sa'ud, in particular have been your Government's firm friend all my life, what madness then is this which is leading on your Government to destroy this friendship of centuries, all for the sake of an accursed and stiffnecked race which has always bitten the hand of everyone who has helped it since the world began.

'It were far far preferable from every point of view if Great Britain were to make Palestine a British Possession and rule it for the next 100 years, rather than to partition it in the way they propose: such partition cannot possibly solve the difficulty but must only perpetuate it and lead to war and misery. Some people seem to think that I, Bin Sa'ud, have an eye on Palestine myself, and would like to benefit by the disturbed state of affairs existing there, to step in and offer to take it over myself. That certainly would be a solution, but God forbid that this should happen, for I have enough and to spare as it is.

'Today I am the 'Imam' or 'Spiritual Leader' as well as the Temporal Ruler of the greater part of Arabia. I also have not a little influence in all the great Muslim countries of the world. I am being placed in the most difficult and most invidious of all positions by the British

Government my friends. On the one hand I am being appealed to by means of myriads of letters and telegrams by day and night from all quarters of the Muslim world to step in and save Palestine for the Arabs. I am even urged by my own people of Najd, and all good Muslims in the outer world to break with the English and save Palestine for its people by war. On the other hand I see that it would be utterly futile to break with my old friends the English, for to do so would bring untold woe on the world, and would be to play right into the hands of the Jews, the enemies of Arabia as well as of England.

'I definitely shall not wage war against you English and I have told my people this, because I am the only man among them who can see far ahead and I know that by so doing I should lose the one potential ally I now have. For are not Italy, Germany and Turkey (especially the latter) like ravening wolves today seeking whom they may devour. They are all flirting with me at the present moment, but I know they will wish to devour me later. A friendly England will, I believe, always prevent them from accomplishing their ends. Hence though as a Muslim I have no particular love for any Christian European nation, political interest demands that I keep in with the best of them, that is England.

'The difficulty is my Arabs and the Ikhwan tribes of Najd—Over this Palestine business their senses are only in their eyes, and they cannot see one cubit ahead. They even now blame me for wavering and obeying the orders of the English, and yet your Government should remember that I am the Arabs' religious leader and so am the interpreter of the scriptures. God's word to them cannot be got round.

'Verily the word of God teaches us, and we implicitly believe this O Dickson, that for a Muslim to kill a Jew, or for him to be killed by a Jew ensures him an immediate entry into Heaven and into the august presence of God Almighty. What more then can a Muslim want in this hard world, and this is what my people are repeatedly reminding me of? Most assuredly your Government is placing me in the same dilemma that they did in 1929-30 which ended in the Ikhwan going out in rebellion against me.

'The Jews are of course your enemies as well as ours though they are cleverly making use of you now. Later your Government will see and feel their teeth. For the present they (the Jews) prefer biding their time. Perhaps your Government does not know that the Jews contemplate as their final aim not only the seizure of all Palestine but the land south of it as far as Medina. Eastward also they hope some day to extend to the Persian Gulf. They cozen certain imperialistic-minded Englishmen with stories of how a strong Jewish and Pro-British State stretching from the Mediterranean to the Persian Gulf will safeguard England's communications with the East, saying that the Arabs are England's enemies and will always be so. At the same time they play on the minds of the sentimental British masses, by telling them that the Old Testament Prophets foretold how they, the Jews, would eventually return to their Promised Land, or again that they, the persecuted and wandering Bani Israel, should not be denied a small place in the world where to lay their weary heads. Now, O Dickson, would the people of Wales like it if you English suddenly gave the Jews their country? But no, it is easier to give away other peoples countries and not so dangerous.

'That the Jews of Palestine are even now straining every nerve to cause a permanent split between the English people and the Arabs can be proved to the hilt by the recent murders of officials in Palestine. It is as clear as daylight to me that the Godless Arab gunmen, hired from abroad, who committed those vile deeds were hired and paid for by Jewish money. We state this to be an absolute fact, for did not the Grand Mufti of Jerusalem swear to us in the 'Haram' of Mecca by the Holy Kaaba that he would never resort to any but constitutional methods in opposing the Zionist machinations in Palestine? And I believe him even today.

'What we fear so greatly and what Great Britain must not allow to come to pass is the turning of the Arabs of Arabia and neighbouring Arab countries into enemies of England. Once this happens then an irreparable crime will have been committed, for, as we said above, the Arabs will never forget an injury, and will bide their opportunity to take revenge for a hundred years if need be. Enemies of England would not be slow to take advantage of this, and an England in difficulties, or engaged elsewhere in war, would then be the signal for the Arabs to act.

'The very thought of the above happening is hateful to me Abdul Aziz, yet be assured that Partition in Palestine will bring this about in spite of all your misdirected efforts. And after all I cannot help you forever as I cannot live more than a few years more. I repeat then that the only solution that I can see is for your Government to rule Palestine herself. The Zionists of course will not like this, but their views must not be asked. The Arabs will agree to this solution and those who do not must be made to agree by such people as myself.

'The main thing at all costs is to prevent the Jews from having an independent state of their own sliced out of Arab territory with no one to guide their future acts and policy. For from such will come a perpetual struggle with the Arabs living round them. Firstly, because the Jews are determined to expand, will intrigue from the very beginning, and not rest till they have created discord and enmity between Great Britain and us Arabs, out of which they will hope to benefit. Secondly, they, having the money, will create a highly effective though perhaps small mechanized Army and Air Force, which they will assuredly use one day for aggressive purposes against the Arabs, seeing that their aim is the whole of Palestine, Transjordan and their old stronghold Medina—the land they went to when driven out of Palestine and dispersed after the Romans destroyed Jerusalem.

'On top of this your Government must at once further restrict all further immigration of Jews into Palestine leaving alone all those already there but allowing no more to come in.'

I here took advantage of a pause in the King's rather forcible harangue to try and explain His Majesty's Government's point of view on the lines suggested by Rendel when I saw him recently in London. But before I had gone very far the King in vigorous fashion checked and rather overwhelmed me with the words, 'By God, your Government has no point of view, except the willful committing of an injustice. Every God–fearing man be he Muslim or Christian knows that it cannot be right to do a wrong, however cleverly the committing may be served up to the people. If I, an ignorant Badawin Arab of Arabia can see, as clearly as I see the sun rise, that the proposed partition of Palestine is wicked and wrong in God's sight, surely the more clever Western politicians, if they fear God at all, can see this also. Thank God I believe in God and his Oneness, and I know that it is this very belief of mine that makes me see things as clearly as I do. I am as firmly convinced that I am right, and that God has opened my eyes to the right, as I believe that God will punish me if I lie to him. Therefore there is *no other side* to this question except bargaining with Satan.

6

ARAB UNITY THEN AND NOW

From its very inception, just before the first world war, the doctrine of Arab nationalism was a doctrine of Pan-Arabism. In its first articulations, towards the turn of the 19th and 20th centuries, by writers such as Abd al-Rahman al-Kawakibi (1849-1902) and Muhammad Rashid Rida (1865-1935), the doctrine was not so much a claim for Arab independence and autonomy as an assertion of the primacy of the Arabs within Islam. Following the Young Turk Revolution of July 1908, and the deposition of Sultan 'Abd al-Hamid in April 1909, Arab intellectuals and officers began increasingly to make a claim for Arab autonomy within the empire. These claims have for their context the turbulent factional politics of the Ottoman empire which encouraged and exacerbated group tensions. Also, the parlous international situation of the Ottoman state in the years immediately preceding the first world war itself encouraged the autonomist and even secessionist views of these elements. The doctrine, then, as it took shape during these years, claimed that the Arabs, because they spoke Arabic, formed a distinct nation which was entitled, as such, to enjoy an autonomous political existence within the Ottoman empire, or perhaps even to secede from it. The territory which the proponents of Pan-Arabism then had in mind comprised the Arabian Peninsula (considered by them to be the cradle of the Arab nation), Mesopotamia, and the Levant, i.e. the territories known as Syria, Lebanon and Palestine. Egypt was not, in their view, part of the Arab world as they envisaged it. The Arabic-speaking parts of the Ottoman empire (which the doctrine had chiefly in view) were and had always been distinct in point of language from the Turkish-speaking areas. But until the 20th century this distinction was not considered politically significant, and was not seen to warrant claims for autonomy, let alone secession; the Ottoman empire was an Islamic state, and Islam whether by Turk or Arab was taken to be the supreme political value.

Before the 1914-18 war these ideas were by no means widespread. On the contrary, they were the affair of a very small number of officers and officials. The great majority, both among the educated and among the common people, were unquestioning in their loyalty to the Ottoman Sultan as the head of the Islamic realm with which they identified themselves. In Egypt, furthermore, in so far as these ideas were known they attracted great hostility. Egypt was then under British occupation, and many among the official and educated classes looked to the Ottoman empire for support against the occupant. They were therefore opposed to any movement which might pose a danger to its cohesion or continued existence.

Arab nationalism (as understood by its earliest proponents) received a great push forward during the first world war. The British, who found themselves at war with the Ottomans, encouraged the Sharif of Mecca to declare a rebellion in the Hijaz against his Ottoman suzerain. He eventually did so in 1916, alleging that the Arabs were being persecuted by the Young Turk regime then in power, and claiming that his movement would liberate his fellow-Arabs from the foreign yoke. At one point he even proclaimed himself King of the Arab Countries, but this title was not recognized by the Allies. Allied, and particularly British, help was extended to enable him to wage war on Ottoman troops in the Hijaz. The Sharifian movement attracted Arab officers who either deserted the Ottoman army to serve in the Sharifian forces, or volunteered for such service while in British prisoner-of-war camps. These officers, and such Arab civilians as made their way to the Hijaz in 1916-18, formed the nucleus of the post-war Arab nationalist movement which now had official standard-bearers in the person of the Sharif and in that of his sons.

Two of these sons in particular were to have an important role to play in the post-war development and extension of the Arab nationalist movement: Faysal, and his elder brother Abdullah. Faysal became the protégé of Colonel Lawrence and General Allenby. He was installed (nominally as Allenby's deputy) in October 1918 in Damascus, falsely claimed to have been captured by Sharifian arms, and allowed to rule over Syria in an attempt to checkmate the French, who claimed the area and whom the British considered to be their dangerous rivals. In Damascus, where he stayed less than two years before being evicted by the French, Faysal made large claims on behalf of Arab nationalism. His supporters used their position in the administration and in the Sharifian army, armed and financed by the British, to propagate Arab nationalist doctrine, which was now however directed against the Western Powers rather than against the Ottoman empire which these Powers had destroyed. The doctrine was specifically directed against France which had occupied the Lebanese coast and wanted also to control the Syrian hinterland. But it was also directed against the British, even though the British were Faysal's paymasters and supporters. Faysal in Damascus at one point aspired, or was encouraged by some British officials to aspire, to rule over Palestine, which was under British occupation; and Sharifian propaganda couched in the terms of Arab nationalist doctrine was indeed widespread in Palestine. This propaganda found a wide response because it filled the vacuum created by the disappearance of Ottoman rule and the loyalties it inspired, and because of the fears raised among the indigenous population by the Zionist commitments of the British occupants. In today's perspective, it may seem puzzling that the British should at one and the same time encourage Arab nationalism in Damascus and Zionism in Palestine. But difficult as this may be to understand now, the British really did believe at the time that the two movements were not antithetical, and that there was no contradiction in supporting both. These movements, they felt, were weak and in need of their protection against the ambitions of other Great Powers, and the British themselves were in any case powerful enough to deal with any difficulties that might arise, and keep the whole area under their control.

Mesopotamia, i.e. the former Ottoman provinces of Mosul, Baghdad and Basra, too was under British occupation, and Arab nationalists in the Sharifian administration in Syria organized armed forays in the country, and tribal and urban resistance against British occupation. Eventually the disorders in Mesopotamia induced the British government to install Faysal as the King of Iraq (as the territory was now to be known), in the belief that such a regime would serve to safeguard British interests without the expense of a British occupation. This belief seemed all the more reasonable in that, all along, Faysal had been a British protégé, who might now be expected to feel gratitude for being given another throne to replace the one he had lost in Damascus. His disagreeable experiences in Syria might also, or so it was thought, make him stick closer than ever to the British connection.

Under Faysal, Iraq became the focus and the base of Arab nationalist doctrine, and its proponents, small in number as they were, became nevertheless able, through their control of a state and its administration, to propagate and, if they possibly could, to realize the aims of Arab nationalism as they had been formulated in the decade 1908-18.

Faysal's brother, Abdullah, was also established by the British as a ruler in a territory of his own. The territory was Transjordan, much less important, rich or populous than Iraq. Transjordan too remained under formal British tutelage longer than Iraq; the British Mandate in Iraq was terminated in 1932, but it was not until 1946 that Transjordan escaped the fetters of British control. Abdullah was as much a believer in Pan-Arabism as his brother, and like his brother reckoned to benefit from its spread. But his importance in this connection was to become manifest only later.

Between the two world wars, with Syria and the Lebanon under French control, with Abdullah in Transjordan unable to play much of a role, with Egypt intent as ever on its own problems and very little interested in the Arab world or Pan-Arabism, Iraq was the centre of the movement. Before his death in 1933 Faysal tried to persuade the French to follow in Syria a policy similar to that of the British in Iraq—a policy which would at once redound to the advantage of his house and widen the base of Pan-Arabism and increase its appeal. His son and successor Ghazi, more strident and more adventurous, sought to annex Kuwait, and made Baghdad attractive to nationalist figures from Syria and Palestine; they in turn made his capital a base for anti-French and anti-British action in these Mandated territories.

Palestine in fact was the occasion for the extension of the Pan-Arab movement, and eventually for a far-reaching change in its character. The disturbances which broke out in Palestine in 1936 were a response by the Palestine Arabs to the Jewish national home policy which the British had undertaken to follow in their administration of the Palestine Mandate. The leaders of the Palestine Arabs decided to use force in opposing the Mandatory government and its policies, and they also sought, in order to strengthen their position, to involve independent Arab governments in their quarrel so that greater pressure might be brought on the British. Of these governments the most important were Iraq and Saudi Arabia. They were by no means unwilling to be involved, moved as they were by Muslim and Arab solidarity, but also by the calculation that successful intervention in Palestine would increase their standing in Arab politics, and perhaps give them the leadership in the Pan-Arab movement. Anti-Zionist disturbances were by no means new in Palestine, but owing to the deteriorating international situation, the British now came to view the continuing troubles in Palestine during 1936-8 with a new and increasing alarm, and they were led in the end to respond to the pressure of Arab governments by recognizing the right of Arab states to intervene on behalf of the Arabs of Palestine. The public and formal consecration of this right occurred at the Palestine round-table conference which took place in London at the beginning of 1939 and where virtually all of the Arab states—even one as far away as the Yemen—were officially represented. Palestine was henceforth unequivocally a Pan-Arab cause, and was in fact to serve as the focus of Pan-Arab schemes and ambitions.

The presence of one particular state at the 1939 London conference marked yet another change in the character of Pan-Arabism that was to have far-reaching consequences. The state was Egypt, and its presence at the conference showed that it was now interested in playing a regional role in the Middle East, a role which, as the next few years were to show, was to be unmistakably Arab. This Egyptian ambition manifested itself after the Anglo-Egyptian treaty of 1936 which freed Egypt from almost all the fetters of British tutelage. Henceforth the rulers of Egypt, whether monarchical or presidential, claimed for Egypt the leading role in the Pan-Arab movement. Such a claim seemed a strong one, since Egypt was in fact the most populous, the most advanced and the most powerful of the Arabic-speaking countries.

This new role of Egypt's could not but be disturbing to the original proponents of Pan-Arabism, who felt it to be a threat to their own longstanding and in a sense legitimate ambitions. This was true of Iraq, ruled (until 1958) by descendants of the Sharif of Mecca, and in whose government some of those who had joined the Sharifian revolt after 1916 still played a very prominent role. It was just as true of Abdullah in Transjordan who considered himself entitled to the premier position in a Pan-Arab union. During the second world war when the British helped Syria and the Lebanon to throw off French tutelage and attain independence, Abdullah advocated a union, with himself as head, comprising Syria, the Lebanon, Palestine and Transjordan—a union which would also be linked with Iraq. But such a union (which would have realized the earliest Pan-Arab dreams) was by then not feasible. Not only was Britain unwilling to use its power and influence in such a cause, but it also aroused the strong opposition of Egypt, Saudi Arabia, Syria and the Lebanon, as well as of the Zionists. None of them wanted to be ruled or overshadowed by Abdullah.

By then, Pan-Arabism had found expression in the League of Arab states, a loose association of states founded in 1945, of which the leading member was Egypt. This primacy was symbolized by the fact that the head-quarters of the League was in Cairo. The League entailed absolutely no dimunition in the sovereignty of any of its members. In effect it was a focus for the mutual fears and rivalries of its constituent members, the more prominent among whom aspired to establish their leadership of the Pan-Arab movement, and of Arab unity, when and if it should come. It became clear very soon that the League was split into two factions, one of which, comprising Egypt, Saudi Arabia and Syria, was opposed to the other, composed of Iraq and Transjordan. The main problem confronting the states forming the League was Palestine. The problem was two-fold: first, how to defeat Zionist ambitions in Palestine; second—and just as important —how to ensure advantage for oneself in the struggle for Palestine and how to ensure that one's rivals within the League did not in any way make the Palestine Arab cause a vehicle for their own territorial and power-political ambitions. The members of the Arab League, therefore while professing a fervent and intransigent Pan-Arabism, actually held one another at arm's length and treated one another with the utmost suspicion.

We can go further and say that the intervention of the members of the Arab League in Palestine in 1948 was an outcome of their mutual suspicions, and their anxiety to deny their rivals the opportunity to annex parts of Palestine or establish a dominant influence there. The defeat of 1948 was a great humiliation for the Pan-Arab movement as well as for individual Arab governments, some of which could not survive the blow to their prestige. But Pan-Arabism by no means declined in its fervour. Always a radical doctrine (in that it aimed at a fundamental change in Arab politics) it became even more radical as a result of 1948. In the view of many influential Arab thinkers political arrangements were by themselves of no use. Only a fundamental restructuring of Arab society, the eradication of corruption and obscurantism, would make possible a true Arab unity. This was the gospel of the Arab Socialist Ba'th Party, as well as of countless officers in Egypt, Syria, Iraq and Jordan. It became the doctrine by which Nasser (who, with fellow-officers, had toppled the Egyptian monarchy in 1952) hoped eventually to establish Egypt's—and his own—hegemony over the whole Arab world. But even though the doctrine was now different, and the stakes higher (by reason of the fact that internal subversion and military *coups d'état* now seemed as potent a weapon as external military force or political influence in bringing a whole country into one camp or another) the essentials of the game remained the same, in that Egypt was claiming the leadership of the Arab world, and other states, notably Iraq and Saudi Arabia, were resisting this claim, Iraq going at times so far as to make a rival claim for leadership. This period, which runs roughly from the Suez War of 1956 to the Six-Day War of 1967, was the period of what has been called the 'Arab Cold War'. It was also the period when the Arab world began to be commonly described as being divided between 'Conservative' and 'Radical' states. One must not however be misled by these expressions, for in the Yemen in 1962-7 the 'Arab Cold War' was actually a shooting war, and the labels 'Conservative' and 'radical' are by no means an infallible guide to the actual policies and alignments of these states.

The high-water mark of Pan-Arabism was reached in February 1958 when Egypt and Syria joined together in the United Arab Republic and it seemed that this union would prove an irresistible magnet for the rest of the Arab world. In fact, it had three immediate consequences. Iraq, which was then Egypt's principal rival, organized a counter-union with Jordan that proved even more short-lived than the United Arab Republic. In the second place, the Lebanese Muslims, who had never reconciled themselves to a Lebanon where Christian, specifically Maronite, influence preponderated, were seized with an enthusiasm for Arab unity such that, encouraged by the new unionist regime in Damascus, they raised a great opposition to the existing Lebanese government, an opposition that degenerated into a civil war, to end which US troops had to be landed in Beirut. In the third place, another direct consequence of the United Arab Republic was a military *coup d'état* in Iraq that ended the Hashimite monarchy and the recently inaugurated Iraqi-Jordanian union. The officers who carried out this *coup d'état* declared themselves votaries of Nasser and the expectation was widely held that they would shortly join the United Arab Republic. But these officers soon divided into a pro- and an anti-Nasser faction. The latter had the upper hand and ruled Iraq until they were toppled in turn by the pro-Nasserites in February 1963. So long as the United Arab Republic lasted, i.e. until July 1961, Iraq, ruled by anti-Nasserites, showed even more hostility than under the monarchy to Nasser's ambition to become the undisputed leader of Pan-Arabism. The Syrian anti-Nasserites who overthrew the United Arab Republic in 1961 were in turn themselves overthrown in 1963 by a military *coup d'état* in which Nasserites and Ba'thists predominated. Since Nasserites and Ba'thists were also now in power in Baghdad hopes were strong that a new and even enlarged United Arab Republic would once more be in the vanguard of Pan-Arabism. Talks to this end between Egypt, Syria and Iraq took place in the spring of 1963, but Syria and Egypt were wary of one another and the negotiations came to nothing. This phase of Pan-Arabism, in which Egypt strove for primacy and seemed at times so near to the achievement of her objective, ended with the Six-Day War of 1967 which dealt Nasser's prestige and Egypt's regional ambitions a mortal blow.

But if, after 1967, there was no visible leader to take up the banner of Pan-Arabism, the doctrine, radical in its rhetoric and divisive in its application, still remained the staple of Arab political discourse. With Egypt no longer able to sustain the role, and with Nasser himself dead in 1970, other contenders came to the fore. One of these was Qadhafi of Libya. His inspiration, his political style and his rhetoric were Nasserite. Time and again, he strove for Arab unity or an approximation thereof. At one point he tried to cobble together a union with Tunisia; on another occasion, a similar union with Egypt, Syria and the Sudan. Both attempts proved ephemeral, for neither Libya's geographical position, nor its political weight or military power are such as to make it a credible leader of Pan-Arabism.

Libya was able to play the Pan-Arab role it did after 1969 only because it could make use of the wealth that its oil put at the disposal of its rulers. This wealth was prodigiously increased first as a result of successful confrontation with the oil companies by Libya on its own and by OPEC collectively in 1970-71, and then by the quadrupling of oil prices imposed by OPEC in the immediate aftermath of the Yom Kippur War of 1973. But Libya's oil resources of course pale into insignificance when compared with those of Saudi Arabia, and after 1973 the actual and prospective wealth of the latter became such as to transform its position both in Arab and in world politics, to make it in fact Egypt's successor as contender for Arab leadership.

In fact it is exclusively its oil wealth that allows Saudi Arabia to aspire to such a position. Neither the extent of its population, nor the past achievements of its leaders in Pan-Arab politics, nor its military power, nor its geographical position would have fitted it for such a role. Again, the Islamic sect dominant in Saudi Arabia, namely Wahabism, would until recently have elicited opposition and objection among both the Sunnis and Shi'ites, who constitute the great majority of the Arabs. From its appearance in Najd and its adoption by the house of Sa'ud in the middle of the 18th century until the conquest of the Hijaz in 1924 by King Abd al-Aziz ibn Sa'ud, and even for some time afterwards, Wahabism occasioned fear and dislike in wide areas of the Arabic-speaking world, and the Saudi rulers were in more or less continuous conflict with their neighbours in the Arabian peninsula and beyond. But circumstances and the accident of the enormous oil reserves within its borders have thrust Saudi Arabia into the position of leadership. What does Saudi Arabia's new prominence mean for the Pan-Arab cause and its prospects?

The prominence of Saudi Arabia means, in the first place, a new prominence for Islam in Arab politics. The Arabian Peninsula has been the last area of the Arab-speaking world to be affected by the influence of Western ideas and attitudes. The inhabitants of the Peninsula, again, have been for centuries a homogeneous Arab population for whom Arabism and Islam are virtually synonymous. Lastly, Wahabism, as is commonly known, is a strict fundamentalism preaching a return to the purity and simplicity of early Islam. Saudi influence therefore is likely to work in favour of a greater assertion of Islamic values and principles in Arab politics. This of course could go counter to the secularism that, for the last few decades, has increasingly characterized those parts of the Arab world—the most populous and the most sophisticated parts, Egypt and the Levant, in particular, which have long been in contact with the West. It would also go counter to the political ideologies hitherto dominant in the Arab world—Ba'thism, Nasserism, etc.—which, whatever their present influence, have succeeded in inculcating a secularist outlook among the educated classes of the Arab world. It must also be remembered that the Arab states outside the Arabian Peninsula are far from homogeneous either ethnically or in point of religion. As a result of Saudi Arabia's prominence, Islam will undoubtedly assume a new importance. But this very fact may itself provoke fear of Saudi influence within the heterogeneous and increasingly secular societies in the rest of the Arab world, and resistance to any Saudi claim to assert Pan-Arab leadership.

But it is by no means clear that Saudi Arabia, prominent as its role has become in Arab politics, will really want to establish Arab unity under its own aegis in the way in which Egypt sought to do from the foundation of the Arab League to the Six-Day War. Saudi Arabia is very rich, and its riches are exclusively under the control of the Saudi royal family who have hitherto been able, with little serious challenge, to govern their domain in autocratic fashion. This enterprise has been made singularly easy by the fact that the kingdom has been kept a closed society, insulated to a very large extent from foreign intellectual and political currents. An aggressive foreign policy, and specifically an active attempt to secure Pan-Arab leadership, would make this isolation more difficult to maintain and hence threaten the position and power of the royal family. Again, the very fact that Saudi Arabia is for its rulers so valuable a property must induce caution in foreign policy. Revolutionary, Soviet-supported regimes are, so to speak, on Saudi Arabia's doorstep; political upsets, say in Africa or Iran might have dangerous repercussions for Saudi Arabia and its immediate neighbours. Arab states like Syria or Iraq could prove a serious ideological or military threat. All this means that Saudi Arabia is faced, in the conduct of its foreign policy, with a range of issues and problems that did not trouble Egypt in its quest for Pan-Arab leadership. Owing to the fact that the Soviet Union was not active in the Middle East when Egypt made its bid for Arab leadership in Faruq's reign, it did not have to consider what bearing Soviet activities would have on its policies. Nasser, again, could afford to pursue blithely a policy of doctrinaire radicalism in the Arab world since he reckoned he had little to lose and much to gain by its success.

Saudi Arabia, then, may be considered Egypt's successor in the leadership of Arabism. But circumstances preclude the Saudis from pursuing a full-blooded policy of Pan-Arabism. Rather they have to use their great resources to prevent the rise of a preponderating power in the Middle East or in the Arab world. The policy must therefore be a balancing act, one of warding off threats or of inducing a desired behaviour chiefly by offering or denying financial rewards. But it must also be a policy of defense against radical and subversive doctrines by strengthening Islamic solidarity and the appeal of Islam, understood as far as possible in a fundamentalist sense. But such a policy is itself not without drawbacks and risks.

Since 1967, or at any rate 1973 (we must conclude) Pan-Arabism, though still alive in the mind of the official and intellectual classes of the Arab world and though still very prominent in their rhetoric, is yet a cause in search of a leader.

The interval that has elapsed between the heady days of the October war of 1973, the oil embargo, and the stupendous rise in the price of oil have not disclosed any new element which might change this conclusion. In October 1973 and the months that immediately followed, it seemed as though a new era was dawning in the Arab world, and that its weight and influence in international affairs would equal that of the Great Powers who have hitherto dominated the scene. The situation which obtains today belies these expectations. The divisions and rivalries that have characterized inter-Arab politics since the establishment of the Arab League in 1945 have persisted, and in some respects have become more serious. It soon became apparent that the October war had ended in a political stalemate, and no agreement among Arab states on the way to end the stalemate was forth-coming. This deep disagreement, which was as much a matter of principle as of interest, became most manifest following President Sadat's visit to Jerusalem in November 1977. Some Arab states—Iraq, Libya, Algeria—were absolutely uncompromising in their opposition, insisting that unrelenting struggle was the only possible stance to adopt toward Israel; Syria was hardly less opposed, fearing to be left alone to face the Israelis; Jordan could see no advantage in following or approving Egypt's policy, since it feared that if it made a deal with Israel and resumed its rule in the West Bank, it would needlessly lay itself open to Syria's enmity and PLO-fomented resistance within its own territory; the oil-rich states of the Peninsula—chief among them Saudi Arabia—could not bring themselves, for various reasons, to approve of the Egyptian's initiative, even though they did not wish to be as outspoken in their opposition as, say, Syria or Libya. The Camp David Agreement only sharpened existing disagreements, fears and suspicions.

The wealth brought by the rise in oil prices, though it has undoubtedly made possible for its owners the exercise of influence, and sometimes great influence, has not made possible unquestioned assertion of leadership in the Arab world. The wealth has also enabled its owners to buy very great quantities of arms; but this has not resulted, so far, in any visible shift of power within the region. Among the oil-rich states, only Iraq and Saudi Arabia have the potential to engage in rivalry, and the arms acquired by the one may be assumed to balance those acquired by the other. Only if these arms are put to use will it be possible to establish if in fact there is a balance. However, the events which have taken place in 1977-9 in the Horn of Africa, in North and South Yemen, in Afghanistan and in Iran raise the question whether the local rivalries, alliances and combinations within the Arab world will not be overshadowed by more complicated, wider and more dangerous problems. If this should happen, then the weight and importance that the Arab states acquired following the October war may be appreciably diminished.

7

LEBANON: THE PERILS OF INDEPENDENCE

The recent civil war in Lebanon has attracted a great many explanations, all more or less plausible, and some cogent and convincing. It has been said that the disturbances were a consequence of the naked greed of Lebanese businessmen who, in an unbridled capitalist economy, were allowed to get richer and richer, while the poor got poorer and poorer. The civil war on this view was the just and inevitable reward of a laissez-faire state and society devoid of conscience or compassion.

The so-called confessionalism which was a pillar of Lebanese politics has also been held guilty. It has been claimed that this 'confessionalism' made for rampant favouritism and corruption in public affairs; that it encouraged officials to put communal loyalty before loyalty to the state; that it meant an army and a police force divided against itself, useless as an instrument of policy, and quite unable to discharge the most elementary duty of government, namely to maintain law and order.

Some observers have also blamed Franjieh, the former Lebanese President, for alienating influential and powerful politicians, and for mishandling and dismantling the intelligence apparatus bequeathed to him by his predecessors, Shehab and Helou.

The presence of large numbers of armed Palestinians has also been adduced as the cause of the civil war. Lebanon, with its weak laissez-faire institutions, with the absence of a strong loyalty to the state, it has been said, was in no position to cope with a group formidable enough to be able to command the active sympathy of a large and powerful group of Lebanese citizens.

Intervention by other Arab states in Lebanese internal affairs has also been made responsible for the civil war, and particularly for the endless supply of arms which allowed various groups to devastate Beirut and other places. Syria, Iraq and Libya are most frequently cited in this connection, though Saudi Arabia is also occasionally mentioned as financing—for some time at any rate—the anti-Palestinian groups such as the Phalanges and Camille Chamoun's followers.

Israeli policy is, again, arraigned. Its pressure and activities on the southern borders, it is alleged, put the Lebanese government under intolerable pressure and greatly increased tension between the Palestinians and those among the Lebanese who disliked and feared their presence in Lebanon.

If one were to write a detailed and consecutive narrative of, say, the last ten years of Lebanese politics, one would, undoubtedly, have to consider all these claims and weigh their merits in the light of the available evidence. But evidence which might enable exigent and sceptical historians to do so is simply not yet available.

Evidence, however, does exist—ambiguous, it is true, and equivocal, like most historical evidence—that might enable us to reach a judgment or, at any rate, to speculate about the character of the polity which, as a result of the events of the last few years, now lies in ruins with its sovereignty and independence mortally, perhaps irretrievably, damaged.

The Lebanese state as it existed until the civil war—as it still exists in a shadowy and formal kind of way—attained independence during, and as a result of, events which took place during World War II. Independent Lebanon was exactly identical in territorial extent and in the character of its population with the Mandated territory known as the *Grand Liban* (or Greater Lebanon in the usual English translation) which the French Mandatory formally proclaimed in the summer of 1920. In considering this Mandated territory, historians seem generally agreed that it is the immediate lineal descendant of the Sanjaq or Mutesarrifiate of Mount Lebanon set up by the *Règlement organique* of 1861. The question is to what extent such a judgment may be accepted or qualified.

Three things can safely be said about the Sanjaq created by the *Règlement organique*. In the first place it was the outcome of a ferocious civil war in which very large numbers of Maronites were slaughtered by their Druze neighbors, and much Maronite property was looted and destroyed. This disaster, in turn, was the remote consequence of the involvement of Mount Lebanon in regional and international politics following Muhammad Ali's occupation of the Levant after 1831 when Lebanese political leaders and communities had willy-nilly to take sides for or against Egyptians or Ottomans. It was then that the seeds were sown of the fearful troubles which were to culminate in the massacres of 1860.

In the second place, the *Règlement organique* embodied the labours of an international commission composed of the representatives of five nations and presided over by the Ottoman Foreign Minister. The *Règlement* was guaranteed by these six Great Powers; namely, Great Britain, France, Russia, Austria, and Prussia, and the Ottoman empire who, in 1867, were joined by Italy. These Powers, and in particular Great

Britain and France, thereafter closely watched and monitored its workings. The *Règlement* instituted an autonomous regime in Mount Lebanon, established an equilibrium between Druze and Maronite interests, between Lebanese and Ottoman interest, and between the interests of the Great Powers. It is generally accepted that under the regime of the *Règlement* (which lasted until it was abrogated by the Young Turk government in 1915) Mount Lebanon knew peace and prosperity.

In the third place, it has to be said that the autonomous Sanjaq of Mount Lebanon as defined in the *Règlement* was sensibly smaller in territorial extent and appreciably different in the character of its population than the Mandated territory of Greater Lebanon and its successor, the Republic of Lebanon. In addition to the Maronite and Druze areas of the Sanjaq (forming roughly the central area of present-day Lebanon), Greater Lebanon included extensive areas in the north with the port of Tripoli, the Biqa' in the east, and Sidon and the areas to the south up to the Palestine frontier. And to the original Maronite and Druze inhabitants of Mount Lebanon were now added large numbers of Sunni and Shi'ite Muslims.

There are, however, two elements of continuity between 19th-century Mount Lebanon and the independent Republic. The first is that the fate of both is profoundly affected by international rivalry and conflict. Neither the Sanjaq nor the Republic can be isolated by its own authorities from the quarrels of its neighbours or the ambition of the Great Powers. The safety of the territory therefore depends not on Lebanese military power, but on the balance of power—regional and international.

The second element of continuity to be seen from the Egyptian invasion of 1831 to the present day is that the Lebanese authorities (whether Druze and Maronite chieftains, or the president and ministers of a parliamentary Republic) are unable, by the exercise of their own authority or by the exertion of the power at their disposal, to contain and put an end to disorder and civil war. This was true in 1840-45 and 1860, and equally true in 1958 and after 1975.

But between the Sanjaq and the independent Republic there are appreciable, not to say crucial, differences. As has been said, Greater Lebanon and the successor Republic are, in point of territory, much larger than the Sanjaq. This state of affairs is the outcome of a French decision taken in 1920. How this decision was arrived at, and to what extent it was influenced by the wishes and urgings of France's Maronite protégés, we do not know in any detail. French records relating to foreign affairs (in any case never as full and informative as their British counterparts) are, in consequence of destructions and mutilations which they suffered between 1940 and 1945, in places seriously fragmented and deficient, while Maronite records (whether the papers of the Patriarchate or private archives) are simply not available.

Two things however are clear: one, that Greater Lebanon more or less corresponds to the non-Turkish area of the so-called blue zone which by the Sykes-Picot Agreement of 1916 France had the right to administer directly, and even to annex; second, that the setting up of Greater Lebanon was thought to satisfy frequently expressed Maronite ambitions, as well as to provide, in the era of League of Nations Mandates and self-determination, a sound and solid base for French power in the Levant.

In view of the later events, it is no exaggeration to describe the French decision to set up Greater Lebanon as a fateful one. What else may be said about it? It would seem that there was nothing inevitable requiring the transformation of an appreciable area of the blue zone of the Sykes-Picot agreement into the political entity of Greater Lebanon. Before the decision to establish it was taken, the issue, as we now know, was considered and discussed by at least one French official, but because of the character of the French records we have no means of telling how carefully the points put forward by this official were attended to and taken into account before the final decision was made.

The official in question was Robert de Caix (1869-1970), who can perhaps be considered as the most outstanding and intelligent servant of the French Mandate in the Levant. How de Caix came to be involved in the affairs of the Levant is not entirely clear, but his involvement does not seem to date from before 1919. Up to then, he had been a well-known figure in Parisian journalism, being the foreign editor of the *Journal des Débats*. He was also prominent in those political circles that had an interest in French imperial and colonial affairs, and it may be that the Prime Minister, Clémenceau, called on him to serve as chief negotiator with the Amir Faysal during the Amir's visits to Paris, precisely in order to attract support from these circles, or perhaps to ward off their attacks.

As we can see from his memoranda in the archives of the Ministry of Foreign Affairs, de Caix was, as a negotiator, extremely shrewd and very well informed. It did not take him long to discover and size up the difficulties with which the French were confronted in the Levant, to appreciate Faysal's ambition, the character of his support, and the strategic position occupied by the British in the affairs of the Middle East.

As regards the blue zone specifically, we may point to a long passage which occurs in a memorandum of January 1920 in which de Caix, discussing the policy of coming to an agreement with Faysal, is led to consider the character of this zone. He is led to point out how heterogeneous this zone in fact is in point of population, and to sketch out the lineaments of a policy that would take this heterogeneity into account, and make use of it to establish a new political order satisfactory both to France and the populations concerned. Though he does speak here of the forthcoming establishment of a 'Greater Lebanon', it is clear that what he has in mind is much less extensive than what a few months later came to be included under this heading.[1]

In another memorandum dated 17 July 1920, de Caix (now Secretary-General of the French High Commission in Beirut) expressed more specifically and more pointedly his doubts about establishing an entity such as was to be proclaimed less than a fortnight after he had written his memorandum. In his paper of the previous January it was clear that de Caix was not including in the Greater Lebanon he envisaged the area of Sidon and the South. This area, with its predominantly Shi'ite population, de Caix thought might form an autonomous province to adjoin Lebanon. In the July memorandum he now declared that Tripoli ought not to be annexed to Lebanon: it was, he wrote, 'a Sunni Muslim centre, somewhat fanatical, and in no way aspiring to be incorporated in a country with a Christian majority.' Again, he was very doubtful if a large city like Beirut (which, as is well known, had not formed part of the Sanjaq) should be the capital of Lebanon. In a few years' time, he pointed out, Beirut would have a population half the size of the whole Lebanon, the character of which it would greatly alter.[2]

In a long report, written in October 1926 that reviewed the working of the Levant Mandate up to then, de Caix showed no doubt about the manner in which Greater Lebanon came about. Pressure was exerted by 'the old French element in Beirut'. This was reinforced by the Christian communities affiliated with Rome, who were too imbued with the *politique de clientèle* to see the dangers of the new arrangment, let alone to alert Gouraud to it. The High Commissioner was bombarded with talk about 'historical frontiers', the history of which no one took the trouble to establish. And the Maronite Patriarchate 'with that lack of genuine political sense which often characterizes cunning men with an aptitude for intrigue' pressed Gouraud as much as it could to give the Lebanon everything.[3]

In any event de Caix's misgivings had no effect on the final decision. The Greater Lebanon, as it was proclaimed by General Gouraud on 1 August 1920, included not only the Biqa' but also Sidon and Tyre in the south, Tripoli in the north, as well as Beirut as the capital of the new territory. In this way the character of the Sanjaq was profoundly, not to say fundamentally, changed. The Lebanese Republic, which attained full independence in 1943, was to find this legacy of the French Mandate more of a curse than a blessing.

Professor Kamal Salibi devotes the second part of his well-known *Modern History of Lebanon* (1965) to 'Greater Lebanon', i.e., to Lebanese history since 1918. At the head of this part stands, by way of an epigraph, a quotation from Michel Chiha, perhaps the most intelligent and penetrating Lebanese writer on Lebanese politics. In this quotation, Chiha declares that Lebanon is a country 'which tradition must defend against force'. The question about Greater Lebanon and the Lebanese Republic is, in fact, whether it does have such a tradition which might shield it against brute force. Of the Sanjaq we may say, though diffidently and with all kinds of reservations, that it had some such tradition which was the outcome of a long period of Druze-Maronite symbiosis. Even so, such a tradition was not strong enough to preserve Mount Lebanon from the disorders of 1840-45 or the horrors of 1860.

Greater Lebanon, however, was devoid of any such tradition. As the French set it up, Greater Lebanon contained a large number of Shi'ite and Sunni Muslims who had never looked upon themselves as partners in a Lebanese polity, and who had no great traditional loyalty to such a state which, furthermore, had been set up by a foreign Christian power to further its own imperial policy. The Sunnis of Beirut and Tripoli, in particular, deeply resented being incorporated in the Lebanese Republic. For a very long time their leaders not only would have nothing to do with the Mandatory authorities or Lebanese politics, but also looked with longing on the prospect of being joined to Syria, where Sunnis were in the majority and where (so it was believed) they would be the undisputed masters. Such sentiments were manifested both before and after Lebanon had attained independence, most notably in 1928 and 1936 when Sunni leaders in Lebanon publicly demanded that they should be recognized as forming part of Syria, and in 1958 when the union of Egypt and Syria in a United Arab Republic directly led to a civil war which was fed and kept going not only by Nasserist intrigues from Damascus but also by the burning Nasserist fervour so widespread among the Sunnis of the Lebanon. These events together with the troubles that erupted in 1975 amply indicate that Greater Lebanon and the Lebanese Republic are politically incoherent, and thus unstable, entities. In 1958, and even more so after 1975, the Lebanese government was hamstrung and rendered impotent by the fact that the loyalty of an appreciable part of Lebanese citizens went to causes foreign to Lebanon, and inimical to its continued existence.

There is yet another difference between the Sanjaq and the Republic. Now there is no *Règlement* the functioning of which is supervised by an imperial government and guaranteed by the Great Powers. The Republic is sovereign and independent, and its rulers are on their own. And how dangerous such independence has proven to be! For the Lebanese leaders—and particularly for the Maronite among them—independence was, in fact, a gamble which in the sequel has proven quite disastrous. The gamble is embodied in the so-called National Pact of 1943. This was really an understanding between, on the one side, the Sunni Muslim notables represented by Riad al-Sulh, and a faction of Maronite notables led by Bishara al-Khuri and (ironically, in view of later events) Camille Chamoun. The Pact was a far-reaching and unprecedented departure in Lebanese politics without analogue in the political traditions of Mount Lebanon. The terms of the Pact were as follows:

1. Lebanon to be a completely independent sovereign state. The Christians to forego seeking protection or attempting to bring

the country under foreign control or influence. In return, Muslims to forego making any attempt to bring about any political union with Syria, or any form of Arab union.

2. Lebanon is a country with an Arab 'face' and language, and a part of the Arab world—having, however, a special character.

3. Lebanon to cooperate with all the Arab states and to become a member of the Arab family, provided the Arab states recognize its independence and sovereignty within the existing boundaries.

The National Pact thus meant that the Maronites were to give up French protection, indeed to make common cause with the Sunnis against the French, in return for their acceptance of Greater Lebanon. Present security was to be bartered against future performance. But covenants without the sword are but words.

This radical departure in Maronite policies, so fraught with dangers and so heavy with future disasters, was undoubtedly effected under British influence, which was then predominant. We do not know whether those Maronite leaders who set their community on this perilous path weighed the risks of this adventure, or whether in their eagerness for power they persuaded themselves that General Spears (the British Minister who egged them on) was an immortal god who would forever watch over their welfare.

Thus, it appears that the two rival powers of the time, France and Great Britain, had, unbeknown to themselves, co-operated in putting together the infernal machine that exploded first in 1958 and then in 1975-76: France, by setting up Greater Lebanon; Britain, by pushing for a Maronite-Sunni National Pact. As its tenor shows, this Pact irremediably involved the inhabitants of this unlucky area in the perils of an inter-Arab state system. This system, as is well known, has been highly unstable. Some of its members have been inordinately ambitious and quite reckless, and in pursuit of their aims wasteful of power and resources which the Lebanese Republic, in its military weakness and political incoherence, could not possibly withstand. Finally, if the story has a moral it is surely that independence can be as constraining as dependence, and sometimes perhaps even downright disastrous.

8

GREAT BRITAIN AND PALESTINE: THE TURNING POINT

The disturbances that broke out in Palestine in April 1936 had a decisive and far-reaching effect, and they may justly be considered to constitute a turning point in the history of the British Mandate, of British policy towards the Arab world and of Arab-Zionist relations. The fairly immediate consequence was the increasing involvement of the Foreign Office in the Palestine problem and the assertion of its preponderance in the formulation of Palestine policy—a preponderance that operated to the detriment of the Colonial Office, which had hitherto been recognized as the department primarily responsible for the territory. This preponderance was to subsist for the next 12 years, ending only when, at the instigation of the Foreign Secretary of the day, the British government abruptly decided to withdraw from Palestine and abandon its inhabitants to the arbitrament of war. In this war, the Arab side consisted not only of the native Palestinians but also of the neighbouring Arab states who claimed to have a right and a responsibility to come to the aid of their fellow-Arabs in Palestine. And this claim has its origin precisely in events that took place in the months immediately following the outbreak of disturbances in April 1936.

There can be little doubt that if such momentous consequences flowed from these disturbances it was in no small measure owing to the policy that the High Commissioner, Sir Arthur Wauchope, followed with the approval of the two Secretaries of State who, in the course of 1936, succeeded each other at the Colonial Office—J. H. Thomas (who anyway had held the office only from November 1935) and W. G. Ormsby Gore (who replaced him in June 1936). Wauchope had been High Commissioner and Commander-in-Chief in Palestine since 1931. In the words of Bernard Fergusson, author of the article on Wauchope in the *Dictionary of National Biography,* the early years of his administration 'were generally adjudged successful', so much so that, just before the outbreak of the disturbances his term of office was renewed for another five years. For him, therefore, the disturbances were, inevitably, something that marred a record marked by peace, prosperity and cordiality with all the elements of the population placed under his care. But, on the other hand, his very success so far and the friendly relations that he had cultivated with the Arab leaders led him to decide that the disturbances could be contained and dealt with by moderate policies, and that forceful methods should be avoided. As Fergusson writes, 'Wauchope's support for local officials who took stern measures seemed to many to be half-hearted. In some cases he relieved them of their posts. He appeared convinced that the situation would improve with time'.

Evidence is not lacking in the official papers to confirm Fergusson's judgment. In August 1936—when disorders were at their height and British forces were seemingly unable to secure law and order in the territory for which Wauchope was responsible—Wauchope reviewed his relations with the Mufti of Jerusalem and tried to justify the policy he had recommended and followed in the four troubled months following the Arab general strike.

> I came to Palestine [Wauchope wrote to Ormsby Gore on 7 August 1936] full of rather vague ideas how to'clip the Mufti's wings'; but [Drayton and Trusted] high officials of the Palestine administration] have shown me how great are the legal difficulties apart from the political drawbacks, and during the last four years the Mufti has been more of a help than a hindrance to Government. Even now [Wauchope affirmed] I know he is not so extreme as his enemies say and, though rather a foxy gentleman, he is more genuine than men like Ragheb Beg [Nashashibi], and more to be relied on.[1]

And in a despatch a fortnight later, he portrayed the Mufti and his colleagues in the Arab Higher Committee as helpless in the face of the extremists who were fomenting the disorders: they 'find themselves in the position in which retreat is impossible because they cannot control the extremist element'; 'I do not believe the Mufti will have the courage to oppose in the open the demands of this party'; any concessions made 'would have to meet with the approval of the extremists'; 'the extremists lead and they frighten those who, like the Mufti, refuse to stand in the open and declare themselves wholeheartedly for violence or wholeheartedly for acceptance of Government offers.'[2]

Wauchope, however, was badly mistaken. The Arab Higher Committee, presided over by the Mufti, was not to be distinguished from 'the extremists'. Available police evidence had pointed to the Mufti's involvement in the violence.[3] And even if this evidence were to be considered inconclusive or unconvincing, there was (perhaps more important) the declaration issued by the Arab Higher Committee on 25 April to the effect that the strike would continue until all Jewish immigration was stopped, as well as all land sales to Jews, and a representative national government set up in Palestine. This was nothing less than a public call to civil disobedience and a challenge that the lawful government could ignore only at its peril.

In building his policy on the false premise that the Mufti and the Arab Higher Committee were to be distinguished from the 'extremists' who were the real authors of the disorders, Wauchope allowed Palestine to slip out of his control. He did nothing to halt the activities of the Arab Higher Committee that, early in May, with the Mufti in the van, 'toured the country', re-organising and gingering up the National Committees in the outlying districts with the object of decentralizing command and ensuring that each Committee should have its zone of activity and should be active in it. At the same time orders were issued by the Arab Higher Committee that non-payment of taxes and civil disobedience were to begin from the 15th of May.'[4] As a result of these unchecked activities, disorders that had started in the cities spread to the countryside. By the beginning of June the situation was so bad that Air Vice-Marshal R. E. C. Peirse, who commanded the small contingent of British troops in Palestine, recommended the proclamation of martial law and the adoption of repressive measures severe enough to bring lawless acts to an end. Wauchope opposed this and he was supported by the Colonial Office.[5] The British troops, therefore, continued merely to act in support of the civil power, as and when called upon to do so. This was in itself a very inefficient way of dealing with rebellion, since the civil power usually did not call upon the troops until a disturbance had broken out; the troops could not assume the initiative in searching for and neutralizing the rebels. Again, the absence of martial law meant that law-breakers would have to be dealt with by the civil courts according to procedures which were not designed to deal with this kind of emergency. The British forces, which then consisted of two Army battalions and two squadrons and four sections of armoured cars of the Royal Air Force, were in any case too small to act in aid of the civil power over the whole of Palestine. They were ham-strung by Wauchope's policy, which kept them dispersed, in small driblets over the whole territory, and prevented them from bringing their full force to bear at a time and place of their own choosing. The deteriorating state of security in turn meant that the Arab contingent of the Palestine police became unreliable, either because its members sympathized with the rebels or because they were intimidated or terrorized into passivity.

It is not surprising that the situation continued to deteriorate. In his despatch of 22 August quoted above, Wauchope was forced to admit that his policy had failed. The armed bands had not been destroyed and individual acts of terrorism and murder had increased, as had the supply of money and arms to the rebels. In a memorandum annexed to the despatch Peirse expressed his great disquiet, declaring that he failed to see 'how at this stage His Majesty's Government can capitulate to the demands of the Arabs'. He therefore proposed the proclamation of martial law and the adoption of measures 'designed to subdue lawlessness in the shortest possible time'. Once again, Wauchope opposed such a policy, and proposed instead 'the granting of some concession to people with whom it is most important we should live on friendly terms in future years, but not granting a concession of such a nature as to give the impression of yielding in the face of violence and disorder which we have been unable otherwise to end'. Some such policy, as will be seen, was in the end adopted with all the ruinous consequences that might have been expected. Wauchope, a few weeks after sending the despatch, came to recognize that the policy he had followed since the previous April had failed, and that martial law should be declared. Instead of blaming himself for misreading the situation and pursuing for half a year an ineffective and disastrous policy, he blamed the Mufti and his colleagues for not behaving as he would have liked them to. 'From start to finish,' he wrote to Ormsby Gore in a letter of 4 September, 'the Arab leaders have refused to face realities, and made no effort to end methods of violence.'[6]

By the time Wauchope came to see the error of his ways it was too late; the situation in Palestine was compromised beyond repair. Quite early in his career the Mufti had realized that his hand would be greatly strengthened if he could mobilize the Arabs and Muslim world in his struggle against the Zionists and the British. Now that he was embarked on a policy of defying the Mandate the Mufti hastened to involve in the conflict as many Arab states as possible. On 29 April 1936, five days after the Arab Higher Committee had published its proclamation, Sheikh Yusuf Yasin, a counsellor in King Ibn Sa'ud's court, approached Sir Andrew Ryan, the British Minister in Jedda, on the King's instructions. His ostensible object was to consult Ryan about a telegram received the previous day from the Mufti. The gist of the text, which Yusuf Yasin handed over to Ryan, was that 'Arab Palestine' had been upset by a British Zionist policy calculated to destroy the Arab nation. All parties had united to organize a strike that would go on until this policy was changed for one that would guarantee the safety of the Arabs, and it was in this cause that the Mufti was invoking Ibn Sa'ud's help. Sheikh Yusuf declared that he knew little about the existing situation in Palestine.

> His object [Ryan wrote] was to consult me as to the best means of avoiding interference and at the same time to maintain Ibn Sa'ud's prestige in the Arab world. There was always a general Arab feeling to be considered. It had been the basis of negotiations with the Yemen and Iraq and those now proceeding with Egypt. It had to be considered also in relation to Palestine, a country for whose welfare the King must wish.

Ryan rejected this approach root and branch. Palestine was a British Mandate, and its affairs were 'for His Majesty's Government to deal with'. Twice in the course of the conversation Ryan declared in 'express terms' that the King would neither increase his friendship with Great Britain nor his prestige in the Arab world by concerning himself with the affairs of Palestine. As for the reply to the Mufti, Ryan refused to advise in any way on its terms in spite of Yusuf Yasin's repeated attempts to get him to express an opinion. Ryan also took care to emphasize the private character of the conversation, telling the Sheikh that 'I had conducted the conversation on the assumption that he, too, was speaking privately. I could not have listened to him had he been speaking officially'.[7]

Ryan's view was clearly the only possible one to hold in the circumstances, and the Foreign Office officials in their minutes approved the conduct of the Minister. The head of the Eastern Department, G. W. Rendel, remarked that the matter was primarily one for the Colonial Office, and added that for Ibn Sa'ud to declare his sympathy in any way for Arab agitation would be to declare himself on the side of those hostile to Britain in a manner incompatible with his professions of friendship. His superiors, Sir Lancelot Oliphant and Sir Robert Vansittart, fully concurred.

Having drawn a blank in his approach to Ryan, Ibn Sa'ud tried another tack. His Minister in London, Sheikh Hafez Wahba, received instructions to approach the Foreign Office, and to represent that fellow-Arabs were 'upbraiding him as a coward and alleging that he was a British Agent for not doing something for the Arabs'. The Minister told Sir Lancelot Oliphant, the Deputy Under-Secretary who received him on 16 June 1936, that his master had no intention of interfering in British affairs. He only wanted to know the real position in Palestine, and requested advice on how to reply to his own people, and others in Egypt and elsewhere. Ibn Sa'ud, the Minister added, wished to do this in consultation with the British government. This was what Oliphant, at any rate, understood Hafez Wahba (who was assisted by his interpreter) as saying. The Saudi Minister was later to claim that he had also said something else, quite far-reaching in its implications.

But even confined to the terms in which Oliphant reported it, this message constituted exactly the same transparent and disingenuous maneuvre that Ryan, on his own initiative, had firmly rebuffed the previous April. The Colonial Office, however, when consulted by Oliphant, did not prove as forthright as Ryan. They, in fact, provided Ibn Sa'ud with an opening, which he proceeded to exploit with fateful consequences. Writing to Oliphant on 17 June, J. C. C. Parkinson of the Colonial Office began by reiterating the official position about the Mandatory's exclusive responsibility in Palestine, but ended with these words:

If King Ibn Sa'ud can use his influence to persuade the Arabs to

> give up the campaign of violence he will be doing a service not only to H[is] M[ajesty's] G[overnment] but to the Arabs themselves.

In a minute of the same day Parkinson recorded that this letter 'was sent with the approval of the S[ecretary] of S[tate]'.

It is not difficult to understand how Ormsby Gore was led to approve so injudicious a step as to suggest to Ibn Sa'ud that he would be 'doing a service' to the British government by using his influence with those in Palestine who were conspiring to break the King's peace. The Colonial Secretary was new to his office. He was not tough or forceful, and his style may have been cramped by his reputation as a Zionist sympathizer. The High Commissioner, whose first term of office had won golden opinions and who had just been appointed to a second one, had been a successful military commander during the war and was a Lieutenant-General on the active list. His advice had just been approved in preference to contrary advice tendered by the Commanding Officer in Palestine. Here, in the Saudi proposal, was something that might prove useful in defusing the situation—consonant, therefore, with Wauchope's advice. What harm in accepting, or at any rate exploring it?

Soon Ibn Sa'ud's modest approach began to assume more grandiose proportions. Hafez Wahba came back on 23 June to tell Oliphant that his master thought it preferable to join the King of Iraq and the Imam of the Yemen in representations to be made to the Palestine Arabs. Could he assume the 'full concurrence' of the British government in such a scheme? These joint representations would, moreover, have to be based on assurances by the Secretary of State for the Colonies that Arab grievances would be examined as soon as disorders ceased.

This was no longer a diffident request by Ibn Sa'ud for advice on how to answer the reproaches to which he was being exposed on account of Palestine. This was a proposal to intervene, to mediate between the government and those who were defying its authority. Once again the Colonial Office took the bait:

> If [Parkinson wrote to Oliphant on 26 June] Saudi Arabia, Iraq and the Yemen were to advise the Arabs of Palestine, with one voice, to put an end to the present disorder, that would be all to the good and naturally we should welcome it.

The Colonial Office even went so far as to float the idea that the British government should itself take the initiative with Iraq and the Yemen in order to suggest that they should offer 'sound advice' to the Palestinians. Parkinson drafted this letter after discussion with Sir John Maffey, the Permanent Under-Secretary, and approval by Ormsby Gore. Sending copies of the correspondence to the Chief Secretary of the Palestine Government, Parkinson wrote in a covering letter of 8 July that

I need hardly say that in a matter of this kind I have not acted without instructions and, as a matter of fact, before Oliphant had his talk with the Saudi Arabian Minister on the 3rd July, there was personal discussion between Mr. Ormsby Gore and Lord Cranborne [Parliamentary Under-Secretary at the Foreign Office].

The upshot of Parkinson's letter of 26 June and Ormsby Gore's conversation with Cranborne (the exact tenor of which is unknown) was that Oliphant told Hafez Wahba that the British government

> appreciated to the full and gladly accepted the offer of King Ibn Sa'ud to take the initiative in concerting joint action with the King of Iraq and the Imam Yahya [of the Yemen] to secure, if possible, the cessation of the Arab rising in Palestine.

Hafiz Wahba replied that the Palestinians wanted the release of prisoners convicted since the outbreak of disorder, the remittance of communal fines that had recently been imposed, and the stoppage of Jewish immigration.

Though Ibn Sa'ud advised the Palestinians that submission first was necessary, the Palestinians pointed out that it was only reluctantly that they had joined issue with the government and would thus be content with nothing less than satisfaction on these three points. The benevolent go-between was happy to assist the British government in its predicament: 'were he to receive assurances of a satisfactory nature on the above three points, the Arabs,' he confidently promised, 'would at once stop all disorders.' It does not seem to have occurred to Oliphant to tell Hafiz Wahba that if the British government were to show the white flag of surrender to the Palestine Arabs they could do it on their own, without the help of Ibn Sa'ud's good offices.

Three days later, Hafez Wahba put forward an improvement on his master's original plan. He proposed that the Crown Prince of Egypt and the Amir Abdullah of Transjordan (which was itself under British Mandate), should also participate in the good offices mission, and that a high Saudi official should go to Palestine to speak to the Arab leaders on Ibn Sa'ud's behalf. The British government was apparently too embarrassed to rebuff Ibn Sa'ud, and the Colonial Office told Wauchope that unless he saw 'serious objections', the government proposed to accept these new suggestions.

What began as a Saudi request for advice was now threatening to become a complicated negotiation in which the Arabs of Palestine—represented, so to speak, by Ibn Sa'ud, Iraq, the Yemen and perhaps Egypt and Transjordan—would bargain with their government for the conditions on which they would agree not to disturb the peace. For this outcome the responsibility is shared by Wauchope, who shrank from taking the necessary steps to end the disorders, Ormsby Gore, who clutched at what seemed to be the helping hand of Ibn Sa'ud, his officials, who failed to alert him to the possible consequences of accepting such help, and the Foreign Office, who should have been even more alert in preventing outside intervention in British affairs. And it is not as though the possibility of such intervention had never been considered before. At the 17th session of the Permanent Mandates Commission of the League of Nations in 1930 Lord Lugard, a member of the Commission, asked H. C. Luke, who was representing the government of Palestine, why the British government had not asked the King of Iraq or the Amir of Transjordan to use their influence with their co-religionists in Palestine to foster a more sympathetic apprecia-tion of the obligations imposed on the Mandatory by the Balfour Declaration (the text of which had been incorporated in the Mandate for Palestine). In reply,

> Mr. Luke submitted that that would have been tantamount to the British Government or the Palestine Government, as the case might be, inviting the sovereigns of other territories to reinforce with their advice, on persons not under their jurisdiction, a policy accepted and undertaken by the Mandatory and endorsed by the League of Nations.

Lugard, however, persisted in his questioning, pointing out that he had not enquired why the government had not asked for the advice of the two rulers in question but rather why they had not asked them to use their influence with co-religionists. Luke's rejoinder was that

> it would be very difficult, and possibly even improper, for His Majesty's Government to invite foreign sovereigns to give advice of that sort. It would be difficult, and possibly improper, to do so even if those two sovereigns agreed with the advice that it was suggested they should give. It would be infinitely more difficult if they disagreed with the advice that it was suggested they should give. It would also, he submitted, be improper for the rulers in question, even if not asked, to take the initiative in interfering—because giving such advice would necessarily have the character of interference—with the political affairs of territories in no way under their jurisdiction.[8]

Reluctance to avoid even the appearance of a rebuff to Ibn Sa'ud quickly led to other demands on the part of the Arab states, to whose inter-vention the conjugated impolicy of the Foreign and Colonial Offices had opened the door. On 14 July Hafez Wahba reported to Oliphant that the Iraqis and the Yemenites would be prepared to co-operate if the British government would promise to stop immigration pending the report of the Commission of Enquiry which, at Wauchope's suggestion the previous May, had been appointed to investigate Arab grievances. The Iraqis further demanded that the British government should promise to discuss with the Palestine Arabs a limitation on immigration and the sale of Arab lands and the establishment of a National Government. Hafiz Wahba himself insisted on the temporary stoppage of immigration. If, he beguilingly suggested, the British government 'were to announce this as their decision, as a concession to the three Arab Kings who are their friends, this decision could not be interpreted as a concession to mob violence by the Arabs of Palestine'.

At this point the Colonial Office wakened to the perils of these negotiations: 'We think,' Parkinson minuted to Ormsby Gore, 'it would be a very dangerous precedent to suspend immigration, as Ibn Sa'ud suggests, as a concession to the three Arab Kings; in any event,' he now came to see, 'it would be difficult to distinguish as things are, between the Arabs in Palestine and the Arab Kings outside acting as mediators.' The Cabinet rejected the Saudi proposals, and Oliphant had no alternative but to tell Hafiz Wahba on 20 July that it was out of the question to suspend immigration. He could not refrain from adding that if Ibn Sa'ud would continue to exercise any moderating influence on the Palestine Arabs (of which, it may be said, nothing had hitherto transpired), 'this would be much appreciated by His Majesty's Government, who thanked him for his offer of good offices'. This gush was repeated by the Foreign Secretary himself. In answer to a message from Ibn Sa'ud promising to use all his influence with the Arab leaders, Anthony Eden conveyed to him his 'keen appreciation' of this assurance. It has to be noted that whether or not Ibn Sa'ud did use his influence with the Palestine Arabs no abatement in the disturbances ensued.

When on 14 July Hafez Wahba broached the demand that immigration be suspended to Oliphant he said he hoped that the British government would agree 'as he himself suggested when he first made representations to the Foreign Office'. It will be recalled that when Hafiz Wahba first raised the matter on 16 June Oliphant understood him to be asking for advice, not to be making a request or proferring advice about how the British should conduct themselves in Palestine. This at any rate is what he conveyed at the time to the Colonial Office. But he does not seem to have grasped the significance of what Hafez Wahba was now alleging. In any case, he did not query or point out to the Saudi Minister that he had made no such statement at the earlier interview. Parkinson, however, immediately spotted the discrepancy, minuting that there 'is presumably some misunderstanding, but it is a very unfortunate misunderstanding, as it would have made a very great difference to our answer had we known that King Ibn Sa'ud was coupling his enquiry with any suggestion'. Whether this would have been the case is not easy to say, since the Colonial Secretary seemed to be looking for almost any way out of the Palestine difficulty. Parkinson, at any rate, tackled Oliphant on this point, who now said that he thought it possible that just as Hafez Wahba was leaving at the end of the interview of 16 June 'he threw in some remark of this kind'. Oliphant admitted to 'a certain difficulty in being absolutely sure that he misses nothing' at such interviews. His difficulty apparently stemmed from the fact that conversations with Hafiz Wahba were carried on through the Saudi Minister's own interpreter.

It was clearly negligent of Oliphant to allow interviews to be conducted in these conditions, but the course of the negotiations revealed him to be guilty of another piece of incompetence. When he met Hafez Wahba on 20 July to tell him that it was impossible to announce suspension of immigration, the interpreter asked whether the three points that the Palestinians had raised through Ibn Sa'ud would be considered separately. Oliphant, no doubt in order to close the door on further discussion, said that he had regarded these three points as 'one joint stipulation', and since no pronouncement about immigration was being made, he doubted the need of pursuing the other two. It was highly maladroit to introduce the idea that rebellious subjects could stipulate terms for their submission, or accept in any way that they could bargain with the government. It was also gratuitous for him to speak of a 'joint stipulation', thus opening the door to the claim that nothing less than total acquiescence by the government in their demands would be acceptable to the rebels.

In the event, Saudi mediation or intercession proved of no benefit to the Palestine government. It simply opened the way to other attempts at intervention which ended by complicating the issue out of all recognition.[9]

As a direct consequence of Ibn Sa'ud's representations, and of the fact that they were not immediately and categorically rebuffed in London, the Iraqis now entered the game. The Iraqi Foreign Minister, Nuri al-Sa'id, now offered his services to bring the disturbances to an end. In a telegram of 17 August Bateman, the Counsellor in the Baghdad Embassy, informed Wauchope that Nuri was going to Ankara and was anxious to stop in Jerusalem en route to do what he could to restore the peace. Bateman ended his telegram by saying that Nuri 'would speak to Arabs in Palestine as an Arab, and not as the Iraqi Minister for Foreign Affairs'. Wauchope accepted with alacrity. At that point he looked upon the outlook in Palestine as black. In a despatch written about that time, he declared he saw no prospect of existing methods (which he himself had advocated) being successful. He was afraid that many armed men would reinforce the rebels from Syria; he was also afraid that Arab officials might join the strike, and that the Mufti would raise the religious cry. Air Vice-Marshal Peirse agreed that the situation was perilous and decided that the only remedy lay in proclaiming martial law and taking other consequent measures, among them the deportation of the Mufti and other leaders of the insurrection. Wauchope, however, as has been seen, set himself resolutely against this advice. Instead, he proposed a policy of 'moderate concession' that, however, 'would have to meet with the approval of the extremists'! Among these he did not count the Mufti; but the Mufti, unfortunately, did not have the courage to oppose extremist demands openly.[10]

But it soon transpired that Nuri's mission was not and could not conceivably be considered a private one—that, indeed, unless he could speak as the official representative of Iraq, it was useless. Staying in Jerusalem as Wauchope's guest, Nuri began his discussions with the Arab Higher Committee. On 22 August, he produced a draft memorandum to be addressed by the Iraqi government to the Arab leaders. This document spoke of the Iraqi government mediating with a view to ending the disturbances and of their using their good offices in order to obtain 'the grant of all legitimate demands of the Arabs of Palestine, whether such demands arise out of the present disturbances or are connected with the basis of general policy in Palestine'. Ormsby Gore immediately objected that an acceptance of this phraseology implied not only a commitment to meeting unspecified and possibly wide Arab demands, but also the admission that Iraq could properly intervene in the affairs of Palestine. To this objection, Nuri's answer now was that his intervention 'otherwise than as Foreign Minister of Iraq, would have been quite valueless'. The same pattern, then, as became apparent in the exchanges with the Saudis was to be seen here: a seemingly benevolent and innocuous approach suddenly and quickly came to have all kinds of far-reaching and dangerous implications.

Very quickly, too, Nuri assumed a monitory tone in which he was urgently echoed by a panic-stricken Wauchope. Since the Arab leaders had committed themselves to continue the strike and disorders until immigration was stopped, calling off the strike without obtaining this concession would lead the fanatical bands and the extremists roving the country to put all their lives in jeopardy. Forwarding this message to Ormsby Gore on 30 August, Wauchope stated that he associated himself with Nuri's appeal. If Nuri's draft memorandum was not approved 'the situation throughout Palestine will become more serious and will require additional troops to control'. How could mere 'formal objections' stand in the way of Nuri's 'great contribution to peace'? In telegrams that had immediately preceded this one, Wauchope had repeatedly pressed for the unconditional acceptance of Nuri's proposal. Thus, on 26 August he endorsed Nuri's claim that he could not act in a personal capacity. Nuri could not possibly do so: the Arabs, he opined, were 'incapable of understanding such a refinement'. If Nuri's proposal is not accepted, he said in the same telegram, this will be proof positive to every Arab that the 'Royal Commission is merely camouflage, and that there is no intention to do anything for Arabs'. If Nuri's efforts fail, he warned in a telegram on the following day, because the British government 'cannot accept representations from Iraqi Government' the chances of an early end to the disorders would become very remote.

Ormsby Gore was not a strong man and could not withstand this pressure, particularly when, as will be seen, it was conjugated with pressure in the same direction exerted by the Foreign Office. He gave in to Wauchope's urgings. Since, however, the intervention of a foreign government was still difficult to swallow, he proposed, in a telegram of 27 August, composed in consultation with the Foreign Office, some changes in Nuri's memorandum, the most important of which was that the term, 'mediation', was to be qualified by the epithet 'informal'. Neither Nuri nor Wauchope were very willing to accept this, and proposed yet another formula that would pin down the British government to a promise of clemency towards rebel bands and to the suspension of immigration.[11]

At this stage, Nuri's efforts seemed to have failed. On 31 August, the Arab Higher Committee issued an uncompromising statement that, while expressing confidence in the mediation of Iraq and 'their Majesties and Highnesses the Arab Kings and Amirs', affirmed that the 'nation will continue its strike . . . until these negotiations will arrive at the much desired result which will preserve for this brave nation its existence and will secure its rights and lead it to obtain its aims'.[12] With this uncompromising language the Arab leaders seemed to be throwing down the gauntlet, daring the British government to a fight. This impression was heightened by the publication in *The Palestine Post* of a report giving accurate details of Nuri's proposals and negotiations with the British government. It was assumed in London that the Arabs were responsible for the leak. This, as it happened, was wrong. As Michael J. Cohen has established, this was the doing of the Jewish Agency who, rightly, calculated that the leak would embarrass Ormsby Gore and force him to make a public denial.[13]

It fell to the Cabinet to decide what should now be done. Hitherto the Cabinet had taken a firm line. On 9 July doubts were expressed about the advisability of publicly announcing a temporary suspension of immigration, since this would be treated as another surrender to force. On 15 July the Cabinet rejected a draft jointly produced by the Foreign and Colonial Offices designed to give Ibn Sa'ud some satisfaction over the suspension of immigration. It was generally agreed that this would be contrary to previous decisions, and that no commitment on immigration could be given to Ibn Sa'ud. Now, at a meeting on 2 September, the Cabinet considered the aftermath of Nuri's attempt at mediation. Sir John Simon, the Home Secretary who, in Baldwin's absence, presided over the meeting, expressed the view that Nuri's intervention had done nothing but harm. 'It was a very remarkable thing,' he declared, 'that the Foreign Secretary of a Foreign State should have attempted to intervene between the British government and those for whom they were responsible in Palestine.' A policy of surrender might temporarily stop the strike but it could not lead to any permanent settlement; it would, furthermore, vitiate the proceedings of the Royal Commission. A more vigorous military action (which Wauchope had continuously opposed) was now to be adopted. Large reinforcements were to be sent immediately to Palestine under General Dill and martial law proclaimed. Also, no decision to suspend immigration was taken.[14]

On 10 September Wauchope met the Mufti and two other Arab leaders and demanded that they put an end to the strike and the disturbances. Seeing that the government now meant business, the Arab leaders agreed to an unconditional cessation, provided that it was preceded by an appeal from the Arab Kings that the British government, they suggested, might ask these Kings to issue. Wauchope turned this down, but he agreed to consult London over another suggestion that an emissary from the Arab leaders visit Baghdad and arrange for such an appeal. On 11 September a meeting of Ministers was held in the Colonial Office to consider this request. Simon was in the chair, and there were present Duff Cooper, the Secretary of State for War; Kingsley Wood, the Minister of Health; Inskip, the Minister for the Co-ordination of Defense; Brown, the Minister of Labour; and Stanhope, the First Commissioner of Works. Ormsby Gore, owing to his father's ill health, was absent, and content to leave the decision to his colleagues. Three officials from the Foreign Office—Vansittart, Rendel and Sterndale Bennett—were also present. They tried very hard to induce the meeting to issue some kind of promise that on the cessation of violence immigration would be suspended. But, led by Simon, the Ministers refused to depart from the previous Cabinet decision of 2 September. Wauchope was told that it was manifestly impossible for the government to accept any responsibility for the projected appeal. It was, however, perfectly open to the Arab leaders to consult fellow-Arabs if they chose to do so.[15]

The decision taken by the meeting of Ministers on 11 September was a defeat for the views of the Foreign Office as they were urged at this meeting by Vansittart, Rendel and Sterndale Bennett. In a minute of 14 September, Rendel recorded that Eden, to whom the Ministers' decision was conveyed by telephone, concurred in it reluctantly.[16] In the same minute Rendel took the opportunity to put down at some length the Foreign Office view which the record of the 11 September meeting as drafted by the Cabinet Office had 'much boiled down'. The main point which the Foreign Office representatives tried to make was that

> there seemed good reason to believe that the present opportunity was an exceptionally favourable one for bringing about a settlement by negotiation and agreement. This [Rendel and his colleagues believed] would be preferable to a mere defeat of the Arabs, which would lead to great bitterness and impair our relations with the rest of the Middle East.

The Foreign Office, then, wanted Ministers to accede to the Saudi and Iraqi demands, and somehow or other promise that immigration would be temporarily suspended in exchange for peace. That such a peace might, under such conditions, be equally temporary, to judge by Rendel's minute, does not seem to have occurred to or to have troubled these officials. Since Ministers were unwilling to make such a promise then, of course, the Foreign Office agreed, there was no point in pursuing negotiations which would hold out false hopes. Rendel's minutes make clear how misguided the Foreign Office thought the Ministers' decision had been.

A few days later, the issue, which seemed to have been so decisively disposed of, was re-opened. On 19 September, Cranborne, who was in Geneva for League of Nations meetings, sent an account of conversations which he and Sterndale Bennett had had with Nuri al-Sa'id. Nuri again pressed the British government to agree to a face-saving device which would enable the Arab Higher Committee to end the strike without the fear of being shot by their own extremists. The British should accept Iraqi good offices and should let it be known that they would accept the eventual findings of the Royal Commission (which had not yet begun its work). He was told this was impossible, as it ran 'the risk of misconstruction which would be placed on acceptance by them of any degree of responsibility for an appeal by any outside power'. Nuri was persistent; could he be told 'purely privately' whether the British wished for Iraqi mediation? This maneuvre, too, Cranborne rebuffed. He found Nuri's language 'extremely obscure' and his remarks 'so disjointed that it was a matter of utmost difficulty to understand what he really proposed and what he really wanted His Majesty's Government to do'. Cranborne's advice was that

> we should confine our dealings with him on Palestine question to narrowest possible limits. He conveyed his ideas to me in so confusing and unintelligible a manner that I was often left to infer what he really meant and I cannot help feeling he is so worked up and so desirous of playing a preponderating mediatory role that he may, without necessarily conscious intent, present to Arabs a dangerously garbled version of anything that may be said to him orally on our side. Detailed discussions with him are therefore [Cranborne concluded] in my opinion to be avoided.[17]

In the course of his talks with Cranborne, Nuri at one point said that even if the British government was not prepared to give him any promise about their policy if the Palestine Arabs were to cease their rebellion, he would still be ready to recommend that Iraq should proceed with an appeal to them, provided it was understood that if and when the appeal was successful, the Iraqi government would wish to make representations in favour of the Palestine Arabs. Cranborne was equally firm here, refusing to be lured into any promise however qualified. Rendel, however, saw in Nuri's suggestion a way of modifying the decision of 11 September. In a minute of 21 September, he wrote that in his personal view, 'for what it was worth', something might be done on the lines of this suggestion of Nuri's. Rendel saw no reason why Nuri should not be told that if strikes and violence ceased and the Royal Commission could go to Palestine, it would be perfectly open to the Iraqi government, and to other supporters of the Arab cause, to say anything to the Royal Commission on behalf of the Arabs of Palestine.

On the same day Bateman sent a telegram from Baghdad reporting the text of a draft appeal to be issued by the Arab rulers, which had been drawn up following representations by the Arab Higher Committee that the only way of ending the strike would be for such an appeal to be made. The Iraqis were now asking if the British government favoured intervention on the proposed lines and whether they had any views on the proposed text. The decision of 11 September had clearly laid down that the British government would not be drawn into negotiations or discussions concerning any approach by the Palestine Arabs tó the Arab rulers or any appeal which might be made by these rulers. Notwithstanding this decision, however, Rendel drafted a reply in which he suggested a change in the text of the appeal, thus proposing to do precisely what the meeting of Ministers on 11 September had decided should not be done. Rendel's draft telegram was approved by Ormsby Gore. The Colonial Secretary, it is true, had not been present at the meeting of 11 September, but he had specifically left the decision to his colleagues and was cognizant of this decision.[18]

His proceedings become even more peculiar when they are set side by side with a minute of his commenting on a debate between his officials at the Colonial Office which had to do precisely with the proposed intervention by Arab rulers. Parkinson wrote in a minute of 21 September that Ibn Sa'ud should not be discouraged from advising the Palestine Arabs to stop their violence, but only provided that this was unconditional. But, he added, past experience suggested that it was not very likely for the Arab rulers to intervene without some concession from the British government and this, he added—rightly, in view of the decision of 11 September—'is just that which is out of the question'. By contrast, in a minute of the same date, Maffey was asking why they shouldn't allow the Arab kings 'to uphold and explain the Palestine Arabs' case before the Royal Commission'. This, he thought, might bridge the differences between the Arabs and the Mandatory. But the Colonial Secretary, on the same day on which he approved Rendel's draft reply to Bateman, is found rejecting Maffey's suggestion and firmly laying it down that it was out of the question to have foreign governments appearing before the Royal Commission.[19]

Ormsby Gore's indecisiveness and his extreme changeableness is nothing less than amazing. For on the very same day, 22 September, he was showing such firmness in his Colonial Office minute, he was also acquiescing in a dramatically opposite line of policy. For on that day a meeting of Ministers was held to discuss legal issues arising from the forthcoming declaration of statutory martial law in Palestine. Malcolm MacDonald was in the chair, and Simon, Duff Cooper, Swinton, Oliver Stanley, Ernest Brown, Sir Donald Somerwell (the Attorney General) and Ormsby Gore were the other Ministers present. In the absence of Eden and Cranborne, who were both away in Geneva, Vansittart represented the Foreign Office. It was he who drew attention to Cranborne's report of his talks with Nuri, and particularly to Nuri's proposal that had inspired Rendel's minute of the previous day, mentioned above. Vansittart, obviously drawing on Rendel's minute, declared that it would be 'helpful' if Nuri could be told that when law and order had been re-established in Palestine, it would be open to the Iraqis to make representations to the Royal Commission on behalf of the Palestine Arabs. He also suggested that the Saudis could be told the same thing. The minutes also tell us that Ormsby Gore said that the Iraqi government could make representations in London, though there could be no question or bargaining! The papers unfortunately do not disclose whether Ormsby Gore made these remarks before or after he had written the minute affirming the very opposite. The record also discloses that Simon, who had taken the lead in formulating the decision of 11 September, now agreed with Ormsby Gore's view. The meeting, we also learn, agreed to Vansittart's suggestion, and thus in effect undid the decision taken eleven days earlier. The record does not disclose the reasons for this remarkable turnabout—which proved to be a fateful one.[20]

It will come as no surprise that Eden concurred in his colleagues' decision, and also approved the text of Rendel's draft telegram to Bateman, mentioned above. He went further. In conveying to Nuri on 24 September in Geneva the decision of 22 September, the Foreign Secretary's tone became quite effusive. His Majesty's Government had no objection to the appeal by the Arab kings; quite the contrary, he added, with an emphasis not to be discerned in his colleagues' words. Though he resisted Nuri's renewed attempt to extract some promise or undertaking, Eden assured him that 'we should welcome' the action of the Arab kings if they could make the disorders stop by their appeal. Like an urgent and fluent salesman, the Foreign Secretary was prodigal in hints and promises; His Majesty's Government, he asked Nuri to remember, had shown in their relations with Iraq and by their recent treaty with Egypt that they were disposed to giving Arabs a square deal. But back in London, Rendel, stern and exact bookkeeper, duly took note of and entered the undertaking in his books. 'Note', he minuted on 28 September, 'the statement . . . that HMG will be disposed to give the Arabs a square deal when the time comes.'[21]

The decision of 22 September, taken at Vansittart's urging and Rendel's inspiration, involved the British government in detailed negotiation's about the text of the Arab rulers' appeal, which made it, in effect, a party to the appeal. Whether the Ministers who took this decision would have thought that this was more than they had bargained for we do not know. At any rate, over a fortnight or so Rendel, the Iraqis and the Saudis are found engaging in detailed bargaining over textual minutiae. Originally the Iraqis suggested that the appeal would open by the rulers declaring that they relied 'upon the good intentions of His Majesty's Government to realise the legitimate claims of the Palestine Arabs'. Rendel suggested instead that the formula should express reliance 'upon the sense of justice of His Majesty's Government and their declared intention impartially to observe all their obligations'. This formula did not find favour with the Saudis, who were afraid that it might be read as emphasizing British obligations towards the Jews. They proposed instead that the appeal should speak of relying 'upon the goodwill of His Majesty's Government and their declared intention to see justice done'. This formula was somewhat invidious since it implied that justice had previously not been done under the British mandate. Rendel, however, pressed for the Saudi formula to be adopted because 'we ought not to risk any opportunity of finding any formula which might help to bring about an early cessation of the strike and the campaign of violence'. Ormsby Gore, too, 'agreed that it would be dangerous to allow this opportunity to slip merely for want of a word of approval or encouragement'. The appeal, finally published on 10 October, did embody the Saudi formula.[22]

Three days before the appeal was published, the Colonial Office was told by Wauchope that Dill believed that the declaration of martial law could not be safely postponed. This news agitated Rendel greatly. The proclamation of martial law would 'embarrass' the Arab kings; 'any attempt to disarm the Arabs by force on a large scale, or to "teach them a lesson" by strong punitive measures . . . may place us in a most invidious position with the Arab rulers, and', so he believed, 'make the situation even worse than it is at present.' Vansittart agreed with his subordinate. Rendel went with his worries to Ormsby Gore, who said he agreed with Rendel; but unfortunately the War Office was insisting that even if disorders ceased, martial law still had to be proclaimed. Undeterred, Rendel tackled the Director of Military Operations and Intelligence and succeeded in persuading him that Dill should stay his hand, and be content with an admonition that if disorders did not cease by a given date, or if they ceased and then resumed, the Army would have to be given special powers.[23]

One of Dill's purposes in getting martial law proclaimed was undoubtedly to establish that it was not the appeal of the Arab rulers, of the imminence of which he was surely aware, but military action and the threat thereof which had put a stop to disorder. This would have helped to uphold the prestige of the government, and prevented the idea gaining ground that civil peace in Palestine was dependent on the goodwill of foreign states. Since Rendel prevented this step from being taken, Dill was reduced to publishing, on 12 October, a Special Order to the troops in Palestine which declared:

> The strike and armed rebellion have been called off unconditionally by the Arab Higher Committee as from to-day. This result is in great measure due to the resolute and energetic action of the three Services, in spite of hampering and difficult circumstances. Cordial co-operation between them has enabled many severe blows to be inflicted on the rebels, and made it possible to maintain all essential services.

Wauchope banned publication of this Order in Palestine, and he, who had not so long ago confessed that he had been mistaken in his estimate of the Mufti, now sent him and other Arab leaders a secret message in which he expressed his gratification that the Arab Higher Committee had issued an appeal to call off the strike and the disorders.[24]

It became quickly apparent that the manner in which the strike and disorder were brought to an end was a blunder of some magnitude. What ensued in Palestine Simson describes succinctly and accurately:

> The situation which began to exist after the 12th October was not officially regarded as equivalent to an armistice. Officially the Arabs had called off their strike unconditionally. But in actual fact the situation fulfilled all the conditions normally found in an armistice. The Arabs kept their organisations, their arms, and their funds intact. They did not have to give up anything as a pledge of future good faith. On the contrary, they openly said that they were just watching and waiting, ready to take up arms again, if the British Government did not come to an acceptable arrangement with their leaders. They also maintained their intimidation in undiminished intensity, to ensure that no Arab had dealings with a Jew. The service of intimidation was useful also in the collection of funds. It is true that the label on the money-box had been altered from 'strike fund' to 'distressed Palestine', but otherwise there was no change.[25]

At a cabinet held on 28 October Ormsby Gore read a telegram from Dill in which it was pointed out that the Arab Organization remained intact and went on collecting; that the National Committee was in close touch with armed bands and the Arab Higher Committee in Jerusalem; that the bands were in armed occupation in part of the country and could be reinforced at short notice from the villages; that military operations against the bands had been greatly reduced in scale through political reasons; and that meanwhile the Arabs regarded the period as an armistice. Duff Cooper, the Secretary of State for War pointed out that the Arabs had emerged with considerable prestige, which they owed partly to the Arab kings who, he reminded the Cabinet, were originally to be kept out of the conflict.[26]

Too late, both Ministers and officials came to see how the policy they had advocated or acquiesced in was imprudent and even ruinous. Thus T. V. Brenan, of the Eastern Department at the Foreign Office, declared in a minute of 23 November 1936 on a telegram about another proposal for mediation in order to persuade the Arab Higher Committee not to boycott the sittings of the Royal Commission on Palestine:

> I think we should steer clear of appearing to welcome any more 'mediation' by these Arab Rulers. Such 'mediation' gives rise to a good deal of publicity, and despite our insistence on not being committed in any way, both the Rulers themselves and the Palestine Arabs imagine and hope that H.M.G. will give some concession.[27]

And Ormsby Gore, whose hesitant and infirm handling of affairs contributed so much to the blunder, burst out a year later when violence was worse than ever in Palestine: 'I bitterly regret that we did not give the rebels an effective taste of martial law before the leaders called off the strike and disturbances. Our action or inaction appears to the world to have been weak. I realise I was myself to blame in not pressing for more vigorous repressive action then.'[28]

The difficulties in which the British government had involved itself when it allowed the intervention of the Arab rulers became apparent the following summer at Geneva. Following the publication of the Royal Commission Report with its proposal for the partition of Palestine between Jews and Arabs, the Iraqi government—which had come to power through a *coup d'état* and was eager to shore up its very shaky position—adopted an extreme and violent line towards this proposal. It instructed its representative at the League of Nations to express Iraq's special concern with the situation in Palestine 'for racial, political, religious, economic and strategic reasons'. This concern, the Iraqis said, was emphasized when the King of Iraq together with other Arab rulers 'intervened with the Arabs of Palestine last October to secure peace'. They had, therefore, 'accepted the gravest moral responsibility' towards the Palestine Arabs who had acted in accordance with this appeal.

The representative of the Palestine government appearing before the Permanent Mandate Commission, J. H. Hall, found the language of the Iraqi delegate inconvenient and embarrassing, since it led the Commission to investigate the intervention of foreign powers in the affairs of a mandated territory. The Commission, or one of its members at any rate, accused the British government of having actually invited the Arab rulers to intervene, and Hall had to declare that the Arab rulers had intervened purely on their own initiative. This, in turn, drew a protest from the Iraqi Foreign Ministry charging that, on the contrary, the action was taken 'in full concert' with the British government. The Iraqis demanded that the British should 'take such steps as they may deem fit to save the situation and remove the bad impression which the above statement of the British representative is bound to make on the Arab rulers'. There was, of course, no denying that by their behaviour the previous year the British had invited this insolence. Furthermore, the Eastern Department was most unwilling to curb the Iraqi violence of language lest, as they informed the Colonial Office, 'too great a degree of pressure might lead to the establishment of a violently Pan-Arab government'.[29] As was shortly to be seen, the speculative dangers apprehended by the Eastern Department were outweighed by real disadvantages flowing from the reluctance to make disapproval of Iraqi proceedings public.

The British government was now the prisoner of its policy. Discussing the Palestine problem with the French representative at Geneva, Jean Chauvel, Shuckburgh of the Colonial Office told him that he was not certain that discussions on the subject could be confined to the Arabs of Palestine. 'It would probably be impracticable for us', he said, 'to take the line that Arabs from outside Palestine had no claim to have a say in the matter. This question could not but be affected to some extent by our action of last year when we acquiesced in the intervention of the Arab Kings in advising the Palestine Arabs to call off the strike'.[30] Shuckburgh's was to prove an all too accurate forecast.

But for the time being, unpleasantness at Geneva had to be endured not only from the Iraqis, but from the Permanent Mandate Commission, who rebuked the government for allowing foreign interference in the affairs of a Mandated territory administered on behalf of the League. 'They are furious with Iraq in particular', wrote Ormsby Gore, 'and query its right to any say, and all the more because Iraq was only admitted to the League because of our treaty of alliance with Iraq which they say is broken in spirit if not in letter.' The Commission considered that the continued defiance of the Mandatory by the Arab Higher Committee was a challenge not simply to Britain, but also to the League and the Mandate system. They were also convinced that the Foreign Office were 'the villains of the piece' who had brought about the intervention by Arab states.[31]

Rendel, the architect of this intervention, also went to Geneva during the 1937 session of the League. There he had a conversation with the Turkish Foreign Minister. Rustu Aras had a word of advice to give him. Speaking in the light of the long experience which Turkey had had in governing such countries as Palestine, three things, Aras considered, were necessary to govern that country: a strong military position in the country itself, conciliatory language in dealing with the various parties, and procrastination in negotiations. What was in fact required was to be *suaviter in modo,* but *fortiter in re,* coupled with Oriental delay. With disarming frankness, Aras said that in spite of the general badness of her administration, Turkey had found this method most effective.[32] It has to be said that, unfortunately for his government, such a method was far beyond Rendel's understanding.

Rendel's intervention, then, had been just as crucial as Ormsby Gore's tergiversations and Wauchope's palsied handling of law and order in causing the British government to sustain a gratuitous defeat in Palestine. Rendel, however, was unrepentant. He was a man of strong and clear views, and great confidence in his own judgment; his long tenure in the Eastern Department had greatly contributed to this. He had been a member of the Department since 1922 and was its head from 1930 to 1938. He therefore had an enviable reputation as a knowledgeable expert whose advice could be implicitly trusted. His immediate superior, Oliphant, seems to have been somewhat mediocre and lack-lustre, while Vansittart, the Permanent Under-Secretary, was by character someone who would readily respond to a self-confident and robust enunciation of a seemingly realistic policy. Long ago he had served in Egypt, but had had since then little experience or acquaintance with Middle Eastern issues. Sterndale Bennett and Baggallay, who served directly under Rendel, whether out of conviction or policy were content to echo their superior. And Eden, the Secretary of State, was new to his office, young and inexperienced. As his minutes show, he usually deferred to, and rarely disagreed with, his officials on Middle Eastern policy. In contrast, Rendel knew his own mind and was not inclined easily either to change it or to give way. In his memoirs is a passage in which he compares his attitude with that of Lord Monteagle, his predecessor as head of the Department. Monteagle, he writes,

> while extremely efficient in the work he had to do . . . disliked, and
> seemed to shun, problems of major policy, where he preferred to
> leave all initiative to his political chiefs. He was far readier than I to
> accept instructions without question, and was never anxious to
> become a protagonist in a political battle.[33]

Rendel's role in Palestine in 1936-8 establishes, indeed, amply vindicates, the truth of this passage as it refers to himself. His successful attempt to promote intervention by the Arab states in Palestine was, from the start, predicated on a clear and far-reaching doctrine. He saw this intervention not simply as a way of re-establishing without violence law and order in Palestine. Rather, this intervention was to be made the means by which the correct view of the Palestine problem would prevail in London and the correct policy conclusions drawn.

For Rendel, the significance of the troubles in Palestine was by no means confined to that country. Their gravest and most dangerous consequences, he firmly believed, lay outside Palestine, in the Arab and Muslim world at large. If the Palestine problem was not solved to the satisfaction of the Arabs, British interests would be at risk in the whole of this world. In September 1936, while he was pressing for intervention by the Arab kings, and for the temporary suspension of immigration which they were demanding, Rendel wrote a memorandum in which the centrality of the Palestine problem in the affairs of the Middle East is forcefully asserted.

The Italian threat to British interests in the Middle East, Rendel began by saying, has hitherto been considered slight. But recent events in Palestine require this view to be qualified. Arabs and Muslims believe that the British government will do nothing to prevent the Palestine Arabs from being crowded out by Jewish immigration. Violent resistance by the Palestine Arabs to such a threat can no doubt be curbed, and sooner or later they can be made to capitulate,

> but from the point of view of our position in the Middle East this will be only a preliminary stage in the solution of the major problem. The Arabs of Palestine, even after their inevitable defeat, and the great body of Arab and Moslem opinion in Iraq, Egypt, Saudi Arabia, Syria, Transjordan and the Middle East generally, will watch the sequel with keen and critical anxiety. It is perhaps not too much to say that ultimately the whole future position and prestige of His Majesty's Government in these countries will depend on the policy which His Majesty's Government then follows towards the defeated Arabs.

If the policy is the wrong one, the Italians will soon exploit an opening which their own intrigues could never have afforded them:

> . . . if a wave of anti-British feeling were to spread over the Middle East, as it is bound to do if the Arabs and their friends are able to represent that His Majesty's Government are not prepared to give the Arabs a 'square deal', the position will be completely changed, and the danger of the Italians, for example, firmly establishing themselves in the Yemen, and even obtaining a dominating position in Saudi Arabia, will then become a real and imminent one. Nothing succeeds like success, and the establishment by the Italians of a leading position in the Arabian Peninsula will immensely strengthen their influence in Iraq, Persia and the Persian Gulf. Our position in the Gulf is at present far from satisfactory and our relations with many of the Gulf rulers, especially in the case of certain key positions such as Kuwait, are vague and indeterminate.

In short, Rendel affirmed, there was 'certainly the strongest ground' for believing that the British position in the Arab and Muslim world would become 'extremely precarious' if it comes to be believed that the government 'will never be prepared to consider the interests of the Palestine Arabs'.

In the whole of this memorandum, there was no evidence provided to buttress these emphatic and categorical assertions, nor did Rendel explain exactly by what mechanism dissatisfaction with British policy in Palestine would allow the Italians to establish themselves in the Yemen, exercise paramount influence over Ibn Sa'ud and supplant the British in the Persian Gulf. Nor did his superiors either ask for such evidence or pause to estimate the likelihood of these panic-stricken prognostications. Vansittart minuted that Italy was 'a great menace to our future in the Near and Middle East. This is not apprehension: it is fact,' and that 'If we cannot escape from *excessive* Jewish influence, or rather what looks like it in the East . . . we shall be playing right into malevolent hands and we shall pay very dearly for it.' And Eden, in his turn, wrote: 'This is a useful memorandum, and I agree with it, and with the minutes.'[34]

In the period following the end of the Arab strike and the associated disorders, Rendel was tireless in repeating and developing his view of the Palestine conflict and its essential characteristics. The Royal Commission on Palestine was not yet very far advanced in its enquiries when we see Rendel attempting to pre-empt its conclusions by putting forward suggestions of his own for settling the conflict. He believed that the only solution lay in establishing a fixed ratio between the Jewish and the non-Jewish population in the country. This would automatically regulate the size of Jewish immigration and still Arab fears that they would become a minority in their own country. If this were done, the problem of law and order would become secondary, and furthermore 'we should in that event be able to count on the support of other Arab and Moslem countries, who are by no means anxious to quarrel with us provided we give the Arabs something approaching a square deal'.[35]

There was, of course, no *prima facie* reason why Rendel's recipe should not be adopted. The Arabs of Palestine did strongly object to Zionism and Jewish immigration, and there was a great deal of force in the argument that the introduction of large numbers of European immigrants was creating intolerable strains and perhaps making the country ungovernable. But neither then nor later did it occur to Rendel that the very involvement of the Arab states in the problem, for which he worked so pertinaciously, would itself fearfully complicate things and render almost any proposed solution unworkable. Nor did he attend to the fact that the manner in which the disorder was ended in October left the Palestine Arabs with the conviction that the government was powerless to control them; which, in turn, made them unwilling to accept anything less than the full satisfaction of their demands—namely, the immediate cessation of all Jewish immigration and the establishment of an independent Palestine.

Rendel's superiors likewise failed to consider these difficulties, and now Oliphant, Vansittart and Eden in succession also approved the views of their subordinate and agreed with them whole-heartedly.

Eden, in fact, wrote personally to Ormsby Gore on 20 January 1937, enclosing a memorandum embodying Rendel's views. The Colonial Secretary responded three days later with a long letter, setting out some of his disagreements with these views. He was opposed to the memorandum's being circulated to the Cabinet, in the belief that to raise such issues ahead of the Report of the Royal Commission was 'both premature and misleading'. Rendel was not easily to be put off. He agreed that Ormsby Gore's objection to a discussion of the problem by the Cabinet in advance of the recommendations of the Royal Commission had 'much force'. He saw, however, no harm in circulating his memorandum to Ministers. This need not involve a Cabinet discussion, and had the advantage of giving Ministers the opportunity to consider at leisure the character of the problem and the pros and cons of various solutions. He was supported by Oliphant, but Eden was not willing to cross his colleague in this matter. Rendel was not deterred. At the beginning of April he raised the matter anew. In January Eden had indicated that he preferred to take no action 'at present'. Would he now be willing to allow the memorandum to be submitted to the Royal Commission 'as expressing the views of an anonymous official who has had a good deal of opportunity of studying the question'?[36]

Between January and April 1937 Rendel had visited Saudi Arabia as Ibn Sa'ud's official guest, and en route had stopped briefly in various Arab countries. He came back even more persuaded—if that were possible—of the rightness of his views. In a memorandum of 12 April, which was sent to the Colonial Office, he was emphatic that 'the course of our future relations with King Ibn Sa'ud will depend almost entirely on the nature of the report of the Royal Commission and of the decisions which H.M.G. take thereon'. He justified this view by a sweeping and grandiose vision of Arab history and politics. In a letter of 28 April which he sent to Downie of the Colonial Office, Rendel declared:

> The Arabs outside Palestine have a quite special connexion with the Arabs in Palestine itself. The Arabs are a single race, occupying a vast area not naturally divided into clearly distinct territories and which has frequently in the past been under single rule. They have a very strong racial and cultural unity, and I think it would be unreasonable to expect the individual branches of the Arab race to be indifferent to the future of those of their fellow-Arabs under foreign administration . . .

Rendel's reading of Arab history and politics was somewhat impressionistic. There had never been a 'special connexion' between the Arabs in and outside Palestine, much less a 'special connexion' between Palestine and

Saudi Arabia. Again, from a presumed racial unity and the absence of so-called 'natural frontiers' it could not possibly be argued that the Arabs should be treated as one political unit, pursuing a single coherent policy. The premises were at best hazy and dubious, while the chain of reasoning which might support the conclusion that the Palestine issue determined every other Middle Eastern issue with which Britain was concerned was not in any way spelled out. And if it had been, it would have been as weak and dubious as Rendel's vision of Arab history.

Rendel also confidently put forward in his memorandum a view of Saudi politics which was equally remote from reality, but from which no evidence or argument could subsequently shake him. He came back from Saudi Arabia persuaded that Ibn Sa'ud was 'genuinely anxious' to co-operate with the British government. On Palestine, however, he was not, Rendel affirmed 'his own master'. Ibn Sa'ud, it seemed, had 'a special responsibility towards the whole Arab—and indeed Moslem world, which is looking to him to defend the Arabs of Palestine from eventually becoming a powerless minority'. If this was not prevented, since his influence and prestige in the Arab and Muslim world were 'very great', he might well become 'a dangerous enemy'. He concluded, sombrely:

> If HMG cannot give him reasonable satisfaction . . . any attempts to retain his friendship are, I feel sure, doomed to failure, and we should in that event have to face the fact that Saudi Arabia, and the States which look to her for guidance, will then become virtually enemy countries.

In adopting this alarmist language Rendel betrayed a gullibility which, in a person of his position, was as remarkable as it was dangerous. Ibn Sa'ud was, in fact, the ruler of a somewhat weak state, sparsely inhabited and poverty-striken. He was the Imam of the Wahabis, a sect which, from its rise in the 18th century until the 20th, had been at daggers drawn with its Muslim neighbours. In particular, since Ibn Sa'ud had ousted King Husayn and occupied the Hijaz, there was no love lost between him and the Hashimite rulers of Iraq, while he and Husayn's son, Abdullah of Transjordan, entertained deep antipathy towards one another. These being the facts, why should Ibn Sa'ud's attempt to pose as the champion of the whole Arab and Muslim world be considered more than an interested and self-serving but empty claim? Furthermore, which particular states looked to Ibn Sa'ud for guidance? Egypt? Iraq? Transjordan? Syria and the Lebanon which were under French mandate? Kuwait, Bahrain, the Trucial States where British paramountcy was securely established by treaty?

Rendel did not pause to ask these questions; nor did his superiors at the Foreign Office ask them. But Rendel went even further. In Iraq, he wrote, he had derived a similar impression. Here, too, serious trouble would be encountered if satisfaction was not given to the Palestine Arabs: 'In that event,' he gloomily prophesied, 'and if we lose the friendship of Ibn Sa'ud, it is difficult to see how Transjordan could continue to cooperate with us.' In so arguing, Rendel showed himself oblivious of the fact that rivalry between Iraq and Saudi Arabia over Palestine was very great, and that scope for this rivalry—which was bound to operate to the detriment of the Mandatory government—was afforded precisely by the British willingness to tolerate or invite the interference of Arab states in the affairs of Palestine. Rendel of all people should have understood the mechanism and the dynamics of this rivalry since it had been clearly brought to his attention only the previous September when the Saudis were complaining of Nuri's intervention and the Iraqis were putting it about that the failure of Saudi representations on behalf of the Palestine Arabs were due to British mistrust of Ibn Sa'ud.[37] As for Transjordan, which was a Mandated territory, and where Abdullah was a client, was it at all credible to speak of his 'cooperation,' let alone of its possible cessation?

Rendel's visit to Ibn Sa'ud also served to enhance his fear of Italy's coming to exercise predominant or sole influence over the whole Arabian Peninsula. He drew a picture of Ibn Sa'ud, 'in desperation' over the policy being followed in Palestine, breaking with the British, turning to the Italians for 'help and guidance', and forced to acquiesce in their 'absorption of the Yemen'. Here too Rendel's naivety is remarkable. If Ibn Sa'ud was so simple-minded as such behaviour would have shown him to be, by what arts then did he win, keep and so prodigiously enlarge his kingdom?[38]

Rendel's advice regarding another issue in Anglo-Saudi relations casts more doubts on his judgment. Ibn Sa'ud had for some time been making claims over territory in Qatar and Abu Dhabi, Persian Gulf sheikhdoms the foreign relations of which were, by treaty, under British control. It should have been obvious that Ibn Sa'ud might be using the Palestine issue, and the threat of resorting to Italy, not only to increase his prestige and influence among his neighbours but also as a kind of lever by which to obtain satisfaction of his territorial claims. Instead of advising that the satisfaction of these claims might be used as a *quid pro quo* for acceptable Saudi behaviour over Palestine and relations with Italy, or vice-versa as the case might be, Rendel repeatedly advocated the unconditional cession of the territories Ibn Sa'ud was claiming. At a meeting of the Standing Sub-Official Committee for Questions Concerning the Middle East of the Committee of Imperial Defence on 1 February 1937 Rendel declared that Ibn Sa'ud was a key factor in the Middle East situation, that he had 'played up very well indeed' over the previous six months, and that his territorial demands in Arabia should therefore be satisfied. G. M. Clauson of the India Office sensibly said that it was arguable whether immediate concessions to Ibn Sa'ud would make him more ready to co-operate over Palestine in the future. He might, in fact, be more ready to co-operate if he felt that there was still something to be obtained from the British government. But Rendel was very urgent; the Royal Commission would be reporting in the near future, and if the Arabs were to consider it unsatisfactory,

> it was generally agreed that there would be worse riots in Palestine than those which occurred last summer. The attitude of the independent Arab States to His Majesty's Government was, therefore, very important. It might be that we should find ourselves in an embarrassing position in our relations with Ibn Saud, and it was quite conceivable that most Arab countries would become hostile to us. There was much material to suggest that if things went wrong over Palestine the Arabs would be prepared to make friends with other countries.

Rendel did not disclose what this abundant material was, nor is there any reason to think that he had more in mind than the increase of Italian and German activism, the consequences of which could not be guarded against or undone by any conceivable settlement in Palestine or in Arabia. He was, however, as usual absolutely categorical in his advice. He continued:

> It would be better, therefore, to settle the Saudi-Arabian frontier questions before we ran the risk of alienating Arab opinion, and a settlement with Ibn Saud on the frontier question might weigh favourably with him if the Palestine situation developed unfavourably. The arguments for meeting Ibn Saud as far as possible, were, therefore, very strong.

A year later when, in response to Arab objections and chiefly through Rendel's urging, partition of Palestine, recommended by the Royal Commission, was virtually abandoned, Rendel was still pressing for cession to Ibn Sa'ud of the territory he was claiming. He was sure that if the territory were offered 'quickly', if would make 'a great difference' in relations with the Saudis. The position had deteriorated, again owing to Palestine, and the possibility of Ibn Sa'ud's 'turning against us in the event of catastrophe was now a serious one and could not be ignored'. The matter, he urged, should be taken to the Cabinet and the objections of the government of India overruled.[39]

Rendel was convinced that Ibn Sa'ud's views and desires both in respect to Palestine and to Arabia should be acceded to without question. He was also determined to ignore any evidence which might cast suspicion on Ibn Sa'ud's good faith and on the sincerity of his professions of friendship with Britain. His attitude was shared by his subordinates in the Eastern Department. In February 1937, when Rendel was away on his visit to Ibn Sa'ud, the Colonial Office sent to the Foreign Office information transmitted from Transjordan tending to suggest that arms and men from Iraq were being smuggled to Palestine through Saudi territory, and suggested that Ibn Saʻud be asked to prevent such movement. E. R. Warner declared himself opposed to such an approach:

> Ibn Saʻud [he minuted] has been admirably helpful over Palestine so far, but one may perhaps be a little doubtful whether he would be prepared to cooperate *actively* in the sense desired *after* a decision by H.M.G. which provoked an Arab rising, and if he considered the decision unfair to the Arabs. Further one may wonder whether Ibn Saud would be prepared to commit himself, even in principle, to such action in advance of H.M.G.'s decision.

Brenan was likewise doubtful whether Ibn Saʻud 'will be able to, or will want to cooperate with us against his friends in Palestine'. Baggallay echoed his two colleagues, adding that to mention the matter at all to Ibn Saʻud might indicate 'that we doubted whether he would continue to act as a good neighbour and wished to give him a hint to do so—which would be insulting'. And would it not be 'presumptuous' to expect him to set up a system of control in his territory? The attitude of these officials was puzzling, for, after all a state was fully entitled to ask a friendly neighbour to watch out for illegal activities within his territory which threatened its own security. This was especially so, since there had been, since 1933, a treaty of *bon voisinage* with Saudi Arabia which covered cases of this kind—a treaty which, for Britain to invoke, did not require that it should follow, in the territory it controlled, policies acceptable to Saudi Arabia.[40]

The same problem arose in September 1937, when there was already considerable disorder once again in Palestine. Glubb in Trans-jordan reported that Fawzi al-Qawuqji might move from Iraq, where he could acquire arms, money and men, to Palestine through Saudi territory. The Colonial Office wished the Foreign Office to invoke the treaty of *bon voisinage* in order to prevent this. Again the Eastern Department refused to move. Since the Arabs were opposed to the partition of Palestine, which the government had not yet formally ruled out, it was impossible, Brenan minuted, 'to ask Ibn Saud specifically for his collaboration in preventing the passage of munitions and potential bandits through his territory'. Rendel concurred.[41]

Yet again, a month later, the Colonial Office sent a 'Secret and Immediate' letter to the Foreign Office with a great deal of detail about possible arms-smuggling to Palestine through Saudi Arabia, and the suspicious behaviour of Saudi troops in the vicinity of the Transjordan frontier. The Colonial Office wished these reports to be investigated by the British Legation in Jedda. Rendel was adamantly opposed to such a step, nor did he want to approach Hafez Wahba in London: 'he is at present in so indignant a frame of mind about our Palestine policy that it may be a little difficult to ask him for a favour on this question'. Ibn Saʻud was in something approaching despair over British policy. Also, if as a result of partition Transjordan were to become independent, Ibn Sa'ud would regard this as 'a personal threat'. What more natural than that he should take preliminary steps for a possible struggle against Abdullah? In any case Abdullah, having expressed support for partition, 'has become regarded as a traitor to the Arab cause by the great majority of Arabs'. If partition is enforced, or 'when the situation in Palestine enters on the next stage in its inevitable process of deterioration', there would be a movement against Abdullah in Transjordan. Ibn Sa'ud was probably preparing for such an emergency. Further, a Jewish state in Palestine, Rendel continued, ominous and dire, was 'likely rapidly to spread its influence and control over all the neighbouring countries'. Might not Ibn Sa'ud feel that Italian assistance offers real advantages, while his continued friendship for Great Britain has given him comparatively little? Rendel believed him to be 'more sincere and straightforward than the great majority of Eastern (or Western) rulers'; the British government, however, was 'driving him very hard indeed', and he was 'increasingly tempted to turn against us.' A letter to the Colonial Office embodied these views. It was described by Shuckburgh as a 'Rendelian outburst'. As his colleague Downie minuted, what Rendel was saying was not that precautions should be taken in Transjordan to guard against possible aggression by Ibn Sa'ud but rather that 'as Ibn Sa'ud does not like our policy, it would be advisable to modify it'. The refusal of the Foreign Office even to investigate further the reports sent by British officials in Transjordan was absolute.[42]

One reason why Rendel would not ask the Legation in Jedda to investigate the reports sent from Transjordan was that the Chargé d'affaires, A. C. Trott, in charge during the absence of the Minister on leave, had shortly before sent a despatch on Ibn Sa'ud's attitude to Palestine which Rendel considered misleading. Trott had been commenting on statements made by Hafez Wahba that Ibn Sa'ud 'found himself gravely embarrassed by the *Ulema* of this country' who were thought to be prepared to issue a *fetwa* (i.e. a ruling based on the religious law) authorizing a holy war against Palestine. Trott pointed out that the *Ulema* were indeed powerful, and that intensive propaganda against partition was being spread at the direction of the Mufti of Jerusalem. But from his observations Trott doubted whether Hafez Wahba was correct in his assertions. 'I have certainly heard nothing locally,' he wrote, 'to justify the statement that the "King is in a serious if not a desperate position."'[43] In an earlier despatch, dated 3 August 1937, Trott had reported that his conversations with Arabs in Jedda led him to believe that the Arabs really understood that partition was the only way in which British commitments to both Jews and Arabs could be realized. An official of the Foreign Ministry said as much to him in the presence of Yusuf Yasin, 'who evidently agreed with him'.[44] Trott's reports displeased Rendel because they did not tally with the views he had been so pertinaciously pressing. He was furthermore afraid that Trott's views might be 'quoted against us when we represent, as we sincerely can and must do, that the reaction of Saudi Arabia to our partition policy is likely to be greatly embarrassing to us'. Since it was too risky to prevent the circulation of Trott's despatches, he drafted a reply to Trott explaining why his views were wrong, and that 'it would not be safe to under-estimate the importance and the genuine character of the appeal of the *Ulema* of Nejd'. Trott's despatch of 28 September was then circulated to the Colonial Office and other departments, accompanied by its prophylactic.[45]

Trott, however, persisted in his misguided ways. In his campaign against the partition plan, Rendel sent telegrams in November 1937 to various posts in the Middle East asking them to report likely reactions to partition if it were carried out either by agreement or by force. Trott reported that if partition was carried out by agreement, public opinion would accept the settlement. If partition was enforced, however, anti-British feelings would be inflamed, Pan-Arab feeling would grow, there would be a call for a holy war, and Ibn Sa'ud might be compelled to lead it. Trott did not seem to take this very seriously, since he declared that British airplanes in Transjordan would deter the raiders. In this case, 'the King who has made no secret of his dislike for partition would bear us a grudge'.

This telegram was worse than useless to Rendel, especially as Trott had begun by saying that a 'strong though vague feeling of solidarity' for the Palestine Arabs had recently grown up 'as a result of religious propaganda initiated from abroad'. Rendel wanted, on the contrary, to stress that hostility to partition was 'spontaneous and deep-seated', not a reaction to propaganda initiated from abroad. To say, also, that Ibn Sa'ud might simply 'bear us a grudge' seemed to him vastly to under-estimate the danger of crossing this potentate. Rendel, therefore, wanted to prevent the circulation of this telegram, as it might allow some opponent of his policy to argue, on the strength of Trott's view, that anti-partition agitation in Saudi Arabia was artificial. But Eden wanted the telegram circulated to his colleagues. Rendel then suggested that Sir Reader Bullard, the Minister in Jedda who was on his way back from leave, and who shared Rendel's views, might be sent a private telegram in order to elicit a refutation of Trott. Oliphant turned this down. Rendel was not one easily to concede defeat, and he now suggested that when the telegram was circulated it should be accompanied by an answer to Trott telling him that his appreciation was mistaken. Alternatively, the telegram should be accompanied by 'a word of caution', explaining that Trott had only been in Jedda for a few months and did not really understand the position. Oliphant judged that this would belittle the telegram and Vansittart ruled it out.[46]

As it happens, Trott did put on record his reasons for an assessment of Saudi politics which departed so much from the orthodoxy which—it is not too much to say—the head of the Eastern Department was bent on enforcing. In a letter of 23 November 1937 he takes up the points which Rendel had made in an attempt to prove that Trott's despatch of 28 September previous (discussed above) was misleading. Trott argued that the influence of the *Ulema* of Najd (who, according to Hafez Wahba were compelling Ibn Saʻud to take an inflexible stand over Palestine) was not quite as strong as Rendel thought. It was true that Ibn Saʻud had been known to defer to the *Ulema* and to discontinue practices of which they disapproved but, Trott went on,

> this was more particularly in the early days when he depended on religious fanaticism as a driving force for his armies; moreover, when the fanaticism of the extreme Wahhabis would have embroiled him with the European powers after the conquest of the Hejaz he was able to restrain it. The power of the Ikhwan, who formed the backbone of Wahhabism and were the great support of the Ulema, has been broken. The Ulema of Nejd [Trott went on] are often supposed to regard the Palestinian non-Wahhabis as almost greater infidels than the Jews.

The Hijaz *Ulema*, Trott also pointed out, were in a similar situation and quite unable to challenge Ibn Saʻud's authority. He added, no doubt in answer to Rendel's objection that he, being in Jedda, could not know what went on in Najd, that Ousman (presumably an Indian Muslim Vice-Consul), who had spent nearly three months at Riyad during the summer, reported nothing unusual and only heard that the King had made very curt replies to such representations about Palestine as were made to him whether by *Ulema* or others.

Trott had another shrewd point to make about the manner in which statements by Ibn Saʻud's officials should be taken. Hafez Wahba, he wrote, himself felt strongly about Palestine and was thus inclined to put words in his master's mouth which were in reality his own. Hafez Wahba, Fu'ad Hamza and Yusuf Yasin, Ibn Saʻud's principal advisers and agents in foreign affairs, were respectively, an Egyptian, a Lebanese Druze and a Syrian. They looked at the matter with much more fanaticism than the King, and it was necessary to remember their bias in weighing what they had to say. He had been struck by the difference between the stance of Ibn Saʻud and his family and the attitude of his envoys:

> ... when, under instructions, I addressed a note to the Amir Faisal saying that the followers of the Mufti had been arrested solely in the interests of good government, His Royal Highness, who need not really have replied at all, went out of his way (or so I thought) to write a mild reply in very correct terms: whereas almost at the same moment His Excellency [Hafez Wahba] in London was saying that

the King was horrified that the wrong men had been arrested, or something of that sort.[47]

Trott's acuteness and discrimination, his ability to penetrate the surface, and his sound understanding of the springs of Saudi politics are in sharp contrast to Rendel's uncritical acceptance of all that it pleased Saudi officials to whisper in his ear, his panic lest Ibn Sa'ud choose Italy as an ally and subvert the British empire in the Middle East, his refusal even to investigate reports that Saudi Arabia was not behaving as a friendly neighbour, and his eagerness to do everything to satisfy the Arabian potentate's wishes. It was Rendel's attitude and viewpoint that became the rule among his colleagues and political superiors. As a typical example we may take a despatch from Sir Reader Bullard, the Minister to Saudi Arabia, written in November 1938. The British government had now, in response to objections by Arab states and to Foreign Office advice, abandoned the proposal by the Royal Commission to partition Palestine (they had initially welcomed it). Bullard was reporting on conversations with Ibn Sa'ud about the forthcoming conference in London where Arab states would be represented, and thus officially recognized as partners in the administration of the Mandate. Bullard's tone is hushed, reverential, devout. Ibn Sa'ud, he writes, had reminded him how at an earlier interview he had not been able to keep the tears out of his eyes when speaking of Palestine:

> His sympathy [Bullard solemnly declared] could be understood even if we did not know of the influence which the Quran must have on the attitude of a pious Moslem towards the Jews. Ibn Saud is usually restrained in his language but when I pointed out the inconsistency between the claim of the Arab Higher Committee to represent all the Arabs of Palestine and the elimination by murder of very many opponents of the Committee, Ibn Saud said that in the circumstances the Arabs might well regard the removal of one traitor as more important than the killing of fifty Jews. What he will do if there is no agreed settlement in Palestine and His Majesty's Government decide to allow Jewish immigration on a considerable scale to continue, I do not know, though I have tried to indicate what he will feel. The Government of Palestine consider they have good reason to believe that for some months he has been furnishing aid to the Arab malcontents in secret. If he feels that his confidence in the good intentions of His Majesty's Government has been misplaced and decides to come out openly in favour of the Arab nationalists, if, for example, he declares he can no longer prevent Arabs from Saudi Arabia from entering Trans-Jordan and Palestine to assist their co-religionists there in what he regards as a

righteous struggle to be free, we may remonstrate but we can hardly be surprised.

This language, we have to remind ourselves, was that of a representative of a Great Power whose dominance over the Middle East was then un-challenged. Some two years before, we may also recall, the whole sequence of events had begun with Ibn Sa'ud's asking for advice as to how he should respond to a request by Palestine Arabs for his intercession. And here now was Bullard humbly taking for granted Ibn Sa'ud's right to direct British policy and to unleash his subjects against a British-administered territory should British policies not meet his expectations: 'It seems to me,' he said elsewhere in his despatch, 'that so far as Ibn Saud is concerned this is our last chance.' The Secretary of State, speaking through C. W. Baxter, who had succeeded Rendel as head of the Eastern Department, expressed his 'appreciation of this report which will be of great value to His Majesty's Government at a time when their future policy in Palestine is receiving active consideration'.[48]

One other example, among many, can be cited to show how the absolute centrality of Palestine in Middle Eastern affairs had quickly come to be established as dogma, the questioning of which, by someone like Trott, would be received with a closed mind and cold hostility, and suppressed if possible. The following is a minute of 13 February 1937, by Rendel's second, Lacy Baggallay—'one of his wise minutes', as Vansittart wrote. In it, Baggallay commented on the likely attitude of the surrounding Arab states to future policy in Palestine. This, Baggallay declared, would depend on the British government's response to Arab grievances:

> If the decision is not only fair, but can clearly be seen to be fair, our influence with Ibn Saud and the Iraqi Government may continue to be sufficient to ensure observance of reasonably correct inter-national behaviour and the prohibition of any general dispatch of assistance in the form of arms, money and volunteers. But if the fairness of the terms is not apparent on their face, our influence will certainly be insufficient.

Baggallay was in effect saying that Great Britain had to satisfy the desiderata of Iraq and Saudi Arabia over Palestine because it was impotent to prevent these two states from using their resources to foment disorder in a British-controlled territory. Worse, if the British government tried to use its influence in Iraq (which, Baggallay conceded, was considerable) in order to prevent assistance to the rebels, this

> might lead either to the fall of the Government of the day or a serious breach with any Government that persisted in conniving at

the despatch of assistance. The result of the first would probably be administrative chaos (with all its consequences for the safety of the R.A.F. and the I[raq] P[etroleum] C[ompany].) The result of the second might be a situation in which we either had to abdicate our position and influence in Iraq by doing nothing, or else had to attempt to coerce the recalcitrant Government, possibly by the use of force (a peculiarly risky proceeding in view of the lack of ground protection for the R.A.F.)

When he wrote this minute, Baggallay was forty years old. Not only had he long ago attained the age of discretion, but by 1937 had had some sixteen years of varied service as a diplomat. He was now, furthermore, in Rendel's absence in Saudi Arabia, acting head of the Eastern Department. He was (as the French expression goes) *payé* to know that the occasions for instability in a polity like Iraq's were as numerous as the sands of the sea, and that it was as hazardous to predict the next upset in that country as it was to predict the course of a game of poker. He should also have known that if British interests were at risk in Iraq, they could not be protected simply by satisfying desires which might be far-reaching but which were certainly undefined and liable to sudden changes at the whim of successive ministers. The wisdom which Vansittart was pleased to detect in his subordinate's judgment was no doubt also exemplified by his further speculation that rebellion in Palestine might lead to rebellion in Syria—a country then under French Mandate. Baggallay did not explain by what mechanism this would come about, but sagacity was also evident in the observation, deep-seeming but profoundly inane and useless, that 'whether this would mean more or less support for the Arabs in Palestine it is impossible to say.'[49] For all his wisdom Baggallay was no more than Rendel's echo.

In the voluminous files which Palestine generated in the Foreign Office during 1936-9 it is in fact impossible to find a paper querying the views of Rendel and his Department, or subjecting their assumptions and asseverations to critical scrutiny. The unanimous and ready assent to Rendel's views by ministers and officials—with the solitary exception of Cranborne when he cautioned against giving in to Nuri's urgings—argues intellectual failure, but perhaps also administrative deficiency, since the organization of the Foreign Office seemed to facilitate the growth and entrenchment of orthodoxies and to inhibit debate that might give ministers the benefit of considering alternative interpretations and a variety of options.

The only reasoned critique of Rendelian doctrine about the Arab world and its attitude to Palestine is, in fact, to be found in a long paper produced in February 1938 by Major W. J. Cawthorn, an intelligence officer at the War Office. So far as can be seen, Cawthorn did not set out to controvert Rendel's doctrine. He was, rather, engaged in assessing, for the benefit of military planners, likely developments under two hypotheses: a continuing state of peace and a major European war, respectively. His long paper, extending over twenty foolscap pages, was well-informed, cool and shrewd in assessing the capacity and effectiveness of Arab governments, the likelihood of their acting in unison, and the circumstances in which they might show hostility to Great Britain. Developments in the Arab world, Cawthorn tried to show,

> have produced an intense, localised nationalism bound up in local problems which are active in preventing wider combination. There is no organisation, body, or individual who can justly claim to represent Arab opinion throughout the world, in spite of the constant efforts made to organise something . . .
>
> In the Arab world today [Cawthorn went on], a leader who combines influence with power in a political or military sense, and who is willing to risk that power is lacking.

There was, in Cawthorn's judgment, little risk in peacetime of concerted military action, against such things as incursions by tribesmen into Palestine or local attacks against British property, personnel and communications.

> While they might be forced to connive at it, it is obvious that none of the governments concerned are likely to encourage it, as in the end it must adversely affect their own internal economic and political interests. Any central control or direction, or the employment of any organised military resources is equally unlikely, at least to begin with.

As regards the situation in a major war, Cawthorn declared:

> History shows that the Arabs are disinclined to take decisive action to support even their friends until they see definite evidence that the side they favour is in the ascendant. Until then, their practice is to 'sit on the fence' . . .

In a conclusion which the events of the second world war vindicated, Cawthorn stated that a serious reverse or signs that Great Britain might lose the war might in turn lead to definite hostile action by some Arab governments. Cawthorn, it will be recalled, was writing in February 1938, when there were already ample signs that the government was hesitating about implementing the partition it had seemed firmly to favour the previous summer. His paper now pointed out that delay in announcing and implementing a policy in Palestine gave foreign propaganda the opportunity to consolidate Arab hostility toward Great Britain, and the greater the delay the more difficult this hostility would be to control. In this, too, Cawthorn's judgment proved to be sound.[50]

Cawthorn sent a copy of his memorandum to the Foreign Office. Baggallay minuted that he agreed with a great deal of it, but in fact, as his remarks show, he dismissed the conclusions that Cawthorn drew from his analysis. Cawthorn, he believed, did not give enough importance to the dangers, 'which cannot be stressed too highly', that partition would present in the event of a major war:

> There can be no doubt [he affirmed] that if partition is enforced our prestige and reputation will never be the same again and that the Arab world will wait, if necessary for years, for the day of revenge upon us and the Jews, which any preoccupation on our part elsewhere will give them. We may hope that that day will never come, and if it comes we may survive it, but we cannot be sure.

He believed that if partition were effected, 'our enemies would supply the Arab countries with arms, money, organisation and cohesion'. But even worse was to be apprehended. A friendly government might afford the enemy an opportunity to establish himself in some part of the Near East, 'and once he was there the rest of the Near East might turn against us, the result if it did so, being the complete interruption of our communications with India, except by the Cape'. And even in ordinary times, partition would make imperial communications 'much more difficult', if they are flanked by sullen instead of friendly countries. Baggallay was, of course, right to worry about enemy actions in the Middle East, but he did not stop to consider that British interests in the area could not be safeguarded simply by ruling out partition in Palestine, and that these interests could be very dangerously threatened, even if the Jewish National Home were completely frozen— that, in other words, the area was turbulent and its governments unreliable for reasons which were far deeper and more serious than anything to do with Palestine. Furthermore, he did not stop to consider that in a major war with a European enemy, the Middle East might be attacked in strength, and would have to be, in consequence, defended in strength—something beyond the capacities of Saudi Arabia or Iraq, whose estrangement so terrified him and Rendel. Cawthorn had also sent a copy of his memorandum to the Colonial Office, and had quite impressed them as 'unquestionably useful and able'. Baggallay was anxious to combat this dangerous subversion by Cawthorn and directed that 'we should put our views on record in a private letter, but', he craftily added, 'not too dogmatically'. As for the Foreign Office itself, Cawthorn's views did not get beyond the Eastern Department; neither the Deputy Under Secretary, nor the Permanent Under Secretary, nor any Minister was vouchsafed a sight of it.[51]

Cawthorn's cool and measured scepticism was overwhelmed by the violent colours of Rendel's lurid catastrophism. The vatic energy of this sibyl, this pythoness, was irresistible; it transfixed, haunted and terrified the

Foreign Office. If partition is carried out, one prophecy of November 1937 went, what would happen could be foretold as follows:

> There will first be a lull while the Arab forces are planning the next outbreak, and recovering themselves from our recent severe measures .... When it is broken, there is likely to be a rapid recrudescence of terrorism, another gradual formation of bands, particularly in Transjordan. The Amir Abdullah is notoriously unpopular, and his authority is precarious. The bands may therefore operate from Transjordan, where it is very possible that there might be a widespread rebellion, which it would be very difficult for us to control with our very exiguous troops. As soon as the bands begin to operate, organised assistance to the rebels and to the guerilla bands will be furnished from Syria and Iraq however much the Governments of those countries may try to prevent it. This will be probably followed soon afterwards by a relaxation of the frontier control by Ibn Saud, and the penetration of Saudi tribesmen into Transjordan and possibly across into Palestine. Each development will produce another on a somewhat larger scale. We shall be obliged to send out strong reinforcements, which will be met in turn by more highly organised and more widespread resistance, until we shall gradually drift into a situation of open warfare.
>
> When this happens, reactions will begin to grow more widespread. There is likely to be a reaction in Egypt, and certain countries will probably turn definitely against us, possibly beginning with the Yemen, where a movement against the Aden Protectorate may well take place, once we have become thoroughly involved in military operations in Palestine.

This, however, was by no means the end of this catalogue of disasters. If a Jewish state is formed, attacks will be directed not only against the British, but against it as well:

> Raids and massacres on a small scale are likely to begin, and these will have a cumulative effect, spreading outwards not only to the outlying areas in Palestine, but also to the neighbouring countries, where there will probably be serious anti-British, and possibly anti-Christian, movements. A new massacre of Assyrians would be a not improbable consequence, and the trouble is likely to become very serious in the more fanatical districts of Syria and Iraq. This in turn could hardly fail to lead to an Anglo-Iraqi crisis, with difficulties over the Anglo-Iraqi Treaty, and the position of our Air Force in Iraq. By this time the trouble is likely to have spread down the Persian Gulf, and to Moslem India.

The consummation of this apocalypse was likely to be at least a European war: adversaries of the British would be tempted to take advantage of the opportunities offered by this turmoil and it would be very difficult 'not to find ourselves landed in some new quarrel with them'. Rendel modestly refrained from developing further 'this chain of probabilities', but he had said enough to show that the consequences of partition extended 'well beyond the immediate sphere of the Middle East'.[52]

Like Hobbes, then, Rendel and fear seem to have been born twins. But unlike Hobbes's, Rendel's fear was not the precise and rational sentiment that issued in a philosophical masterpiece; it was more a wild, uncontrollable, exorbitant panic that imprisoned its victim in a mad nightmare.

Rendel's vision of Arab history and politics, then, entailed the absolute centrality of the Palestine question. This vision was accompanied by a no less clear idea of the events taking place in Palestine itself, and of the real significance to be seen in them. It will be recalled that in October 1936 Arab rulers had themselves suggested appealing to the Palestine Arabs to end the strike and disturbance, and that, just as martial law was on the point of being proclaimed, Ministers agreed to allow this appeal to be made—an appeal that was understood to be unconditional. As has also been seen, Rendel's urgings were greatly instrumental in effecting this sudden, last-minute, fateful change of policy. Barely was the appeal issued before Rendel began to argue as though the appeal had not been unconditional and that the cessation of civil disobedience and disorder had somehow to be rewarded. On 15 October he was already arguing for as wide an amnesty as possible, but Eden did not want to press this just then. On 21 October, he returned to the charge over the temporary suspension of immigration which the Arab rulers had demanded and he had supported, but which Ministers had adamantly refused. In a minute on a Cabinet paper by Ormsby Gore he produced a remarkable example of sophistical ingenuity. In his paper Ormsby Gore argued against a temporary suspension of immigration in the belief that matters should remain in *statu quo ante* while the Royal Commission was investigating. But what is *status*, Rendel brightly pointed out, if it is not static—and the *status quo ante* requires that the stream of immigration be halted. In a minute of 27 October he tried to suggest that surrender of arms by the Arab population could be exchanged for suspension of immigration. The proposal found no takers, and on 17 November he recurred to the issue of clemency, now pleading that since the decision not to suspend immigration 'has come as a great blow to the Arab world', some of the damage thereby done might be remedied if 'real generosity' could be shown to the rebels who were still under arrest. Eden was unwilling to exert himself in this matter, but Rendel was persistent. In a draft letter to the Colonial Office dealing with the specific case of two Arabs sentenced to death on whose behalf the Saudis had made representations, Rendel inserted a paragraph 'so as to make the appeal a slightly more general one'. But Oliphant, mindful of Eden's instructions wrote against it: 'Sorry! no good', and the paragraph had to be deleted.[53]

Rendel's representations over clemency and immigration were too close in time to the Arab rulers' appeal for the circumstances in which this appeal had been issued to have been forgotten. A year later, however, Rendel could glibly write as though the appeal had been a favour done to the British government. In a memorandum of 27 October 1937 which formed part of his campaign to defeat the partition proposals, Rendel could write: 'Last year, the Arab rulers were able to induce the Arabs of Palestine to call a halt. This time there is every indication that, if we persist in our present policy, they will on the contrary give them an increasing degree of sympathy and support.'[54]

The enforcement of law and order in Palestine was, in Rendel's view the least important issue raised by the Arab rebellion. The issue, as has been seen, involved for him the whole range of British relations with the Arab and Muslim world. But it was even wider than this; the Palestine question was really one between world Jewry and the Arab countries as a whole.[55] From this two corollaries followed. The first Rendel formulated when commenting on a conversation between Weizmann and Sir Alexander Cadogan concerning the Arab rulers' appeal. This appeal, Weizmann declared, had been represented in Palestine as being made 'with the consent' of the British government. Cadogan denied, correctly, that the Arab rulers had been given any sort of promise about future policy in return. Weizmann, while accepting this, pointed out nonetheless that the appeal could be misunderstood in Palestine, and

> the very fact of its having been made would give the Arab rulers in future a right to interfere in the affairs of Palestine.

Rendel took umbrage to this:

> I confess [he minuted on 9 October 1936] that it seems to me a little paradoxical for the international Jews, supported by Jewish opinion in every country in the world . . . to object to the Arabs of Palestine seeking the assistance of their fellow Arabs and fellow Moslems from the neighbouring countries of Arabia.

Rendel then was equating the 'international Jews' and 'Jewish opinion' with sovereign states controlling territories and armies in respect of the character and consequences of their intervention in the affairs of Palestine. An equation of this kind was permissible, indeed natural, in polemics between Zionists and anti-Zionists, but for a British official to make it argued a disturbing blindness to the dangers inherent in the Mandatory government's admitting the right of sovereign states to interfere in its affairs.

The second corollary which followed from viewing the disturbances in Palestine as stemming from a conflict between world Jewry and the Arab world as a whole was Rendel's belief that, in quelling the disturbances in Palestine, the British government was simply serving Jewish interests at the cost of quarrelling with the Arab world. This belief, at times rueful, at others resentful, surfaces in various places in his comments. Thus the minute on Weizmann's interview with Cadogan began:

> I feel there is no doubt that it would not suit the Jews at all that a settlement of the Palestine disorders should be reached at the moment.

The Jews want the British and the Arabs to fight. The Arabs would thus put themselves out of court and the Jews would take all.[56] At about the same time, in trying to prevent the proclamation of martial law in Palestine, Rendel argued that 'there are many elements in this country and in Palestine whose interests would be far better served by the continuation of the disorders than by what they would probably describe as a premature settlement.'[57] Rendel was so persuaded that Arab-fomented disorders would benefit only the Zionists that he even wondered whether Jewish agents were not at work inside the Arab camp. He almost, but perhaps not quite, believed that the Mufti himself was a Jewish agent, or at least a valuable ally of the Zionists who could be relied upon to press his claims in so unrestrained a manner as to force the British to take repressive action against the Arabs.[58]

Rendel's extreme annoyance with the Zionists for being the reason why Great Britain was embroiled with Palestine did not remain confined to the privacy of his files. In October 1937, the Colonial Office sent him copy of a report by a Jewish Agency representative on his interview with a high official at the Ministry of Foreign Affairs in Paris. It was notorious at the time that Syria served as a base from which arms and men were smuggled into Palestine, and the Jewish Agency representative raised with the French official this issue, among others. He was promised that Palestinian Arab leaders would be closely watched and that requests by the Palestine Administration to prevent entry into Syria of wanted persons would be strictly attended to. He was also told that France was in favour of the partition plan. Rendel found these 'heart to heart' talks very tiresome, whether because the Jewish Agency had elicited a statement in favour of partition (which was still British policy), or because the French promised to control more closely the activities of Palestine Arabs on their territory. In order to put a spoke in the wheels of the Jewish Agency, and to sow mistrust between them and the French, he suggested to the British Ambassador in Paris to warn the Quai d'Orsay that their confidences were not treated with the discretion they would expect.[59] It was left to his successor, C.W. Baxter, to look askance at Zionist discussions not only with foreign officials, but with the Colonial Secretary himself. In July 1938 Weizmann had gone to him with reports that anti-Zionist agitation in Cairo was probably fostered by Germany. Baxter minuted sourly that this was the third interview within a month between Malcolm MacDonald (who was then suspected of friendliness to Zionism) and Weizmann.[60]

In the same minute Baxter emulated Rendel in another respect. Weizmann's report about German responsibility for agitation in Egypt did not surprise him; the Germans would naturally make use of British difficulties, 'but of course', he added sententiously, 'the original responsibility for these difficulties lies elsewhere.' This was a theme which Rendel hammered remorselessly, as though attacks on Britain over events in Palestine were a just punishment for guilt, and thus to be borne in silence and self-abasement. The Embassy in Berlin reported in October 1937 that the Nazi organ, the *Völkischer Beobachter*, had published a virulent attack on the measures taken following the murder of the District Commissioner for Galilee, L. Y. Andrews. 'Semophiles' in London had insisted on a strong policy with the result that hundreds of Arab 'activists' were thrown into concentration camps—even though the murder might have been a Jewish act of provocation. In any case the real responsibility for the murder lay with the British government's self-interested and tyrannical policy in Palestine. Rendel's comment on this demagogical outburst was:

> There is a very great deal of truth in all this. We are riding for a fall, and might usefully take this to heart.[61]

Similar sentiments expressed at the other end of the political spectrum found equal favour with Rendel. Also in October 1937, the *New Statesman* published a letter from a correspondent with Leftist leanings who had recently resigned from the Palestine Civil Service. It was misleading, protested the writer, to call Andrews' assassination a 'dastardly murder' (as *The Times* had recently done).

> Would any liberal-minded person [asked Thomas Hodgkin] speak in such terms of the killing of some prominent Gestapo official by an opponent of the Nazi regime?

Andrews was a very competent official who knew Arabic well and had wide contacts with influential Arabs and Jews. He was thus an 'unofficial secret agent' of the Administration,

> but from the point of view of the great majority of Arabs he was a spy, who represented the hated British autocracy in its most objectionable form.

At the margin of this sentence, Rendel wrote 'or Zionist policy', meaning that Andrews represented the hated Zionist policy 'in its most objectionable form'. Rendel, then, assented in, and thoroughly approved, the analogy (fanciful and far-fetched as it was) that equated British administration (operating strictly under the rule of law and subject to Parliamentary scrutiny and to that of the League) with a secret, lawless, terrorist organization like the Gestapo. 'This letter', he was pleased to minute, 'has a great deal of sense in it, though it is, of course, written from a very "Left" and "anti-Imperialist" point of view.'[62] We may, then, legitimately suspect that the policy which this very able official so tirelessly pushed was, or in the course of his campaign had come to be, tinged somewhat with an ideological or doctrinaire passion—a passion that led him to oppose what he called 'Zionist policy', not simply as incompatible with British interests, but as something in itself evil, and so making quite comprehensible (and perhaps also excusable) the murder of a fellow civil servant.

As is well known, following the invasion of Abyssinia, Anglo-Italian relations deteriorated greatly and a barrage of virulent Italian propaganda, particularly from Radio Bari, was constantly directed against British positions in the Middle East. This was indeed the most important reason why, in Rendel's view, Saudi Arabia should be conciliated to the utmost. But, strangely enough, when this propaganda concerned Palestine, Rendel adopted a supine, not to say defeatist, attitude. Whenever anti-British propaganda was reported as being inspired or instigated by Italy, all that Rendel did was to wring his hands and say that there was 'a great basis of truth' in the propaganda, that 'we have delivered ourselves into the hands of the Italians by our policy in Palestine', and 'that the origin of the present trouble should be sought in our own policy'. The proper response to these jeremiads was given by a member of the News Department, who minuted one of them to the effect that even if British action in Palestine supplied the material,

> the virulent use being made of it in the Italian and German press, which are fully controlled, is malign and dangerous both in the Near East and beyond; that we should do what we can to offset it and counter inaccuracies and exaggerations; and that close German-Italian co-operation in the matter is noticeable and significant.[63]

Rendel's reaction to Italian propaganda was sometimes more than simply defeatist, it was bizarre. More than once the Italians spread untrue rumours of unrest in Transjordan. Rendel cautioned against denying these rumours. He believed the Amir Abdullah to be 'intensely unpopular' because of his support of partition. He also believed, on what evidence is quite unclear, that there was 'every possibility of an early rising in Transjordan'. Therefore, it 'would be embarrassing if we had to follow a denial by an admission that the story we were denying was merely prophetic'! Again, the Embassy in Rome reported that the Italian press was spreading stories about disturbances in Transjordan and Abdullah's position being undermined by his son Talal's sympathy for the Palestine rebels. Rendel feared, why is again not clear, that it would 'hardly be practicable' to deny such rumours, 'even', he obscurely added, 'if it was thought desirable to do so on general grounds'![64]

It is not only that Rendel had absolutely no evidence of an imminent revolt in Transjordan; it is also that his way of speaking about a polity like Transjordan was uncritical and misleading. He referred to Abdullah's alleged unpopularity, but even if there was evidence of this unpopularity, it did not follow that popularity or unpopularity determined (as at times and to some extent it did in constitutional and parliamentary regimes) a political leader's fortunes, or had any effect on his power and standing. In Transjordan, as in the Middle East generally, it is power which attracts popularity, not the other way round. Abdullah's career is a case in point: given position and power by the British, he lost them not by forfeiting popular suffrages but by falling victim to an assassin's bullets. The same misconception is manifest even more incongruously in Rendel's comments on Saudi Arabia. In the course of his campaign in favour of territorial concessions to Ibn Sa'ud at the expense of Qatar and Abu Dhabi, he argued that it was

> important to realise that Ibn Saud is far more dependent on the opinion and support of his subjects than other dictators are. What he is most afraid of is that if he supports H.M.G. in their policy of partition, and there is then serious trouble between H.M.G. and any group or combination of Arabs, his own position will become impossible and he himself go under.[65]

In what manner Ibn Sa'ud was dependent on Saudi public opinion, and exactly how an unfavourable public opinion would lead to his downfall, Rendel did not consider.

Rendel saw the politics of the Palestine Arabs through the medium of the same, inappropriate, Western categories. From the undoubted fact that they disliked Zionism, feared continued Jewish immigration, and resented the possibility of Jewish superiority or even equality in a Muslim land where non-Muslims had been traditionally looked down upon, Rendel concluded that the rebellion that began in 1936 was the expression of the unanimous and inflexible resolve of a citizenry—a resolve which would inevitably prevail, and hence utterly foolish to resist. This is what he meant by insisting that the trouble in Palestine was 'political and not criminal' and that to delay a solution to the political problem would only lead to disaster; that in Palestine there were no 'extremists' and no 'moderates', only nationalists; and that the role of the Mufti in the troubles could be easily over-rated.[66]

Rendel's peremptory denial of a distinction between extremists and moderates among the Palestine Arabs was in response to his subordinate, Brenan, who had dared to write in a minute that

'Undoubtedly the majority of the Arab population in Palestine are sick to death of the acts of the extremists.' There can be no doubt that Brenan's judgment was more faithful to the evidence, as then known, than Rendel's. Nor can there be any doubt that deep divisions existed among the Palestine Arabs—divisions that the events of 1936-9 deepened and embittered. This bitterness stemmed from the fact that the Mufti and his supporters, in order to enforce their policies, murdered and terrorized their rivals and opponents as well as anyone whom they suspected of wishing for an accommodation with the authorities. It is thus not clear why Rendel placed such weight on his description of the trouble as 'political' rather than 'criminal'. In the first place, from the government's standpoint, a murder remained an offense which, as a matter of elementary duty, it had to repress and punish, whether the murder was 'political' or 'criminal'. In the second place, from the fact Arab crimes were politically motivated it did not follow that the cause to which they were committed was destined to triumph. On the contrary, history is littered with unsuccessful revolts and abortive uprisings. And, in fact, the disorders in Palestine were brought to an end by military action less than two years after Rendel's despairing prophecies.

As it happened, an alternative view of the events in Palestine was put forward by another official, but Rendel, for all the view's cogency, consistently pooh-poohed and succeeded in discrediting it. The view was offered by Colonel Gilbert MacKereth, the British Consul in Damascus. MacKereth had been in Damascus since 1933, and had long experience in and knowledge of the politics of the Levant. His knowledge and judgment of political trends in the area are displayed in a long memorandum about Pan-Arabism which he sent on 15 May 1936. The memorandum was not a response to the general strike in Palestine or to any other event in particular; MacKereth wrote it 'largely with a view to clarifying my own mind on this very confused question'. Pan-Arabism, he argued, 'has thrived only under what is thought to be oppression, and has always died in liberty.' And since the war, 'the viper kept alive abroad to bite the Turk now finds in the bosom of its protectors a softer flesh for its fangs.' MacKereth did not think that Pan-Arabism could compete against the interests which were bound up with the existence of separate states. These interests were daily becoming stronger and increasingly difficult to dislodge:

> In each State has been formed a Government with a permanent or semi-permanent officialdom, recruited on European lines and jealous of its power and prospects. Autarky has more than made an appearance and national defence forces have been individually organised and infused with local *esprit de corps*. Legal and political systems grafted upon different roots have grown quite dissimilar. Each country has apart from the influence of the mandatory Powers tended to become increasingly conscious and jealous of the boundaries fixed by the 'victorious allied Powers'. It

is sufficient in this connexion to recall the frontier difficulties that
have arisen between Iraq and its Arab and Islamic neighbours.
Xenophobia has also reared its head in the labour market in Iraq
where, as in Egypt some years ago when considerable hostility was
shown by Egyptians to officials of Syrian or Lebanese origin,
Syrians are still regarded bitterly and begrudged the savings they
make and export to their own country. In Syria, Saudi Arabians
or Iraqis are generally despised, secretly if not always openly, and
scoffed at as 'ajanib' ('ajanib' is one of the Arabic words for
foreigner and has an opprobrious tang to it). Transjordan, too, has
shown the same distaste for foreigners. Great fear of the Zionist
movement has made the Palestine Arab slightly more tolerant of
his brethren from adjoining countries. . . . [Palestinian leaders]
appear, even today, to be loath to consider amalgamating their lot,
except as the dominant partner, with that of the more primitive
Arab population of Transjordan.

MacKereth was also highly sceptical of Islam as a unifying political
influence, though he did not doubt its power to mobilize resistance to a
foreign presence in the area. All this was shrewdly observed and soundly
argued. Over forty years after its composition the memorandum may be
seen as a remarkably accurate summation and forecast of political trends
and attitudes in the Arab world. As his concluding paragraph shows,
MacKereth was also aware of the social and intellectual context in which
Pan-Arab ideologists operated; he was alive to the gap which yawned
between the reality and the rhetoric of Arab politics; and he could convey
his understanding precisely and vividly:

The standard of thought found in Arabic journalism is, to say no
more, mediocre, and full, as Johnson would have said, of
deliberate anfractuosities of temper, but it is widely esteemed by
the masses. It is a diverting sight to visit an Arab cafe and find a
literate Arab reading to a large circle of semi-literates bits from
Arabic newspapers, published in Damascus, Jerusalem or Cairo,
reviling the Western Powers for their iniquitous treatment of
orientals or proclaiming the power of the Italian air force to blow
the British fleet out of the sea, and a thousand and one more
abstruse mysteries that must have about the same influence on the
hearers as the tales of Scheherazade. Discussions follow that
usually take the most ludicrous turn; all with an air of gravity that
might lead the onlooker to think it represented profound
understanding. In this manner a fairy web is woven all over the
Arab-speaking world. It will be instructive to follow closely the
effect of Arab journalism and literature in molding and unifying
Arab opinion and in weaning it from its present parochial

interests. But, if a guess is permissible, it will be many generations before anything palpable appears. Until then it would seem certain that local Arab nationalism will be the rule. And the longer it is the rule the more important will local factors become. With this, the dream of a "United States of Arabia" or an Islamic confederation brought about by culture, religion and peaceful persuasion in a greater common weal, will tend to become an abstraction suitable only for the entertainment of philosophers.[67]

Rendel minuted on the memorandum that it was 'excellent and well worth reading'. But this was almost the last occasion during Rendel's tenure in the Eastern Department that words of praise for the Consul in Damascus were to be heard in the Foreign Office. In January 1937, Lord Peel and Sir Horace Rumbold, the Chairman and a Member of the Royal Commission on Palestine, visited Damascus. MacKereth discussed the problem with them, and one of his suggestions, as he reported, was that the Commission should get to the bottom of Sir Henry McMahon's alleged promises to Sharif Husayn during the first world war. This was a sensible suggestion, since the allegation that Palestine had been included in these promises was used to argue that the British government was guilty of bad faith in subsequently promoting a Jewish National Home in this territory. MacKereth clearly believed—rightly, as the evidence shows—that there was no historical basis for these widespread accusations. But his suggestion horrified the Eastern Department; Sterndale Bennett warned solemnly that the Consul was here 'straying on to rather dangerous ground', and the warning was endorsed by Rendel.[68]

During the second half of 1937, MacKereth, without realizing what was happening, managed to attract Rendel's hostility. This growing hostility may be followed in Rendel's minutes on MacKereth's telegrams and despatches in this period relating to the Palestine problem. Following the publication of the Royal Commission Report with its plan for the partition of Palestine, law and order began steadily to deteriorate in Palestine. This was a direct consequence of the manner in which the earlier disturbances had been brought to an end in October 1936. Those responsible for these disturbances had not been in any way dealt with. The impression was current that this was because the British government was incapable of dealing with them, and had to supplicate for the intervention of the Arab rulers to save its face. The cessation of the disturbances was thus looked upon as a mere armistice which could be terminated if the British response to Arab demands was to prove unsatisfactory. As was to become very clear, as early as the late summer of 1937, Damascus was the centre whence arms, funds and men were sent to Palestine to feed and sustain the disturbances. MacKereth was most diligent and energetic in tracking down those responsible for this traffic, and in giving advice and making suggestions to the Palestine government and the Foreign Office for dealing with what he considered to be a foreign-supported *fronde*. It was these activities, and the view of the Palestine problem that they implied, which aroused Rendel's ire.

Rendel's own view about the character of the disturbances that erupted in Palestine in the latter half of 1937 is expressed in a minute in which he commented on a private letter of 7 October from Ormsby Gore to Eden. In this letter the Colonial Secretary stressed that the hold of the British on Palestine now depended as much on co-operation with the French in preventing the Mufti (who was now a refugee in the Lebanon) and his followers from fomenting rebellion from the outside as on 'our own continuance of determination to rule with courage and vigour'. Rendel's response to this was quite negative:

> I confess [Rendel wrote on 13 October] that I am a little disturbed at the tone of Mr. Ormsby Gore's letter, which seems to imply that what is required in Palestine is a firm administration rather than a well-worked-out ultimate policy. I feel more and more convinced that the administrative problem in Palestine and the question of the maintenance of order and the suppression of crime will be a simple matter once we can satisfy the people of the country that our ultimate policy is based on principles of justice.[69]

For a man of affairs, Rendel exhibited a dangerously simple-minded faith about the ease with which one could discern and formulate 'principles of justice', translate them into practical arrangements, and in the process win the assent and approval of the parties to a dispute. Rendel clung with passion to the belief that the solution of the Palestine problem was a simple matter of applying the 'principles of justice', and dismissed with intense anger—which is the concomitant of passionate political commitment—warnings before the event that law and order was dangerously deteriorating in Palestine.

The Foreign Office files include one such warning which, as it happens, emanated from the Damascus Consulate. Rendel's reaction to it will serve to illustrate his view not only of the Palestine problem, but also of the worth of advice emanating from Damascus. With a despatch of 30 September 1937 MacKereth sent a report written by a junior clerk in the Consulate, Davis-Williams, in which he recorded his impressions during a visit to Palestine the previous August. Davis-Williams had lived in Palestine for five years and had 'a fair knowledge' of Arabic, Hebrew and Yiddish. He found the situation in the country quite alarming. In spite of official assurances that the country was calm, he found his sojourn punctuated by numerous outbursts of violence, which the newspapers failed to report, and the majority of which were perpetrated by Arabs.

'Everyone,' he wrote, 'is waiting—the Jews with trepidation, the Arabs with relish, the English with apparent indifference—for the conflagration which seems bound to come in the near future.'

> Davis-Williams found a dangerous effervescence
>
> fanned to flames, not only by the Moslem press but also in the mosques Friday by Friday where the crusade is preached against the Jews and against the hated foreign power which has brought them to Palestine and which protects them there.
>
> The Arabs, according to what I learned, have gone too far now ever to turn back. The cry is everywhere 'Jehad' (a holy war); all or nothing. They told me everywhere that nothing but complete independence will satisfy them. They saw Syria get its way in 1936 as a result of strikes and criminal violence; Palestine, therefore, can do likewise—will, indeed, do likewise. . . . The troubles of 1936 were cited and it was pointed out to me that the Arabs were well able to defeat the British.

Davis-Williams went on to report that his Arab interlocutors were forecasting that the same tactics used in 1936 would be used again, but with more organization, and that disturbances would start when the Mufti and the Arab rulers had done their best at Geneva and in London and had failed—'and they surely will fail—such is the power of Jewish money.' We see in retrospect that Davis-Williams's forecasts were correct, and his description of the Arab state of mind accurate. But even at the time, given the other information at the government's disposal, his warnings did not deserve to be contemptuously dismissed—which was the fate they met at Rendel's hands. Davis-Williams had, injudiciously, talked about the Arabs as a treacherous race. For Rendel this was enough to dismiss him as a Zionist:

> Would he, I wonder, [he indignantly asked] have thought it treacherous of his fellow Welshmen if they had resisted an attempt by a victorious Germany to settle Frankfort Jews in Wales?
>
> The report tells us nothing that has not been said over and over again by Zionist publicists of every kind. It is of little real value. If I had time I would answer this despatch fully. As it is I would simply ignore it.[70]

Rendel's dismissal of Davis-Williams's memorandum as 'a very poor report, which seems to me to have missed the essential facts' is clearly the outcome of a political commitment. It was this commitment to the 'principles of justice' so injudicious in a civil servant which blinded Rendel to what was actually going on in Palestine, and led him to dismiss anything emanating from the Damascus Consulate which did not conform to his preconceptions.

And very little, if anything, did. MacKereth's appraisal of the Arab and of the Palestine scene was diametrically opposite to that of Rendel's. In a despatch of 26 May 1936 he warned that 'we shall be deluding ourselves if we think that even if we turned every Jew out of Palestine, quit the country ourselves, and planted an Arab ruler there we should gain more than momentary Arab goodwill by it. Arab loyalty, as history and contact with them teach, is fickle to a degree, and Arab appetites are insatiable. Whatever solution the Royal Commission may discover for the Palestine problem, Arab politicians will continue to use "Zionism" as a stick to brandish in our faces, and Italy as a bogey to frighten us.' The only policy which seemed to him worth following in order 'to conserve our already considerable influence among the Arabs, which is based not at all on words but on physical facts' was simply to 'manifest our strength and dissemble our weakness'. All this Rendel dismissed as 'misleading' and MacKereth as 'all off the rails'.[71]

MacKereth was committed neither to 'justice' nor to Zionism or anti-Zionism. He was sceptical of grandiose views about the inevitable spread of Arab nationalism, and firmly convinced that the British position in the Middle East could be preserved only if British power and influence were believed to be paramount. In particular he considered it his duty to elicit support, within his consular district, for the policy of his government, and firmly to discourage activities that might pose a threat to the King's peace in Palestine. Thus, of his own motion, he took steps to ensure favourable comment in Syrian newspapers about the proposal to partition Palestine, following its adoption as official British policy. No other British diplomatic post in the Middle East attempted to do so, and neither did the Foreign Office, where Rendel was busy trying to change official policy and instruct them in this sense.[72] Again, when the Mufti organized in September 1937 the Pan-Arab Congress that met in Bludan in order to protest against British policy in Palestine, MacKereth spoke to the Syrian Prime Minister in order to suggest that 'an unfortunate impression might be made were the Syrian government to take part in discussions concerning the internal affairs of a neighboring and friendly country'. MacKereth also approached the French Delegate in Damascus, who in turn 'spoke most emphatically to the Prime Minister, explaining also that it would be embarrassing to France were a member of the Syrian government to attend the congress'. In this instance too, MacKereth was the only British representative to take such action, and to do so on his own, since the Foreign Office took no initiative in the matter.[73] Grudgingly approving MacKereth's activities, Rendel could not forebear, however, to complain of the length of his report and of the Consul's 'pseudo-Meredithian' style. MacKereth also intervened in something much more significant, and again did so without benefit of instructions. He had established beyond possible doubt the complicity of Syrian officials in the smuggling of men and arms into Palestine. He took the opportunity of an informal dinner party to put before the Syrian Prime Minister his view of the 'active and almost open conspiracy in Syria to secure irruption and continuance of public disorders in Palestine'. He explained that he had no instructions to speak officially, but he did not hesitate to tell Jamil Mardam that he was aware of the activities going on in Damascus. These, MacKereth said, were intolerable and might eventually prove dangerous to Syrian independence. Were disturbances to continue in Palestine and responsibility for them laid by British public opinion at Syria's door, Syria's admission to the League of Nations might be blocked. MacKereth went on to suggest to Mardam that 'he was possibly inclined to overestimate pan-Syrian and pan-Arab feeling in Syria. It was perhaps not as ardent as some people thought, nor was it so wholeheartedly interested in the Palestine problem. I did not think,' MacKereth heretically added, 'the security of his government really rested on it at all.'

This daring language was received by Rendel almost with consternation. He was 'somewhat disturbed' by MacKereth's threat that Syria's admission to the League might be vetoed, for this might annoy the French. A word of warning should be given to Colonel MacKereth. And there was another thing: Colonel MacKereth 'seems to regard the whole question as purely a local criminal one'. 'The Arab rebels,' Rendel was anxious to point out, 'are something more than mere "thugs". The motive on which they are acting, however misguidedly, is a passionate desire to prevent territory which they regard as their own from being given—as they think unjustly—by a third party (i.e. His Majesty's Government) to an alien invader.' Incredible as it may seem, a formal despatch was actually sent to MacKereth which, while thanking him for the energy he was showing on this issue, proceeded to read him a sermon on the danger of his losing sight of the lofty feelings which moved those who were threatening the lawful government in Palestine.[74]

MacKereth was tireless in tracking down those responsible for terrorism in Palestine, in pressing the Syrians and the French to prevent and deter these activities, and in suggesting to the government of Palestine various methods of frontier control. As consistently, Rendel poured cold water on his suggestions and dismissed his information, sometimes with tepid praise, sometimes with savage disapproval. In a minute on a telegram in which MacKereth enquired what had been done to stop the activities of a notorious bandit, Rendel dismissed the Consul as merely making a fuss. More than once Jerusalem asked that MacKereth visit them in order to have the benefit of his advice about anti-terrorism. Rendel's minutes concerning these requests show how reluctant he was to allow much contact between the British authorities in Jerusalem and the British Consul in Damascus.

> I think [went one such minute] that, in spite of his energy, gallantry, and personal charm, he is hopelessly wrong-headed as to the general question of our policy in Palestine, and I do not entirely trust his judgment about affairs in Syria. I fear I cannot therefore regard these visits as an unmixed blessing.[75]

Rendel's minutes also sought to discredit MacKereth as hopelessly prejudiced, and thus untrustworthy, in his judgments. Thus MacKereth wrote to the British Resident in Amman discounting rumours that Ibn Sa'ud might have sent money to Transjordanian figures who were opposed to Abdullah, and added: 'Yusuf Yasin who, from all accounts, is a Sheikh who is a snake, is quite likely to have encouraged them all with words. In fact I am told that he did.' Given Abdullah's and Ibn Sa'ud's mutual hostility and the inveterate habits of intrigue among courtiers in both countries, there was nothing improbable in MacKereth's report. But Rendel in a marginal note on a copy of this letter wrote: 'There is no reason for this except that Colonel MacKereth thinks all Arab nationalists snakes.'[76]

It will be recalled that Rendel expressed his approval of a letter in the *New Statesman* which compared a British District Commissioner who had been murdered in Nazareth to a Gestapo official. In his minute about the letter Rendel, quite gratuitously, wrote that he feared that 'Mr MacKereth is in some danger of finding himself exposed to much the same risks as the unfortunate Mr Andrews'.[77] The obvious implication was that MacKereth, by his unnecessary and tiresome foolhardiness in tracking down terrorist leaders, was endangering his life in a doubtful cause. Shortly afterwards, what was implicit here was explicitly spelled out. A despatch from MacKereth of 30 October 1937 reported that he had received an anonymous threat to his life. Rendel seized on this report as an occasion for MacKereth's removal from Damascus. How far were we justified, he asked, in continuing to allow him to take such risks?

> That these risks are very serious indeed there is no doubt. Colonel MacKereth has, in my opinion, misunderstood the nature of the trouble in Palestine, which he regards as nothing more than a criminal outbreak against constituted authority as such. We have reason to know, however, that the present campaign of violence is only part of a very widespread and deep-seated national movement spreading through all the Arabic-speaking countries against our policy in Palestine.

MacKereth's activities in Damascus were then really quite useless:

> even if Colonel MacKereth were to secure the arrest and execution
> of every Palestinian terrorist in Damascus and were to lose his life
> in doing so—which he is all too likely to do in any case—I am
> convinced that the trouble would go on undiminished and indeed
> probably with increased vigour.

These emphatic and sombre prophecies alarmed Vansittart, who asked
whether MacKereth should not be recalled and replaced by a Consul who
would confine himself to purely consular work. Rendel's answer to this
enquiry was even more sombre and emphatic:

> Knowing Col. MacKereth's character, knowing the nature of the
> movement he is 'up against', and the character of many of its
> champions, it seems to me that the more successful he is in securing
> the arrest—and probable execution—of Arab nationalist agents,
> the more serious will be the danger with which he will be
> threatened.[78]

In the event, MacKereth was not moved from Damascus, and though
Rendel's Oriental fatalism had a fatal influence on Palestine policy, his dire
forebodings proved false in the case of MacKereth, who had the temerity to
live on for many years afterwards until he died peacefully in his bed in 1962.

The Report of the Royal Commission on Palestine was published on 22
June 1937. Its most important recommendation was that Palestine be
partitioned and that two independent states, one Jewish and one Arab, be
set up, with the Arab state comprising Transjordan and those areas of
Palestine which, under the scheme of partition, were to fall to the Arabs.
There were undoubtedly many serious objections to this scheme, and
critics—Arab and Jewish, Zionist and non-Zionist—did not fail to point
them out. Among those critics was Rendel. He strongly disagreed with and
violently objected to partition, and he had a great faith in his own solution.
It was, he believed, the 'only hope'. The solution was to impose a ceiling of
between forty and forty-five percent for the Jewish population and to set up
a system of autonomous Jewish and Arab cantons, with minority rights
being guaranteed in perpetuity.[79] It may well be that Rendel's scheme was
preferable to partition, though we might also suspect that it too had
drawbacks and that it too would elicit opposition. From a British point of
view, however, it did not much matter which scheme was adopted,
provided it safeguarded British interests in the territory, and did not
damage British authority and prestige in the Middle East as a whole. But
the policy which the British government had followed in Palestine after the
outbreak of disorders in April 1936—a policy which Rendel inspired and
continued tirelessly to urge—rendered nugatory any proposed solution
(whether the Royal Commission's or Rendel's own) and in fact ended by
making the problem insoluble and by severely damaging British interests

and authority in the Middle East. The two features of the policy that led to these fatal consequences were the unconditional armistice with the rebels into which the government implicitly entered when it allowed the appeal by the Arab rulers to the Palestine Arabs in October 1936, and its acquiescence in subsequent intervention by Arab states in the affairs of Palestine.

Even before the Royal Commission Report was published, Rendel began his campaign against its proposals. He was very adroit. He did not start by opposing outright the conclusions of a Report which seemed thorough, exhaustive and authoritative, and by which Ministers were clearly impressed. His first gambit was to suggest that the government should postpone a decision on its recommendations until, say, the Permanent Mandate Commission had had time to consider it. Exceptionally, Oliphant found himself in disagreement with Rendel. He felt strongly that it was unwise for the government to publish the Report and not disclose its own views about a partition. 'Such a situation,' he wrote, 'would furnish both Arabs and Jews with every incitement to try in the meantime to intimidate H.M.G. to take a decision in their respective favour and would be most dangerous.' Both Vansittart and Eden agreed.[80] But Rendel, as usual, did not easily admit defeat. Even when the government declared its support for partition in principle, he tried to persuade Ormsby Gore to adopt a temporizing stance in the House of Commons debate on the Royal Commission Report which was to take place on 21 July. Ormsby Gore disagreed. He was 'most anxious' that the government should commit themselves to an integral acceptance of partition 'and seemed nervous lest any more elastic attitude should expose H.M.G. to undue pressure from the Jews and Arabs and lead to dangerous intrigues by both parties'.[81]

But if Rendel failed in delaying public response by the government to the partition scheme, he unquestionably succeeded in introducing in this response qualifications and reservations which he would later on exploit in order totally to undo partition. In some 'Preliminary Departmental Comments' written on 23 June Rendel multiplied and magnified the difficulties of the scheme in a manner such that a reader of his memorandum would sagely think that here was a most difficult business, requiring extreme caution. Was it wise, for example, to envisage setting up a Jewish state?

> It seems almost too much to hope [he opined] that the new Jewish state, once it has become powerful and prosperous, will regard with equanimity the presence of British civil and military (or police) authorities in [Nazareth, Haifa and other localities which, according to the partition scheme, were to remain under British control]. At the same time, it would clearly be most difficult, and open to serious objection, to hand over such places as Nazareth

(which is wholly Christian) and Haifa (which is of great strategical importance and contains the British-controlled mouth of the Iraq pipe line) unreservedly to a new independent sovereign state consisting largely of immigrants from Central Europe and Germany, who may well in future tend to look towards Germany or Central Europe rather than towards this country.

Again, sound though the idea was in principle, was it not really imprudent to think of joining Transjordan to the Arab parts of Palestine? The new state

> will come under the rule of the Amir Abdullah, who is regarded by most of the Arab world as very doubtfully loyal to the Arab cause, and who has further, quite recently, compromised his position by the close relations he has established with the Turks. The Amir Abdullah, though possessing many virtues, is politically short sighted, and a good deal given to petty intrigue. It may be then that to hand over large areas of Palestine to a new state under his rule will lead to difficulties of a new type between Transjordan on the one hand and other Arab states, such as Syria and Saudi Arabia, on the other.

But Rendel was by no means wholly negative. He was ready with a variety of ingenious suggestions to cope with the difficulties which his insight and experience had enabled him to anticipate. To deal with the difficulty posed by Abdullah's character and propensities 'it is perhaps for consideration,' he very thoughtfully suggested, 'whether we should not explore the possibilities of only handing over the Arab portions of Palestine to the Amir of Transjordan when he joins some kind of federation with Syria and Iraq, if not with Saudi Arabia.' The notion of Abdullah and Ibn Sa'ud joined together in a federation is weird enough to make us wonder whether Rendel was not indulging here in a little private joke.[82]

The Head of the Eastern Department succeeded in communicating to the Foreign Secretary his doubts whether the partition scheme was 'equitable and well conceived', and Eden in turn successfully argued in Cabinet that a statement drafted by Ormsby Gore in support of the partition scheme should be redrafted on 'less definite lines'. Rendel therefore attended a meeting at the Colonial Office where he succeeded in watering down Ormsby Gore's draft. Thus, for instance, where the original draft spoke of 'a scheme of partition on the lines recommended by the Commission' representing the best and most hopeful solution to the deadlock, the amended draft spoke of a scheme of partition 'on the general lines recommended by the Commission'. Again, Ormsby Gore's draft spoke of 'commending the scheme of partition', which Rendel changed to 'supporting a solution of the Palestine problem by means of a scheme of partition'. Ormsby Gore was concerned with affirming the government's absolute determination to maintain law and order pending the execution of the partition scheme. 'If disorders should again break out, of such a nature as to require military intervention,' his draft went, 'the High Commissioner will immediately, and in respect of the whole country, delegate powers under the Palestine (Defence) Orders-in-Council to the General Officer commanding the military forces, and steps will be taken to enforce disarmament.' Rendel's amendments were drastic here, and their effect was considerably to weaken the monitory force of the statement. As amended, the passage now read: 'If serious disorders should again break out, of such a nature as to require military intervention, the High Commissioner will, and in respect of the whole country, delegate powers under the Palestine (Defence) Orders-in-Council.'[83] That this amendment in particular was meant by Rendel considerably to emasculate Ormsby Gore's warnings is made clear by the way in which he dealt with another public warning by Ormsby Gore a few months later. The Colonial Secretary, in answer to a parliamentary question about the despatch to Palestine of a new commission to examine the partition scheme, said on 21 October 1937:

> It is perfectly clear that until the ordinary rule of law obtains in Palestine and people who commit murders and outrages can be convicted in ordinary courts and evidence produced, to send out any Commission is out of the question.

This statement Rendel found 'most disquieting' and he wished to delay sending it to British diplomatic posts in Arab capitals until a decision had been taken over the despatch of this new commission. Oliphant, whose strongest point was the observance of established conventions, objected that Ormsby Gore's statement had actually been made in Parliament and it would not be 'fair' thus to suppress it; but why not write privately to explain the importance which should be attached to it? Rendel therefore drafted a letter to Jedda, Baghdad and Cairo in which he set forth that it would be 'premature' to take Ormsby Gore's statement 'too literally', that while terrorism was 'of course' likely to delay a solution, 'the situation is not quite parallel with that which existed a year ago, and it is conceivable that we may have to go ahead with tackling the political issue before the administrative and military problem is entirely disposed of.'[84]

In his attempt to defeat partition Rendel went to extremes of ingenuity. At one point he went so far as to suggest that Lord Hailey, the chairman of the Permanent Mandate Commission, should be enlisted against partition. Could he not be approached, and his attention drawn to the imperfections of the partition scheme proposed by the Royal Commission? Could the Permanent Mandate Commission perhaps devise an alternative scheme, or suggest to the British government itself to devise a better scheme? For once, Eden adamantly rejected a proposal made by Rendel: 'Such a course would be madness,' he minuted.[85]

Extravagant as this suggestion was, it did not approach in extravagance Rendel's warnings about the catastrophe that would ensue if partition were enforced. He had no doubt, he declared in a memorandum of 22 September 1937, that force would have to be used, but where the use of force would stop, he was unable to say:

> We know that the northern tribes of Saudi Arabia are only being prevented from launching a holy war against the Jews by Ibn Saud's firm hand, but we clearly cannot expect him to restrain them if we are at virtually open war with the Arab world. We also know that organisations are springing up all over southern Syria, ready to send bands into Palestine as soon as hostilities begin. . . . Feeling is likely to be almost equally strong in Egypt and Iraq, when in spite of our treaties, a great deal of help is likely to be furnished to the rebels . . .
>
> The use of force, then, may well mean the despatch of a large scale expedition, and the consequent hostilities may well be far reaching.[86]

It is difficult to believe that these lurid fancies actually lurked behind Rendel's staid and conventional appearance, that the exemplary official who had passed first into the diplomatic service should have such a fertile imagination. This, however, is what the evidence shows. It also shows that the power of this imagination was such as to overawe his colleagues and superiors.

But surely, it may be said, Rendel must have had some ground for his prophecies. What, then, does the record show? Immediately after it was announced, the partition scheme aroused the strongest opposition on the part of the Mufti and the Arab Higher Committee. This is not difficult to understand, since the scheme provided for a union between Transjordan and the Arab parts of Palestine under Abdullah, and thus destroyed the Mufti's prospects of exercising power. By the same token Abdullah in Transjordan and those Arab notables opposed to the Mufti were in favour of the scheme. But the stance of the Palestine government was not such as to encourage public expression of support. Not only did it fail to give a clear and unambiguous lead, but it also failed to protect the Mufti's opponents against murder by his agents. This was very serious. Almost equally serious was the bungled attempt on 19 July 1937 to arrest and deport the Mufti (who succeeded in taking refuge in the Haram). The authorities were afraid to enter the Haram and arrest him because they believed this would be regarded as violating a religious sanctuary. The Prime Minister was consulted and Wauchope was told that it was advisable to give up the plan of arresting the Mufti, who remained in the Haram free to direct opposition to the goverment until he escaped to the Lebanon in the middle of the following October just as the government had again decided to arrest him and his colleagues following the murder of Lewis Andrews, the District Commissioner for Galilee.[87]

The hesitant and nerveless manner in which opposition by the Mufti and the violence instigated by him were dealt with was not the only reason for the evaporation of support for partition among Palestinian Arab leaders. Their unwillingness was increased by the lack of public response by the British government to attacks on partition made by Arab leaders outside Palestine. The initial attack, a violent one, was made by the Iraqi Prime Minister, Hikmat Sulayman. He had come to power through a military *coup d'état*, his position was none too secure, and his regime was widely accused by its opponents of being anti-Arab, pro-Kurdish and pro-Turkish. Opposition to partition might therefore establish his credentials as an Arab nationalist, thus discrediting his opponents' propaganda. On 10 July, he made a violent statement against partition, attacking Abdullah who, by accepting the scheme, had, he said, brought himself into contempt. Privately, he told the British Ambassador that 'he had done what was necessary to satisfy public opinion'. He himself did not think partition would be carried out without the consent of the League of Nations, which would not be forthcoming, hence there was no reason for agitation! Hikmat's outburst elicited no public rebuke even though Iraq was formally a friend, indeed an ally, and in effect a client. A private remonstrance was sent, and the Iraqi Minister in London was spoken to. This absence of public reaction on the part of the British led people to suspect that Hikmat spoke as he did because he had had prior approval. Wauchope reported that the statement had had a very bad effect, that Abdullah was most indignant, and that it had been a 'most powerful factor' in the public opposition to partition by Arab leaders who had previously expressed themselves, privately, in favour of partition.[88]

There is little doubt that Hikmat's attack on partition led others to make similar gestures. On 23 July, MacKereth reported that the Syrian government addressed a note to the League of Nations regarding partition, and sent a copy to MacKereth.

> I have refrained [MacKereth wrote] from discussing with members of the Syrian government the Royal Commission's report on Palestine. I felt that to talk to them about it could only still further encourage them in their conviction that Syria is entitled to be consulted in the affairs of Palestine. Nevertheless Sa'adallah al Jabri [a Minister], when he was dining with me the other night, referred to what he described as the impertinent declaration of Hikmat Suleiman about Palestine; I did not gainsay him.[89]

British passivity in the face of Hikmat's attack also perplexed and displeased the Saudis and undoubtedly led them to a change in the very moderate stance which, as will be seen, they had originally adopted, contrary to Rendel's prophecies. Hikmat, Hafez Wahba complained to Rendel in an interview on 29 July, continued to enjoy the confidence of the British government which, although speaking of objecting to his actions, did nothing to interfere or mark any displeasure. Rendel's maladroit language on this occasion can have done little to persuade the Saudis of British resolve or steadiness of purpose. Rendel confided in Hafez Wahba that Hikmat's action had greatly increased British difficulties. But Iraq was, after all, an independent country and its behavior could not be controlled. He told Hafez Wahba, confidentially, that Hikmat's 'singularly ill-advised and ill-timed action' had very nearly wrecked the negotiations for an Iraqi loan. But the prospectus for the loan had, in fact, been issued that very day, and the Saudis would have been right to think that action spoke louder than confidences.[90]

As has been said, the Saudis were by no means originally opposed to partition. This was not what Rendel had expected. In a minute of 3 July he had declared that Ibn Sa'ud's first reaction was likely to be adverse, and he advised that to soften his opposition the King should be told that the government had not yet committed itself either to partition or to an enlarged territory which Abdullah would govern.[91] Hafez Wahba's reaction to the partition scheme seemed to confirm the soundness of Rendel's judgment. When he met Hafez Wahba on 7 July, the Saudi Minister declared himself 'extremely depressed' by the partition scheme to which Ibn Sa'ud would react violently. The King would never again be able to exercise a moderating influence over the Palestine Arabs, and Anglo-Saudi relations would deteriorate. 'I have seldom,' Rendel feelingly wrote, 'seen Sheikh Hafez so moved or so unhappy.' Rendel tried hard to make him take a 'less tragic' view of the situation, but he was 'extremely gloomy' when he left, 'and I confess that I found the interview a most painful one.'[92]

But, lo and behold, three days later a telegram arrived from Bullard, followed by another four days later which ought to have lifted Rendel's gloom and soothed the pain which the interview with Hafez Wahba had occasioned. For Bullard reported that after the initial shock that the partition scheme created, Ibn Sa'ud proved to be 'most friendly'. It turned out that what disquieted Ibn Sa'ud about partition was that Abdullah would be aggrandized and made independent. If this were to happen, he said, he would claim Aqaba and Ma'an and a corridor to Syria. 'He gave me the impression,' Bullard wrote in his telegram of 14 July, 'that he felt helpless and greatly dependent upon Great Britain.' He wanted urgent financial assistance, and when Bullard mentioned that the projected Arab state would receive a grant of two million pounds, Ibn Sa'ud said that this was 'all very well but do not let me go bankrupt either'.

After seeing Ibn Sa'ud in Riyad Bullard traveled eastward

accompanied by the Druze adviser to Ibn Sa'ud, Fu'ad Hamza, who had been present at all of Bullard's interviews with the King.

> By the time we reached Hofuf [Bullard went on] Ibn Sa'ud had received telegrams from Palestine Arabs asking for advice and assistance and [asked?] Fuad to suggest a reply. Fuad, who is himself very hostile to proposals of His Majesty's Government, said with obvious regret that whatever happened Ibn Saud would never support a policy opposed to that of His Majesty's Government and I understand he drafted reply in such a way as not to encourage the Palestine Arabs to count on help of Ibn Saud against us.

The percipient Trott, who pointed out that what Ibn Sa'ud's foreign advisers said was not always identical with the King's views, is seen here to have been doubly right.

But Bullard's news did not lift Rendel's gloom. He grudgingly admitted that Ibn Sa'ud's attitude had proved more favourable than anticipated, but immediately went on to lament that Ibn Sa'ud's territorial claims might create 'a lot of trouble', and that 'we shall not be able to propose a new Arab State for membership of the League of Nations unless we can say that it has well-defined and established frontiers, which cannot be done so long as Ibn Sa'ud's claim to Akaba and Maan continues'.[93]

Bullard's report was confirmed by none other than Hafez Wahba, who called on 14 July to give the gist of a telegram from Ibn Sa'ud that repeated the points he had made to the British Minister. But Hafez Wahba now had recourse to the ploy which had proved so profitable the previous year. He asked Rendel for his 'personal and confidential' advice about the manner in which Ibn Sa'ud should respond to the appeal from the Palestine Arabs relating to the partition scheme: the Iraqis, Hafez Wahba said, had replied 'in a sense generally favourable to the Arab cause and strongly opposed to partition'. Rendel, very correctly, adopted the official line and said that the best advice Ibn Sa'ud could give was for the Palestine Arabs to accept the position in favour of which the government had definitely and finally decided. But Rendel was not content with simply reiterating the official position. He went on to say that there was, in any case, 'no hurry about replying.' The Royal Commission's Report and the government's endorsement of its proposals would have to be considered by the Permanent Mandates Commission and the Council of the League. If partition was accepted in principle, negotiations with Jews and Arabs would have to take place: 'There was thus,' Rendel reiterated, 'no immediate hurry.' Given Hafez Wahba's known personal opposition to partition, would he not have taken this language as a hint that, after all, the King need not, for the moment at any rate, press too strongly on the Palestine Arabs the advice that 'they should accept the situation'?[94]

The absence of a forceful and immediate British reaction in Palestine and elsewhere to attacks on the partition scheme clearly encouraged both Ibn Sa'ud and Hafez Wahba to press for the abandonment of partition. On 20 July, Hafez Wahba conveyed a message from Ibn Sa'ud that his position was becoming 'increasingly difficult'. The 'Wahabis of Nejd' were raising strong objections to a Jewish state on religious grounds, and Muslims abroad were also constantly urging him to oppose partition.

> He was thus [Hafez Wahba continued] being strongly driven both by his own people and by his correligionists abroad, and his position was being made almost unbearable. He had told Sheikh Hafiz that he had not slept for five nights as a result of the acute anxiety that this question was giving him. Sheikh Hafiz himself was clearly much disturbed by this last telegram and implied that King Ibn Saud was virtually faced with a choice between maintaining his own position in his own country and retaining his friendship with His Majesty's Government.

Later on, during the summer of 1937, Hafez Wahba continued both in London and in Alexandria (where he met the Oriental Secretary at the British Embassy) to make alarmist statements about the threat by the *Ulema* of Najd to Ibn Sa'ud's throne. At one point, also, Hafez Wahba, in an interview with Rendel, complained that he was being 'accused' by his Arab and Egyptian friends of being too pro-British, and that he was finding it increasingly difficult to carry on as Saudi Minister in London.

As will be recalled, Trott's dismissal of the possibility that Ibn Sa'ud's position was being threatened by his own *Ulema* displeased Rendel very much. For his part, he was very alarmed indeed that Ibn Sa'ud might fall if he did not oppose British policy in Palestine:

> The really disquieting feature of this communication [he minuted on 20 July] is the suggestion in it that Ibn Saud's position in his own country may be severely shaken if he acquiesces in our policy. Ibn Saud has always been much more dependent on the consent and support of his people than other dictators, and I think there may be some justification for the Saudi Minister's nervousness, particularly when it is remembered that Ibn Saud is in serious financial difficulties, and is already tending to lose popularity as a result.

There was no evidence of any kind to back up these judgments, yet both Oliphant and Eden accepted them, the latter even going so far as to ask that the Cabinet be informed of Hafez Wahba's communication.[95]

Rendel was no less disturbed by Hafez Wahba's plaint and by the possibility of his resignation. He recorded that the Minister was 'very much moved'. Rendel had done his best to defend British policy 'and to conceal my own feelings on this subject, and I suppose I must have succeeded, as the Minister parted from me more coldly than usual'. He felt the urge to confess that he had found the interview 'extremely embarrassing'. Oliphant commiserated with his colleague over this 'painful interview', and solemnly declared that it 'would add to our difficulties were the Sheikh to resign'. Vansittart added, with foreboding, that this was a straw which showed how the wind was beginning to blow, and 'it will blow a lot stronger'. Happily, however, this proved to be no more than a passing tiff—perhaps because the British official was not as adept as he thought at disguising real feelings, and the cordial friendship lost nothing of its warmth. When, in January 1938, Rendel's appointment to the Sofia Legation was announced, Hafez Wahba expressed his uneasiness lest this affect the question of Palestine, 'since,' Rendel minuted on 19 January, 'it is now generally known that I have been personally active in trying to secure a reconsideration of the Royal Commission's recommendations.'[96]

Intimations that Ibn Sa'ud was in difficulties and his throne perhaps in danger continued to be conveyed to London in the summer and autumn of 1937, and continued to be given credence by the Eastern Department. Baggallay went so far as to suggest in August that Ibn Sa'ud should be told that 'we will not take it ill if he makes known his views publicly'; for, if 'out of a sense of loyalty' Ibn Sa'ud refrained from attacking partition publicly, 'a religious crusade' might be started against him, which would weaken his position, 'a result which could hardly help us.' So terrified was the Department that they were driving Ibn Sa'ud to his ruin that Rendel could hardly be restrained from hinting to Hafez Wahba 'confidentially' at the end of October that partition was on its way to being abandoned. Oliphant and Vansittart both thought this unwise, but their words of caution could not prevent the Oriental Secretary at the Baghdad Embassy from telling Yusuf Yasin at the beginning of November that the government was 'in no way committed to the particular proposals put forward by the Royal Commission'. It did not occur to these officials so solicitous of Ibn Sa'ud's welfare and safety—and if it did, the papers bear no indication—that what moved Ibn Sa'ud was not fear for his throne but jealousy of the hated Hashemites in Iraq who were using the Palestine issue to gain prominence and primacy in the Arab world. And yet it was not for lack of telling. In August, the Saudi charge d'affaires was informing Baggallay that it was Iraqi action that was adding to Ibn Sa'ud's difficulties; and Captain Holt, the Oriental Secretary at Baghdad, in the same memorandum in which he recorded his strong hint to Yusuf Yasin that partition was dead, went on to speak of Ibn Sa'ud's intense suspicion of Iraq's competition for leadership of the Arab world, and of the impression he had gained from the Saudi official that Ibn Sa'ud was jealous of the limelight gained by Iraq at the League of Nations (of which Saudi

Arabia was not a member) as a result of attacking British policy in Palestine.[97]

Did Ibn Sa'ud justify this blind belief in his absolute loyalty? Did he deserve the fond protectiveness with which Rendel and his colleagues so tenderly regarded him? As has been seen, the Eastern Department fought shy of pursuing enquiries about arms smuggling through Saudi territory and suspect activities on the frontier with Transjordan. As has also been seen, Ibn Sa'ud had not objected to the partition scheme when it was first announced, and only changed his stance when the Iraqis attacked it without drawing even a public protest from the British government. No doubt in order to protect his position, Ibn Sa'ud sent a telegram to a friend in Damascus which became known to the Palestine government. Its text is not now in the file, but it was enough for Wauchope to refer (in a letter of 14 July) to its 'unfortunate and most disappointing substance'. When Ormsby Gore circulated the letter to his colleagues, Eden's attention was attracted by this passage and he asked for further information. Rendel, while providing the text of Ibn Sa'ud's telegram, hastened to explain it away. It was not, he minuted on 26 July 1937, a sign of bad faith on Ibn Sa'ud's part. The King, he explained, had for a long time made it increasingly clear that he might be obliged to adopt a policy over Palestine at variance with that of the British government. Rendel ingeniously reconciled. Ibn Sa'ud's language to Bullard with this private expression of opposition to British policy. What he was doing in his conversation with Bullard was 'merely' drawing attention to one or two points of special concern to him, but 'he never disguised his profound dissent from the line of policy we had been obliged to adopt'.[98] This was quite untrue, since neither Bullard's report nor Ibn Sa'ud's message subsequently sent through Hafez Wahba in any way indicated that the King was opposed to partition as such or that he was undermining it by private advice to his friends.

Ibn Sa'ud continued to be promoted in the Foreign Office as a sincere and straightforward man. In a telegram of 5 January 1938 Bullard described in affecting terms the distress which the disorders in Palestine personally occasioned to Ibn Sa'ud:

> For four months he had been unable to listen to broadcasts from Jerusalem because they were so painful to him. He had decided to listen on January 3rd to the first Arabic broadcast from London and filled his tent with Arabs for the occasion. When the news was announced that an Arab had been executed in Palestine he felt as though the rope was round his own neck and he and the Arabs with him could not refrain from tears. At this His Majesty was deeply moved and tears in the sincerity of which I at least believe came into his eyes. He readily admitted that the British did not punish Arabs for their political opinions but asked whether the crimes for which they were hanging and imprisoning Arabs would

have been committed if it had not been for the policy of His Majesty's Government. I know a reply of a kind to this question [Bullard feelingly wrote] but none that will convince Ibn Saud or any other Arab.[99]

A few months later evidence came to hand that this man of sensibility was actively supporting the Mufti (now a fugitive in the Lebanon) by obtaining large amounts of arms and ammunition and having them smuggled from his territory into Palestine. Bullard, on the strength of Ibn Sa'ud's word, categorically denied such allegations and stoutly declared that he 'fully' believed in the King's friendship. When Ibn Sa'ud's involvement was 'conclusively' proved Bullard was compelled to change his opinion of the King's good faith, but he now abounded in excuses for this underhanded behavior. An apologist might argue, he wrote, that Ibn Sa'ud's conduct was no worse than that of many highly placed Muslims who have subscribed to insurgent funds. Ibn Sa'ud, after all, hated Jews; he was disappointed that his territorial claims in the Peninsula had not been satisfied; the Nazi annexation of Austria together with the recent Anglo-Italian conversations relating to Arabia and the Red Sea were British diplomatic defeats. We have, Bullard concluded, a poor case and ought to be thankful that Ibn Sa'ud has done no more than secretly supply arms to the Palestine Arabs. If a European war should break out, prophesied Bullard, 'we should have reason to consider ourselves fortunate if Saudi Arabia remained neutral, since we have everything that Ibn Saud would like to have while the countries likely to be opposed to us have nothing that he covets.'[100] This judgment was self-confessedly that of an apologist. But the recognition that power or weakness in a state elicited respect or its opposite in other states, was (whatever its merits) couched—at last—in the language of realism. This language, however, sat ill with sentimental effusions about Ibn Sa'ud's readiness to shed tears and simple-minded belief in his good faith.

Arab opposition to partition, then, was allowed to mount to a crescendo, and the opportunity was missed to impress upon Ibn Sa'ud— and other Arab rulers—that policy in Palestine was exclusively the affair of the British government. Partition, whatever its intrinsic merits or demerits, had been proposed by a Royal Commission, and the government had adopted the proposal. To allow opposition by foreign states to influence it over a matter which, barring the oversight exercised by the League of Nations, was entirely within its jurisdiction was fatally to undermine British authority and prestige in the whole area. Equally fatal, therefore was the passivity of the Foreign Office in allowing opposition to partition to develop, in not seizing the opportunity, early in July 1937, to impress on the Arab states the determination of the British government itself to settle the Palestine conflict, and thus to undo some of the damage done by Arab intervention in the previous autumn.

This passivity now also led to a further, serious complication.

It encouraged yet another state to claim a say in the Palestine conflict and its settlement. This state was Egypt, and its involvement was to change the complexion of inter-Arab politics for many decades to come and to make the Palestine problem even more intractable. In the summer and autumn of 1936 the Egyptian Prime Minister, Mustafa al-Nahhas, offered his good offices in the Palestine affair, but his offers came to nothing and Egypt was not included among those states that appealed for peace in Palestine in October of that year. When the partition proposal was made and the Iraqi Prime Minister attacked it so vehemently, Nahhas expressed to Sir Miles Lampson, the British Ambassador, his 'utmost disapproval' of Hikmat Sulayman's irresponsible proceedings. He mentioned to Lampson that his political opponents, in order to embarrass him, were raising the issue of Palestine in the Senate and asking for a statement of Egyptian policy on the matter, and he sought Lampson's advice on how to proceed.[101]

Lampson was not, however, the best person from whom to seek advice on this particular matter. He seems to have held strong views on Palestine, and to have expressed them indiscreetly. Thus in a conversation with the Egyptian Prince Regent in July 1936, who had asked whether nothing could be done to terminate the lamentable state of affairs in Palestine, Lampson said that 'he quite understood his feelings which were in fact in large measure shared by every thinking Englishman'. Speaking 'entirely personally and unofficially' Lampson suggested 'a sort of general truce' in which immigration into Palestine would be temporarily suspended pending the investigation to be carried on by the Royal Commission, and in exchange there would be cessation of violence. Lampson was careful to say that such bargaining between the lawful government and its subjects was entirely his own idea, but, as O.G.R. Williams of the Colonial Office noted, Lampson 'will probably have given the impression that he was expressing more than a personal view—despite his disclaimer'.[102]

Neither Lampson, then, nor the Foreign Office took the opportunity of Nahhas's request for advice to impress on him that Palestine was a British affair and that, as Eden declared in a telegram of the previous November when dealing with Nahhas's offer to mediate, there was no wish in any way to encourage his intervention.[103] Since nothing was said now to discourage him from officially raising the Palestine issue, since he was also aware that Arab states were in fact intervening in the matter, and since Palestine was being used as a weapon in internal politics, Nahhas recurred to the subject in another conversation with Lampson towards the end of July. This time he did not criticize the Iraqi intervention or complain about his opponents' tactics or ask for advice. Rather, he launched an attack on partition which 'he could not too strongly deplore' and he offered his services to devise a change in this 'fatal policy'. Lampson's response was so lame that it can almost be said to have invited further intervention:

I said I know you would be grateful for his desire to help: but I must remind him that His Majesty's Government had adopted the Royal Commission's recommendations as basis of their policy. That must naturally also be my brief: but as His Excellency would have seen in the press the whole question was still before Parliament in London: I suggested His Excellency had better wait and see result.

To do Lampson justice, he did tell London that he was due to have another conversation with Nahhas shortly, and it might be helpful to provide something for him to say to the Prime Minister. Rendel, reciting yet once more that Arabs looked upon partition as unjust, that Arab opinion, forming itself 'by curious processes', was now opposed to it in 'spontaneous and widespread' fashion, and that 'we are likely to be in for an increasing amount of trouble over Palestine', concluded in despondence and despair that Lampson could not be given any further guidance to help him deal with Nahhas, and Vansittart echoed that he was afraid that Mr. Rendel was right. Eden silently initialled the minutes.[104]

But Rendel's lamentations about the engulfing and irresistible tide of Arab 'public opinion' was not based on any evidence. And as concerns Egypt specifically, such evidence as existed went the other way. A despatch from David Kelly (acting for Lampson, who was absent on leave) sent towards the end of October 1937 discussed at some length Egyptian attitudes to the Palestine conflict. Political leaders were constrained by their position to interest themselves in Palestine, since they could either make local political capital out of it or, like Nahhas, wanted to play the role of leader of Arab opinion. Among the educated classes little interest was displayed, their general outlook being more towards Europe than the East. The traditional religious classes were, however, more sympathetic. As for the mass, it was largely unaware that the issue existed, and since it was in nobody's interest to stir it up, it remained supine. Kelly, however, cautioned against too sanguine a view. Egypt was, after all, Muslim and thus likely to sympathize with fellow Muslims in their tribulations and grievances. Not to be forgotten either was the King's 'inherited tendency' to pose as the major monarch of the Muslim world. All these, he concluded, were factors which might provoke 'an artificial and inconvenient interest in the Arab cause in Palestine'. Again, Palestine might be used as a pretext to attack Nahhas for subservience to the British, and if his administration were replaced by one less well-disposed, the new government could discreetly feed the agitation instead of dampening it.

All this was well-observed, percipient and cautious. Instead of considering, however, how the situation which Kelly described could be used to forward British policies and prevent damage to British interests, Rendel's first concern was to protect Ministers against the dangerous thoughts contained in this despatch:

> I am afraid [he minuted] this despatch may be seized upon by the Colonial Office in support of their contention that it is quite unnecessary to worry about reactions to our Palestine policy in neighbouring Moslem countries. If the despatch is carefully read, it shows that there are very unpleasant possibilities ahead, and that the present lull is in fact due largely to accidental circumstances.

From Rendel's language one might have concluded that the Egyptian lack of interest in Palestine was an anomalous interruption—a 'lull'—and that Egypt was, in normal times, passionately and unremittingly concerned with Palestine:

> A hasty reading of the first part of it [he wrote on] leaves one with the impression that Palestine is of little or no interest to Egypt, and as, in the present conditions of stress of work, most papers have to be read hastily, I should be inclined not to give too wide a circulation. I would, therefore, refrain from printing it, and would merely send a copy to the Colonial Office in due course in typescript.

The only reason why the Colonial Office was allowed to see Kelly's subversive despatch was that he had already, compounding his offense, sent a copy to Jerusalem, and it might look suspicious if his Department were to withhold it from the London Department responsible for Palestine.[105]

Lampson's intellect was of a quite different class from that of his subordinate—less given to questioning, blunter, considerably less sceptical, dangerously prone to falling for seemingly simple black-or-white judgments, and far from suspicious enough of what traps and pitfalls could lurk behind the common man's no-nonsense view. Thus, here were the Jews, making a lot of trouble in Palestine, for themselves and for us, and here was Ibn Sa'ud saying, perfectly reasonably, stop immigration. Is it better to satisfy the Jews and take on the whole Arab and Muslim world, or is it better—for us as well as for the Jews—to abandon all talk of partition, to do as he asks, and secure the friendship and good-will of the Arabs? Could any man of sense doubt what the answer ought to be? This was the tenor of a telegram which Lampson, back in Cairo, sent a fortnight or so after Kelly's despatch. A copy went to the Colonial Office where J.M. Martin minuted that Lampson's telegram expressed very much the views held by the Eastern Department of the Foreign Office, and that

> this attitude and the failure to understand Partition and present its merits to Arab Governments and their representatives is far more formidable than Ibn Saud himself.

In another minute written at approximately the same time, Martin made the point that the Foreign Office had never made the slightest effort to commend partition to Arab states, though complaints against the proposals were given a ready hearing. As the evidence surveyed here conclusively shows, Martin's comments were fully justified.[106]

Equally justified was Martin's implied criticism of the Eastern Department's behaviour. Regardless of its merits, which may have been debatable, partition was, after all, Cabinet policy. Officials, therefore, were in duty bound not only to defend it, but actively to further and promote it. The defense, as has been seen, was at best tepid and unconvincing and, worse, seemed positively to invite opposition and attack. As the evidence also shows, opposition in the Arab world to partition when it was first announced was by no means clear, determined or unanimous. A more resolute stance on the part of the Foreign Office and of diplomatic representatives might have led to a different, and more desirable outcome, in one respect at any rate: it would have established that the British government meant to be master in Palestine, that it held the initiative and would brook no repetition of the intervention which it had allowed to take place in October 1936. These points established, it would have been of relatively little importance which policy for Palestine was finally decided upon. But the cost to British authority and prestige in the Middle East of abandoning under pressure and threat a policy the adoption of which had been publicly announced does not seem to have been weighed—the papers, at any rate, disclose no evidence of this.

On the contrary, Rendel was so sure that partition was absolutely bad that he allowed no other consideration to be taken into account. He was also unshakeably certain that once partition was abandoned and Jewish immigration restricted or stopped peace would descend on Palestine.[107] Moreover, the fight against partition assumed for him the aspect of a righteous struggle in which the Colonial Office, 'intransigent on the Jewish side,' and looking at the problem from the point of view of 'Jewish opinion in this country' had, at all costs, to be defeated.[108] Rendel also believed that the Jewish case benefited from the presence in the House of Commons of able and persuasive supporters, and that if the Arab side of the case was to carry any weight, 'it will have to be presented with great force and skill.'[109] Rendel may even have come to identify himself with 'the Arab side of the case', in that excess of zeal which Talleyrand so deprecated in diplomats, and to have even perhaps believed that he was the best judge of what this case was and ought to be. Following the Mufti's flight from Palestine, the dissolution of the Arab Higher Committee and the arrest of its members in the beginning of October 1937, Jerusalem reported that these actions were not altogether unwelcome in respectable urban Arab society and among village notables. A junior member of the Eastern Department, J. R. Colville, commenting on the telegram, remarked that 'moderate' Arab opinion seemed not to regret the arrests. Rendel's rebuke was cutting and peremptory:

> I never know [he minuted] what is meant by 'moderate' Arab opinion. There are indifferent Arabs and keenly pro-Arab Arabs—but it would hardly be a sign of wisdom on the part of any Arabs to welcome the policy of H.M.G.[110]

Following the debate in Parliament of the Royal Commission report and its consideration by the Permanent Mandates Commission in September 1937, Ormsby Gore sought to obtain from the Cabinet a decision about future policy in Palestine. On 9 November 1937, he circulated a memorandum and a draft despatch to the High Commissioner for consideration by his colleagues. He argued for the adoption of the partition scheme, which the draft despatch declared to be 'the best and most hopeful solution of the problem—indeed, ultimately, the only possible solution'. The draft despatch also declared that partition would be carried out even if Arab and Jewish co-operation was not forthcoming. The memorandum made the point that uncertainty about British policy and its ultimate intentions could only tend to increase Arab intransigence. Ormsby Gore also argued against involving Arab states in the Palestine problem, since they had shown themselves hostile to any policy likely to be acceptable to the British government and to the League.[111]

Rendel was ready for Ormsby Gore. As early as the middle of the previous October he had written a long memorandum attacking the partition scheme. In a further memorandum, also written before Ormsby Gore's paper had been circulated, Rendel sketched out what ought to be the Foreign Secretary's immediate objectives in the forthcoming Cabinet discussion. This was to try and 'leave the door a little more ajar than it is at present to the possibility of some other solution' than partition. Rendel believed that a new Commission should re-examine the partition proposals. This Commission should be told that the British government desired not to impose a solution but to reach one by general agreement, and that the maintenance of friendly relations with the Arab and Middle Eastern countries had the same 'paramount importance' as the re-establishment of peace in Palestine. Rendel also desired the new Commission to be authorized 'to embark on consultations not only with the non-Palestinian Jews but also with the non-Palestinian Arabs'. Rendel was firmly of the opinion that any hint that the government was prepared to consider an alternative solution to partition would 'produce an immediate relaxation in the tension which is at present steadily developing in Palestine and in the neighboring countries'. The solution which Rendel favoured was to set a limit of 40 percent on the Jewish population of Palestine. Drawing a wholly imaginary distinction between non-Palestinian and Palestinian Jews, he affirmed that the latter would 'gladly' accept such a solution, as would the Palestine Arabs, and that this would solve the problem. Rendel's views were endorsed by Vansittart, who minuted that 'We should be very firm in not letting the Jews break our back.'[112]

As will be seen, Eden was faithfully to follow Rendel's suggestions and completely to adopt as his own Rendel's version of the Palestine problem. In the memorandum and minutes of 14 October 1937 that inaugurated Rendel's autumn offensive two salient arguments are advanced against partition. Partition will not settle the conflict because a Jewish state 'will mean the creation of a new jumping off place for the Jews, from which they will inevitably spread their influence over a much larger area'. The Jews are also likely to prove a Trojan horse for the British empire:

> the culture of the leading Jews in Palestine, as I know by personal experience, is predominantly German. The Jewish immigrants of the better class are mostly of German origin or tradition, and have not only kept a culture of a strongly Germanic character, but have even retained a curious loyalty to Germany and to German ideals. A Jewish state is therefore likely to acquire a very Teutonic complexion, and it is by no means inconceivable that if there was some turn of the wheel in Europe, a no longer actively Jew-baiting Germany might find a ready-made spiritual colony awaiting her in a key position in the Middle East. Anti-clerical France supports the Church abroad, and it may be that if trouble breaks out in Europe, we shall not be able, after all, to count so completely on the friendship of the Jews of Galilee as we are at present inclined to assume.

Rendel's disquisition about the problematic loyalty of the 'Jews of Galilee' was his response to a suggestion by R.I. Campbell, the Head of the Egyptian Department, to whom the memorandum had gone for comment. Campbell agreed entirely with Rendel, and in order to reinforce the view that Jewish immigration into Palestine had to be strictly controlled, he put forward the ingenious argument that to respond to Jewish pressure would

> only act as an incentive to Hitler to maintain his anti-Jewish policy. Not only will our creation of a Jewish state (even if, as Mr Rendel says, that state proves illusory) help Hitler to disengage his responsibility, but, by giving a stimulus to his anti-Jewish policy, it will provide him with an ideal means of fostering our difficulties in the Middle East. If Egypt becomes prominently involved in the controversy, and if the possibility of an eventual Judaeo-Egyptian frontier is not excluded, Hitler is brought indirectly into Egyptian affairs.

Rendel and his colleague seemed to be saying that a Jewish state was a bad security risk; that it would act as a Trojan horse for Nazi Germany. Rendel had yet another point to bring forward against a Jewish state. He drew a damaging analogy between Jews in Palestine and Italians in Abyssinia. Aggression against Abyssinia was justified by the prosperity and progress Italians would allegedly bring to the Abyssinians, and the same argument was being used to justify Zionist domination in Palestine: *Mutato nomine de nobis fabula narratur.*

As against this picture of pro-German, potentially treacherous Jews and of domineering jack-booted Zionists, Rendel held up the picture of an Arab world having a latent vitality, now stirring into new activity. The Arabs

> have produced, and are still producing, great leaders, and are capable of a patriotism, which it may be unwise to ignore and difficult to suppress. There is a growing number of Arab nationalist leaders in Syria, Egypt and Iraq, and the example and prestige of Saudi Arabia, the guardian State of the Holy Places of Islam, may yet prove a formidable force.

Since political boundaries in the area were for the most part 'artificial post-war creations', what happened in Palestine would immediately influence 'opinion' in other parts of the Arab world, which look upon Palestine as an Arab country 'being treacherously handed over to an alien and particularly dangerous invader'.

No one in the Office questioned Rendel's judgments or enquired whether the evidence did indeed show that Jews in Palestine were predominantly German in culture, or that they might provide a base for German activities in the Middle East. Neither was Rendel's vision of an Arab world led by 'great leaders' and moving in unison under their inspiration compared with the facts, which indicated internal weakness and instability, an increasingly strident style of ideological politics, and great mistrust—not to say downright hatred—that kept Arab rulers at arm's length from, if not at daggers drawn with, one another. Nor was any doubt thrown over Rendel's confident prophecy (in his memorandum of 3 November, cited above)—made in the teeth of the armistice of October 1936 and its ruinous consequences—that, if only partition were abandoned, there would be an immediate relaxation of tension in Palestine. It is not hindsight which leads one to ask why such doubts occurred to no one in the Foreign Office. The facts which might give rise to such doubts were known at the time. If, then, the political and official heads of the Foreign Office remained unaware of the facts, or did not work out their implications, this would seem to argue for a serious intellectual and organizational failure in a central department of state. Perhaps the only shadow of doubt cast over Rendel's judgment and on the policy hitherto followed under his inspiration—and even then the evidence is ambiguous—may be found in a passage which occurs in Vansittart's minute on the memorandum of 14 October. 'Partition might have come off,' wrote Vansittart, 'if it had ever got a fair start. But the start was foul, and it will clearly never recover.'[113]

Eden in due course saw Rendel's memoranda of 14 October and 3 November, and it was on his instructions that Rendel drafted the memorandum which he circulated to the Cabinet in reply to Ormsby Gore's of 9 November cited above. Eden's memorandum of 19 November was a compendium of the arguments against partition and against resisting intervention by Arab states in the conflict, which Rendel had agitated during the previous fifteen months or so. British relations with the whole Arab world were made to hinge entirely on the rejection of partition. Even the Yemen played its part in Rendel's advocacy. The reaction in the Yemen to British policy in Palestine was declared to be 'most unfortunate'. The King of the Yemen was represented as having been as anxious as the British government to prevent Italy from establishing herself in his country, but the announcement of the partition scheme had been followed by the conclusion of an Italo-Yemeni treaty and by increasingly cordial relations between the two countries. The Yemeni claim to Aden and the Protectorate had been revived and coincided with the Italians challenging British actions in the area. Eden's memorandum was flanked and buttressed by appendices in which evidence was gathered together and marshalled to show the unanimous opposition of the Arab world to partition. An aide-memoire from Hafez Wahba was called in evidence to show the deadly danger which Ibn Sa'ud ran of being accused by his people of treason should he prevent them from participating in the war against partition. A note from Ibn Sa'ud was also appended in which the King referred to 'the great moral responsibility which we willingly assumed with the consent of our friend, Great Britain', when the appeal of the Arab rulers was published, which brought about the cessation of disturbances in Palestine.[114]

Eden's memorandum elicited a counter-memorandum by Ormsby Gore; and to reply to the points the Colonial Secretary now raised Rendel drafted yet another memorandum which was boiled down by Vansittart and which Eden took with him to the crucial meeting of the Cabinet. In this document Eden was made to assert that if the government announced its intention to proceed with partition,

> the Middle Eastern countries will turn against us and join our enemies. This danger seems to me so grave that I should be neglecting my duty if I did not put it in the forefront of the case for which I am asking my colleagues' support.

Later on in the memorandum a warning was sounded, clearly designed to be as emphatic, as solemn, as blood-chilling as the resources of official English could make it. Partititon would mean the 'total and permanent' alienation of the Muslim countries of the Middle East, and there is no doubt in my mind that, if we persist in our present policy, we shall find one of the most vitally important strategic areas on our line of inter-imperial communications held by definitely hostile States, ready at any moment to join actively in any combination against us.[115]

Ormsby Gore, in response to this heavy artillery, managed a few shots which ought to have been quite telling, but which failed in their effect. The Colonial Secretary was personally a lightweight, and he was in no position to dispute or controvert a case put forward with such strength and authority. Ormsby Gore doubted whether it was possible to argue with any plausibility that, as Eden's memorandum put it, the Middle East was 'an organic whole'. He was not convinced by Eden's argument or by the evidence that there was any 'widespread or permanent feeling' in the Arab countries against partition. He was, of course, right, but his mere assertions unsupported by the kind of evidence to which Eden appealed would not have impressed his colleagues.

Eden's memorandum also argued that partition might not succeed in gaining the consent of the Council of the League of Nations which would have to ratify any change in disposition for a Mandated territory. This argument was based on a memorandum of 12 November by R.M. Makins which gave warning of snags that partition might encounter at Geneva. It is interesting that Rendel's memorandum of 14 October, where the anti-partition arguments were orginally marshalled in expectation of the Cabinet debate, drew a comment from another member of the League of Nations department at the Foreign Office. 'From the Geneva point of view,' R.C.S. Stevenson minuted, 'I have little to say except that there the "Palestine problem" has no real existence as a near Eastern question. With very few and unimportant exceptions it is regarded by League members solely as a European demographic problem.'[116] Such a view was obviously useless to Rendel, and we may suspect that he took steps to elicit a different opinion. Makins declared that if 'forcible partition' was proposed, he foresaw the 'very gravest difficulty' in obtaining the necessary unanimity, and failure was 'very probable'. Though no Arab state was on the Council, Persia would 'no doubt' support Arab views. The British government could rely on no active support, even from the French representative. As regards the Assembly, Makins would view 'with dismay' the possibility of Egypt, Iraq, Turkey and Persia working against Great Britain in Geneva. 'It would, in my opinoin,' he affirmed, 'be far more serious than the possible opposition, which would be confined to this issue, of the States with large Jewish populations, such as Poland and Romania. Such limited opposition would be unlikely to affect the general position of Poland and Roumania, or their relative positions in the balance of power. The alienation of the Mohammedan countries might well be total.' Makins, therefore, on the strength of these speculative, albeit emphatically expressed, views supported Rendel.[117]

These views were, naturally, incorporated in Eden's memorandum, and Ormsby Gore tellingly controverted them. He could do so because he had direct experience of, and could describe authoritatively, the balance of opinion and power at Geneva. The Permanent Mandates Commission, whose opinion carried much weight with the Council, was almost exclusively concerned with the fulfillment of the Balfour Declaration. He pointed out that British policy was criticized not for being unjust to the Arabs, but not for giving enough to the Jews. 'Indeed,' he rightly pointed out, 'the whole tenour of my cross-examination was that we had been weak in the face of Arab aggression.' He also rightly questioned the assertion in the memorandum, based on Makins's briefing, that the French might be opposed to partition, and the other assertion, also based on Makins's advice, that the Persians would give support to Arab views. Neither Persia nor Turkey nor France were likely to encourage Pan-Arab ideals.

Ormsby Gore also queried two central arguments in Eden's memorandum. It was not true, as Eden declared, that the success of the partition scheme was predicated on the assumption that it would be arrived at by general agreement. Neither the Report of the Royal Commission nor the government's Statement of Policy which immediately followed it made any such assumption. Again the Foreign Office paper asserted that the government was now faced 'with solid and growing opposition from the majority of the native inhabitants of Palestine'. Ormsby Gore pointed out that the activities of the terrorists made it impossible to ascertain the trend of opinion in Palestine.

Ormsby Gore's strongest argument was directed against Eden's proposal to subject partition to another scrutiny—a course which meant that decision on Palestine policy was postponed and uncertainty prolonged. To make his point, the Colonial Secretary quoted from a letter he had recently received from the Acting High Commissioner in Palestine:

(a) It is the uncertainty which is causing so much tension here . . .

(b) More delay means more uncertainty and a strengthening of the feeling that His Majesty's Government really do not mean to enforce a scheme of partition.

(c) The East does not understand compromise, but merely accounts it as weakness. It would be damaging to His Majesty's Government's prestige having accepted the arguments in favour of a scheme of partition and having stated that the next step will be the appointment of a Commission to investigate the practical possibilities of such a scheme, if His

Majesty's Government were now to recede from that position. Such a move would be looked upon, not only in Palestine but elsewhere, as a surrender to the gunmen and the assassin, and a triumph for the forces of disorder.[118]

After his defeat by Eden in Cabinet, Ormsby Gore sent a long letter to the Prime Minister in which he tried to explain how he felt about Middle Eastern policy generally. Here he made two points which he might with advantage have stressed in his Cabinet paper and in the Cabinet discussions. These two points, which were largely vindicated by the subsequent course of events, constitute the gravamen of the case against Rendel's (and thus Eden's) policy.

> If we vacillate [Ormsby Gore warned] Arab demands will grow and grow, and Jewish bitterness against us will grow and grow, and our position will become hopeless; and we shall be forced by events to a humiliating withdrawl from Haifa and Jerusalem, and some other power will step in sooner or later.

If partition is carried out, Ormsby Gore also argued, Jewish immigration would cease to be a British obligation, and the Arabs would get the self-government over the greater part of Palestine that they desired:

> So my trouble is that I do not see any practical alternative policy which does not leave us with obligations which can only make our future relations with the Arab world even worse. We shall be out of the frying pan into the fire.

Neville Chamberlain sent this letter on to Eden, who referred it to Rendel, who wrote a long minute reciting yet once more how a Jewish state would be 'partly Communist or partly Germanic', how Ibn Sa'ud was not to be bought, and how the only way to secure Arab friendship and confidence, regain and retain continuing friendship with the Muslims of India, safeguard inter-imperial communications, oil supplies and prestige was by preventing partition in Palestine. Eden then minuted that he was not impressed with Ormsby Gore's arguments, and no reply was necessary.[119]

The decisive Cabinet meeting in which Rendel's triumph was consecrated took place on 8 December 1937. The minutes record that Eden stated flatly that 'Without this difficulty over Palestine he was able to view the whole of the Middle East as being in a peaceful condition.' Partition was 'very inconvenient'. He wanted to make clear that partition would not be enforced irrespective of the opposition offered to it. He desired the new Commission (being appointed to devise a scheme of partition) to be enabled to hear opinions that partition was unworkable, or to say so themselves. The Prime Minister, who opened the discussion with a long statement, was clearly on Eden's side, and his support seems to have been decisive. He realized that if partition were immediately abandoned, the government would be criticized for having surrendered to threats and force.

More especially, it would much

> embarrass people who had brought themselves with difficulty to accept the policy. We had not, in his view, yet reached a point where we could say that it would be folly to go on with the policy of partition.

It was clearly the purpose of the new Commission to enable the government, after a decent interval, to reach precisely such a point. Here, a timely intervention by Sir Thomas Inskip, Minister for Co-ordination of Defence, enabled the Prime Minister to find a safe and convenient way of ensuring this result. Inskip pointed out that if he himself were a member of the Commission he would want to know the mind of the government on this issue. The point need not necessarily be made in the text of the public despatch in which the new Commission and its terms of reference were to be announced, but the Cabinet ought to know its own mind on the subject. Chamberlain then ingeniously suggested that this point could be covered by a personal communication to the Chairman of the Commission. And, in fact, this was precisely one of the decisions taken by the Cabinet that day. And in due course Ormsby Gore had to address a secret and personal letter to the Chairman of the new Commission, the terms of which were approved by the Foreign Office, inviting the Commission to indicate, should it be 'driven' to such a conclusion, that partition was unworkable, even though this was not part of their official, public remit.

Ormsby Gore, then, was defeated. He acknowledged defeat and surrendered with a characteristically fudged statement that tried to avoid a clear-cut decision. He advocated, therefore, that the minutes record 'that the Despatch [announcing the new Commission] should be re-drafted and that we should make clear that we intended to continue the policy of partition and could see no alternative; but it must be done in such a way as to leave the door open for the Commission to say, if necessary, that a workable plan could not be devised.' This, a triumphant Rendel noted in the margin, was a contradiction in terms.

It is interesting and ironical that one supporter of Ormsby Gore in the Cabinet was Malcolm MacDonald, who was shortly afterwards to succeed him at the Colonial Office and who was to adopt all the features of the Rendelian policy: the abandonment of partition, the limitation of Jewish immigration, and the full involvement of the Arab states in the affairs of Palestine. At this Cabinet however, MacDonald (then Dominions Secretary) declared that he personally

> would take a lot of convincing that partition was not the least objectionable solution. There was no other solution that met the

Arab difficulties as well as those of the Jews. Any change of policy would create a storm against the Government . . . We should be accused of vacillation and weakness. Nevertheless he agreed that it was necessary to proceed cautiously. He would not give an impression of running away from partition, but would leave the door open to the Commission which was to examine possible schemes of partition to say if it found it impossible to devise one. He would, however, leave the door open [MacDonald was careful to say] only a very little.[120]

Partition was dead. But Rendel maintained his vigilance. One of the Cabinet decisions had been that Ormsby Gore should re-draft the despatch announcing the new Commission in consultation with a number of Ministers, including the Foreign Secretary. Rendel drafted the list of changes required by the Foreign Office and haggled with tenacity over every word. At one point Cranborne, perhaps in order to avert bad blood among ministerial colleagues, had to intervene in order to moderate his relentless campaign to plug up every conceivable loophole and banish every possible ambiguity.[121] He also went on advocating territorial concessions in Arabia to Ibn Sa'ud in order to make sure of his friendship which, on his own logic, the abandonment of partition ought anyway to have amply ensured.[122] Even when he was no longer Head of the Eastern Department, he strove to ensure that the pro-partition dogs should be trounced and sent into headlong flight. He volunteered (and Halifax, the new Foreign Secretary, accepted the offer) to indoctrinate the Partition Commission in the heinousness of partition, and he wrote a long, anonymous memorandum which Halifax tried to persuade the Colonial Secretary to circulate to the Commissioners.[123] Rendel's heirs in the Eastern Department were certain that the abandonment of partition would inaugurate a new heaven and a new earth. In September 1938 MacDonald had a conversation with Weizmann about the impending report of the Partition Commission. At one point Weizmann said it would be extremely unfortunate if the Jewish Agency had to break off relations with the British government, their best friends in the world at the moment. Baggallay annotated this passage to the effect that 'they will be fools if they do, but it would be a great relief to us'. Ever the careful civil servant, however, Baggallay thought better of this too frank utterance, crossed out 'would', and substituted the more judicious and non-commital 'might'. But there can be no mistaking his jubilation: the demise of partition, he minuted, 'would certainly make the taking of the next step easier.'[124]

The next step was also something for which Rendel had pertinaciously worked, namely the open and official involvement of the Arab states in the affairs of Palestine. When the Report of the Partition Commission appeared in October 1938, the government hastened to say that in the view of the insuperable difficulties raised by any scheme of partition, a new way of settling the conflict would now be pursued. A conference of Arabs and Jews would be called at which, perhaps, an acceptable compromise might be reached. The character of this conference was decided at a Cabinet Committee on Palestine which met on 24 October 1938, with the Prime Minister presiding. MacDonald declared in this Committee that

> a settlement of the Palestine problem would never be reached if we treated Palestine in isolation, and a satisfactory solution would only be found if Palestine was treated as a part of the Middle East. If this was true then the sooner we took steps to secure the good-will and co-operation of responsible persons in the countries contiguous to Palestine the sooner would a settlement be reached.

Chamberlain approved: 'Palestine had now become a Pan Arab question and the "Arab Princes" would be more likely to form a united front if they were omitted from the conference than if they were invited to attend it.' The die was cast, and Great Britain in effect here surrendered control and initiative in Palestine, and went into partnership with a collection of querulous and unreliable client states. There was a dissenting voice at the Cabinet Committee of 24 October, that of Sir John Simon who, in September 1936, had presided over the meeting of Ministers which decided to have nothing to do with mediation by Arab rulers. The reversal of this decision, it will be recalled, inaugurated the fatal peripeties here recounted. Simon now uttered words of caution and warning which the sequel was seen fully to justify.

> It should [he said] . . . be remembered that His Majesty's Government would have just announced their intention to continue their responsibility for the Government of the whole of Palestine and that it was proposed to follow up this very definite announcement by inviting representatives of a number of foreign Governments to confer with them on the problem of the future administration of Palestine. If the Conference proved a success no great harm would have been done, but if the Conference proved a failure and broke up without any result it would then have been placed on record that the Governments of these foreign countries were in disagreement with the solution proposed by His Majesty's Government. While he did not see how we could avoid inviting these Arab representatives from outside Palestine, he felt that the implication of so doing should be realised in advance.[125]

What is so remarkable, and so ominous for British interests in the area, is that this warning—which was not heeded—had to come from a Minister outside the Foreign Office, and that, whether by Ministers or by officials of this great department of state, not a memorandum, not a despatch, not a minute exists which shows that these implications were thought of, let alone examined.

9

SUEZ REVISITED

The literature of the Suez expedition of 1956 is now very large, but even so the episode is far from being fully understood. Crucial decisions in London, Paris and Washington remain obscure, as do the motives and calculations of some of the main figures. The puzzles that remain will perhaps not be solved until official records and private archives become available. But if we do now have some understanding of the events which followed the nationalization of the Canal, it is to the memoirs and personal accounts of protagonists and observers published during the last two decades that we are mostly indebted. Their revelations and self-revelations, however, themselves raise new questions and sometimes give new twists to old puzzles. The last two or three years have seen the publication of a new batch of memoirs written by some of those who were most closely concerned with the political decisions or the military operations. Apart from the new light which they succeed in throwing on various decisions and incidents, what these new works chiefly do is to enhance further the sense of irony which the Suez expedition has all along evoked. They also impress on one the difficulties of military action conducted by allies and, above all, make it even more apparent that the expedition and its failures constituted a fateful turning-point in the affairs not only of Britain and France but also of the whole Western world.

That Nasser's action was a grave challenge to their interests and prestige was the strong and immediate reaction of the British and French governments. MacMillan emphatically put it to Dulles at the beginning of August 1956 that it was 'a question not of honour only but of survival'. As we learn from Selwyn Lloyd's memoirs, *Suez 1956: A Personal Account*, Sir Ivone Kirkpatrick, Permanent Under Secretary at the Foreign Office, spelled out the ominous consequences of Nasser's coup as they were seen at the highest level in London. If we sat back while Nasser consolidated his position, Kirkpatrick wrote to the British Ambassador in Washington a month later, he could eventually wreck us by getting control of the oil-bearing states. This would lead to financial ruin and we should not be able to pay for the minimum defense that was required. And a country that could not provide for its own defense was finished. There can be no doubt that Kirkpatrick's estimate of the consequences for Britain and her allies of losing control of the Middle East was right, even though this was to become clear only some two decades later, and even though this loss of control was self-inflicted and operated to the prodigious benefit of states which, in point of power, were puny and insignificant when compared even to Nasser's Egypt.

But the question arises: if the consequences of Nasser's challenge were so dire, how did the British government contrive to trap itself in this awkward and perilous position? Nasser could do what he did because Britain had agreed in 1954 to evacuate the Canal Zone, without obtaining in return securities which were more than formal or indeed more than purely illusory. It is, of course, true that the position in the Canal Zone was given up following heavy pressure by Eisenhower and Dulles, who believed that the British should be—to use Eisenhower's delicate euphemism—'encouraged' to go, in the belief that this would perhaps secure Nasser's friendship and benevolence. But American pressure was not responsible for British unpreparedness in the Eastern Mediterranean—an unpreparedness which made it impossible to retaliate swiftly against Nasser. In his memoirs, Selwyn Lloyd observes that Malta, the only deep-water harbour available to Britain was six days' sailing from Port Said, but he accepts no blame for Mediterranean geography. Why then was it agreed to evacuate the Canal Zone before making ready a deep-water harbour in Cyprus? How otherwise could the Eastern Mediterranean be controlled in an emergency? Again, during the debates in the House of Commons on the Anglo-Egyptian agreement, Eden argued that evacuation of the Canal Zone would transform the 80,000 British troops in Egypt from a useless 'beleaguered garrison' into a mobile strategic reserve. The last British troops left Egypt in June 1956, and the following month Nasser nationalized the Canal. Far from a mobile strategic reserve being ready for instant use, the most laborious, elaborate and time-consuming preparations had to be made before a force could be fitted out and made ready to mount an assault upon the Egyptians.

For this mismanagement, responsibility must lie at the highest political level. But beyond the issue of military prudence, there is another, more important, and more precisely political, failure. In the account of his Cairo embassy (*The Middle East in Revolution*, 1970) Lord Trevelyan remarked that the main cause of deterioration in Anglo-Egyptian relations during the spring of 1956 was the Baghdad Pact. There is little doubt that he is right. In promoting the Pact Britain made a choice between Arab states who were ranged in different camps, who were indeed at daggers drawn with one another. To choose alliance with Iraq was automatically to alienate Egypt, and the contrary would also probably have been true. Were these alternatives considered, and the costs, as well as the advantages, of the Baghdad Pact policy taken into the reckoning? Was it at all perceived that a choice had to be made between Iraq and Egypt? And if the decision was taken that the greater advantage lay in choosing Iraq, why then at the same time gratuitously increase Egypt's ability to do damage by giving her unfettered control over the Canal Zone?

None of the memoirs published so far give any inkling that this fundamental question was faced, or that the steps which a hostile Egypt might take and the way to counter them were considered. In his memoirs Lloyd quotes a message which he sent to the Egyptian press on the occasion of the Egyptian National Day following the withdrawal of the last British troops from Suez. In this message he denied that it was British policy 'to isolate Egypt and deprive her of her legitimate place in the Arab world'. He adduced, in proof, British support for the foundation of the Arab League, and, he went on, 'we have every interest in promoting unity and co-operation between Arab States'. Taken at face value this rhetoric indicated either insincerity or muddle, since it ignored or brushed aside inter-Arab rivalries and enmities that experience showed a realistic Middle-Eastern policy had to reckon with. Such professions could only arouse the suspicion or contempt of those whom they were meant to persuade.

Selwyn Lloyd's memoirs disclose an even more deep-seated muddle. In the space of two pages he advances two incompatible justifications for the Suez expedition. He compares it on the one hand with the decision to go to war in 1914, a decision taken because 'it was contrary to the national interest for Germany to be allowed to subjugate France and acquire a complete hegemony in Continental Europe'. But, on the other hand he declares that he agrees 'almost exactly' with the view of Professor Gilbert Murray, who had been shocked by Nasser's 'irregular' action, but then relieved to find that, happily a UN 'police force' was now established which 'should proceed to discharge its functions of maintaining the law'. A Conservative Minister should have known better than to confuse the logic of the national interest with the logic of that fantasy world which, with Tolkien-like imaginativeness, Professor Murray had conjured up at the end of the first world war and continued thereafter to inhabit. Things are what they are: if the Suez expedition was in the national interest, then Hammarskjöld's 'police force' showing the door to British and French troops was a defeat for the national interest. Why should we deceive ourselves?

The same failure to engage with reality—a failure which became manifest in British Conservatism during this century—may be seen in Eden. Lloyd quotes with approval Eden's statement in the House of Commons on 1 November 1956 to the effect that if the United Nations were willing to take over the physical task of maintaining peace in the Middle East, 'no one would be better pleased than we'. This kind of talk, of course, took in nobody, but it may not, for all this be dismissed as mere words. In a constitutional and parliamentary regime words are the currency of politics;

if, as happens in banana republics, what is said comes to bear little or no relation to what is done, public discourse is corrupted, the public credit is injured and citizens grow contemptuous of their rulers. Suez was a defeat and a humiliation for Britain, but the British had enough pride and self-confidence in 1956 to look this setback squarely in the face. There was no need for their rulers to talk as though this defeat was really a victory, as though British troops had returned to Egypt only to make straight in the desert a highway for Hammarskjöld.

There was here, then, on the part of the Prime Minister intellectual weakness as well as a failure of leadership. As an epigraph to his book, *The Rise and Fall of Sir Anthony Eden*, Randolph Churchill quoted some famous words of Tacitus in order to apply them to his subject. Eden, we are given to understand, would have been universally deemed *capax imperii* had he not actually exercised power. But on Churchill's own showing the capacity to wield supreme power had never been evident in Eden's record. Churchill exhibits him as intellectually mediocre, as steadily advancing in position and honours simply by eschewing anything adventurous or original, and making his name by espousing the cause of the League and of 'collective security'—frivolities with which European leaders distracted their peoples on the way to catastrophe. On this view, Churchill was right to argue that Eden bears his share with Simon, Hoare, Halifax and others for the smash-up of August 1939. And it is true, as Cadogan remarked in his *Diaries*, that the first fatal turning which led to the catastrophe three years later was taken while Eden was Foreign Secretary, when Hitler's remilitarization of the Rhineland was allowed to go unchallenged. This record would scarcely justify the notion that Eden was *capax imperii*. It is anyway ironical that the League of Nations launched him on his career, while the United Nations was the instrument of its ruin.

Other ironies abound. Eden was Foreign Secretary at the time of the Anglo-Egyptian Treaty of 1936, a consequence of which had been to deliver the Egyptian people to two corrupt tyrannies, that of the royal palace and that of the Wafd, who between them alternated in misgoverning Egypt, and finally opened the way to a military *coup d'état*. This treaty was the final abdication of responsibility for the welfare of Egypt—a responsibility which had justified the British presence after 1882. Eden was again Foreign Secretary when the Treaty of 1954 was negotiated which, as has been said, left substantial British interests in Egypt and its vicinity without any real security. Furthermore, during the war he had publicly encouraged moves towards Arab unity in the hope no doubt that Britain would find profitable its role as patron and protector of this movement. And here he was now, taking on the most important member of the Arab League. Again, fate decreed that he should do so in collaboration, in 'collusion' as the *bien-pensants* said, with Israel, while he had been, at the time of the Peel Commission, a powerful and determined opponent of a Jewish state in Palestine, and subsequently remained, in the words of Oliver Harvey (his private secretary at the Foreign Office during the war) 'immovable on the subject of Palestine', 'blindly pro-Arab', 'lov[ing] Arabs and hat[ing] Jews'.

Harvey's *War Diaries* disclose to the observer another ironical twist in Eden's fate as a political figure. He was, we learn, sympathetic to Labour. On one occasion he even confided to Harvey that he hated 'the old Tories' and 'would rather join the Labour Party if they remained dominant'. Too much, of course, should not be made of these confidences uttered at a time when political alignments, like so much else, were in flux. But his views in the post-war do show that the sentiments Harvey recorded were not a flash in the pan. These views in respect of economy and society were what is known as moderate. They conformed to the cozy and lenitive Butskellism which Conservatives in the '50s persuaded themselves would take all the bother and difficulty out of governing. That he of all people should now be the butt of a most ferocious assault by Labour, that he should be denounced as an extremist and war-monger partook, therefore, of the general unfairness of things. In his memoirs, *1956 Suez,* Christian Pineau, then French Foreign Minister, has a passage which felicitously sums up the painful irony of Eden's fate.

> *Cet homme* [he writes], *auquel on peut appliquer le rare quali-ficatif de 'charmant', était une sorte de Nehru britannique, en plus fragile. Merveilleux diplomate, il n'était pas fait comme Chur-chill pour être Premier ministre au cours d'une grave crise internationale. Il n'avait pas pour cela le célèbre entêtement britannique, cette manière dure et rugueuse qui donne aux peuples menacés un sentiment de paternelle protection.*

From the very beginning Nasser's challenge was understood—rightly—to go beyond the simple nationalization of a commercial company. But it remained the case that it was the take-over of the Suez Canal Co. that constituted the *casus belli*. In the ensuing political and military crisis the specific issues raised by this take-over, and by the circumstances surround-ing it, came somehow to be relegated to the background. But these issues are by no means negligible, and a book devoted to them, written by the then Director-General of the Suez Canal Co., Jacques Georges-Picot, *La Véritable crise de Suez*, proves to be one of the more interesting and enlightening works in the literature. Georges-Picot's account raises two issues, both of primary importance. The first relates to the Anglo-French strategy in the days immediately following nationalization. As is well known, the Canal continued to function, the Company having asked its pilots to stay at their posts. Georges-Picot declared that he believed this at the time to be a mistake, and that the proper course of action would have been for the Company immediately to cease operations and bring the Canal to a halt, while the British and French would simultaneously launch a lightning operation against Nasser. But both the British and the French governments, he declares, insisted that the Company should carry on and maintain full services. Then suddenly in September the two governments decided to allow the Company to withdraw its pilots. Neither Pineau nor Lloyd controvert Georges-Picot's account. As he says, it is not clear why the decision to withdraw pilots was taken at that time, since there were then no impending military operations. But by the time the pilots were withdrawn Nasser had been able to recruit pilots of his own and could then maintain the service uninterrupted and rebut the Anglo-French claim that the Egyptians were incapable of operating the Canal. The whole episode showed a fumbling and unsure touch, but as Georges-Picot also suspects, it indicates that the British and French governments did not want the Canal closed when Nasser took it over as this would mean petrol rationing. But petrol rationing was precisely what had to be immediately ordained in order to show Nasser and the world that the British and French governments were in earnest. To have flinched from it was the first, fatal sign of the irresolution which Dulles encouraged and exploited, and which led to bitter humiliation at the end of the year.

The other, even more important, issue that arises out of Georges-Picot's book relates to the status of the Suez Canal and the interests of the Suez Canal Co. In 1951, and again in 1952 following the *coup d'état* in Egypt, Georges-Picot raised the question of the Canal Convention of 1888 and suggested that the impending termination of the Suez Canal Co. concession, as well as the changed international conditions, required new arrangements and securities to preserve the international character of the Canal and protect its functioning against local disturbances and politically motivated interference. The French government, however, considered that these matters were more the affair of the British, whose shipping was the predominant user and who owned 43 percent of the shares. But the British— as well as the Americans—were in favour of letting sleeping dogs lie, for fear that a negotiation over these issues would give the Soviets an opening to interfere in the Middle East. Between caution and timidity there is a very thin line, and it was crossed when the Anglo-Egyptian Treaty was signed in 1954 without the Convention of 1888 being brought into the negotiation. For, after all, if fear of Soviet interference dictated the response to Georges-Picot's proposal in 1951 and 1952, what, one might ask, was there to prevent the Egyptians, once free of a British garrison, from establishing whatever relations they pleased with the Soviets?

The question of the Company was distinct from that of the Convention. As has been said, the British government was a major shareholder, but more than half of the shares were held by private individuals and institutions. Nasser's action meant a violent and arbitrary disturbance of private property. If the French government, a socialist one, did not much care to defend French investors, this interference with property should have been considered an undesirable, indeed a dangerous precedent by the Conservative government in Britain, and the United States government should have been just as attached to the defense of property. Yet, as Georges-Picot shows, the Company was held at arm's length, as though the governments to whom it was entitled to look for protection were ashamed to have anything to do with a successful commercial enterprise. Georges-Picot declares that in a conversation of 1955 the British Ambassador in Cairo 'ne me cacha pas que le Gouvernement britannique n'entendait aucunement intervenir directement pour faciliter les affaires de la Compagnie'. Following nationalization, the French and the Americans made it clear that they were opposed to the restoration of the Company's rights, and as Selwyn Lloyd himself writes, 'the British Government was anxious that it should not seem to be fighting only for the shareholders'; to work for 'a new international company or authority' was likely to be more acceptable to 'underdeveloped countries'. At the London Conference in August the Company was not even given the status of 'observer'. Also, as is well known, the US refused to advise or instruct ships of American registry to pay their dues to the Company which, by a unilateral fiat, had been so suddenly expropriated. What is more, the accounts held by the Company and by a subsidiary in American banks were by official order frozen until 1958. Ironically, though Egyptian official accounts as they stood at nationalization were placed in escrow, new accruals (partly arising out of Canal dues) were never frozen, nor were Egyptian private accounts. And the official accounts were partially released from restrictions in November 1957. US official behaviour over these issues, whatever the immediate calculations that prompted it, was ominous for the investment of private capital in poor and economically backward countries. Historically, it was this investment that had done most to increase the productivity, and hence the material prosperity of these countries. What the United States was now doing was increasing the vulnerability of this kind of enterprise, and joining, so to speak, in the Bolshevik chorus of hostility which, for decades now, had been directed against it. Its actions, in other words, were ultimately inimical to the economic order that underpinned American society, and helpful to the spread of *dirigisme* in those parts of the world which were not already under the sway or influence of the Soviets.

Were the Americans aware of the ultimate consequences of their policies? Georges-Picot reports a meeting in May 1954 with Henry Byroade, then Assistant Secretary in charge of the Middle East at the Department of State, and subsequently Ambassador in Egypt. Byroade declared that his Department was in favour of the rapid evacuation of Egypt by the British army

> *qui permettrait peut-être ensuite un rapprochement de l'Egypte avec l'Occident! Il ne méconnaissait ni l'instabilité du Gouverne- ment égyptien ni la croissance d'un nationalisme aveugle, ni même celle de l'influence communiste. Il ne niait pas les risques que courait le trafic du Canal; mais n'en estimait pas moins que l'évacuation britannique était pour le moment le seul imperatif de sa politique.*

Selwyn Lloyd likewise testifies to the singleness of purpose—or perhaps of vision—shown by American officials, both in Washington and in the Middle East in the early 1950s: 'McGhee, an Oklahoma millionaire, had steadily undermined our position in the Middle East'; 'Acheson was pursuing us all the time to settle with Musaddiq, on the ground that if he fell, the next Iranian leader would be much worse'; Sweeney, the American liaison officer in the Sudan 'was outspokenly anti-British. His favourite theme ... was that Britain had done nothing for the Sudan, and we were finished anyhow'; 'the McGhees in Iran, the Sweeneys in the Sudan, the Cafferys in Cairo, Aramco in Saudi Arabia, had shown themselves openly anti-British. Herbert Hoover Junior, the Under-Secretary of State, was thoroughly anti-British ... '.

British ministers, then, would have been aware of the unfriendliness of US policy in Egypt and elsewhere in the Middle East, and should have expected little sympathy when Nasser nationalized the Canal. Yet they seem to have assumed that in a quarrel with Egypt, the United States would be on their side. This was Eden's assumption, and MacMillan's, and Selwyn Lloyd's. Their ground for such an assumption seemed, however, reasonable. For the whole sequence of events had been triggered by Dulles who, suddenly and without consultation, decided to withdraw an offer to finance the Aswan dam project. This could mean, *prima facie*, that Dulles was hostile to Nasser because of his friendship with the Soviet Union, that Dulles was eager to diminish and discredit him. Reasonable as this assumption was, Dulles's behaviour soon afterwards showed that it was a faulty one. In his memoirs Selwyn Lloyd considers that the real reason for Dulles's action was simply electoral tactics. Dulles thought that a Reso- lution from the Congress limiting the Administration's power to finance projects like the Aswan dam—and opposition in Congress to that project made this a possibility—would have been damaging in the presidential election campaign. Lloyd may be right, but clearly this explanation of Dulles's behaviour either did not occur to ministers in the summer and autumn of 1956, or was not given much importance.

And yet Dulles's actions during this period were not such as to inspire confidence in his allies. For his initial discussions with Eden at the beginning of August, he came to London accompanied by the legal advisor to the State Department; 'and the two lawyers', Robert Murphy writes, 'had devised various delaying tactics designed to support Eisenhower's policy of avoiding military intervention'. It should have been clear quite early that Dulles, with all the ingenuity of a pettifogging attorney, was trying to drown the issue, as the British and French understood it, in a flood of specious *chinoiseries*. What his oblique proceedings indicated indirectly was also perhaps to be grasped directly from the language of his subordinates. Thus during the London Conference in August Georges-Picot 'found Murphy more than ever opposed to any policy which would not give Egypt complete satisfaction', and he understood that Dulles's policy was to catch his allies in the quicksand of internationalization and thus prevent any attempt to compel Nasser to go back on what he had done.

It is of course natural to ask what Dulles had in view in following this policy. That he and Eden were not on good terms does not explain much. That there was a standing anti-imperial prejudice in political and official circles in Washington may be taken for granted, but it was only a prejudice, no more than a disposition to favour some kind of policy and to put up resistance to others. That Eisenhower wanted nothing untoward to happen in the run to the presidential election is also no doubt the case, but this begs the question rather than answers it. For the question is this: why should he think it untoward for one foreign—albeit allied—country to take forcible action against another foreign country in response to what, *prima facie* at any rate, was a provocation? Why, to put the question in terms that Murphy uses, did Eisenhower labour under the conviction that if he took no action to deflect the British and the French from military action, he would be allowing the US to be 'used as a cat's paw to protect British oil interests'? The answer is that Eisenhower was operating according to a doctrine which made it seem politically dangerous and morally heinous for a country like Britain or France to try conclusions with a country like Egypt. Whatever its origin, whether in the State Department, or in the academico-political complex—compared with which the celebrated military-industrial complex (to which Eisenhower, with a deliciously modish Marxism, used to refer) has proved to be but a dumb and blundering Goliath—the doctrine may be found itemized in the President's missives to Eden as printed in the second volume of Eisenhower's White House memoirs which, with evident self-satisfaction, he entitled *Waging Peace*.

From the outset and throughout the duration of the crisis, Eisenhower kept on insisting that the use of force against Nasser should not be even contemplated unless and until every possible resource of the United Nations had been exhausted. This was to argue as though the conflict between Egypt and the British and French were a dispute between private parties and that the United Nations were a kind of court that would listen to both parties and adjudicate according to the law. But the UN is not a court of law. It is an organization in which states vie with one another for power and influence and where they speak and vote strictly in accordance with their interests. Neither the Security Council, nor the bear-garden which the General Assembly was even then bidding fair to become, could be reasonably expected without fear or favour to decide on an issue on its merits. Why then should the British and the French consent to take on the role of guinea-pig in order to prove a self-evident truth?

Eisenhower, too, invoked 'world opinion', which he claimed to be largely on Nasser's side. More specifically, he affirmed that 'the people of the Near East and of North Africa and, to some extent, of all of Asia and all of Africa, would be consolidated against the West to a degree which, I fear, could not be overcome in a generation and, perhaps, not even in a century'. These were manifestly speculative, indeed extravagant, asseverations. 'World opinion' is an inherently incoherent notion, and scarcely less so is the view that 'all of Asia and all of Africa' could be, or would long remain, of one opinion on anything whatever. Furthermore, to speak at all of public opinion assumes the existence of free and constitutional polities, where political leaders who have to reckon with it must learn how to decipher, and take advantage of, its ambiguous and enigmatic deliverances. Eisenhower was of course the leader of such a polity, and had, in prudence, to take US public opinion into account. Even so, he was wildly exaggerating when he told Eden that 'American public opinion flatly rejects the thought of using force'. There was simply no evidence of an emphatic unanimity such that the President had no option but to bow to it. In any case, the force which was likely to be used was not American, but British and French. Did Americans really have passionate objections to British and French soldiers fighting a pro-Soviet ruler, whose extreme and insulting language about the US was still fresh in people's minds? The improbabilities lurking in the President's arguments should not lead us to think that he was being insincere. It is more likely that he did really believe the world to be as he described it. He may really have thought that in the contest with the Soviet Union, the way to make sure of Asia and Africa was to 'wage peace'. To do Eisenhower justice, he was only taking a leaf from his Soviet rivals; but the 'Partisans of Peace', as everyone including the Soviets knew, were only a front whose rhetoric could not possibly be mistaken for the substance of politics.

For Eisenhower, however, the rhetoric and the substance seemed identical. Force, he declared flatly, would 'vastly increase the area of jeopardy'. He envisaged a 'general Arab war' and 'prolonged military operations' the burden of which on Western Europe would be increased by the denial of Middle East oil. All these propositions were far removed from reality. Egypt was not a power that could sustain prolonged military operations. The Arab states were neither able nor willing to combine in a general war on behalf of a ruler whom many of them mistrusted or even hated. The use of force does not always 'increase the area of jeopardy': Eisenhower's own world would have been in mortal jeopardy had force not been used to defeat Hitler. But for one reason or another Eisenhower frightened himself into believing that his country's allies were compromising and undesirable acquaintances who had to be cut dead in public, and various declarations by him, Dulles, and Cabot Lodge at the United Nations clearly had this effect. Even Casey, an Australian Foreign Minister (who actually happened to disapprove of the Suez expedition) was thought too contaminated—had not Egypt severed diplomatic relations with Australia?—for the President to afford to receive him.

Panic, least of all in a Superpower, is not a pretty sight. Even less so when it is the outcome of a systematic misjudgment of reality. However, the world is not so arranged that mean-spiritedness or a consistent misreading of the situation necessarily and always attract the penalties they deserve. But in this case they did. The evil consequences touched not only the friends and allies of the US, and the Egyptian people who had to endure Nasser's yoke for another 14 years, they also affected the US itself, whose championship of Nasser naturally neither secured his friendship nor halted the steady spread of Soviet influence or of political rot in the Arab world. What Eisenhower did achieve was to strike a blow against the Fourth Republic, and pave the way for de Gaulle, who proceeded severely to cripple NATO.

If Suez was considered to affect both survival and honour, then it had to be met with resolution. And it is generally agreed that such was the immediate response of the government. At a Cabinet held on 27 July the decision to use force in the last resort was unanimous, and the Chiefs of Staff instructed accordingly. But from then on, we see hesitation, divided counsels, and confusion at the highest level regarding purposes and plans. The detail of what took place between August and November is controverted and still in many respects highly obscure, but the criticisms which a famous leading article in *The Daily Telegraph* levelled in January 1956 against Eden's domestic policies apply with remarkable exactitude to his handling of the Suez affair a few months later: here too the record unmistakably shows 'changes of mind by the Government; half measures; and the postponement of decisions'.

We learn from Selwyn Lloyd that on 3 August the Chiefs of Staff submitted four alternative plans: to launch an attack on Port Said only, to launch 'limited operations' on Port Said and follow with a major assault on Alexandria, to conduct limited operations at Alexandria and launch a major assault on Port Said, or finally, to 'launch a full-scale assault on Alexandria, seizing port and airfield, followed by an advance to the Suez Canal via the Cairo area'. The Egypt Committee of the Cabinet considered these alternatives on 10 August, and decided on the last one as being 'easier and safer'. 'Although it would take longer to reach the Canal,' Lloyd writes, 'it might deal with Nasser more quickly.' It is clear from this language that the objective, then, was to do away with Nasser's regime, not simply to deal with the narrow issue of the Canal. Indeed MacMillan tells us in his memoirs that he himself was against a mere re-occupation of the Canal; what he was seeking was the rapid emergence in Cairo of a friendly Egyptian government. The choice of a descent on Alexandria and a march on Cairo shows that the Egypt Committee agreed with him.

It would appear, however, that all through Eden was the prey of hesitations and misgivings. General Beaufre, visiting London on 10 August (the very day the Egypt Committee decided in favour of the Alexandria plan) was told by General Stockwell that the Prime Minister was opposed to such a plan because it would be difficult to justify politically. However, the plan was eventually approved, and the landings scheduled to take place on 15 September. On 22 August this was postponed to 19 September, in order to await the outcome of the Menzies mission to Cairo, and of a possible reference to the Security Council; on 28 August there was a further postponement to 26 September, 'for the same reasons', Lloyd writes; on 4 September the Chiefs of Staff declared that 9 October was the final date by which a landing in Alexandria could be made, but this, Lloyd writes 'was still too early a date', since the outcome of Dulles's proposals for a Canal Users' Association would not be known by then. The Chiefs of Staff were told to prepare a new plan. Lloyd cites these delays to disprove 'the theory that we were longing for the chance to use force'. These successive postponements were made 'in the hope that the pressure of international opinion would make Nasser see sense'. To adapt a remark by Cardinal de Retz, when the sword has not been drawn, plenty of reasons will be on hand later on to show that it was virtuous not to have drawn it. By the beginning of September, was it not clear that the Americans were prevaricating, and were the postponements, therefore, not a sign of infirmity of purpose? Can the Foreign Secretary and his colleagues really have believed that 'pressure of international opinion' would do for them what they were reluctant to do for themselves?

The new plan which the Chiefs of Staff were told to prepare was approved by the Cabinet on 11 September. Its character shows that, whether this was realized or not, a change of objectives had now taken place. The intent was no longer to go directly and speedily from Alexandria to Cairo in order to topple Nasser, which at the beginning of August had been the purpose of the expedition. The plan now was to land in Port Said and secure the Canal. But secure it for what purpose? We learn from Beaufre (*L'expédition de Suez,* 1967) that the idea of a landing in Port Said was being mooted in the second half of August by Admiral Barjot, the Commander-in-Chief of the French Expeditionary Force. This admiral, *'plus politique que marin',* as Abel Thomas describes him, was now saying let the British go to Alexandria and let us go ourselves to Port Said; we will seize it as a pawn, stay there as long as necessary, negotiate at leisure and get what we want.

Lloyd is not forthcoming about the considerations that led to the change in plan, but it is clear that they were more political than military. If a landing at Alexandria was difficult or impracticable past a given date, the same would be even truer of a landing at Port Said. Perhaps the notion of seizing a pawn with which to bargain, which may have originated with Barjot, now seemed less risky than a frontal assault on Nasser's regime; perhaps it was thought more prudent to draw the sword only halfway. And to do it in slow motion. For the plan as Lloyd describes it was to have three stages: first, the neutralization of the Egyptian air force, then a few days of aero-psychological bombardment, and only then the occupation of Port Said and the Canal by airborne and seaborne troops. The purpose of a battle is to obtain a decisive victory—and this plan had built into it a fatal indecisiveness. It had been better had the sword never been drawn at all. The plan, it is true, was drawn up by military men, but the soldiers were responding to the divided counsels and the hesitations of their masters. Other features of the plan and of its execution contributed to the final failure. In their memoirs the French participants comment on the complication and ponderousness of the integrated Anglo-French command, particularly as it was at any moment subject to directives from London and Paris over the detailed conduct of operations. Baeyens, who was Barjot's political adviser, declares categorically that this campaign has shown the failure of an integrated allied command. Massu, who commanded the French army contingent in the field, quotes in his memoirs (*Vérité sur Suez 1956*, written in collaboration with Henri Le Mire) a passage from the final report of Beaufre, who was Stockwell's deputy in the command of the allied land forces, in which the point is made that the piling up of one command structure on top of another impeded quick decisions and swift responses to a rapidly changing situation. Again, Baeyens and Massu make the point (which Beaufre has also made) that after the start of the operations, timidity in London led to orders to avoid certain targets like the transmitters of Cairo Radio. Also, since the operation was in the end to be formally a response to hostilities between Israel and Egypt, no troopships were to be allowed to leave Malta before the expiry of the Anglo-French ultimatum to these two states; this, lest there should be accusations of 'collusion'. This precaution would, of course deceive nobody. In any case, since the British and French had been threatening military intervention for months, what could be more natural than they should happen to have troopships in the vicinity of Egypt, by chance so to speak, at the very moment when Israel was attacking Egypt?

The involvement of Israel—which gave rise to so many attacks and denunciations on the score of 'collusion'—seems itself to have come about by reason of the hesitant and unsure stance of Eden's administration. We learn from *Comment Israël fut sauvé*, the memoirs of Abel Thomas, who was Bourgès-Maunoury's chef de cabinet at the Ministry of Defence, that on 18 September a cable was received from London in which he was told that the operation was now postponed *sine die*. The French government however, and Bourgès-Maunoury in particular, seem to have been determined to hit Nasser hard, and it was then that the idea of making use of Israel for this purpose crystallized. There were meetings with the Israelis at the end of September, and discussions between French ministers and their military advisers. There was even a meeting at the Elysée Palace at which Coty, the President of the Republic, expressed misgivings about a joint Franco-Israeli attack on Egypt and its effects in the Arab world. The outcome of these debates was a decision that France would give support to an Israeli attack—and without this support the Israelis would not move— but only on condition of British participation. This is easily understood since Cyprus, a British territory, would be wanted as a base, and since the British alone had the heavy bombers that were thought essential for paralyzing the Egyptian air force.

We do not know in any detail the Anglo-French discussions that followed the French initiative to involve Israel in the quarrel over Suez. The crucial decisions were taken in conversations at Chequers and in Paris in the middle of October. The Paris meeting, on 16 October, Abel Thomas tells us, considered a memorandum by Bourgès-Maunoury suggesting a number of options. One was to send an ultimatum to Nasser, rejection of which would be immediately followed by an Anglo-French attack; another was that Israel should attack Egypt, which would call forth an Anglo-French intervention. Abel Thomas declares that in the course of the discussion, Bourgès-Maunoury asked Eden three times what he would do in case there was a joint Franco-Israeli attack on Egypt, and every time Eden made as though he had not heard. 'But', Thomas goes on, 'everything indicates that it was fear of this possibility which finally led Eden to agree to the second plan. Pineau had proved to him that in view of the delay occasioned by Dulles's ambiguous, not to say favourable, attitude towards Nasser's *coup de force*, an operation confined to France and Great Britain was no longer conceivable. Only the pretext of the Israeli operation would now justify triggering a joint intervention by France and Great Britain.' Selwyn Lloyd's valuable account essentially confirms what Abel Thomas reports. Once the Israelis were introduced into the issue, the Cabinet had to envisage three possibilities: a combined Anglo-French-Israeli attack, a Franco-Israeli attack, or an Israeli attack followed by the comedy—to use President Coty's word—of the ultimatums. The first alternative, which Ben-Gurion desired, was ruled out for its apprehended repercussions on British interests in the Arab world. The second could not be entertained because if the British government stayed on the sidelines it would, as Lloyd writes, look ridiculous in the eyes of most countries, and British prestige in the Middle East would fall still further; domestically, again, this would procure a triumph for the opposition, who would claim that it was they who had forced the government to back down and, simultaneously, denounce its members as the 'guilty men' who had blundered into a second Munich. There seemed to remain only the last alternative, the details of which were enshrined in the so-called 'Sèvres Protocol', the text of which both Pineau and Abel Thomas print—a document which Sir Patrick Dean signed on behalf of the British government on the evening of 24 October, and which was approved 'without dissent' by the Cabinet on the following day.

It was a bad decision, the consequence of past timidity and procrastination. Throughout, of course, Eisenhower and Dulles had finessed and prevaricated, but it was none of their responsibility to defend British and French interests. Given their real views and inclinations, which from the outset were reasonably clear, was it not hopeless to try to enlist them against Nasser? As for the United Nations—was it really believed that anything of substance would issue from this circumlocution office? Was it not futile to go through the motions of an appeal to the UN, in the hope perhaps that Egyptian recalcitrance would provide a *casus belli*? Negotiations on behalf of Egypt were in the hands of Fawzi, famous for a style of shimmering ambiguity, and the go-between was Hammarskjöld, whose similar talents if nothing else made him a Swedish Fawzi. Pineau has a striking description of Hammarskjöld's negotiating methods, which he attributes to the Secretary-General himself. Even if Pineau may not reproduce his interlocutor's very words, his report, like a speech in Thucydides, does vividly convey the essential truth. To deal with a conflict which threatened to lead to bloodshed, Hammarskjöld confided in Pineau,

> *je commence par me saisir du problème au nom des Nations unies. Je me garde ensuite de proposer trop vite une solution. Venant de moi elle serait aussitôt suspecte et repoussée. Mais je complique les choses à plaisir; je multiplie les conversations exploratoires. J'agis comme une araignée qui ficelle un insecte pour l'immobiliser avant de le manger. Je tisse mes fils autour du problème, au point de le rendre invisible, ou, si vous préférez incompréhensible. A la fin les gens ne savent plus très bien ce qui les oppose et renoncent à se battre.*

And in New York by their own account Pineau and Lloyd found themselves caught in a process of tentative explorations, preliminary discussions and hypothetical negotiations which bade fair to volatilize their claims into thin air. But of course the British and French had of their free will gone into the spider's parlour. In the United Nations, as in any other forum, the universal rule holds sway: *caveat emptor*. The upshot, then, of all these unprofitable palavers was the decision to break out from Dulles's and Hammarskjöld's webs by participating in a complicated and needlessly risky scheme. A clear and straightforward case was made to appear well-nigh indefensible by means of a subterfuge which could not deceive a child but which inextricably confused two separate quarrels, to Nasser's great advantage.

Militarily, the British and the French did not need the help of the Israelis. And as Beaufre pointed out in his book—perhaps the most intelligent one written so far about the affair—if the Israelis had remained within their borders and adopted a highly threatening posture, the Egyptians would have had to tie down large forces in Sinai and Gaza, and disperse their remaining troops between Alexandria and Port Said, since they could not tell for sure where or when an Anglo-French attack would come. This would have been more advantageous than the 'aero-psychological' circus which, by delaying actual occupation of the Canal Zone, helped to make the expedition a complete loss.

Whether, however, occupation of the whole Canal Zone would have availed the British and the French anything is a moot point. Lloyd confesses to doubts about toppling Nasser and to being 'horrified' by the idea of re-occupying the whole of Egypt or having to prop up a pro-Western regime in Cairo. In other words, the original object of the expedition was no longer clearly in sight. Having the Canal merely as a pawn with which to negotiate would have come up against the same determined opposition by the United States. And it does seem to be the case that it was this opposition that finally demoralized Eden and induced him, against the wishes of the French, to obey the United Nations cease-fire resolution. This opposition took the form chiefly of conducting a *blitzkrieg* against the pound in the money markets, and obstructing an application to the International Monetary Fund, which the government was entitled to do, for the withdrawal of part of the British subscription to the Fund. This offensive engendered a 'sterling crisis', which meant that the Bank of England had to spend its foreign currency reserves in order to maintain the fixed parity of the pound against foreign holders who were bidding it down. But this bidding down could not, in the nature of the case, be more than a short-term offensive, since the value of a particular currency depends in the last analysis on the real underlying trend of its economy. And to sacrifice at the altar of 'fixed parity' was, as may now be clearly seen, to worship a false god. In any case, if 'fixed parity' of sterling was so important for the conduct of international trade and finance then the Americans would surely, sooner rather than later, have shrunk from grievously damaging the international financial system in which they have so large a stake simply in order to punish the British for crossing them. It was not a failure of the pound, but failure of will on the part of the Prime Minister which brought the expedition to an end. A man with stronger fibre would have looked the Americans in the eye, called their bluff, and if need be, dared them to choose between the NATO ally and the Egyptian dictator.

As in every enterprise of this kind, there were, inevitably, disagreements about the manner in which it should be carried out, and whether it should be undertaken at all. But the Suez expedition called forth in Britain a remarkable outpouring of moral passion, vehement affirmations of moral principle in various parts of the intellectual, official and political classes. In a BBC talk given ten years after Suez Mr. Robert Rhodes James declared that 'in the long run Suez came home to roost on the Tory Party'. It is not clear what this image is meant exactly to convey, but if it implies that the electorate believed the expedition to be morally wrong or criminal, and in due course visited its displeasure on the guilty party, then this seems to be a rather hazardous judgment. There is no evidence that the electorate by and large resented the government's trying to knock Nasser off his perch, and neither in the 1959 nor in the 1964 general election was it an issue. In 1959 MacMillan achieved an enormous Conservative majority, and in October 1964 Wilson got in by a whisker, with a promise to initiate a 'white-hot technological revolution' and to pursue a hitherto unknown brand of purposive politics. The opposition and the disapproval came not so much from the mass of the electors as from some of their representatives. It was of course to be expected that the Parliamentary Labour Party and its leaders should be vocal in opposition, both on grounds of conviction and in order to discomfort and discountenance the government, particularly when American opposition to the venture was revealed to be implacable. The same kind of objection (albeit not from the same motives) was heard in Conservative ranks. Some 15 Conservative members protested through the Chief Whip against Eden's policy. One of them, Nigel Nicolson, became in consequence embroiled with his constituency party in Bournemouth East and Christchurch. To explain and justify his stand, he published in 1958 *Parliament and People*. As he said in a speech to the Conservative Association in his constituency, his objections to Eden's policy were 'a matter of principle'. Britain's quarrel with Egypt should have been kept separate from the Israeli-Arab conflict. This was not all, however, for he was also against the use of force, which he thought full of risks 'to our alliances, our Commonwealth, our oil supplies, our oil-routes, our economy and our reputation, and we knew in advance that the Labour and Liberal Parties in Parliament would not support it'. Instead, Nicolson favoured 'economic sanctions to prove to Nasser that his type of highway robbery does not pay, with the threat of military sanctions to block his future ambitions'. But economic sanctions were useless if the US would not join them, and the threat to use military force is not, in principle, different from the use of force itself. Flimsy as this distinction turns out on examination to be, those who objected to the expedition 'on principle' came to be invested with an aura of virtuous high-mindedness, in contrast to those low, scheming characters who conspired to attack Egypt and who, through the providential operation of poetic justice, swiftly received their deserts.

    Nicolson raised another issue, of a constitutional character. He believed that a government could use its majority in the House of Commons to do anything it wished against the will of the opposition, except to go to war. Indeed, as he wrote, the fact that the Labour Party had consistently opposed a policy of force was among his main motives for opposing it himself. In any large undertaking it is of course the part of wisdom for the government to obtain the acquiescence, if not the assent, of the opposition. It may be, as has been alleged, that Eden neglected to keep the Labour leaders briefed about his views and policies. They, on the other hand, had made it clear from the start that they would not countenance the use of force except through the United Nations. Given what the United Nations even then had already become, this was tantamount to ruling out the use of force unconditionally. Nicolson's constitutional dictum, taken at face value, would give the opposition a power of veto over the government's policy, and hamstring it in discharging what is one of the few duties it has unquestionably to discharge. The dictum would also go against the logic of representative and responsible government as this has developed at Westminster.

Dislike of the government's policy in Britain was by no means confined to parliamentary circles. Both Beaufre and Ely, the French Chief of Staff, express their belief that Lord Mountbatten, the First Sea Lord, was opposed to an attack on Egypt, perhaps owing to Nehru's influence. And since his death it has transpired that his dislike of Eden's policy was indeed strong and was known to the Sovereign. It may well be that this dislike, expressed by such a figure, with such intimate links to the Court, played its part in sapping the Prime Minister's will. However, the most extreme opposition is perhaps that recounted by Lord Ballantrae in his memoirs, *The Trumpet in the Hall* (1970). He had been appointed Director of Psychological Warfare for the expedition, and one of the channels of his propaganda was to be Radio Sharq al-Adna, which broadcast to the Arab world from Cyprus. Weeks before the expedition was launched Brigadier Fergusson (as he then was) had gone to Cyprus to explain to its British Director in veiled terms what might be required from him in certain hypothetical circumstances. The Director's sympathies were 'deeply and genuinely' with the Egyptians and he told Fergusson that none of his British or Arab staff would agree to broadcast bulletins or propaganda connected with an attack on Egypt. The Director made great difficulties over approving other broadcasters whom Fergusson suggested; 'so *parti pris* was he, the Prophet himself would have been rejected for this purpose as unsuitable or unqualified.' On the second day of hostilities the Radio began broadcasting messages to the effect that the staff were heart and soul with their Arab brethren, and dissociated themselves from the broadcasts that Fergusson had arranged to be made the night before. Fergusson acted swiftly, ordering the whole staff to be put under arrest, confining the Director to his house and cutting off his telephone.

Nothing like this incident is recorded to have taken place among the French, nor did French parliamentarians manifest the kind of conscientious scruples that troubled some Conservative MPs. But it would seem that both in Britain and France the diplomats were in large measure opposed to the use of force against Egypt, and that their attitude, known to ministers, resulted in a mutual loss of confidence. Abel Thomas reports that both the Ministry of Defence and the Prime Minister were very wary of the Quai d'Orsay getting to know anything about the expedition and its planning; the Quai was suspected of being pro-Arab, or too impressed with the power of the Arabs. Whether these suspicions were generally justified or not, the diary of one French diplomat, Jacques Baeyens's *Un coup d'épée dans l'eau du canal*, does show that he was not only sceptical about the conduct of the expedition but also hostile to its aims. We cannot but raise an eyebrow to see the Diplomatic Adviser to the French Commander-in-Chief describing the expedition as 'aggression pure and simple, of the kind which the civilized world had always condemned. War was being levied on the most important nation of the Muslim world. This gangsters' operation was being carried on in absolute contradiction to the principles of the United Nations charter.' Baeyens also referred to his prospective functions when Cairo should be occupied as a 'gauleiteriat'. As for the Suez Canal Company, it is a 'gold mine' which has simply changed hands, *'et, au fond, n'est-ce pas juste'*, seeing that the shareholders had enjoyed its benefits since 1869? There is no evidence that such sentiments led Baeyens to be anything but punctilious in the discharge of his official duties, but the reader cannot escape an uneasy suspicion about the solidity of a political and social order whose official upholders entertain such doubts about its legitimacy.

Like the Quai, which its masters kept at arm's length, practically the whole of the Foreign Office, as Lord Trevelyan has written, was ignored by ministers. This was an unheard of state of affairs that gives one pause. For clearly here was no ordinary disagreement between ministers and advisers over the prudence or profitability of a given policy; the disagreement seems to have been more fundamental. It is as if military attack upon Egypt offended feelings which were very powerful and principles which in some sense were considered sacred. But the coherence and intelligibility of these feelings and principles do not seem to be in proportion to the sincerity and vehemence with which they were held. Sir William Hayter, then Ambassador in Moscow, declares in his memoirs (*The Kremlin and the Embassy*, 1966) that he could not believe his eyes when he read the text of the Anglo-French ultimatum to Egypt. This action, he tells us, 'seemed to me flatly contrary to all that I knew, or thought I knew, about British policy . . . I believed that we were strongly opposed to the use of force to obtain national ends, and here we were condoning such ends (even though by a friend against an enemy) and apparently preparing to use it ourselves.' He also discloses that in his private opinion Khrushchev was not far from the truth that the British and French governments had behaved 'like bandits'. How, we find ourselves wondering, could it possibly have occurred to an ambassador, in a world where powers like the Soviet Union and political leaders like Nasser existed, that his country could renounce the use of force; and why, not the sudden and arbitrary seizure of one's property, but the attempt—clumsy and timid enough in all conscience—to recover it should be branded as banditry?

Another high official at the Foreign Office, Lord Gore-Booth, who retired as Head of the Diplomatic Service, also deplores the Suez expedition deeply. In October 1956, he had just taken up a Deputy Under-Secretary-ship dealing with economic issues. In his memoirs (*With Great Truth and Respect*, 1974) he, like Lord Trevelyan, remarks on the fact that the Office knew nothing of what was impending: 'to a degree unprecedented since Munich, they were not being consulted or even allowed to know.' He even went so far as to write a note for Kirkpatrick (who seems to have been exceptional in not thinking the government's policy a sin and a crime) so that those in authority should realize 'that the overwhelming majority of people in the Office felt that our action had been a bad mistake'. The policy, Gore-Booth felt, was imprudent; if one single Arab were killed in the preliminary bombing of the airfields 'there would be hell to pay'. Further-more, 'the action we were taking seemed so utterly out of the character of post-war, United Nations Britain.' It was, in truth, 'the Great Aberration' over which, however, 'a veil of forgiveness' was mercifully thrown following Eden's retirement.

Manifest in this ideal of a 'United Nations Britain' is an intellectual weakness, a wan sentimentality that fails to get a grip on reality. There is here unwillingness to grasp what survival requires in a world from which civility has almost gone, peopled by predators who laugh at the rule of law and take pride and pleasure in brutal flouting of custom and convention. But if Lord Gore-Booth cannot be right in thinking that Suez was out of character for Britain—how could it be, given Britain's martial past?—he is justified in adding that it was out of character for Eden. This was perhaps the reason for the widespread anger that Eden's action aroused among the intellectual and official classes: that this British Nehru had outraged the pieties that he was believed—on the whole rightly—to share. Shortly after Suez two close friends happened to be discussing the affair in Moscow. Their notoriety does not diminish their value as spokesmen or exemplars in respect of attitudes and judgments widely current among their peers. 'It's absolutely out of character . . . ' Guy Burgess told Tom Driberg, shaking his head over the lost leader, 'Eden's *not* a warmonger: he's a man of peace'. The clerisy at large, then, have succeeded in endowing Suez with a halo of evil which still clings to it. Their tender conscience has made the so-called collusion with France and Israel—stratagem of a kind to which states have immemorially resorted, albeit here clumsy and transparent—an act of especial wickedness. How the pieties that Suez outraged came to strike root, to flourish and luxuriate, how beautiful souls came to set the tone in a public life distinguished not so long ago by some robustness and realism, how scruple decayed into scrupulosity—this remains the central mystery of modern British politics.

10

THE UNITED NATIONS:
HAMMARSKJÖLD AND AFTER
Dominated by the lust of self demolition . . . —T. S. Eliot

In the autumn of 1973, Mr. William F. Buckley, Jr., American newspaper columnist and the editor of the *National Review*, served as a United States delegate to the 28th General Assembly of the United Nations. In *United Nations Journal*, a most readable work in which he describes this experience, Mr. Buckley recounts an episode that took place late one afternoon in the General Assembly. The Cuban Foreign Minister, Raúl Roa, was attacking the United States and a number of Latin American countries. He was particularly vehement about Chile. Roa declared that he, 'a simple human being', wished to dissociate himself

> from those here who represent the bestiary and the forest. The henchmen of colonial racism and of imperial propaganda have tried to cast a curtain of pretenses, fallacies, calumnies, scurrility, adulterations and vile accusations to disguise their machinations, their felonies, their knavery, their infamy, their crime and their irresponsibility. That was also the clumsy intention behind the ridiculous, lying, petulant, cowardly and low so-called 'I accuse' of the . . . rented Vice Admiral, who dishonours this Assembly, bearing the stigma of traitor on his brow and his bloody garments after the murder of thousands of Chileans . . . .

Naturally the Chilean delegate retaliated. He referred to the 'tyrant Fidel Castro', to his despotic and arbitrary regime, and to his delight in watching public executions ('to which he even invited some diplomats'). This attack greatly incensed the Cuban Foreign Minister, who moved towards the speaker, as though intending physically to attack him, and shouted *'hijo de puta'* (son of a whore) and *'maricón'* (a queer). Some Latin Americans moved to interpose themselves between the disputants and four Cuban bodyguards who had followed on Roa's footsteps were seen poised to raise their pistols. A shoot-out, it would seem, was only narrowly averted. The next day, Mr. Buckley tells us, there was a flurry of applications to the police for permission to carry guns in New York. 'It would be illuminating', he quietly adds,

> to know exactly how many pistols are in the General Assembly when all the representatives are at their seats. We have nowadays the technology to get the answer to that question, by a little discreet X-raying. Perhaps someone will suggest to one of those roaming cameras up in the newsroom behind the cornices that they shoot out an X-ray and identify the configuration of hand-guns among those gathered in New York to guard the peace of the world.

The General Assembly was openly to gratify Mr. Buckley's wish. X-ray cameras were not needed to photograph Yasir Arafat with the gun peeping from under his jacket. The prophetic shot fired at Concord in 1775 was metaphorically heard around the world—but this other, ominous, television shot in New York 200 years later was literally seen by the whole world.

The incident that Mr. Buckley recounts shows at any rate that Yasir Arafat was only building on precedent. These unseemly exhibitions inevitably prompt a comparison between the United Nations as it is now and as it was meant to be.

One's thoughts go back to the League of Nations—of which the United Nations is the heir—and to those men of elevated minds and exalted principles who devised it and spent their considerable talents in fostering and defending it: men like President Wilson, General Smuts, Lord Robert Cecil and Professor Gilbert Murray. For these spirits the League was the long-awaited 'Parliament of Man' in which quarrels were to be settled by public discussion, in which partial interests, however bitter their conflicts, would still be subordinate to the interest of humanity as a whole. Thus, in an article in the *Dictionary of National Biography*, Mr. Philip Noel-Baker tells us of Lord Robert Cecil that, when Smuts appointed him as South African delegate to the League, he 'persuaded his colleagues that all meetings of the Assembly and of its committees and of the Council should be held in public', and that he 'was a firm believer in the value of public international debate, saying that "publicity is the life-blood of the League."'. The line seems direct and unbroken between the high-minded scion of the House of Cecil and the Cuban gunmen swaggering on the floor of the General Assembly. How did this come to be? What went wrong? How did the mass suddenly turn into a black mass? Or is it that in fact nothing at all went wrong, that from the very beginning it was all a terrible mistake, that 'public international debate' had to end in the sinister glint of guns among the decorous diplomats, in Khrushchev thumping his shoe on the table, and in the vulgar abuse that Mr. Buckley cites for our enlightenment and edification?

For the United Nations (as the League of Nations before it) is not a parliament, but the parody of a parliament. It does not come into being like a parliament and is not subject to periodical elections. It does not legislate, and it does not produce or support or control a government. The analogy with a parliament is at best very weak; it is misleading rather than clarifying. Of course President Wilson and the other League of Nations enthusiasts did not themselves invent this way of looking at and dealing with relations between states. It is only the variant of a particular tradition of Western political discourse which, however adequately it may have summed up and accounted for some (very limited and very local) kinds of political experience, was dangerously ill-suited to the maneuvrings and bargainings of sovereign states—those *monstres froids* as de Gaulle described them. How paradoxical, therefore—and how pitiful—that of all political idioms it should be this one, in the circumstances the least appropriate and the most misleading, which came to prominence in the era of Lenin, Hitler, Stalin and their proliferating imitators and successors. It was a ruinous miscalculation. But at least there is fitness and justice, indeed strict justice, in Raúl Roa's being the legatee of Professor Gilbert Murray and Lord Robert Cecil.

He is, of course, not the sole legatee. Buckley's *Journal* abounds in felicitous examples of 'public international debate'. For instance, the practice of the 'non-aligned' nations to clear the chamber as a gesture of contempt for speakers from Israel, South Africa, Chile and (at that time) Portugal. Or the 'total acceptance of the double line' which confers on the Soviet Union the freedom of 'inveighing passionately against such practices as they are themselves most proficient in'. Or again, General Mobutu, the President of Zaire, who came to New York accompanied by 63 aides (including a lady-in-waiting for his wife, a maid, two valets, a radio editor, a tv editor, three cameramen, a photographer, and a lighting engineer), and whose speech at the General Assembly received the ovation of the delegates. He entitled it 'The Flame of Freedom', and bought an entire page of *The New York Times* in order to publish it for the benefit of 'those who wish to contemplate its infinite significance in this time of world crisis'. The speech inspired Buckley to publish an article of biting irony (which he includes in his book), describing how an aide to Mobutu placed his speech on the podium, and after he was done, retrieved it.

> General Mobutu [Buckley wrote] is an accomplished diplomat, as witness that he got much more applause than any other speaker, thus far during the session. It is a difficult art, diplomacy. But if you master it, you can say things that are received as enthusiastically as

headmasters' jokes. General Mobutu doesn't like it that he is considered as part of the Third World, because the figure 'three' implies the precedence of 'one' and 'two', and Africa is greater than either the Western powers or for that matter Russia in any number of ways, mostly unspecified.

Buckley also reported another remarkable passage of this speech:

> The General explained that much of the so-called aid to African countries is an economic swindle of sorts. Consider, he said, so-called fellowship grants to African students. The grant is made, and the student travels to America, and spends the entire sum of money in America! In other words, the economic grant is really a grant to American educational institutions, not to African students. What is confusing under the circumstances [Buckley remarks] is why Zaire, having caught on to this Yankee shell game, doesn't retaliate by making huge grants to American students to study in Zaire?

For a final specimen of 'public international debate' consider the doings of His Excellency Jamil Baroody, the Permanent Representative of Saudi Arabia and 'the most conspicuous figure in the United Nations'. To him, Buckley tells us, 'nobody, but nobody' ever replies. Buckley even wonders whether Baroody and the UN were not made for each other. On any subject that engaged his interest he would talk at relentless and uninhibited length. He would talk about it before the Special Political Committee, the First Committee, the Second Committee, the Third Committee, the Fourth, Fifth and Sixth Committees, and the General Assembly 'until the nervous membranes of the entire body would shatter with the pain of it'. Baroody's engrossing subject is Israel; and *United Nations Journal* explains why, at the UN, this is a particularly obsessive subject. 'It is', Buckley writes, 'a source of great historical anguish in the UN that the dreaded and odious Israel was formed as the result of a United Nations resolution. Accordingly it has become necessary to establish that the United Nations was then under the domination of the United States, that the United States was under the domination of Harry Truman, and that Harry Truman was under the domination of American Jews.' This is Baroody's great theme, reiterated at great length and on every conceivable occasion.

The sub-title of Buckley's *Journal* is *A Delegate's Odyssey*. While on his adventures, Odysseus, we remember, received from Aeolus a bag of wind. Aeolus should be the tutelary deity of the UN. But the prevalence of windbags is not as harmless as might be thought. Buckley considers that the rhetorical satisfaction that delegates get from presenting their views has a price, namely a poisoned atmosphere:

One cannot survive a tense evening's debate in which, for instance, Mr. Baroody figures prominently, without wishing that the United Nations' debates were adjourned to the Union League Club, with obstreperous members barred at the door by the steward. The question of course is whether there is an impalpable impulse forward, toward reconciliation, after one of those monstrous sessions; whether the sheer fatigue of it all works us in the right direction. Optimism on this point is less easy for a Westerner. The nervous system is a much more important part of our psychic make-up, and I can (myself) imagine giving up the debate, rather than having to spend one more hour listening to drivel. There is no question about it but that iron-butted diplomats trained in oriental patience and conditioned to encephalophonic ideological indoctrination stand up better under that kind of thing that we do.

Encephalophonic babel is not a description of what one would call a parliament. If such a comparison is to be made, lovers of 'the comparative method' might like to display side by side the Security Council and the Diet of pre-partition Poland with its *liberum veto*. Such a regime Lord Robert Cecil's father described as 'the ceremonious anarchy which was called a Government'. It is doubtful if the adjective 'ceremonious' quite fits the Security Council. But the parliamentary analogy is not the only one to have been thought of.

In a book entitled *United Nations: Sacred Drama* (1968), Dr. Conor Cruise O'Brien has argued that what goes on in the General Assembly is a drama written by some Shakespeare of the theatre of the absurd and 'performed in no coherent order by a motley cast, most of whom have forgotten most of their lines and mangle the remains of what they remember'. Rather grandiloquently, Dr. O'Brien affirms that the person-ages in this idiot performance 'symbolize mighty forces, since the audience is mankind and the theme the destiny of man', and that the drama originates 'in fear and prayer'. Hence for him the United Nations is not only drama, but also, more precisely, sacred drama. Knowing what goes on in the UN, we may well raise our eyebrows at this epithet. But, after all, 'sacred' is an ambiguous word; vestal virgins and temple prostitutes were both held to be sacred. With this ambiguity in mind, we grant that Dr. O'Brien's analogy is, when lightly handled, suggestive and stimulating (if quite tedious when pursued at book-length).

Dr. O'Brien goes on to argue that a General Assembly resolution may constitute a 'moral warrant' for a policy which the Assembly has no power to enforce, but which a Great Power may find expedient to execute on its behalf. The 'moral warrant' theory, Dr. O'Brien continues, 'recognizing a reserve of sacred authority in the Assembly, has explosive potentialities, like everything sacred'. Rather high-flown language, but one can see what he means. Explosive like, say, Lenin's oratory, or perhaps Hitler's speeches? But how did the General Assembly's 'sacred' authority come to be established? Dr. O'Brien rightly points out that between 1945 and 1958— when the United States had a safe two-thirds majority in the Assembly—US spokesmen sought to establish the notion that, as a chief American delegate (Warren Austin) put it, the Assembly was 'the moral conscience of the world'. Dr. O'Brien also explains clearly and concisely how the machinery was put together and perfected that at last enabled Raúl Roa and General Mobutu and Jamil Baroody and Yasir Arafat to stage their dazzling displays of 'sacred' rhetoric:

> Rhetoric [O'Brien points out] has its own dynamics and the dynamics of a rhetoric which involves arguments of international law . . . are powerful and dangerous. The 'power of the United Nations' and in particular of the General Assembly, is the power to evoke such rhetoric and squeeze it towards action. The legal rhetoric of a great power is a commitment, though a loose one, and this is especially so of a great power in which a government, not in control of the press and other media, has continually to persuade its own public that it is doing the right thing. Once certain words have been spoken, the justifications, which must accompany future action or inaction, have been partly predetermined.

This passage notwithstanding, O'Brien seems to agree—and this in a book published only 12 years ago—with the 'often-heard left-wing charges that the proceedings on the East River are a puppet show of which the wires are pulled from Washington . . . . ' If this is so, then we can only marvel at the wretched puppetry by which the puppet-master manages to be tripped up by the wires of his own dolls.

There was a fateful moment in what, echoing Hegel, we might call the dialectic of the puppeteer and the puppet. This was when Dean Acheson conscripted the General Assembly to take part in the campaign against Soviet proceedings in Korea. It was then, as is well known, that the United States instigated the famous 'Uniting for Peace' resolution, and thus invested the General Assembly with the first rudiments of its 'sacred' authority. It was, Buckley contends, 'the dumbest thing' that Dean Acheson did. And it is, of course, true that the United States had absolutely no need of this demagogy in resisting Soviet encroachments in Korea. But it is a moot point whether the prize for dumbness ought not to go to Acheson's successor, John Foster Dulles. For he it was who, for reasons still incomprehensible, chose to side with the Soviets, in order to hound and humiliate his allies, the British and the French, in the Suez affair, to the benefit of those who (on Buckley's testimony) now for their favourite sport regularly abuse, insult and pillory the United States. And it was precisely on the stage of the

General Assembly that the sacred and primeval drama was enacted and goats were sacrificed for the atonement of sins and the redemption of the world. In this ceremony the chief celebrant, the *pontifex maximus*, was none other than the Secretary-General of the UN, Dag Hammarskjöld.

Dr. O'Brien leaves us in no doubt that in the sacred drama of the UN the Secretary-General is of central, pontifical importance. Indeed he goes so far as to speak of his 'spiritual authority', actually comparing Hammarskjöld's career to that of Pope Innocent III. Hammarskjöld, the 'high-priest of the shrine of survival', by meddling in the power-politics of the Congo squandered 'the spiritual resources of his office', exactly like Innocent III who grievously damaged the Papacy by the merciless war he had waged against the Hohenstaufen. Such an exalted analogy would by no means have abashed Hammarskjöld since he, on his part, expressly considered the UN a church, albeit a secular one.

When Hammarskjöld first came to the UN the world was far from suspecting that such mystic yearning lurked behind his lack-lustre appearance. He seemed a thin-blooded functionary, whose life consisted entirely of drafts, memoranda and compromise formulas. Nor was this appearance entirely illusory, for Hammarskjöld's dim, nondescript and ungainly official prose finally attained a kind of heroic distinction through its sheer nebulosity and utter impenetrability, qualities which seem to be required in one who is engaged in squaring the circle and similar diplomatic games.

Azzam Pasha—who represented Saudi Arabia in the Buraimi quarrel, in which Hammarskjöld tried to mediate—may safely be assumed to be well acquainted with the obscurity and circumlocutions of Oriental chancery styles. Azzam, it seems, 'appreciated Hammarskjöld's subtleties and shared his passion for delicate nuance, but even he [Brian Urquhart tells us in a footnote to his copious and sympathetic biography *Hammarskjöld*, published in 1972] found the task of translating into Arabic Hammarskjöld's exact meaning formidable and very time-consuming'. Urquhart quotes a sentence from the 'long and complex' letter addressed by the Secretary-General to Prince Faisal of Saudi Arabia which enables us to gain an idea of the style, all qualifications and tortuosities. It defeated Azzam's subtlety, fortified as it was by the legendary resources of the Arabic language. In the course of this letter, Hammarskjöld suggested sending an emissary who might explore

> some general conditions—or some general unbinding terms— which might constitute an area of agreement.

'General unbinding terms' is too precious a locution to be lost to diplomacy (especially in these times of detente). It is interesting to learn that Hammarskjöld found in the Egyptian Foreign Minister Mahmoud Fawzi 'a friend and a colleague with whom he could speak his mind on even the most difficult issues without fear of being misunderstood'. This was clearly an elective affinity, for Fawzi himself rivalled the Secretary-General in the power to hide his meaning or lack of meaning in layer upon layer of half-hint, tentative suggestion and hypothetical supposition, being, verily, able to multiply sevenfold Empson's seven types of ambiguity.[1] It is thus a joy to watch these two virtuosi of the strategy of the indirect approach in action.

When the Israelis were pressed by the US to withdraw from the Gaza strip at the beginning of 1957, it was left to Hammarskjöld to make interim arrangements for the territory. The fundamental issue was when, and under what conditions, the Egyptians would be allowed again into the area from which the Israelis had expelled them. The Assembly resolutions on the subject were unclear. When the Israelis evacuated Gaza the UN forces—the arrangements for which were anyway, appropriately and no doubt gratifyingly, 'almost metaphysical in their subtlety'—took over. Hammarskjöld found himself having, as he put it, 'to indulge very much in a somewhat extraordinary policy; that is, the policy of taking step after step in an atmosphere of great ambiguity.' The Egyptians wanted to take over immediately and the Israelis were opposing this vociferously, so that the Secretary-General, much as he tried, could not for long remain in the delightful position of being able 'to slip around all corners and avoid saying whether the cat is white or black, because it was so dark all around'. He negotiated with Fawzi, and the two friends agreed that the 'initial' take-over of Gaza would be by UN forces. The beauty of the arrangement was that the work 'initial' was to have 'a completely indeterminate interpretation'. It might be taken to mean that the initial phase 'would last until the Egyptians "raised their eyebrows" '. Quoting from an unpublished document, Brian Urquhart tells us that when 'Hammarskjöld said that a fairly long initial period might be needed so as to provide opportunities for an orderly settlement of some of the problems of the Gaza strip, Fawzi merely nodded'. The percipient reader will not be surprised to learn that shortly afterwards— between a nod and a wink, so to speak; en un clin d'oeil, as you might say— the Egyptians were back, firmly ensconced, in Gaza. Hammarskjöld expostulated with his friend, but Fawzi (we are told) 'answered this message evasively'. Nordic mist had found its match in the Middle-Eastern mirage.

This man of the corridor and the backroom first made his reputation as a Swedish civil service economist. He was a Keynesian, a dirigiste, an egalitarian; one, that is to say, of the ancient tribe of the mathematici[2] (a genus humanum, Tacitus said, potentibus infidum, sperantibus fallax) who have come to enjoy much prosperity, influence and power by putting their black arts at the service of the leaders of the democracy, to enable them to bribe the masses by debauching the currency, ruining the public credit and vaporizing private property (the euthanasia of the rentier, to use the so amusing expression which the Master with precious and brittle Bloomsbury wit invented, or shall we say coined). Hammarskjöld was, in short, exactly such as the great and the good delight to clasp to their bosoms.

Nor did he disappoint them. Very shortly after taking office he showed himself to be indeed a super-egalitarian and the very prince of *dirigistes*. In a report of December 1953 he spoke of a government's 'basic responsibility to guide the economic and social development of the nation', and went on to establish a parallel between 'internal social justice' and 'international justice'. What he meant by this is made clear in a report of 1956 in which he asserted that 'we all recognize that it is impossible within any nation today to defend for long an inequality of economic conditions which the majority of people believe to be unjust. What is a cause for unrest within a nation may become just as much a cause of unrest and instability in the international community.' For him the UN was a first step 'towards the establishment of an international democracy of peoples'. We wonder whether it ever occurred to him that this would be no more than an international of people's democracies. Such predilections of course entailed Hammarskjöld's being what is called an 'anti-colonialist'. In a passage characterized by a touch of acerbity, Paul Henri Spaak summarized the Secretary-General's record in this respect:

> His influence over the countries of Asia and Africa was undoubted. He consolidated it by not being always altogether fair to Europe and to whites in general. He experienced exacerbated and triumphant anti-colonialism. He participated in [anti-colonialism] out of duty, but also I am sure from conviction.

Spaak's mild, posthumous criticism is exceptional. During his lifetime the Secretary-General enjoyed enthusiastic public approval. Towards the end of his career, the Soviet Union attacked him quite harshly; but none of the Western Powers whose influence and position he strove to undermine so effectively ever raised their voice in public against him. On the contrary, the Western opinion-makers, in the media and elsewhere, joined in a chorus of eloquent plaudits and fond gratulations which the circumstances of his death caused to rise to a crescendo.

All this, of course, was amply deserved. It was right and meet that a man of his particular talents and opinions should receive such recognition and reward. But Hammarskjöld was not one to enjoy in a straightforward, uncomplicated way the power and honours which fell to his lot. He was a queer, uneasy, buttoned-up sort of man, all knots and complexes and inhibitions. Yet his exterior, which certainly did not show those 'lineaments of gratified desire' of which Blake speaks, hid (to adopt an image that Hammarskjöld uses in a transparent reference to himself) tenacious Lucifer-like ambitions. The Secretary-General aspired, in the prophet Isaiah's words, to be 'above the stars of God', 'above the heights of the clouds', indeed to be 'like the Most High'.

After his death (in 1961) his diary was published under the title *Markings*. Hammarskjöld clearly intended the diary to be published, and considered that it provided the only true 'profile' of him. From its very first page *Markings* declares itself to be a remarkable and very peculiar work. For the book begins by reproducing a letter to a friend in which Hammarskjöld gives his permission to publish the diary, which he describes 'as a sort of "White Book" concerning my negotiations with myself—and with God' . . . . negotiations between two sovereign powers, as it were. Before his call to the UN we find the author declaring his 'hunger for righteousness', and avowing his desire to atone 'for the guilt you carry because of your good fortune'. Such feelings, of course, are *de rigueur* in modern secular sainthood.

After a year or two in New York, the tone of the diary changes sensibly. We now see Hammarskjöld, as though the recipient of a divine vision or inspiration, comparing himself (in March 1956) to Phinehas:

> Then stood up Phinehas, and executed judgment: and so the plague was stayed. And that was counted unto him for righteousness unto all generations for evermore. *(Psalms 106:30-31)*

A few months later, he affirms himself to be the servant of 'an idea which must be victorious if a mankind worth the name is to survive'. This fervour rises to its highest pitch in 1956-7, before and after the Suez affair. He confides to his diary that he is the recipient of God's orders, that he is God's instrument, that he has been called. An entry of 28 July 1957 reads:

> You are not the oil, you are not the air—merely the point of combustion, the flash-point where the light is born.
> You are merely the lens in the beam. You can only receive, give and possess the light as a lens does . . . .
> Sanctity—either to be the Light, or to be self-effaced in the Light, so that it may be born, self-effaced so that it may be focused or spread wider.

Another entry, a few days later, justifies Hammarskjöld's description of *Markings* as a White Book recording his weighty transactions with God:

> Your responsibility is indeed terrifying. If you fail, it is God, thanks to your having betrayed Him, who will fail mankind. You fancy you can be responsible *to* God; can you carry the responsibility *for* God?

It is a fair guess that the great and good who chose and anointed the Secretary-General did not bargain for quite such exaltation. But perhaps the most remarkable passage in this diary is an entry of July 1958 which manages to combine the sacred and the profane in one turbid amalgam:

> The ultimate surrender to the creative act—it is the destiny of some

to be brought to the threshold of this in the act of sacrifice rather than the sexual act; and they experience a thunderclap of the same dazzling power.

Equally equivocal is Hammarskjöld's mixing of *mystique* and *politique*. He affirms that 'In our era, the road to holiness necessarily passes through the world of action.' But at times he seems aware how perilous is his path and that *qui vent faire l'ange fait la bête.* Thus, at the time of Suez, when he was most convinced of his divine election, he also writes: 'It was when Lucifer first congratulated himself upon his angelic behaviour that he became the tool of evil.' He also seemed aware at times of the pitfalls of what (to use a phrase current among 16th-century Protestant divines) may be called the holy pretense. An entry that dates from the beginning of 1957 runs:

> The most dangerous of all moral dilemmas: When we are obliged to conceal truth in order to help the truth to be victorious. If this should at any time become our duty in the role assigned us by fate, how strait must be our path at all times if we are not to perish.

At that moment, as one recalls, sanctimoniousness was being discharged in a copious, unceasing flow over the heads of the British, the French, and the Israelis; and we cannot help wondering which particular deception prompted this oblique and mealy-mouthed confession. Hammarskjöld's adventures in search of sainthood remind us irresistibly of those 'Dreams to Damnation' by which Thomas à Becket (in T. S. Eliot's play) found himself tempted. A few lines from the Archbishop's soliloquy, which concludes the first part of the play, will present in as good a light as can be contrived the predicament that Hammarskjöld made for himself:

> *Servant of God has chance of greater sin*
> *And sorrow, than the man who serves a king.*
> *For those who serve the greater cause may*
> > *make the cause serve them,*
> *Still doing right: and striving with political men*
> *May make that cause political, not by what they do*
> *But by what they are . . . .*

If *Markings* charts Hammarskjöld's spiritual journey, Urquhart's work exhibits the glories and vicissitudes of his terrestrial career. In this career Suez is the triumph and the Congo the disaster. And as we see from *Markings* it is precisely during the Suez episode that Hammarskjöld was seized with high religious fervour and became convinced that he was chosen by God to be our savior. This seems to have induced in him a certain spiritual pride, a joyous conviction that he was not like the sinners and the publicans. Thus (on 31 October 1956) he stood up in the Security Council to rebuke publicly the two culprits, Great Britain and France. As a servant of the UN it was certainly his duty to avoid taking a public stand in conflicts between its members:

> However [he sternly warned], the discretion and impartiality thus imposed on the Secretary-General by the character of his immediate task may not degenerate into a policy of expediency. He must also be a servant of the principles of the Charter, and its aims must ultimately determine what for him is right and wrong. For that he must stand.

Luther at the Diet of Worms. But Hammarskjöld was not put under the ban; he was patted on the back. The US representative, Henry Cabot Lodge, described his speech (with proper awe) as a 'major bomb'; and the French representative, Cornut-Gentille, said that 'he appreciated both the motive and aim of the statement'. Only the British representative, Sir Pierson Dixon, seemed to appreciate how near to the ridiculous attempts at the sublime could be, and to have had enough courage to confront the high-flown and high-minded Secretary-General. He told Hammarskjöld that he 'wasn't playing fair'. The haughty reply was that he knew what he was doing and that 'it was hardly the moment for the British representative to be talking about "playing fair" '.

The streak of arrogant self-righteousness manifest in this incident appears even more clearly in an exchange with Ben-Gurion a month or so before. The Israelis were following a policy of retaliatory raids in an attempt to stop their neighbours from attacking settlements and the like. Hammarskjöld disapproved of this policy, and wrote to Ben Gurion:

> You are convinced that the threat of retaliation has a deterrent effect. I am convinced that it is more of an incitement to individual members of the Arab forces than even what has been said by their own Governments. You are convinced that acts of retaliation will stop further incidents. I am convinced that they will lead to further incidents. You believe that this way of creating respect for Israel will prove the way for sound coexistence with the Arab peoples. I believe that the policy may postpone indefinitely the time for such coexistence . . . . I think the discussion of this question can be considered closed since you, in spite of previous discouraging experiences, have taken the responsibility for large-scale tests of the correctness of your belief.

In the nature of things, it is quite impossible to say whether Ben-Gurion or Hammarskjöld was right. Is deterrence efficient? Is deterrence useless? Considered as maxims of policy both propositions can be taken to be valid on occasion; and this is one of those antinomies that must remain unreconciled to the end of time. But this is beside the point. In this exchange, the interlocutors were not on an equality. Ben-Gurion was responsible for the safety of lives and the welfare of a state; the oracle of the UN's 38th floor, on the other hand, had no responsibility for the safety of anybody—not even his own life would be in danger if his advice were to result in catastrophe. The self-assured and hectoring tone is out of place; and the advice was, in all senses, gratuitous and, literally, impertinent.

It was the Suez affair which more than any other event gave Hammarskjöld such an exaggerated idea of his power and influence. The monstrous regiment of the 38th floor was based on the illusion (to which the momentary collusion between the US and the USSR over Suez gave rise) that the UN could have a policy of its own. Hammarskjöld seemed really to believe that as Secretary-General he wielded some kind of power, personal to himself, whereby he could force the Powers to make their policies conform to his own view of what was good for the world.

In 1954, in a gloss on article 99 of the UN Charter (which empowers the Secretary-General to take the initiative in the Security Council when he believes that there is a threat to peace), he had declared that the real significance of this article was that it 'does imply that the Governments of the UN expect the Secretary-General to take the independent responsibility, irrespective of their attitude, to represent the detached element in the international life of the peoples . . . . ' 'Sometimes', he went on to say in a remarkable sentence, 'he will have to voice the wishes of the peoples against this or that government'. These words announce the neo-Jacobin Club which Mr. Buckley describes. In a speech of 1959 Hammarskjöld was even more explicit. He now declared that the UN had an existence and possibilities independent of the will and policies of member governments. These possibilities arose from the emergence of an 'independent position' for the organization, rooted in the existence at the UN 'of an opinion independent of partisan interests and dominated by the objectives indicated in the UN Charter'.

Markings shows that for the Secretary-General *vox Hammarskjöldi* was *vox Dei*. These speeches indicate that he believed it to be *vox populi* as well. Dr. O'Brien compared Hammarskjöld to Innocent III. The more apt comparison is to Boniface VIII—who claimed to be *judex ordinarius*, set by God over the whole world, and showed himself to the pilgrims at the jubilee of AD 1300 seated on Constantine's throne, shouting: 'I am Caesar—I am Emperor.'

Shortly afterwards, as is well known, Boniface was to be manhandled and briefly imprisoned by the French King's bravoes (shall we perhaps compare them to the UN's Cuban gunmen?). Boniface's estimate of the position of the Papacy was as mistaken as the Secretary-General's exaggerated idea of his own power and influence. Urquhart's biography

206 ISLAM IN THE MODERN WORLD

contains many examples of Hammarskjöld's defective political judgment. His intervention in the Lebanese disturbances of 1958 is a case in point. These disturbances were the outcome of disputes among the political leaders, and between the communities of the Lebanon—disputes that were envenomed and exacerbated by the activities of the newly formed United Arab Republic. Nasser, the President of the new republic which comprised Egypt and Syria, was at the height of his power and influence and he imagined that he would soon be able to control the whole Arab world. He therefore encouraged the Lebanese Sunni Muslims and other elements to bring down the lawful government. This was done by the smuggling of arms and volunteers from Syria. The Lebanese government complained at the UN and a United Nations Observer Group (UNOGIL) was sent to the Lebanon. Hammarskjöld, it is clear, followed his own personal policy. In public, he denied that the UAR was much—or at all—implicated. But in private, he asked Nasser to desist:

> The UAR [he told Nasser] had overplayed its hand badly in [Lebanon] and had to change its course quickly. Military intervention must stop and the radio propaganda of the 'Voice of the Arabs', which was an open incitement to rebellion in Lebanon, should come to an end.

Nasser promised to stop the infiltration of men and arms into the Lebanon, and Fawzi confirmed the undertaking. But the smuggling went on regardless. When protests were made in the British press about Hammarskjöld's partiality to Nasser (and this, we now know, was the case) Hammarskjöld protested huffily to the British Foreign Secretary. He concluded his letter with a self-righteous and offensive rebuke:

> The straight line [he admonished Mr. Selwyn Lloyd] often looks crooked to those who have departed from it.

The Iraqi *coup d'état* of 14 July 1958 compelled the United States to take immediate measures to prevent a dangerous deterioration in the Lebanon, and landed troops in Beirut. Hammarskjöld seriously believed that (as he informed Cabot Lodge) 'as soon as the first US ship appeared on the horizon all Nasser's restrictions on infiltration from Syria'—restrictions which in any case existed only in Hammarskjöld's own imagination— 'would inevitably be lifted'. And we learn from Urquhart that 'Lodge himself seemed to be almost as disturbed as Hammarskjöld at the new situation'! A child could have told them that the landings—token as they were of a resolute US policy—heralded, on the contrary, the end of the fun-and-games. It was at this late stage that Hammarskjöld took a purely personal decision to increase the numbers of UNOGIL—a group which, whatever its earlier role, was now no more than the fifth wheel on the coach.

In comparison with the Congo operations on which the UN

embarked in 1960, the Lebanese affair was 'chicken-feed'. But, as Dr. O'Brien pointed out, UNOGIL provided a precedent for ONUC (as the UN Congo expedition was known). But in the Congo Hammarskjöld found himself completely out of his depth. The abrupt decision by Belgium to give up rule over the Congo released fearful passions and cupidities in the country. The US, the USSR, and God-knows-how-many-other states also found it expedient or necessary to involve themselves in the disorder. For the UN to hope, in the circumstances, for the independent role of Hammarskjöld's dream was simply chimerical. This is clear from the chapters which Urquhart devotes to the Congo in his biography; the voluminous literature which has grown round the catastrophes of 1960-64, if it shows anything, shows the Congo of those days to be indeed that

> *darkling plain*
> *Swept with confused alarms of struggle and flight,*
> *Where ignorant armies clash by night.*

In sum, no more need be said than that Hammarskjöld's legion, far from being master of the situation, was in reality no more than one of these armies; and that its commander, searching confidently for one knows not what, fell in an obscure, forlorn, far-away place.

The blood of martyrs is the seed of the church. The seed has sprouted thick, tall and strong. And not only in the guise of General Mobutu and his retinue of 63 (was it really for this that the martyr offered up his life?). As Hammarskjöld would have wished it, the big subjects in the UN today are (as we learn from Buckley), 'colonialism, sovereignty over natural resources, and the evolution of the doctrine that the have-not nations, "as a matter [of] right," are entitled to economic help from the have-nations'. The outcome is that (as Buckley ingeniously demonstrates in an appendix to his journal) the United States today is 'the only Superpower in the UN that has no functioning satellite.' By what arts, by what stratagems we may ask, was such a booby-trap sprung, and how did the US wake up one day to find itself caught in these coils?

The answer is that no arts, no stratagems, were necessary, that the US was itself the unheeding author of its own discomfiture.

> It was done . . . [as Senator Moynihan has recently written] with the blind acquiescence and even agreement of the United States which kept endorsing principles for whose logical outcome it was wholly unprepared and with which it could never actually go along.[3]

The infernal machine began to be put together with the 'Uniting for Peace' resolution, and was much improved at the time of Suez with the unleashing of the General Assembly against Great Britain and France. So that the United States—and any state it dares to befriend—is attacked, denounced and vilified at pleasure. Ingenuity is not needed, only transparent sophistry. Any threadbare calumny will do since the US is anxious not to offend, and even to join in its own castigation.

Mr. Moynihan gives one or two examples of this absurd self-punishment. He tells of a UN publication, *The World Social Report*. This document proves that the United States is a less just society than the Soviet Union and the 'developing' countries. This conclusion is reached by 'correlating'—in familiar social-scientific fashion—'social justice' with the absence of public protest. The Report, we are told, is the most popular UN document. The US did not, until 1974, protest against this travesty. On the contrary, the US 'actively participated in this sustained assault on American institutions'. American help in, and approval of, such a document is attributed by Mr. Moynihan to the fact that it was a Third-World document and, as such, to be treated with tolerance and understanding.

There was an even more curious episode which took place at an American-financed Population Tribune meeting in Stockholm. Here a Professor René Dumont from France accused the white man of eating the little children of the Sahel, of Ethiopia, of Bangladesh, by his 'overconsumption of meat and his lack of generosity towards poor populations'. This indictment later appeared on the front page of an official five-language UN publication, *Development Forum*. The results of this meeting so pleased the official US delegation that they reported: 'All basic US objectives were achieved and US accomplishments were many . . . . US delegation unanimously pleased with final result.' Mr. Moynihan has no doubt how such a report ever came to be written. He attributes it to three decades of habit and incentive which have created in Washington 'patterns of appeasement so profound as to seem wholly normal'.

Things have come to such a pass that William Buckley, whose term of service at the UN coincided with the last Israeli-Arab conflict—called by some in the UN corridors the 'Yum Yum Kippur war'—is led to declare that if Israel had been charged with anti-Semitism, Israel would have lost. Buckley served principally on the Third Committee of the General Assembly which deals with 'Human Rights', and a large part of his book is a very lucid and witty treatise on the fine art of proving that white is black, which has been perfected at the UN. Such miracles are effected by skillful drafting, indefatigable oratory, organized and disciplined voting by blocs of states and coalitions of blocs.

It will be asked: does any of this really matter? The answer is that it does very much matter to be able, for instance, to distinguish between everyday life in the United States and everyday life in the Soviet Union. Such distinctions are annihilated at the UN, constituting

the most concentrated assault on moral reality in the history of free institutions . . . it does not do to ignore that fact or, worse, to get used to it.

On the evidence produced in his *Journal* this assault on moral reality is successful, not least because so little effort is made to withstand it. Detente is 'in' right now, the chief US delegate said in response to Buckley's drawing attention to the 'strategic gains we would stand to make by an undisguised, and undissimulated, constancy to ideals nominally promulgated by the United Nations'. Therefore Buckley was not allowed to deliver a speech in which he wanted to say that 'we have not heard more profuse compliments paid to the Declaration of Human Rights than by some who maintain huge fortifications calculated to prevent the exercise of that right'. Nor another speech in which he wanted to declare (*à propos* the Fourth Geneva Convention regulating the administration of territories occupied by a state during a war) that 'It is in our judgment as obvious that the Fourth Geneva Convention should be consulted in the Mideast as it is that it should be consulted in Eastern Europe.' So sceptical is Buckley of steadfastness and stout-heartedness among those who speak for his country that he later wrote this passage in his widely read syndicated newspaper column:

> I pray that every Jew in Russia will be permitted to emigrate. But I pray also that one (1) Jew will elect to remain, while pretending he wants to get out. Otherwise there will be a collapse of our foreign policy, of Congressional sanctions, and of our Army, Navy, Air Force, and probably our national anthem.

It must not be thought that the US is the only Power in the UN that makes a habit of discomforting its friends and sparing its ill-wishers. The issue of 'Guinea-Bissau' loomed large in the 28th Assembly. This was of course before the 1974 *coup d'état* in Lisbon and the African states mounted an attack on Portugal and its friends, and demanded that a representative of PAIGC—the anti-Portuguese movement in the territory —should be invited to address the Assembly. The British, the French and the Americans held a consultation on strategy. The British said they would oppose in the Assembly any invitation to PAIGC.

> They also said that they would vote in the Security Council against granting membership to Guinea-Bissau, provided both the United States and France did. This togetherness in the UN is very important. The British and in particular the French are anxious never to be isolated in any vote that might be construed as anti-African. The French are especially timid, and they gave no absolute assurances; the best we could get from them was that they would 'probably' abstain on all the votes—abstaining is the great cop-out in the UN. . . .

True to his promise, the British delegate spoke in the Assembly against inviting a representative from PAIGC. But he—representing, be it noted, the views of a Conservative government—began by a rebuke to Portugal, an ally in NATO.

> My Government has frequently made clear, both in the United Nations and directly to the Portuguese Government, our strong conviction that Portugal should press ahead with all practicable speed toward the granting of self-determination in accordance with the right of, and taking into account the wishes of, the people of its territories in Africa . . . . We call upon the Government of Portugal to follow the example of those other colonial or former colonial powers whose former dependencies in Africa and elsewhere are now sovereign independent States represented in this Assembly . . . It pains us that Portugal, a country with which we have so many historical ties, should be pursuing policies which we regard as misguided.

This sermonizing emanated from the representative of a country which, as a farewell gift, endowed each African colony it had governed with a disorderly despotism or a methodical tyranny. Even if self-determination in Africa had been a shining success, these words, which were not an historical appreciation but mere political rhetoric, would still have been misplaced. As birds know by instinct, one does not foul one's own nest. But, as political rhetoric, such words were useless and even dangerous for, ingratiating as they were, they could easily—and with justice?—be dismissed as insincere, and thus attract nothing but the contempt of those they were meant to placate. It does not require much political sensitivity to understand this, and it is not lack of intelligence in Downing Street, or the Elysée Palace, which leads to UN delegates being instructed to speak in this way.

As it happened, Sir Alec Douglas-Home came to New York to address the General Assembly that autumn. He arrived with the reputation of 'the toughest man in town on the matter of human rights', and Buckley arranged to interview him on his tv program. The discussion began with the issue of civil rights in the Soviet Union, and the attempts by West European states (in the framework of the European Conference on Security and Co-operation) to secure some significant changes in Soviet practice. The *Journal* prints large extracts from the interview. Buckley quoted a speech of Sir Alec's: he had said that 'we should do something' to remove barriers to the movement of people and ideas. Did this, he was asked, 'mean merely that you should importune the Soviet Union to make these modifications'? Sir Alec hastened to deprecate this language:

> I think 'importune' [he objected] is carrying on rather the language of the Cold War, isn't it, which we want to get away from. We want

to be able to say to the Soviet Union, 'Look, can you do this, this and this? If you can this will be fine because it will start to loosen up relations . . . .'

But if this approach proved useless, would Sir Alec consider the use of sanctions? Sir Alec didn't think that 'you want to talk in terms of sanctions . . . I think you must use persuasion to the limit. If you can't persuade the other side . . . then we simply just revert, as I said, to a state of a passive sort of confrontation, which is very unsatisfactory.' Palmerston's heir concluded the discussion by insisting that one didn't want

> to talk in terms of increasing sanctions because we want a response from the Soviet Union, and if there is no response, it is not our fault. We have made the offer; we have made the suggestions. If they turn them down, well, that's their affair.

Would Mr. Gromyko or Mr. Malik, we find ourselves asking, have fed this pap to Buckley's American audience? But we must not imagine that the Foreign Secretary was incapable of baring his teeth. Shortly afterwards (in a Parliamentary debate following the Yom Kippur War) a Labour MP, Mr. Gerald Kaufman, asked Sir Alec if he 'will not go to Holland and tell the citizens of that loyal and steadfast ally how he reconciles British membership in the EEC with the oil blockade Britain was carrying on against Holland'. It was, no doubt, a partisan and tendentious point, but no more so than a hundred others which are the daily meat and drink of Members of Parliament. To deal with it—to pulverize his parliamentary colleague—Sir Alec hurled a thunderbolt:

> I am not sure that the words 'loyalty' and 'steadfast' come very well from the honourable Gentleman.

We remember again the wisdom of the birds and think how gratified, and perhaps even excited, Mr. Buckley's audience would have been to see this admirable ferocity used against an opponent somewhat more dangerous than Mr. Gerald Kaufman, MP for Manchester (Ardwick).

Pashas in Downing Street or sultans in the Elysée are responsible for the lives and welfare of great multitudes, but in modern democracies the responsibility is remote and diffuse. In contrast to what obtained in the older despotisms, the penalties of failure are, so far at any rate, neither drastic nor really unpleasant. Hence

> *He that trusts to you*
> *Where he should find you lions finds you hares,*
> *Where foxes, geese.*

But the pashas of old, like modern commissars, had of necessity a keener nose for danger, and did not allow their leonine and vulpine instincts to atrophy.

De Gaulle, that old sultan, described states as cold monsters. But what saved these monsters from being utterly monstrous was a fierce and touchy sense of honour. The sense of honour has its origins in the pursuit of, and the competition for, power. Involved in it is a jealously for one's prestige, and a quick readiness to protect it from being damaged—whether by one's own actions or by the actions of others. Based on the pride of power, a sense of honour is, in a Christian or a Kantian scheme, an ambiguous virtue, but it is a virtue all the same. The question is whether, both intelligence and courage failing, an atavistic sense of honour may come to save all these Western states, heavy with undreamt-of prosperity and luxuriating in their feelings of nameless guilt, from passively waiting for the destruction which, if it comes, will surely be in essence self-destruction. All this is to say how grateful we are to William Buckley for a work of intelligence and courage, a work indeed imbued with a sense of honour. It is appropriate that he should choose to end his book with the text of a telegram which Mr. Moynihan, then US Ambassador in New Delhi, sent to Mr. John Scali, chief US delegate to the UN, in order to congratulate him for administering a rebuke to the Cubans for raising doubts about the legitimacy of Puerto Rican independence. Mr. Moynihan described how he himself, when a delegate at a previous session of the UN, had

> sat in the General Assembly and listened to the Stalinist son of a bitch from Cuba go on about Puerto Rico. But still it was his job. He is a Stalinist. He works for a Stalinist. He can get killed if he makes a mistake. What drove me to despair was the complacency of our putative allies in this matter. The honour of American democracy was being impugned? What is honor? said our allies. Let us talk of malaria eradication, and aid levels. . . . In the end what troubles me most about the Puerto Rican episode is that we seem to be willing to forget about a clear violation of the Charter, a direct lie about the United States. What has come over us? Forget about a slander on our honour? What have we become? . . . .

11

THE RETREAT FROM ALGERIA

The Algerian rebellion began in the small hours of 1 November 1954. In various parts of Algeria, but particularly in the Aurès Mountains, apparently concerted attacks led to the killing and wounding of French policemen, soldiers and civilians, and to government buildings and installations being damaged. The rebellion ended exactly seven years and eight months later with total surrender of the French, and the proclamation on 1 July 1962 of the Democratic and Popular Republic of Algeria. Thenceforth, the new state was to be ruled—as it continues to be—by the Front de Libération Nationale. This organization, which started with a handful of supporters in 1954, brought crashing down in this short space of time French rule in Algeria, which had lasted for over a century and a quarter and which had seemed so solid and impregnable. The victory of the FLN also resulted in the total and precipitate flight of the non-Muslim population, who abandoned the property and enterprises created and built up by their talent and energy.

The establishment of the Algerian republic changed the balance of power in the Western Mediterranean to the detriment of France and other Western powers; it increased the power and influence of the block of Arab states; it made Algeria into a centre of 'Third World' movements and rendered terribly attractive to these the violent and radical methods which had stood the FLN in such good stead. While it lasted, the rebellion had far-reaching effects on the politics of France and its constitutional destinies. The rebellion was probably the most potent reason for French participation in the Suez expedition of October-November 1956—an expedition which, owing to the policies that the United States chose to follow, dealt a mortal blow to French and British interests in the Middle East.

It was the rebellion, again, that brought about the fall of the Fourth Republic and the belated return to power of General de Gaulle, who gave France a new constitution and, while he reigned, concentrated in the person of the President of the Republic all the powers and authority of the state. De Gaulle's assumption of power also had far-reaching effects internationally. He greatly weakened and indeed perhaps crippled NATO; he created great difficulties for Britain and the United States; and he made respectable anti-American sentiments in Western Europe and elsewhere, which the Soviet Union found highly profitable. The military struggle in Algeria also led the French army to become deeply involved in politics. Indeed, it was the threat of a military *coup d'état* that opened the way to power for de Gaulle. His subsequent policies goaded some of the most highly placed of his military supporters into plotting a second *coup d'état* in Algiers in 1961, into which were also drawn many gallant and brilliant subordinates; and his surrender of Algeria to the FLN incited some of them to take part in conspiracies against his regime which led to their dishonour, and imprisonment or execution.

These prodigious peripeties generated a vast literature of memoirs, diaries and eyewitness accounts, of social and economic inquiries, of reportage, pamphlets and novels, as well as solid, painstaking and sometimes highly intelligent historical accounts. Of these the best known is perhaps Yves Courrière's four-volume *Guerre d'Algérie* (1968-71), which became a bestseller. Equally notable and perhaps more valuable is the second volume of Claude Paillat's *Vingt ans qui déchirèrent la France: la liquidation 1954-1962* (1972) which sets the Algerian affair in the context of French politics and French policies in Tunisia and Morocco. Another work which should be mentioned is Philippe Tripier's *Autopsie de la guerre d'Algérie* (1972), particularly for the mass of detail it provides about the organization and progress of the rebellion.

Notwithstanding the great interest and high importance of the Algerian affair, before the appearance of Alistair Horne's *A Savage War of Peace* no reasonably comprehensive, or even generally satisfactory, account existed in English. Let it be said at the outset that Mr. Horne has written a most readable work. A great mass of materials has been digested and assimilated; the confused events of a long-drawn-out conflict and the successive policies with which the various parties responded to changing circumstances have been skillfully marshalled and coherently organized to produce a spare and elegant narrative. Though its account of policies and of debates about policies is clear and adequate, the strengths of this work lie more in its depiction of the *faits et gestes* of the rebellion. In this its closest affinity is with Courrière's work, much of which consists of lively and dramatic reportage. Mr. Horne is particularly good in describing the operations of the FLN maquis, the increasingly efficient military response by the French, the Battle of Algiers, the confrontations of Barricades Week, the OAS and the *Barbouzes* on the rampage, the *putsch des généraux,* the storming by the French army of the *pied noir* quarter of Bab-el-Oued and the massacre of the Rue d'Isly in Algiers. Reading Mr. Horne's account of these terrible events it behooves us, who live in security under a government of laws, to reflect how easily all wonted certainties may vanish into smoke, and how loyalties which hitherto had seemed solid, unshakable pillars can all of a sudden tremble and totter.

If, in spite of its many qualities, the reader comes away with misgivings from Mr. Horne's book, it is because he senses that the author has perhaps not come to grips with the political and social issues raised by the Algerian rebellion; that the character of the FLN and its war against both French and Muslim Algerians, the French reaction to the onset of the rebellion, and the policies followed by the leaders of the Fourth Republic from November 1954 to the *coup d'état* of May 1958, have not been sufficiently weighed and considered; and most important of all that de Gaulle's character and aims as President, the role he played in encouraging the liquidation of French rule, and in bringing about conditions that led to the dispossession and the panic flight of so many of his compatriots have not been scrutinized as critically as they deserve to be.

The book, then, seems to suffer from a certain haziness about central and fundamental issues. We miss here the sharp cutting edge; and its absence we may associate precisely with the pervasive presence of those cosy pieties which dominate the political discourse of the Western world and give comfort and reassurance to the teeming multitudes of its *bien pensants*. To give a small, but significant example—in the course of a bibliographical discussion Mr. Horne remarks that the author of a book published in 1959 'generally supports the *pied noir* case', and adds: 'nonetheless, his book contains much useful documentation'. That 'nonetheless' speaks volumes: it is as though 'useful documentation', and perhaps other virtues, are the natural appanage only of those who did not support 'the *pied noir* case'. The adverb may of course have been a slip of the pen. But the book contains other, certainly more considered, judgments which go in the same sense. Of the Suez war Mr. Horne remarks that it was the shortest in history 'and possibly the silliest'. Had he considered what was at stake in this expedition, and the immense damage which its failure inflicted on British interests, he might have avoided this condescending superlative.

Again, dealing with the Sakiet incident of 1958, when the French, retaliating against an attack on one of their planes, bombed an FLN base which operated in this Tunisian village on the Algerian border, Mr. Horne condemns the bombing as 'a gross miscalculation'. It is by no means clear what such a judgment can mean. The bombing led to the usual orchestrated hullaballoo in the United Nations and elsewhere, but there is no indication that this in itself in any way hampered or incapacitated the French in Algeria. It also led to an Anglo-American mission of so-called 'good offices' which so far as the immediate issue went effected nothing much. Agreeing to such a mission may have been a miscalculation on the part of the French government since it led many in the army to fear that the civilians were selling them down the river, and thus facilitated in some measure de Gaulle's coming to power.

Sakiet may also have been a gross miscalculation in another sense, and on the part of another power. The so-called 'good offices' mission was most probably meant by its authors to put pressure on the French government, and make it more amenable to the demands of the rebels. In the second volume of his memoirs, which appeared in 1969, General Paul Ely records a few conversations which he held with Henry Cabot Lodge, the United States representative to the United Nations, a few weeks before the events of May 1958 which brought de Gaulle to power. Ely, who was then chief of the general staff, complained to Cabot Lodge about the considerable help which the Tunisians were giving to the Algerian rebels and suggested that the United States should press the Tunisians to desist. Cabot Lodge however remarked that from a United States perspective what was important was not the immediate problem which pre-occupied the French, but how to loosen once and for all the Soviet hold on Nasser:

I was then led [Ely writes] to show him an aspect of the problem which he found particularly striking. The United States, I told him, do not want to understand the depth of the feeling against NATO which was developing. Furthermore, the situation might lead the country to call on General de Gaulle. This would perhaps in some measure affect international alignments.

Mr. Cabot Lodge seemed astonished and vexed by this prospect. He asked me what was the feeling in the army, and more precisely, if the army would follow General de Gaulle. I answered that it could not be said that the army was for or against de Gaulle, but that in a difficult situation he might appear as a possible saviour.

In the light of this passage and of de Gaulle's NATO policy it is reasonable to speculate that the policy leading to the despatch of the Murphy-Beeley 'good offices' mission was itself the grossest of miscalculations.

But, clearly, this is not the reason why Mr. Horne believes Sakiet to have been a miscalculation. Rather, he seems to believe that it is futile for a European power to bring its military preponderance to bear in a quarrel with an 'Afro-Asian' state like Tunisia. In any such quarrel Afro-Asia, Mr. Horne seems to believe, is bound to win. This in fact is the moral he finally draws from the Algerian affair. In his last chapter he comments on the criticism that de Gaulle moved too fast in abandoning Algeria to the FLN:

As far as the latter reproach goes, in the last stages of negotiation he suffered from the lesson not learned by Kissinger in Vietnam, or perhaps by the Israelis vis-à-vis the Arab world; namely that peoples who have been waiting for their independence for a century, fighting for it for a generation, can afford to sit out a presidential term, or a year or two in the life of an old man in a hurry; that he who lasts longest wins, that, sadly, with the impatience of democracies and volatile voters committed to electoral contortions every four or five years, the extremist always triumphs over the moderate. Just keep on being obdurate, don't deviate from your maximum terms, was the lesson handed down by the FLN and remains as grimly valid today—whether for Northern Ireland or the Middle East or Southern Africa.

If history teaches lessons, is it really true that the 'lessons of Algeria' should lead the British government to deliver Northern Ireland to the IRA, Israel to welcome the PLO, and Rhodesia to capitulate to the Patriotic Front? May it not be possible to read the 'lessons of Algeria' in a diametrically opposite way and to argue that an organization that became as formidable as the FLN can in fact be mastered? May it not be that there was nothing inevitable about de Gaulle's surrender, that it was the outcome neither of a French defeat in the field nor of 'electoral contortions' at home? That this surrender was not something which the realities forced on de Gaulle, but a deliberate step taken in furtherance of a 'grand design' which was impossibly grandiose and illusory, and which could not but miscarry?

But leaving aside Mr. Horne's exaggerations (for the Algerian revolt did not last a generation, and the Algerians had not been 'waiting' a whole century for their independence), what in fact was their revolt, the outcome of which Mr. Horne believes to have been pre-ordained and inevitable? Algeria contained two populations living side by side: the French who had established themselves in the country after 1830, and the much larger Muslim population—both Arab and Berber—who had been the victims of conquest and who were much less prosperous than the French. Algeria was juridically part of metropolitan France and its affairs were the responsibility of the Ministry of the Interior. But the French rulers of Algeria found it very difficult to treat all the inhabitants of Algeria on a basis of equality. The French element constituted an ascendancy whose views and interests were preponderant in the government of Algeria. This was the vice of Algerian government, but it need not have proved fatal. What made the system finally untenable was not that it could not be justified—and perhaps it could not—but that it was run by a civilian government that had to observe legality, to be constitutional in its procedures, and which was ultimately answerable to a popularly elected assembly. If French Algeria had been governed as the Democratic and Popular Republic of Algeria is governed there would probably have been no trouble. But French government in Algeria was neither fish nor fowl. For example, there were elections of a kind, but the elections were widely believed to be rigged, and the malpractice, as was to be expected in a free press, widely denounced. This could only bring government into disrepute, give it a bad conscience, and demoralize its agents. Mr. Horne quotes Germaine Tillion as declaring that if genuine elections could have been held they might have spared Algeria a long and cruel war. It is difficult to see how this view can be justified. Given the cleavage between French and Muslims in Algeria, given the great disparity in numbers, the preponderant influence of the French Algerians in Paris, and the prevalence of activism among Algerian political leaders, genuine elections would more likely have envenomed rather than ameliorated the situation. As Melbourne said of Catholic Emancipation in Ireland before he died, 'Everybody but the fools was in favour of Roman Catholic Emancipation, but it has turned out that the fools were right'.

Mr. Horne holds that the economic conditions of Algeria in the decades preceding the rebellion had something to do with its outbreak. French settlers created the modern sector of the economy, whether industrial or agricultural, and they were, naturally, its principal beneficiaries. But this economy, with its increasing mechanization and efficiency, was unable to provide employment for the rapidly growing population of native Algerians—in 1906 they numbered some 4,500,000, and by 1950 some nine million. Most of them lived off the land, occupying three-quarters of the cultivable area; but native agriculture was inefficient and undercapitalized, and the sustenance it offered was meagre. One outlet was emigration to France, where, by the outbreak of the rebellion, there were 500,000 Algerian workers. But this emigration (which has actually continued following Algerian independence), though it was a valuable economic resource, was not extensive enough to absorb all unemployment, and an official French report found that 'nearly one million Muslims (or *one in nine* of the overall population) were totally or practically unemployed, and that another two million were seriously underemployed'.

Such figures may of course be used to condemn French rule as exploitative and colonialist, but it is by no means clear that a government, whether it is native or foreign, can do anything very much to control the birthrate of its subjects or create, in a poor country, enough employment to keep pace with the increase in the population. As Mr. Horne records, the estimated Algerian population today stands somewhere short of 16 million. Unemployment and poverty have not disappeared with the disappearance of French rule. Yet the Algerian government has enjoyed, since its inception, vast and increasing windfalls in the form of revenues from an oil industry bequeathed to it by the departing French, and has taken powers to 'plan' and to regulate the economy and very often to run agricultural and industrial enterprises. But it does not follow that independence will guarantee prosperity, or even a modest competence. It may even turn out that Algeria since independence has taken the wrong economic turning, and that its government may do less well for the Algerians than the foreign ruler. As Etienne Mallarde argues in *L'Algérie depuis*, the very extent of these governmental powers, and the creation of a large government-owned, capital-hungry but inefficient and unprofitable industrial sector which cannot provide much employment, may well perpetuate the poverty in which Algerians lived before the French conquest, and in which French rule and the enterprise of French settlers made it possible for vastly greater numbers of them to subsist.

Agricultural unemployment led large numbers of peasants to gravitate towards the cities. Thus, the population of Algiers increased by 42 percent between 1936 and 1948, but there was not enough employment to absorb this immigration—an immigration which therefore led, writes Mr. Horne, to 'the mushrooming of wretched *bidonvilles* and the simmering of new kinds of urban discontent'. No doubt he is right, but it must not be thought that these urban poor sparked off the rebellion. The cities not only of independent Algeria, but also of Egypt, India, Bangladesh and Pakistan harbour such penniless multitudes, but do not manifestly put at risk the regimes in question. And in Algeria itself the rebellion was not planned by these urban poor, and its first recruits did not come from within their ranks. Nor do they seem to have come from those rural areas where French settlers predominated. They originated rather in those remote and extremely poor mountainous areas that had never felt the effects, good or bad, of French settlement, and which were lightly policed and imperfectly controlled.

As for the leaders of the rebellion, in one way or another they were connected with the various organizations set up by Messali el-Hadj or under his inspiration. Messali (1898-1974), after service in the French army during the first world war, became an industrial worker in France and a member of the French Communist Party. In 1927 he became the secretary-general of L'Etoile Nord-Africaine, founded the previous year by another Algerian, also a member of the Communist Party.

The Etoile and its successors—the Parti Populaire Algérien founded in 1937, and the Mouvement pour le Triomphe des Libertés Démocratiques set up in 1947—demanded total independence for Algeria and North Africa. But perhaps more important than these demands were the doctrine and method of political action inculcated by those organizations, a doctrine and method marked by its original Communist and Leninist inspiration and favouring organized revolutionary and conspiratorial action. Thus, within the MTLD there grew up the secret Organisation Spéciale dedicated to violent struggle against the French regime. To the PPA, the MTLD and the OS belonged the overwhelming majority of those who were later to lead the FLN, notably Ahmed Ben Bella, Abane Ramdane, Hocine Ait Ahmed, Mostefa Ben Boulaid, Larbi Ben Mhidi, Mohammed Boudiaf, Mohammed Khider, Belkacem Krim and Amar Ouamrane. Thus from its beginnings the FLN was marked by a predilection for violence. Violence in struggle against the French to be sure, but also violence in settling disagreements among themselves, and violence above all against the Algerian people. Of the FLN leaders just mentioned, Ramdane, Khider and Krim were assassinated at the instance of their comrades, Hocine Ait Ahmed and Mohammed Boudiaf live in exile, and

Ben Bella, defeated in the post-independence struggle within the FLN chronicled in Mallarde's work for 14 years after his overthrow in 1965, vegetated in a top-floor flat in Algiers, as a state prisoner without benefit of trial or sentence.

Fairly late in his narrative Mr. Horne, discussing de Gaulle's 'basic misconceptions' over Algeria, declares that 'he could not seem to grasp that his adversaries were ruthless and adroit political revolutionaries, deeply committed to totalitarian principles of "no-compromise" '. The evidence at our disposal does not show whether de Gaulle was really unaware of the character of the FLN. What may be said is that scattered in *A Savage War of Peace* are episodes of FLN warfare, with its ruthless use of terrorism against civilians, whether French or fellow-Algerians, governed by a methodical and systematic strategy which from the start the leaders of the rebellion adopted. Mr. Horne does not sufficiently stress this, and how rooted such a strategy was in Messalist activities, which in turn may have owed something to the Leninist revolutionary tradition. Had he made use of the material to be found in Mohammed Harbi's work on the origins of the FLN, published in 1975, or of Boudiaf's reminiscences, which appeared in 1976, his readers would have been much better able to appreciate the exact character and workings of the rebellion. Thus the reader would have been better placed to understand the significance of a letter written from Cairo towards the beginning of the rebellion, in which Ben Bella gives the directive *'Liquider toutes les personalités, qui voudraient jouer à l'interlocuteur valable'* vis-à-vis the French. Ben Bella began his political career in the Organisation Spéciale. Krim who, as has been said, was assassinated by his former colleagues in 1970, was a member of the PPA and of its para-military organization from 1945; he gave an interview to a Yugoslav periodical in 1959, when he was war minister of the Provisional Government of the Algerian Republic. In this interview he declared that recruits to the National Liberation Army had to give proof of their aptitude for the soldier's life. Before gaining the qualification to serve in the army, a new recruit, he said, must assassinate at least one colonialist or one known traitor; such an assassination marked the end of every candidate's trial period. This ceremony of assassination was, incidentally, celebrated with vibrant lyricism by Frantz Fanon, the ideologue of the FLN.

Given the character of Messali's organization and the close links which at one time or another the leaders of the rebellion had with it, it does not seem that Mr. Horne is justified in his criticism of the police action that immediately followed the incidents of 1 November 1954. He speaks of 'the mass indiscriminate round-up of suspects, most of them innocent but converted into ardent militants by the fact of their imprisonment'. But on his own showing this was hardly the case. The police were successful in breaking up the rebel network in Algiers and in Oran. They also outlawed the MTLD and arrested some of Messali's prominent followers who, as it happened, were at odds with those of their former comrades who had decided to secede from the organization and launch the FLN on their own. But this was hardly indiscriminate behaviour.

The case which Mr. Horne cites in order to illustrate how 'many innocents fell into the bag' is that of Ben Youssef Ben Khedda, 'a pharmacist whose hands were clean', whose only offense was to write a letter to a newspaper 'complaining about the blind arrests' and who, as a result, found himself in prison. When he was released five months later, we are told, he joined the FLN. But who in fact was Ben Khedda? This pharmacist with the clean hands was not exactly a political innocent. During the second world war he became a member of the PPA; in 1954 he was secretary general of the MTLD; the letter he wrote was addressed to a Communist newspaper; and soon after going over to the maquis (following negotiations with Abane Ramdane in May 1955) he became a member of the Comité de Coordination et d'Exécution which was to supervise all rebel activities inside Algeria. We may then suspect that Ben Khedda was more than a martyr to free speech, and that his adherence to the FLN was not simply the desperate and indignant answer of an innocent man to tortures inflicted by brutal jailers.

Similarly, Mr. Horne somewhat uncritically makes heavy weather of the French capture in 1956 of Ben Bella and his companions who were flying in a Moroccan plane from Rabat to Tunis. 'The King [of Morocco]', he writes, 'mortified by what he took as a personal affront, and Bourguiba, who had had triumphal arches erected in honour of the Tunis "summit", henceforth stiffened their resolve to back the Algerian war effort to the utmost.' A historian may not take such theatrics at their face value, or adopt them on his own account. If he must take notice of them, should he not also ask what the rulers of Tunisia and Morocco thought they were doing by publicly honouring and erecting triumphal arches for men whom a friendly and allied country held responsible for criminal and treasonable activities? As for the substance of the matter, is it really true that by imprisoning Ben Bella and his companions the French forfeited the chance of negotiating with Algerian *interlocuteurs valables*, that the prisoners became 'a source of constant embarrassment to successive French governments, a veritable time-bomb in their midst'? The evidence does not show that Ben Bella imprisoned in France was any more of an embarrassment to the French government than Ben Bella imprisoned in Algeria was to the Algerians. As for his being, together with his companions, *interlocuteurs valables*, Mr. Horne himself shows that these men of 'the exterior' were at daggers drawn with those of 'the interior' who directed operations in Algeria, and who were, as he puts it, 'delighted' with the French coup. In any case, when de Gaulle decided to liquidate, the *interlocuteurs* were there all right, as many as were needed, ready (albeit with sullen ill-grace) to act as receivers.

If the French government can be held to have been at fault, it is not for having neglected *interlocuteurs valables*. It is rather for having badly failed in the first years of rebellion—up to about the middle of 1957—to protect the Algerian Muslims against the terror practised by the FLN. Mr. Horne gives many examples of Algerians killing, mutilating and intimidating fellow Algerians both in Algeria and in France. In the two and a half years from November 1954 to May 1957, 6,352 Muslims as against 1,035 Europeans were killed in Algeria, and it is probable that woundings and mutilations reached a total several times that of the killings. As Tripien justly remarks, the figures hardly indicate that there was a revolt by a whole people against a foreign occupier; they also show that the aim of the FLN was perhaps as much to subjugate the natives as to expel the foreigners.

The bare figures, grisly as they are, fail to convey the cruelty of the fraternal violence which the FLN unremittingly practised against their brethren—'Ten Kabyles, one Frenchman', as the gifted Kabyle writer Mouloud Feraoun bitterly described it. As it happens, a little while before the publication of *A Savage War of Peace,* a member of the FLN, 'Commandant Si Azzedine', published a book of reminiscences, *On nous appelait fellaghas*, which provides valuable testimony about the character of FLN warfare. Mr. Horne rightly observes that Algerian accounts of the revolt are somewhat scarce, and this fact will add to the value of Azzedine's testimony. In 1954 Azzedine—whose real name was Rebah Zerari—was a 20-year-old welder working in a factory in Algiers. One Sunday, having attacked the factory guard and left him senseless, he tried to break into the office safe to steal the cash. He then fled and joined the FLN, where he showed an aptitude for guerrilla warfare and was successful in ambushes and encounters with the French army. He was once captured, and succeeded in hoodwinking his captors into believing that they had persuaded him to become an agent who would induce his former comrades to surrender to the French, and he was then able to rejoin the maquis.

The most interesting passages in *On nous appelait fellaghas* are those in which the author explains how the FLN bands succeeded in terrorizing the villagers into giving them help, shelter, food and money, and into acting as their auxiliaries and spies. The operation was thorough and methodical. An informer would provide the FLN with details of the position, circumstances, and relations of the inhabitants of a particular village. The village would be invaded at night, the village dogs having been killed beforehand to prevent their giving the alert, and the sleepy and frightened villagers would be assembled in the mosque where the FLN leader would terrify them by exhibiting detailed knowledge of their affairs. He would then make his demands, leave his orders and retire with his men. And woe to the villager who was tempted to disobey him, or inform the authorities. His punishment was mutilation or, more frequently, to have his throat cut.

Azzedine tells us that at the age of 21 he had '*droit de vie et de mort sur l'ensemble de la population*' of the sector for which he was responsible.

The instances he gives of the pitiless manner in which this terrible power was used confirm what has long been known from French sources. Two incidents, involving Algerian soldiers working with or for the French, may be cited. What happened to them exemplifies, *mutatis mutandis*, what helpless civilians had to face. On one occasion, a detachment led by Azzedine penetrated at night, thanks to a soldier's treachery, a camp of *goumiers*, captured them in their sleep, and subsequently murdered them in cold blood. On another, a force which the French had set up as a rival to the FLN was persuaded to desert to the latter. It was led by 17 officers who were assured that they would be admitted to the ranks of the FLN. By means of a ruse that Azzedine devised, one by one these officers were disarmed, bound and gagged, and then murdered in punishment for unspecified 'exactions' which they were said to have committed. The corpses were left, so we are told, to be discovered by the French two days later. The strategy of the FLN was thus, clearly, by means of intimidation and terror to erect a wall of fear and mistrust between the Algerians and the French authorities. The mutilations, the killings, the destruction of village schools, the prohibition on recourse to the law courts and on visiting the government's hospitals and clinics, were all clearly directed to this end.

Similarly, as we learn from Azzedine's memoirs, a particular target of the FLN were those army units which began to be formed in order to protect the villagers from their champions, and to attract them to the French side by the provision of various services. Azzedine reports the order he received from his commander to mount an attack on 'the Black Commando'. On inquiring what this was, he was told:

> *Une unité que ne chasse pas systématiquement des djounouds* [i.e., The FLN fighters]. *Ses hommes donnent des bonbons aux enfants, soignent en douceur la population. Ils ne maltraitent personne. Les fellahs les distinguent en tout cas du reste de l'armée. Le Commando noir est dangereux pour la révolution. Nous devons monter une opération contre lui, afin qu'il engendre à son tour la répression!*

The outbreak of the rebellion found the French authorities ill-prepared. The army did not know how to tackle guerrilla warfare, which slowly and inexorably spread over the countryside; Tunisia and Morocco, on attaining their independence, became bases and sanctuaries for the FLN in the east and in the west; the administration was thin on the ground in the villages; and the procedures of the courts were not adapted to deal with this kind of emergency. By the middle of 1956 the French were beset on all sides. It was then that Abane Ramdane took the decision to bring the war into Algiers itself, and launched a vast and formidable terrorist operation. In retrospect this may be seen to mark the apogee of FLN power in Algeria itself. For the battle of Algiers was decisively won by General

Massu and his paratroops in the course of 1957. Elsewhere, the French army, considerably reinforced and under the leadership of Robert Lacoste (whom Mollet had appointed governor-general in February 1957), began to get the measure of the guerrillas and to learn how to tackle them. In 1959, General Challe was to proceed methodically to clear guerrillas from one area of the country after another. He was able to do so because by September 1957 a formidable barrier separating Algeria from Tunisia (the Morice line, named after the then Minister of Defense André Morice) had been erected—a barrier which the FLN was never able, until de Gaulle's surrender in 1962, to surmount or appreciably to penetrate. The western borders, where anyway the FLN was much weaker, were similarly controlled. 'By the spring of 1958', writes Mr. Horne, 'the balance of the war was, on the whole, a negative one for the FLN—certainly as far as the interior was concerned. In the cities terrorism had been defeated; in the *bled* operational military successes were few and far between, and morale was down; on the frontiers there was costly stagnation.'

All this was the achievement of unstable governments at the mercy of changeable parliamentary majorities, of a regime which was constantly and remorselessly denounced by the Gaullists for being willing and ready to abandon—*brader*, as the contemptuous and pejorative term had it— Algeria. Attacked, for instance *à cor et à cri* by Senator Michel Debré— who was Prime Minister when Algeria was finally *bradée*—in his periodical of grandiloquent and self-righteous title, *Le courrier de la colère*. But it was not, in those last years of the Fourth Republic, only a matter of mere words, for eating which democratic politicians have such an astonishing capacity. As Claude Paillat has remarked, ever since 6 February 1934, there has been something Florentine about French politics, in which plots and riots seem to alternate. In May 1958 there was a combination in Algiers of riot and plot. Both among the *pieds noirs* and in the army there was fear and suspicion, following Sakiet and the Murphy-Beeley mission, that weak and unstable governments in Paris would sell Algeria down the river. Demonstrations and mob action were encouraged and incited by *pied noir* leaders, by officers who did not want their victory over the FLN to be spoiled, and by the Gaullists.

Each faction had its own aims, which proved in the end incompatible with the others. In the tenebrous maneuvers before and after May 13 (when the government headquarters in Algiers was invaded by the mob, and the Commander-in-Chief in Algeria, Salan, was given full powers by the outgoing Prime Minister, Gaillard), it was de Gaulle's devotees who proved the most successful. These devotees were prodigiously active, in Paris and in Algiers, both among the civilians and the military: Chaban-Delmas, Sanguinetti, Soustelle, Frey, Delbecque, Biaggi, etc. The events of May 13 and those which followed until de Gaulle assumed power on June 1 have been discussed in a great many books, and Mr. Horne recounts them on the whole clearly and concisely. One crucial incident in the succession of murky events in which Salan and other senior commanders were compromised relates to 'Résurrection', the plot whereby troops would be sent to France to compel the parliament and the government to abdicate in favour of de Gaulle. The plot enjoyed the support and co-operation of many highly placed officers in Algeria and France. It amounted to nothing less than a military *coup d'état*. On May 24 'Résurrection' was enacted in Corsica where paratroops seized power. But this was not enough to deliver the *coup de grâce* to the Fourth Republic, and it was bruited that Paris itself would shortly be occupied.

There is little doubt that de Gaulle knew of these plans. On May 26 he had refused a request by the Prime Minister designate, Pflimlin, to condemn publicly the military take-over of Corsica. The following day he asked, through the complicity of friendly military channels, for Salan to send him an emissary to inform him of the state of affairs. General Dulac, Salan's chief-of-staff, was dispatched, and he was seen by de Gaulle on the morning of May 28 at Colombey. As he recounts in his memoirs, published in 1969, and in a private letter dated 17 October 1970, printed by Paillat, Dulac gave de Gaulle details of 'Résurrection'. In his letter he declares that, de Gaulle having said 'They don't want de Gaulle—so what are you doing?' he told him that there was a plan for sending three regiments of paratroops to Paris. As Dulac states in his memoirs, de Gaulle found this insufficient. He then asked when, according to the plan, Salan would reach Paris. He was told that Salan and Massu would arrive with the first wave of paratroops. De Gaulle then said:

> I do not want to make an immediate appearance, so as not to seem to be coming back simply as a result of this forcible act [*cette action de force*]. After a few days, I want to be called upon as an arbiter who, at everybody's request, takes up the leadership of the country so as to spare it useless divisions. I must appear on the scene as the reconciler and not as the champion of one of the opposing factions.

De Gaulle also raised the possibility of his being abducted by his opponents, using some such phrase as '*ces salauds*' to describe them, and Dulac assured him that there would be no difficulty in arranging for paratroops to be dropped in the neighbourhood of his estate. De Gaulle ended the interview by declaring: 'It would have been greatly to be preferred for my return to office to take place through the ordinary processes [*par la voie du processus*].' De Gaulle then got up and led his visitor to the door, saying to him: '*La baraque* (i.e., France) must be saved. You will tell General Salan that what he has done and what he will be doing is for the good of France.' From de Gaulle's language it appears then that on the morning of May 28 he was, however regretfully, expecting his return to power to come about by the intervention of the troops from Algeria.

That interview is crucial in appreciating the circumstances attending de Gaulle's resumption of office, and it is much to be regretted that Mr. Horne (who does not include Dulac's memoirs in his bibliography) has given it in abbreviated and misleading form, for it does clearly indicate that de Gaulle knowingly climbed back to power through the threat of a *coup d'état* which he did not discourage, but on the contrary encouraged. Who can doubt that it was this sword held over their heads that made the leaders of the Fourth Republic, and the SFIO in particular—the *salauds*, it would seem, to whom the conversation with Dulac referred—put up the white flag and allow de Gaulle to assume in his own person the powers of the state?

Nor was de Gaulle's encouragement of Salan's and Massu's proceedings private and discreet. At a press conference on May 19, de Gaulle declared that he understood very well the attitude and action of the military command in Algeria, and hoped that in the national interest the army would remain *'cohérente, unie, élément exemplaire en un temps où il n'y en a guèrre.'* When it was objected that his words were an encouragement to mutiny, drawing attention to the fact that Salan had been given full authority by Gailard he replied: *'Je souhaite donner courage et vigueur aux Français qui veulent l'unité nationale, qu'ils soient d'un bord ou de l'autre de la Méditérranée. Car c'est cela la question!'* As 'the rest'—which included republican legality and constitutional government—he dismissed it with that haughtiness which he affected towards the rest of creation, as *'des histoires d'un univers qui n'est pas le mien'.* It was at this press conference that de Gaulle spoke of *'résurrection'*—a word which, as Mr. Horne points out, became the code-word for the military descent upon France. Mr. Horne, who mentions the press conference of May 19, does not quote the passages that have just been cited—passages which are quite essential to the understanding of de Gaulle's strategy for recapturing power. In the light of these passages, and of his conversation with Dulac, de Gaulle's refusal of Pflimlin's request on May 26 to appeal to the army for restraint—a refusal which he justified by alleging that he could not risk his authority, for fear that he would not be obeyed—assumes a sinister character, and it does not seem very satisfactory for Mr. Horne to say that this attitude 'seems perhaps not entirely unreasonable'. For after all, is it not precisely in such extremities— when the constitution is at stake—that the precious authority of the *patres* has to be flung into the balance, the more so as those who were threatening the regime invoked de Gaulle's own name? It remains to add that de Gaulle's own account of these events in *Memoirs of Hope* (which was published in 1970) is cursory, jumbled-up, tendentious and misleading.

De Gaulle, then, climbed back to power on the backs of a public tumult and a military conspiracy. The aim of both tumult and conspiracy was to ensure that Algeria would not be abandoned by the regime in Paris;

those involved looked to de Gaulle to prevent such an outcome, and had reasonable grounds for believing that he shared their aim. And his language immediately before and after assuming power could not be reasonably understood otherwise. They were not to know that words which everybody understood in their ordinary sense de Gaulle would invest with a private, esoteric meaning. The famous '*Je vous ai compris*' which he tossed to a vast crowd in Algiers at the beginning seemed a response to their desire for reassurance. In his memoirs he tells us that he shouted these words 'in order to establish emotional contact', that, seemingly spontaneous, they were in reality 'carefully calculated' to fire their enthusiasm 'without committing me further than I was willing to go'. This may be so, but there were other words, more difficult to gloss over, and for these de Gaulle vouchsafes no interpretation. There was the notorious '*Vive l'Algérie française*' which he pronounced at Mostaganem; there was the speech in Oran when he declared that '*la France est ici, avec sa vocation. Elle est ici pour toujours*'; and there was his exclamation at a press conference in October 1958: '*A quelles hécatombes condamnerions-nous ce pays si nous étions assez stupides et assez lâches pour l'abandonner.*' Given such words, and given the manner in which de Gaulle used the soldiers to climb back to power, it is no great wonder that their loyalty should have been strained, and that some of those who conspired against the Fourth Republic should compromise themselves once again in a new conspiracy against its successor. In his account of the attempted coup of April 1961, *Le putsch d'Alger*, Jacques Rouvière quotes an address by the then Prime Minister, Michel Debré, in which he describes the mutineers as '*des soldats trompés*', and asks if the question is not precisely whether these soldiers '*se sont trompés*' or '*ont été trompés*', whether they made a mistake, or were deceived. Paillat also, interestingly enough, has a choice of words that evokes ideas of infidelity and betrayal. For the men of Algiers, he writes, de Gaulle's coming to power was the advent of '*le temps des cocus*'.

It is clear that de Gaulle skillfully used the Algiers *fronde* in order to gain power, and used it for purposes that would transcend the Algerian problem, purposes to which the very presence of France in Algeria would be sacrificed. In retrospect, the signs are unmistakable. He kept those supporters of his, like Soustelle, who were most wedded to the *pied noir* cause at arm's length. He gradually transferred those officers most dedicated to an *Algérie française* outside Algeria. And just as important, he refrained from appointing a political figure to act as Minister for Algeria, but appointed as his right-hand men in Paris to deal with Algerian questions officials who were either lukewarm in their attitude, or were even opposed outright to the maintenance of French rule in Algeria. These were René Brouillet, a diplomat appointed as secretary-general for the department of Algerian affairs, and a *conseiller d'état*, René Tricot, as his *chef de cabinet*. Brouillet, as Soustelle writes, was determined to have no views on Algeria. As for Tricot, his memoirs, *Les sentiers de la paix* (1972), with the mealy-mouthed biblical allusion of their title, are most revealing in this respect. When Brouillet offered Tricot the post, Tricot told him that de Gaulle ought to know that he, Tricot, believed that Algerians should take charge of their own affairs, even to the extent of becoming independent. De Gaulle ratified Brouillet's choice. Tricot's position and his influence on Algerian policy were greatly enhanced at the beginning of 1960 when, after Massu's removal from Algeria and the 'Barricades Week' that ensued, de Gaulle established a Committee of Algerian Affairs under his own chairmanship in which all important decisions concerning Algeria were thenceforth taken, bypassing or dominating the council of ministers and the government. Tricot was the secretary of this committee.

There is no doubt about Tricot's views and the direction in which his influence was exercised. As early as 1957 he had come to believe that, chiefly for demographic reasons, Algeria had to become independent. He also believed that it would not ultimately be possible for France to win the war in Algeria, that the FLN could not be eradicated, and that no other native Algerian leadership was viable. It was not viable, because it could not truly represent the Algerians, and could not truly represent them because it did not—for whatever reason—advocate the activism and extremism that was the hallmark of the FLN. These were counsels of despair, the outcome of a desperate and fallacious logic. In such a society as that of native Algeria, it is not a question of representiveness. As anyone can see, the Algerian government rules today not because it is representative, but because the French withdrew and handed over power to the only organized body of armed men who were on the scene—a civilized government thus acting for all the world like the votary of some Mao or Ho, in the barbarous belief that legitimacy comes out of the mouth of a gun.

It would seem that by the latter half of 1959 de Gaulle had made up his mind to abandon Algeria. In September 1959 he wrote a speech in which he proclaimed the recourse to Algerian self-determination. He gave Algerians three options: secession, integration or 'association'. This was essentially abdication; for a government, particularly in a country like Algeria, does not announce that it is willing to envisage its subjects throwing over their allegiance without disastrously losing its prestige and authority. Nor can we be in much doubt about de Gaulle's own secret intentions. The journalist J.-R. Tournoux has reproduced in *Jamais dit* a document dating from December 1959 in which de Gaulle expressed his view that there was no future for France in Algeria. French troops, he said, had a crushing superiority over the FLN and would finish by eliminating the greater part of the gangs, but 'morally and politically, the Algerian Muslims incline towards us less than ever'. He went on:

To pretend that they are French, or want to become such is a frightful joke.

To entertain the idea that the political solution is integration or *francisation*, which are and can be nothing but maintaining our rule by force—which the men of Algiers and a good number among the military call '*l'Algérie française*'—is a lamentable stupidity.

Therefore, given the real state of mind of the Muslims and of all the peoples of the earth, given the 150,000 men who died fighting against us in Algeria, etc., it is simply mad to think that our domination maintained by force has any future whatever.

What it amounted to, then, was this: that Algerians were not and could not be Frenchmen—which was certainly true—therefore the French had to retire from Algeria and give it up to the FLN. The two options were equally desperate, but were they the only ones open? By the end of 1959 Challe had, to all intents and purposes, mastered the rebellion. This could have been the opportunity for the French state to assume its historic responsibilities, and at last to institute a public order which was not the plaything of the *pieds noirs*, which would treat Frenchmen and Muslims as equals, and protect the life, property and livelihood of all without exception.

This *homme d'élite*, then, '*dominateur et sûr de lui-même*' (to use expressions by which he described the Jews, but which are much more clearly applicable to himself) chose otherwise. Algeria was an *affaire de quatre sous*, a mistake, an embarrassment standing in the way of his *Weltpolitik*, to be got rid of as quickly as possible. These *bougnouls*, these *bicots*, would never become Frenchmen. Can you see us, he asked Delbecque, who had done so much to procure his triumph, living together with Muslims, giving our daughters in marriage to Arabs? What then about the French in Algeria? '*Ah, les pauvres diables*', unfortunately they will have to suffer what they will have to suffer. What about the oil discovered by French geologists and developed by French capital? To a political figure, Roger Duchet, who asked him about it, de Gaulle replied with aristocratic contempt: '*Ah! le pétrole, c'est ce qui vous intéresse. Eh bien! Monsieur, on essaiera de vous le garder.*' Hollow words they proved to be, since barely ten years after the surrender French oil companies were expropriated, in a move which proved to be one link in the strategy by which very shortly afterwards the oil cartel bent Western consumers to its will.

A few years ago an adaptation on the English stage of *Le Misanthrope* transferred the locale of the play from the Paris of Louis XIV to that of Charles de Gaulle. The transposition was witty and apposite, for de Gaulle was the unchallenged master that the Sun-King had been in his days of glory. The Parliament, the Cabinet were mere *chambres d'enregis-*

trement. To his Minister of Finance, Antoine Pinay, who complained that decisions were being taken without the knowledge or consent of ministers, de Gaulle replied (according to Tournoux's book *La Tragédie du Général,* published in 1967): *'C'est moi seul qui fais la politique, et sous ma seule responsabilité. Moi seul, ai le pouvoir de décision.'* This omnipotence became clear and formal after 'Barricades Week'. In February 1960, de Gaulle sought (at Tricot's suggestion), and was given, full powers to legislate by decree. No institution in the state escaped his imperious will. Jacomet was a *maître de requêtes* in the Conseil d'Etat seconded to Algiers to be secretary-general of the government. Towards the end of 1960 de Gaulle made a speech in which he referred to an Algerian republic that would exist in the future. The speech so scandalized Jacomet that he resigned from his Algiers post, saying that de Gaulle was not France and France was not de Gaulle. To mark his displeasure, de Gaulle, against established tradition and the formal view of the Conseil d'Etat, dismissed Jacomet from the Conseil.

From about the middle of 1959 onwards, in spite of the military successes, the Algerian situation suffered an increasing *pourrissement*, the origin of which, it is now apparent, lay in de Gaulle's determination at all costs to get out, and to do this by a deal with the FLN. In June 1960, negotiations (which proved abortive) were held in secret at Melun with FLN emissaries. As Mr. Horne rightly remarks, to the uncommitted Muslims of Algeria the episode constituted a clear sign that, in spite of outward appearances, the FLN were winning. Nor was this a mistaken view. Melun was followed by other secret contacts and negotiations in 1961. De Gaulle's determination to cut and run was frankly expressed at a council of ministers on 31 August 1961, and his words are reported in the diary of the minister Robert Buron, *Carnets politiques de la guerre d'algérie* (1965). We are ready to negotiate for a disengagement, the President declared, but if the Algerians are unwilling, we will disengage all the same and 'devil take them'. In February 1962 formal negotiations again took place at Les Rousses. The French representatives were three ministers, Louis Joxe, Robert Buron and Jean de Broglie. Paillat describes them as being 'somewhat utopian intellectuals, completely unaware of the reactions, temperament and traditions of those whom they were to confront. Furthermore they are softies'. Indeed even Tricot is unexpectedly ironical at the expense of the chief negotiator, Joxe:

> *Louis Joxe, agrégé d'histoire, ambassadeur de France, faisait face à Belkacem Krim, ancien sous-officier de l'armée française, maquisard, chef révolutionaire. De l'un on citait des mots, de l'autre des attentats.*

With all their inadequacies, these particular negotiators had their style cramped further by de Gaulle's haste to get out at all costs. At Les Rousses French concessions were not found adequate, and talks had to be resumed a month later at Evian. De Gaulle was even more urgent for a liquidation, and French surrender was duly itemized in a 93-page document. This document the French government insisted on calling 'Governmental Declarations' and not an agreement, since to do so would mean formal recognition of the FLN and its provisional government as legally representing Algeria. These 'Declarations' were ratified by a popular referendum which, however, the Conseil d'Etat by a majority of 42 against 12 declared unconstitutional.

The Algerian government, which took control of the country in July 1962, was thus, legally speaking, not bound by the engagements solemnly signed at Evian. Some of the more important of these engagements related to the Algerians of French origin, the guarantees for whose protection in the end proved to be mere paper guarantees. Unable to look to their rulers for that protection which it is the elementary duty of a civilized government to provide, and made a pawn of in the sanguinary quarrels which rent the FLN after independence, they fled in panic. Many were murdered. Their possessions became the booty of the victors. Who whom: it is ironical that a traditionalist officer full of the virtues of discipline and duty and authority should have been the means whereby this barbarous maxim of policy was once again applied—applied at the expense of the *pauvres diables* who were his kith and kin.

The *pieds noirs* had the consolation that their rights were guaranteed at least on paper, but another large group of Algerians whose fate was bound up with France did not enjoy this honour. Over a quarter of a million Muslim Algerians in one way or another took part in actions against the FLN and thus bound their fortunes to that of France. A large number of them were enrolled, particularly when Challe was commander, as *harkis*, or auxiliary soldiers. No provision, formal or otherwise, was made for these men. The Evian document has nothing to say about them, and, as Tripier records, the authorities refused to allow them to go to France. They thus suffered the full force of FLN vengeance. They were lynched, tortured, stoned, burned alive, or dispatched by other horrible means. Their abandonment by their French liege went beyond the call of any *raison d'état*. And on the part of de Gaulle insult was added to injury. Mr. Horne reports a remark by Tricot that de Gaulle could never bring himself to congratulate the *harkis* for their feats in French service: 'This was not, in his lights, a strictly honourable function'! On this matter of honour, the supreme soldierly virtue, Alfred Fabre-Luce's remark is perhaps more appropriate. In his marvellous pamphlet, *Haute Cour* (1962)—the one undoubted literary classic produced by the Algerian War—he refers to the various possibilities that were all rejected in favour of the Evian liquidation: they would all, he writes, have been honourable. But the course actually chosen required the large French army still in Algeria after independence to remain passive spectators of massacre and rapine; and thus '*On a choisi la seule issue qui ne l'était pas.*'

In its time the war in Algeria generated a great deal of breast-beating, anguish and denunciation of their fellow Frenchmen by French intellectuals, some of whom even actively and systematically helped the FLN in all kinds of illegal ways. In *Intellectuals and Decolonization in France* Paul Clay Sorum has reviewed their opinions on empire during the two decades or so after 1945. A large part of the work is devoted to the Algerian War, and we are indebted to Mr. Sorum for a *sottisier* in which shallowness, fancy and a shrill and narrow moralism are exhibited for our inspection. No doubt France and Frenchmen were guilty of a wrong no greater than that committed by the conquerors whom they supplanted. Defeat and conquest are, after all, normal hazards in a world of states which recognize no superior. What (if one is to make a judgment) seems exorbitant and monstrous is for a state deliberately, suddenly and precipitately to withdraw its protection from those who look to it for the defense of their lives and possessions. But to the specimens reviewed by Mr. Sorum this point does not seem to have occurred at all.

12

GREAT BRITAIN AND
THE UNITED STATES
IN THE MIDDLE EAST

British interest in the Middle East, understood in a political rather than an economic sense, dates roughly speaking from the French Revolutionary and Napoleonic wars. If we take either the Suez fiasco in 1956 or the abandonment of the Persian Gulf in 1971 as constituting the terminus of any substantial British connection with the area, British power (and sometimes predominant power) would then have lasted, give or take a few decades, something like a century and a half. The interest of the United States in the Middle East has been of much shorter duration. We can affirm, in fact, that it does not date, in any substantial sense, from much before the second world war.

British interest in the Middle East, both in its beginnings and subsequently, stemmed from two distinct pre-occupations. It was, in the first place, an outcome of European balance-of-power considerations. The French, the Russians and the Germans were successively seen by British statesmen to pose, by their overwhelming ambitions, a threat to this balance. The preservation of the balance required at the time the adoption of policies which entailed intervention in the Eastern Mediterranean, and the formulation of a policy towards the Ottoman empire and its neighbours.

In the second place, British interest in the Middle East derived from what may be called Imperial pre-occupations. These pre-occupations centered predominantly around India, and may in turn be divided into two categories. First, those that had to do with securing the route to India, or at any rate making sure that no Great Power was in a position to threaten it, and second, those connected with what might be called the regional interests of the government of India. Taken as a regional power, the government of India had considerable weight. It controlled large and disciplined armed forces, and through the greater part of the 19th century—before and after the abolition of the East India Company—it was engaged in territorial expansion and consolidation. Again, in the latter half of the 19th century, fear of Islamic militancy in India, which might be encouraged from the outside, became yet another consideration in the foreign policy of the government of India. Added to all this there was, as might be expected, a miscellany of issues of which a powerful regional state had to take notice. A good example was the suppression of piracy and of the arms trade in the Persian Gulf—activities which, unintentionally and indirectly, laid the foundations of British preponderance in this area.

As may be easily seen, the European and the Imperial considerations were not identical. They could in fact at times pull in different directions. At any time, on any Middle Eastern issue, up to the end of the second world war there could be three different views emanating from three different centres within the British government all of which had some power over the formulation and execution of Middle Eastern policy. There were the Foreign and India offices in London, and the government of India in Calcutta (and later New Delhi). To the three centres we have to add for the period between 1920 and 1948 the Colonial Office, in respect principally of its responsibility for Palestine.

The contrast between Great Britain and the United States in the Middle East is therefore very great. The United States is a Great Power—more, it is a Superpower, but it is not an Imperial Power. It has no possession like India, it does not maintain an army of occupation as Great Britain maintained one in Egypt, it does not have a *place d'armes* fully under its control as Cyprus was after 1878. It has a Sixth Fleet dependent in many important respects on NATO allies—allies who are now shaky, unreliable or disaffected. The concomitant of this contrast in the situation of the two Powers is a contrast in outlook just as great, if not greater and more decisive. For the outlook which goes with an imperial position, bound up with the continuous need to safeguard tangible and substantial territorial interests, an outlook made up of caution, scepticism and a sense of political realities that such responsibilities perforce inculcate—such an outlook is infinitely more difficult to instil and maintain among United States political figures— Superpower though the United States is.

And what we see at the beginning of the period of United States preponderance in the Middle East is not only the absence of an imperial position and the pre-occupations that go with it, but also in fact the presence of an anti-imperialist pre-occupation. As Wm. Roger Louis has recently shown in *Imperialism at Bay*, F.D. Roosevelt and many other influential political figures, as well as high officials in the Department of State and foreign service officers believed that the British (and French) imperial positions, somehow or another, sooner or later, had to be liquidated, and the people ruled by Imperial Powers helped to independence. So far as one can tell from the available evidence, neither Roosevelt nor other prominent political figures gave any thought to the consequences in international politics of weakening or crippling friendly Imperial Powers, or, more specifically, what bearing the policy they favoured would have on the formidable problem of dealing with the Soviet Union—but this was probably not seen as a problem, let alone a formidable one.

Again, there seems to have been little consideration given to the character of the international society that would emerge when the existing empires were dismantled. For what would replace these empires would be a multitude of weak, unstable, frequently irredentist and litigious governments most of whom have never formed part of the society of states that has functioned according to political assumptions and attitudes worked out and articulated in Western Europe—governments, moreover, whose international behaviour would, of necessity, be profoundly influenced by the absence, in their internal politics, of constitutional traditions and practices. The problem of dealing with such an eventuality was not seriously faced. That the problem would exist at all was not even envisaged.

These remarks apply to South East Asia, as they were later to apply to Africa, and they also as fully apply to the Middle East. But so far as this area is concerned, two points need to be added. In the first place, the notion that a stable and friendly Middle East would result from the encouragement of aspirations to independence—a notion so congenial to US policy-makers—received a great deal of support and reinforcement from the British policy of the period. As Phillip J. Baram has shown in his recently published work, *The Department of State and the Middle East 1919-1945*, many US foreign service officers looked up to the British in the Middle East and were predisposed to adopt their categories and assumptions about Middle Eastern politics. And, since the mid-1930s the predominant British view on the Middle East had been the Foreign Office view. And this view was that British interests in the area could be preserved precisely by working with what was believed to be the emerging dominant force of nationalism. Hence reliance on a deal with the Wafd for the preservation of British interests in Egypt, hence the stance adopted towards the French in the Levant, and the encouragement of Pan-Arabism. This was a very recent line of policy, but it happened to be the dominant one in the decade 1935-1945. It was this line of policy that was adopted by the Department of State and by most foreign service officers—with the natural difference, of course, that in their minds the United States and not the United Kingdom would be the one to benefit from the new order.

The second point is somewhat different in character. If the encouragement of a new regional order was ideological in its character and somewhat hazardous in its consequences, another feature of United States policy in this period of transition was strictly practical and non-problematic. This was simply to ensure free and equal access for US oil companies in the Middle East. This was only to uphold a long-standing policy of insisting on the open door in international economic enterprise. If the successful pursuit of this policy meant that the British would be overshadowed and supplanted, then this was, in effect, indirectly to undermine Great Britain's imperial position. But legitimate and straightforward as was the desire to protect and advance the interests of US oil companies (which were purely business enterprises) it was to have increasingly political consequences in the decades following 1945.

The ideological stance adopted by US policy-makers during the second world war remained more or less the same in the period that followed. To give two striking examples among many: first, the encouragement of the Egyptian revolutionary officers and of Nasser, who emerged as their leader in the period 1952-1955. This encouragement was justified by the view that these officers were a force for reform, that Egyptian society badly needed reform, that a new society had to be built up in Egypt, that if it was not built up there would be no stability in the country, and that only a government composed of young, modern, progressive, forward-looking men could effect the necessary transformation. The policy was grandiose, but deeply misconceived in itself and in the benefits for the United States which it was anticipated would accrue from its application. But even confining oneself strictly to US interests, the policy must be judged a failure since Nasser and the revolutionary officers in the end followed a policy of friendship with the Soviet Union—which it was precisely the aim of the United States to prevent. As for the reform of Egyptian society, it would be hazardous in the extreme to claim that the military regime has fulfilled the hopes which its advent widely aroused.

The second example relates to the Suez affair of 1956. The policy that the United States adopted led to the ruin of the British and French influence in the Eastern Mediterranean, and ultimately elsewhere. It was accompanied by a great outpouring of principles and professions about the impermissibility of aggression, etc. The advantages anticipated from this heavily ideological policy remain mysterious. But there is nothing mysterious about the disadvantages which Nasser's triumph, procured chiefly by the United States, shortly afterwards produced for the United States. In so far as anything can be said to be a consequence of anything else, it may safely be said that the *coup d'état* of 14 July 1958 in Iraq and the civil war suffered by the Lebanon at the same time were both consequences of United States policies in 1956.

Apart from the fact that it had not been an Imperial Power, and that its policies as a Great Power and as a Superpower have been to a considerable extent infected by ideological predilections, the United States was different from the United Kingdom in another very important respect. In the United Kingdom the conduct of foreign affairs has traditionally been part of the Crown prerogative—which, in modern times, has meant that it is in the hands of ministers, parliamentary control over whom in this respect being very difficult to enforce, even when the House of Commons was more powerful that it is now. The government of the United Kingdom, again, rests on the assumption that the Queen-in-Parliament is sovereign. But given the supremacy attained by the House of Commons over the House of Lords and given that the Cabinet controls the Commons through the operation of party discipline, ministerial discretion in conducting foreign policy becomes practically unlimited.

Conditions in the United States, as is well known, are very different. Through its treaty powers and control over appointments, the Senate is practically the President's partner in foreign affairs. The government of the United States is a government of checks and balances in which the Executive is by no means able to control the Legislative. This makes for greater responsiveness, ultimately, to the wishes of the electorate. And this electorate consists, to an appreciable extent, of descendants of immigrants with all their varied sympathies and connections abroad. In the circumstances, these are sometimes successful, in a manner unknown in the United Kingdom, in bringing to bear pressures of which both Legislative and Executive have to take account. All this is to say that policy and its execution are subject, in a wholly legitimate way, to influences and constraints from which other Great Powers have been immune. It is very difficult to say, *prima facie* and as a general rule, whether this makes for the successful or unsuccessful conduct of foreign affairs. This, at any rate, is certain: that a foreign policy conducted under such conditions becomes an extraordinarily complex thing to observe and study, and that the pitfalls standing in the way of the historians are more numerous than usual.

As has been said, the Rooseveltian stress on the liquidation of empires neglected the issue whether such a policy would make the Soviet threat more or less dangerous. But it became clear, fairly soon after the end of the war, that the threat could not be denied or gainsaid. This threat in fact has enforced on United States policy a discipline of the kind which the possession of overseas territories imposed on the defunct empires. The threat in due course evoked a counter-threat, the display of force, the creation of a counter-force. The need for a counter-force has, willy-nilly, been one of the two poles between which the United States has oscillated since 1945. The other is, of course, the ideological one best exemplified, for example, by support for Nasser after 1952, by pressure on the British to give up their bases on the Suez Canal, and most strikingly by the policy adopted at the time of the Suez expedition. But this ideological stance has sometimes been justified by power-political considerations. The threat from the Soviet Union enforced discipline on the United States. But since its inception the Soviet Union has been highly adept itself at using ideology as a weapon. Hence it has tempted its opponents to spread a counter-ideology, which has been justified by the argument that showing sympathy for Third-World aspirations, a forthcoming eagerness in the 'North-South dialogue', and similar gambits would themselves be a potent weapon against the Soviet Union. Potent an ideological weapon may be, but it is not clear who will be hurt or deterred by it, nor whether to counter ideology with ideology will not itself be something of a victory for the Soviet Union. In any case, if in using ideology a leaf is being taken out of the Soviet book, it is salutary to remember that for the Soviet Union ideology has never been a substitute for military power.

13

HOW TO (AND HOW NOT TO) SEEK PEACE IN THE MIDDLE EAST

President Sadat's visit to Jerusalem in November 1977 and the events that followed it in quick succession are, in their unexpectedness and possibly far-reaching effects, difficult to parallel in recent diplomatic history. Greatly different as were the protagonists and the issues involved, the Nazi-Soviet Pact of the summer of 1939 springs to mind as a similar event which threw into the melting-pot previous assumptions and calculations. It would have been a fair question to ask why, say, British or French policy-makers did not in advance consider the likelihood and repercussions of such a *coup* or, to take a nearer and more comparable event, why the Israeli and US governments were caught off balance by the October 1973 war.

So now, too, it is interesting—to put the matter no higher—to ask why Sadat's initiatives seemed, initially at any rate, to have occasioned in Washington not perhaps consternation, but certainly surprise and embarrassment. A development of this kind seemed to go against all the assumptions and expectations that had led the US administration, in the months preceding the visit, to advocate a 'comprehensive' settlement of the Arab-Israeli conflict to be worked out at a Geneva conference where, under the joint auspices of the US and the USSR, all the parties to the dispute would be represented. One such party which the US, in the face of adamant Israeli objections, was endeavouring somehow to include was the Palestine Liberation Organization. Though nothing has changed in the aims and stance of the PLO, which have been exactly the same before and after Sadat's visit to Jerusalem, it is a measure of the disorientation produced by this event that President Carter should (at a press conference held on 15 December 1977) vehemently denounce the PLO. By their negative and intransigent attitudes, he declared, they have removed themselves from any immediate prospect of participation in peace negotiations.

This kind of somersault, which may or may not prove politically advantageous, does lead us to suspect that the assumptions on which the earlier policy was based were perhaps insufficiently critical. Did they have built into them elements that might have allowed in advance for some such contingencies as have now eventuated? And here too a parallel could prove illuminating and even perhaps—were it not so difficult to learn from history—instructive.

As is well known, it was a British initiative that led to giving the Zionist movement an internationally recognized standing in the affairs of Palestine, and may thus be said to have brought into existence the conflict which the US is now so deeply engaged in attempting to settle—engaged in a manner utterly unforeseen during the whole period running from the Balfour Declaration to the establishment of the state of Israel. Less than two decades after the Balfour Declaration was published, serious disturbances led the British to reconsider their commitment (enshrined in the League-of-Nations mandate) to facilitate the establishment of a Jewish national home in Palestine. These disturbances may be seen to stand at the beginning of a decade, running roughly from 1937 to 1947, in which British policy in Palestine and in the Middle East took on a character such that the historian cannot help bringing it to mind when he reads his morning newspaper and wonders about the exact meaning of some pronouncement by the President of the US, a communiqué by the Department of State, a declaration by an Arab public figure or a counter-declaration by his Israeli counterpart. Why is it that in spite of the fact that the US is so different in its circumstances and outlook from Britain, recent events have something in them of the *déjà vu*, something which powerfully evokes the earlier period?

It is generally accepted, and it seems also to be true, that the establishment of a Jewish state in Palestine was a failure for British policy and seriously damaged British interests in the Middle East. But we have to ask what this policy was, and whether the failure was fortuitous and due to circumstances that nobody could have reasonably foreseen, or whether the failure was inherent in the policy itself. Inherent in it because the policy was not well thought-out, and was thus fated to disappoint the hopes placed on it.

The policy had its origin in the Arab Revolt which began in Palestine in 1936—a disturbance serious enough to force the British government to rethink its Palestine policy and its stance towards Zionism. This process of rethinking went on over a period in the Foreign and Colonial Offices, and eventually involved also the Cabinet. It was obviously a response to a changing situation. What crystallized at the end of this process was the profound belief (which became fully manifest in 1938-39) that the conflict in Palestine could not be isolated from other Middle Eastern issues in which vital British interests were involved; that for the sake of these vital issues other parties—aside, that is, from the Zionists and the Palestine

Arabs—should be allowed a say in the settlement of the conflict; and that their desiderata should in some sense and to some extent be satisfied. These other parties were neighbouring Arab states who, indeed, ever since the outbreak of disorders in Palestine, had been pressing on the British government, more or less insistently, the case of their fellow-Arabs in Palestine.

The British decision that this pressure should be acceded to and recognized as legitimate, issued in the Palestine Conferences which met in London at the beginning of 1939 (the plural form being used in the official designation in order to mark and ratify the Arab refusal to sit in one conference hall with the Jews). Arab states were officially represented. In retrospect, this may be seen as one of the most important landmarks in the history of the Palestine conflict. Two benefits were anticipated by the British from this unprecedented acknowledgement of the right of foreign states to interfere in the affairs of a British-administered territory. It was hoped that the Arab states would exert a moderating influence on the Palestine Arab leadership, and persuade them to agree to a settlement which, in any case, would considerably limit the British commitment to Zionism; and it was thought that this signal recognition by Britain of the standing of Arab states in the Palestine question would secure their friendship in the disturbed and dangerous international situation which was looming so large in 1939.

These expectations failed. The Arab states proved unable to persuade the Mufti of Jerusalem (who was then the most powerful Palestine Arab leader) to settle for the important and significant concessions to Arab demands made in the White Paper. It is also very doubtful whether this policy served to secure Arab friendship in the second world war. What is at any rate beyond doubt is that pro-Axis sympathies and actions ceased to be a threat to the Allies in the Arab world only when the Axis no longer was the invincible power it had seemed to be after the fall of France. But whatever the hopes and calculations that led the British government officially to recognize the right of Arab states to interfere in the affairs of Palestine, there is no doubt that the policy was a great blunder, the consequences of which are even now being felt.

If the pacification of Palestine was thought to require great concessions to be made to the Palestine Arabs, it was perfectly feasible for such concessions to be made without introducing into the conflict a large number of new parties. For there is no doubt that the introduction of these parties made the conflict more, rather than less, difficult to settle. Implicit in British policy was the assumption that because the Arab states were deeply concerned about their brethren in Palestine—which may have been true—therefore it followed that they would all be of one mind in seeking a settlement. The very opposite was in fact true. The policies and interests of various Arab states in respect of Palestine varied a great deal and they were potentially and actually in conflict. And these inter-Arab conflicts did not alleviate but, on the contrary, tremendously complicated and envenomed the Palestine conflict. These inter-Arab rivalries and disagreements were not unknown to the British government, but ministers and officials chose to disregard them.

Another feature of British policy in the decade 1937–47 comes to mind while considering the present situation. In 1945–47 Palestine once again became a highly critical issue in British policies relating to the Middle East. Britain was then still, to all outward appearance, the paramount power in the area. Great British interests were involved here: oil, which now loomed larger than before; and defense against the Soviet Union. The Kremlin, after its long isolation, was now emerging as a formidable threat, over a wide perimeter to be sure, but also especially in the Middle East where, therefore, the friendship of the Arab states was believed to be as important as it had been thought in 1939. These states were bound by a variety of ties to Great Britain, but the ties were, in many important cases, under great strain over issues peculiar to each state, and not particularly involved with the conflict in Palestine. But British policy-makers chose—in the face of much evidence—to play things so as to make the Palestine dispute the crucial issue in the Middle East in terms of which everything was to be judged. It was the outcome on which everything was to be deliberately staked. Moreover, the solution of the problem had to satisfy not only the Palestine Arabs, but also all the members of the Arab League. This was all-in comprehensiveness. In the third volume of his memoirs Hugh Dalton (Chancellor of the Exchequer in the Attlee administration) quotes an entry from his diary dating from January 1947 which provides a telling critique as much of Ernest Bevin's policy as of later attempts at comprehensive solutions.

> I have tried several times in Cabinet [Dalton recorded] to get them to agree to partition as the best solution. I have urged that, instead of trying to make a synthetic glue of all the Arab States, including Egypt, we should try to split them. . . .

But Dalton, as he wrote, failed to make much headway with Bevin.

Bevin's policy failed—failed in the sense that when it came to war the Zionists could not be defeated; failed precisely because it came to a war, in which it was Britain's friends and allies who were defeated and humiliated; and failed, finally, in the sense that what took place in Palestine in 1948 made British problems with various Arab states not easier, but more difficult to deal with. It was an ambitious policy, but it was ill-judged and reckless. Ill-judged because, whether the Zionists won or lost, it was highly speculative whether the British would in any way benefit; and this because it was simply not true that Palestine was at the centre of all Middle Eastern problems.

The parallel between British policies then and prevalent US views now should be apparent. In both cases there is the strongly held belief that the Palestine problem is at the centre of all Middle Eastern issues (and with the occasionally added rider nowadays that the PLO is at the centre of the Palestine problem). And there is a second belief, as strongly held: to be settled, the Palestine problem requires the participation of all parties with any shadow of a claim to participate—requires, in the current terminology, a 'comprehensive' solution.

But more than a parallel is involved here. British policies over Palestine in the decade 1937–47 established a conventional wisdom about the Middle East which has become widespread and influential not least in American official (and academic) circles. The US did not become seriously involved in Middle Eastern affairs until the second world war, and did not become a dominating factor in them until some time after that war. A reader of the published collections of US State Department papers relating to this area from the outbreak of the Arab revolt in Palestine onwards will be impressed by the extent to which American officials implicitly accepted the assumptions that underlay British policies from 1937. But these were assumptions, let it be remembered, which had been late in making their appearance, and which had been a response to a particular international situation; assumptions, moreover, which were remote from the political realities, and which proved profitless, and indeed highly damaging to British interests!

Curiously enough these same assumptions underlie, perhaps unwittingly, a document which is admittedly not official, but to which later events have given a particular importance. This is the so-called Brookings Report on the Middle East (it appeared in December 1975), the analysis and conclusions of which seem to have been adopted by official agencies.[1] Like the British policy-makers of 1937–47, the Brookings Report considers the Palestine conflict as the crux in the Middle East. It is, of course, undoubtedly true that the Palestine conflict is crucial for Israel and for some of its Arab opponents. But does it have the same over-riding importance for the US? And if it has, is it the case that the Brookings proposals are the best way of dealing with it?

> The United States has a vital interest [the Report declares] in the establishment of a stable peace in the Middle East.

Taken as a bare general statement, the assertion seems unexceptionable. But is it not really to be qualified? One may observe in passing that if today American influence is so great in the Middle East, this is the fortunate outcome of a war (that of October 1973). But leaving this aside, should not one consider whether it is really the case that *any* peace, provided it is stable, will be consonant with the interests of the US? Supposing it was the 'stable peace' of Eastern Europe, or of parts of the Far East today? To answer this question is to suggest that US interest in a stable peace cannot be absolute and unqualified. The point is perhaps elementary; but it is worth making not only for its own sake, but also because the statement which evokes it is couched in that rhetoric of general principles the resort to which is a standing temptation in a democracy but which can be so misleading and so dangerous.

> The United States [the Report again says] has a strong interest in the security, independence, and well-being of Israel and the Arab states of the area and in the friendship of both.

Again this is unexceptionable, but the Report goes on to say that 'their security and future development will remain in jeopardy until a durable settlement is concluded'. Here, too, we have unqualified prognostications which nothing in the situation can possibly authorize. For is it not conceivable that the very search for a 'durable' settlement between Arabs and Israelis will so exacerbate matters, and arouse among various parties such fears for their security and interests, that tensions in the area will be *increased* rather than lessened? Again, may it not be the case that 'a durable settlement' will do nothing to provide 'security and future development'? This is simply because the political and social problems of the Middle East are such as to preclude stability in any conceivable future. The Arab world today is the prey of an ideological and activist style of politics that is not compatible with stability. The legitimacy of many of its regimes is simply that derived from the sword. The disparity in the population, power and wealth of the various states is exactly such as to provide a temptation for one state to lay its hands on the resources or territory of a neighbour, and for that neighbour to take pre-emptive measures—whether forcible or not—to prevent such an occurrence. The list of civil upsets and inter-state disputes in the Arab world during the last decade which have nothing to do with the Palestine conflict is enough to show that a promise of 'security and future development' to follow the settlement of this conflict is vain and delusive.

> The United States [the Report also declares] has a strong interest in the unimpeded flow of Middle Eastern oil to itself and to its European and Japanese allies.

This, too, is unexceptionable. Furthermore, it is given point by the embargo of 1973. But one has to say that it is unsafe to link the two issues in a manner such as to lead to a belief that the supply of oil can be made secure by a settlement of the Arab-Israeli conflict. The supply of oil is by far the larger and more formidable issue. The issue is this: whether it is consistent with their security that the United States and its allies should be so utterly dependent for a vital commodity on a source of supply which is outside their control. A new Arab-Israeli war may, it is true, once again interrupt this supply. But is it not prudent to consider that even if this conflict were to disappear the threat of such interruption would remain? Such a threat must figure in the plans of any potential enemy, and can be minimized only if the Americans are known to be able and willing to counter it. The real question here concerns the steps that can be taken to prevent such a catastrophe—and this problem is such as to reduce to quite modest proportions the Arab-Israeli conflict. If such a threat were guarded against, the Arab-Israeli conflict would not loom so large. The contrary is not the case.

But it is sometimes said that Saudi Arabia—the largest supplier of oil—must be kept friendly, and that the principal means to this end must be a solution of the Arab-Israeli conflict that would be favourable to the Arab side. It is by no means clear what such a solution would have to be since Arab views have been in this matter more or less irreconcilable. It is also true that large interests are at stake for the US in Saudi Arabia. But it by no means follows that a settlement—even a pro-Arab settlement—of the Arab-Israeli conflict will necessarily safeguard these interests. Such a settlement will not do away with radicalism and instability in the Arab world, and will thus by no means lessen the threat to the present Saudi regime. It may even, conceivably, increase it. More than this, if the US has great interests at stake in Saudi Arabia, the stake of the Saudi regime in Saudi Arabia is even greater. To preserve these interests, the Saudi regime needs the friendship and protection of the US just as much as, or perhaps more than, the US needs Saudi friendship and good will.

Connected with the formidable problems created by insecure oil supply is the other formidable problem presented by 'petrodollars'; their effects on capital markets, on the mechanism of international finance, and on the welfare and prosperity of the poorer countries. This, again, transcends by far in significance the Arab-Israeli conflict.

It is, if at all, only faintly related to it. The principal oil-exporting countries are said to accumulate external balances at the rate of $45 billion and more a year. A large part of this accumulated surplus is believed to be invested in short-term loans in the Western money markets. It is not necessary to assume ill will on the part of the lenders to believe that this is a highly dangerous situation. These lenders are relatively inexperienced in dealing with international capital markets, nor can they have the same pressing concern as the free industrial countries for the health and stability of international trade and finance on which their prosperity in the end depends. The short-term loans in which so many of the 'petrodollars' are invested are used to meet the needs of the governments of the poorer countries whose accumulated debts are said probably to amount now to over $200 billion. For these poorer countries to be kept afloat, their debts have to be refinanced by the Western banks. These banks thus find themselves in the position of borrowing (petrodollars) short in order to lend long. The perils of such an arrangement do not need to be spelled out.

An equally perilous prospect in the long term is presented by this enormous shift of capital resources to the oil-producing countries. The income from the oil accrues directly to governments who thus become the preponderating economic power in the countries which they govern, with all that this implies in the way of *dirigisme,* 'socialism' and similar inter-ventions—which must be more or less crude, capricious and harmful—in the market. Where international investment is concerned, this means that private venture capital (which before 1939 was very successful in indus-trializing large parts of the world and greatly enhancing material prosperity) becomes less and less important. As loans are now made *by* governments, they are also made *to* governments. These are by and large the governments of the poorer countries of Asia, Africa and South America, and their investment record is (as is well known) dim and dismal. The capital which the oil producers have succeeded in extracting from the rest of the world will, thus, in very many instances be used inefficiently and wastefully, to the detriment of employment and international trade, and thus to the detriment of the free world; used also in shoring up and maintaining regimes whose interests and instincts are far removed from those of the free world.

Considering the magnitude of the problems involved in obtaining a secure supply of oil, and those created by the siphoning off to the OPEC countries of so much wealth, it seems absurd and pathetic of the Report to declare that US efforts 'to establish greater economic stability and to help manage the growing economic interdependence among nations more effectively are likely to be frustrated' so long as the Arab-Israeli conflict goes on. This is like claiming that efforts to eradicate cancer are likely to be frustrated so long as a cure for the common cold has not been found.

The Report also has something to say about the means of settling the conflict. Here it is absolutely unequivocal. It declares that the settlement has to be 'comprehensive'—a term that has become very popular of late, and which we may suspect to have been launched on its career by this Report.

As has been said, the fearful complication which the Palestine conflict assumed dates precisely from the decision of the British government to give in to the pressure of the Arab states, and formally to recognize their right to intervene in the dispute. This was because there were now involved a large number of parties with incompatible, and even irreconcilable, interests, whose stance was governed by a multitude of calculations that had little to do with Palestine. The search for a 'comprehensive' solution may exacerbate the situation rather than remedy it. To 'unfreeze' the situation by a search for 'comprehensive' solutions may be as unsafe as to keep it 'frozen'—a prospect by which the writers of the Report are appalled. May it not be the case, anyway, that this is a conflict for which no acceptable solution can be devised? That the problem will not be solved, but will perhaps simply disappear in circumstances as yet unknown?

The policy that the Report advocates is 'comprehensive' in an even more drastic sense. For it has gone so far as to propose—and recent American policy at one point adopted the proposal—that the Soviet Union should be invited to have a share in the making of the 'comprehensive' settlement. In justifying such a step the Report argues that 'the Soviet Union is increasingly annoyed at being left on the side-lines', and that it 'has a considerable capacity for complicating or even for blocking' progress towards a settlement.

What has to be said here is that the Soviet Union will not be deterred from 'complicating' or 'blocking' a settlement simply because it is involved in the negotiation. It is even conceivable that its ability to complicate or block will be enhanced precisely because it is able to take part in the negotiation. The matter is by no means straightforward or clear-cut, and the risks either way are considerable. But instead of arguing the case the Report is content to make sweeping but highly doubtful assertions.

Even more doubtful is the equally bare assertion that another Arab-Israeli war will provoke 'a major confrontation between the United States and the Soviet Union'. Confrontation between the two Superpowers results not so much from conflict between other states as from their own world-wide rivalry and their mutual suspicions. Specifically, if there is confrontation in the Middle East between the US and the USSR, this will arise not from an Arab-Israeli war, but from the desire of each Superpower to secure advantages in an unstable but important region and, if possible, to deny these advantages to the other. An Arab-Israeli war could be the occasion of a confrontation—but so might a *coup d'état* in Iran or Saudi Arabia—or a quarrel between Iraq and its neighbours to the south.

For a document produced by a committee in which academics predominated, the Brookings Report seems flatly categorical and dogmatic in its analysis, and curiously reluctant to explore options, risks and possibilities. If I have dealt with it in such detail it is because its outlook and assumptions seem to have governed recent policies mooted by the US administration.

It is quite in keeping with the character of the Report that the Egyptian-Israeli negotiations initiated by President Sadat's visit to Jerusalem could not have been envisaged or allowed for in its scheme and that, as has been said, the administration which adopted its conclusions was surprised and taken aback by these developments. But was it not always on the cards that if any Arab state were to decide to settle with Israel on its own, this would have to be Egypt? It is the only state with the incentive and the ability to do so, and its quarrel with Israel can be settled with relative ease. That such a possibility should not have been explored either in the Report or, apparently, by the Carter administration is very significant. But Sadat's initiative will have had the advantage for the US administration—whether it knows this or not—of extricating it from a futile and damaging line of policy.

It is usually (and rightly) said that the academic's virtues—his critical turn of mind, and his willingness to follow the argument wherever it leads—become defects in the man of action, who must accustom himself to make quick decisions on the basis of hunches and imperfect information. But in a region like the Middle East where yesterday's friend can become today's opponent, where alliances and allegiances shimmer and dissolve like the *fata morgana*, the academic's scepticism, his readiness to scrutinize far-fetched theories and unlikely suppositions—qualities not to be found in the Brookings Report or in the policies to which it gave birth—are perhaps qualities that even busy men of action should cultivate.

14

MISREADING THE MIDDLE EAST

The years which have elapsed since the Yom Kippur war have seen the United States sustain two very serious setbacks in the Middle East. In a surprisingly short space of time the regime of the Shah—a principal US ally in the area—has crumbled, while the new rulers are unstable, unpredictable and unfriendly. Nobody can tell what the repercussions of these remarkable events will turn out to be, but it is sure beyond peradventure that, even in the best of circumstances, US interests (public as well as private) and US influence in Iran and in the region generally will have sustained a severe blow.

Ironically enough, the ally who has now been destroyed was himself chiefly instrumental in inflicting the other major defeat suffered during this decade by the US (and the West generally) in the Middle East. It is notorious that the Shah was the most eager and the most pressing in persuading his confederates in OPEC to increase again and again the price of oil—an increase the economic and political consequences of which are as incalculable as they are ruinous. Ruinous, not only to OPEC's victims but also, as recent events have again ironically shown, to the Shah himself. He might still be on his throne had he not, dazzled by his easy spoils, spent and spent and spent, thus shaking, destabilizing and discomforting hitherto immobile and obedient masses.

Great as are the reverses over oil and in Iran, yet the agents who brought them about, compared to the United States in point of power and resources, are puny and insignificant; and furthermore it could not possibly be argued that these were the instruments or puppets of another Superpower who was effecting indirectly what it could not accomplish directly. If things have come to such a pass, it is then the policies which the United States chose to follow in the Middle East that must have brought things to this pass. US preponderance in Middle Eastern affairs is relatively recent, dating from not much before the end of the second world war. Saudi Arabian oil, and later the necessities of a global strategy which Soviet hostility made necessary, led to US involvement in the area. If, in the decades following the second world war, the US attempted to play an imperial role in the Middle East, the manner in which it played this role was very different from that of Britain and France who had preceded the US as dominant powers. Unlike the United States, these two empires did actually occupy and administer— for longer or shorter periods—Middle Eastern territories. This on the whole gave them a feel for the political realities of the region, and a grasp of what is necessary for gaining and keeping power. The US, on the other hand, never occupied or administered Middle Eastern territories. And what is more, we see it adopting, as a dominant power in the region, a paradoxically anti-imperial stance. The character of this stance in the formative period of US dominance has now been described and documented for us in Phillip J. Baram's excellent study, *The Department of State in the Middle East 1919-1945*. As Professor Baram shows, anti-imperialism was a prejudice that foreign service officers and departmental officials shared with their political superiors, whether in the State Department or the White House. So long as US policy concerned itself only with safeguarding private and business interests in the region, and with ensuring an open door for commercial enterprise, such sentiment was of little consequence. It was otherwise when the US joined the war against the Axis, and needed to formulate a policy over strategic and political issues.

As Professor Baram shows, the formulation of this policy was heavily influenced and at times determined by the officials in the Near Eastern division and in the Post-war Planning division of the State Department, as well as by the views of foreign service officers stationed in Arab capitals. The names of Wallace Murray, Paul Alling, Loy Henderson, George Wadsworth, William Eddy, Christina Grant and William Yale are probably not very well known to the general public, nor on examination does the originality, penetration or sagacity of their views on the Middle East entitle them to any wide recognition. But by virtue of their official positions, these views enjoyed a privileged access to the highest political authorities who, even if they did not always agree with them, learned to view the Middle East and its problems, as well as the options open to the United States, in the light of the assumptions which over the years they encountered in despatches, minutes and policy papers.

As representative of their outlook and views we may instance Loy Henderson, appointed Minister in Iraq in 1943 and director of the Office of Near Eastern and African Affairs in 1945. In the latter post Henderson, Professor Baram writes,

> turned out to be a vociferous foe of France in the Levant. His frequent memoranda were presented as dire and urgent philippics. French tactics, he inveighed, 'are similar to those used by the Japanese in Manchukuo and by the Italians in Ethopia,' as well as

to those 'pursued by Russia in Eastern Europe.' France disgraced the Allies, destroyed the confidence of little countries in great powers, and dealt a blow to the prestige of the infant UN Organization and the recently convened San Francisco Conference. As for France's wish for pre-eminence in the Levant, none at all should be countenanced, said Henderson, even on the level of education, language and culture. The French have no rights in the Levant, indeed had none even when the mandate was legal.

It is not only in retrospect that Henderson's stance may be queried. What purpose, one might have asked even in 1945, would be served by this anti-French policy so unhesitatingly advocated? Again, the parallel drawn between Japanese in Manchuria, Italians in Ethiopia, Russia in Eastern Europe and the French in the Levant was so clearly exorbitant as to bring into serious question this official's judgment.

But Henderson's views were neither eccentric nor isolated. We learn, for instance, that in 1944 the State Department's inter-divisional committee on Arab countries went so far in its eagerness to destroy the French position in the Levant as to recommend the nationalization of key French financial interests in Syria and the Lebanon. Collaboration with the Soviet Union in the same righteous cause was also welcomed: 'It was believed', Professor Baram tells us, 'that mutual anti-imperialism would put Moscow and Washington on the same sides of the barricades against the French. That position in turn stood to enhance Soviet-American cooperation on other problems.' What other problems? Puerile as it may sound, the belief of the State Department officials was that a Soviet-American ganging-up against the French in the Levant would actually make the Soviets easier to deal with on the Polish question. But it was not only in the Levant that Soviet co-operation was desired. In Palestine, it was also believed, Soviet-British-American co-operation would strengthen 'progressives' and 'moderates' among both Arabs and Jews against the 'extremists' on both sides, and lead to the creation of a binational state there. The misjudgment was just as grievous as in the Levant, and in both cases argues a failure to appraise the local situation, to fathom the character and aims of Soviet policy, and to think out United States interests and objectives in what was, admittedly, a new, unfamiliar situation. This intellectual failure stemmed as much from commitment to a naive anti-imperialist ideology as from inexperience plain and simple.

In the case of Saudi Arabia, however, ideology seemed to be the perfect hand-maiden to American interests—which, although private, were fast becoming quite substantial and beginning even to have a bearing on political and strategic issues. Through a combination of shrewdness and good luck, American oil companies obtained a license to prospect in Saudi Arabia.

They found extensive deposits and began exporting Saudi oil in 1938. When, some three years later, the United States joined the war and began to be politically active in the Middle East, the opportunity which this gave to displace the British as Ibn Sa'ud's patron and protector began to seem literally golden. Anti-imperialist sentiment, no doubt genuine and deeply held, was now seen to be profitable. It was now that there began that deliberate and continuous process of magnifying and aggrandizing Saudi Arabia—a poor, sparsely populated country dependent on foreign bene-volences, where a form of Islam highly repugnant to the generality of Muslims held sway, a country the sole importance of which was that it contained vast amounts of oil which, however, it was utterly incapable of extracting. It was then that there was inaugurated the style of respectful and awed flattery in which it became customary for the President of the United States to address the King of Saudi Arabia—a style that may be exemplified by the locution 'Great and Good Friend' with which Roose-velt's missives, drafted by the State Department, began. It was clearly believed that if only British influence could be eliminated a warm and exclusive American-Saudi special relationship could be established and maintained. But of course one had to be vigilant against all imperialist incursions. Thus, during 1942 the idea was mooted that Ibn Sa'ud might be helped to pay off his debts with Jewish funds secured through Zionist good offices, and that this would facilitate a settlement in Palestine. It is highly probable that the scheme would have come to nothing. Wallace Murray, then head of the Division of Near Eastern Affairs, however was greatly disturbed by it, and his extravagant language in rejecting it indicates not only the cast of his mind and his implicit assumptions, but also how great the umbrage he would take to anything which might threaten, however slightly, the intimate coziness of US-Saudi relations. If the Jewish loan to Ibn Sa'ud went through, he feared that 'Zionists could extend their influence and activities outside Palestine', and this 'appears to have the character of economic imperialism backed by international sanction'. Economic imperi-alism: the vulgar catchwords of Marxism strike an incongruous note in the memoranda of this high State Department official.

The attempt to edge out the British from Saudi Arabia and secure the exclusive friendship of Ibn Sa'ud involved more than epistolary magni-loquence. State Department officials were willing to recognize without question Ibn Sa'ud's right to have a say in the settlement of the Palestine problem, and to make far-reaching, albeit elastic, promises about it. Thus in a letter of 1943 drafted in the Near Eastern Division for Roosevelt's signature (which the President only slightly watered down) Ibn Sa'ud was assured that no decision would be taken until after he had been 'fully consulted and his agreement sought'. This line of policy seems to have been adopted as a matter of course, as though it were axiomatic that Saudi Arabia—as well as other Arab states—had the right to a say in the affairs of

Palestine. This indeed was what the British had decided, as an act of policy, to assume in 1939. But it did not follow that the United States should automatically do likewise. There were cogent reasons for it not to do so. Palestine was a controversial issue in US politics, and a wise policy should see to it that the two partners in policy-making, i.e. the Executive and the Senate, act in harmony, or at least do not pull in different directions. In Palestine specifically, it was not evident that the cause of peace would be served or US interests advanced if one side should be favoured or supported at the expense of the other. Yet this was, as Professor Baram shows, precisely the implicit assumption in State Department thinking. Writing of George Wadsworth, who served in various Middle Eastern posts before and during the second world war, Professor Baram remarks that he

> in effect misled his Arab hearers with his constant maximal pledges of American support and with his concomitant downgrading of any American interest in Zionism. Thus, whenever an American political leader endorsed a Jewish homeland in Palestine the Arabs felt, variously, that it was mere electioneering, or that they were being betrayed by America, and/or that a Jewish conspiracy of wealth and the media in America had caused a reversal. For had not Departmental officers like Wadsworth conditioned and assured them for years that American foreign policy was anti-Zionist? I would submit [Baram goes on to say] that the Department's practice of such self-deception and deception of the Arabs—as if, in the making of American foreign policy, Presidential, Congressional and domestic opinion counted for naught—was as much a cause of the Arabs' evolving hostility to the US as the substantive fact that after the war American presidents did support the right of a Jewish state to exist.

It may be that this tendency by officials to play down inconvenient political declarations or interpret them misleadingly, as Baram speculates, led James Byrnes, the Secretary of State in 1945, to issue an instruction to foreign service posts in the Middle East that they 'should not (repeat not) unless otherwise instructed attempt to comment on . . . or interpret . . . in any way' a statement by President Truman favouring the immigration of Jewish refugees to Palestine.

The three years between 1945 and 1948 were to involve the United States deeply in Middle Eastern politics and particularly in the Palestine conflict. In this conflict a large number of parties and interests were deeply engaged, and it was by no means easy for a Great Power like the United States, with a multitude of interests and considerations to reconcile, to adopt a policy such as to minimize damage, if not to maximize gain. All the more difficult in that public opinion, the Legislature, the President and the State Department held different views and varied them from time to time. A hesitant and indecisive stance was therefore to be expected, and it may be that, as Nadav Safran remarks in his *Israel: The Embattled Ally*, such hesitation actually made the conflict worse, and that a clearer and more decisive policy would have prevented armed intervention by the Arab states. In the circumstances of 1947 partition was the most promising solution, and resolute public support for it by the United States and Britain would most probably have limited the immediate violence and avoided the long-drawn-out, festering and ever-widening conflict. In the event, the US first supported partition, then suddenly abandoned it, then at the last minute decided once more to support it and recognize the provisional government of the new state of Israel. It is well known that partition was unpopular in the State Department, and that in recognizing Israel Truman went against advice of the officials dealing with the Middle East. One of these officials, William Eddy, who had served as Minister to Saudi Arabia and was a most fervent advocate of the Saudi connection, resigned from the Department in protest. His gesture may be taken to symbolize widely held sympathies and aversions which even now are still much in evidence.

The years following the 1948-9 Arab-Israeli war showed that the US, which was now a dominant power in the Middle East, had not really thought out a coherent policy—a policy that would articulate its principal interests in the region and relate them to the realities of the local situation. An obvious over-riding interest was to maintain stability and, in the absence of an Arab-Israeli peace treaty, to prevent new hostility. In May 1950 a US-Anglo-French Declaration was published pledging the signatories to regulate the supply of weapons to both sides, and affirming their opposition to any attempt to modify by force the boundaries laid down by the Arab-Israel armistice agreements. A chain is as weak as its weakest link, and the sequel proved that more than one link in this policy had as much consistency as melting butter.

For the policy of the Tripartite Declaration to work, the solidarity of its signatories had to remain strong and unimpaired. The policies which the US followed in the next few years were not calculated to preserve mutual confidence. The US did not prove itself solicitous of British interests in Egypt. After the military *coup d'état* that brought Nasser to power the US strongly pressed the British to evacuate the Suez Canal Zone in exchange for some elastic and minimal, not to say meaningless, engagements by Egypt. This was presumably done in order to secure the goodwill and friendship of the Egyptian military regime—a regime that US officials seriously believed would promote the welfare of the Egyptian people, and was therefore worth supporting. But if this was the calculation—and as a calculation it was manifestly faulty and absurd—then it did not chime in with the other line of policy which was followed at the same time. This was the policy that led to the Baghdad Pact, in which Iraq was given pride of place.

The Baghdad Pact policy proved both costly and unprofitable. Because it gave Iraq the primacy among Arab states, the policy alienated Nasser. He thereupon turned to the Soviets and made with them the famous arms deal of September 1955. The policy also alienated the French, who believed that it would enable Iraq to dominate Syria, whom they looked upon as their protégé. Prohibitive as the cost of the Baghdad Pact policy proved to be, it yielded no profit. Perhaps the only way it could have was for the US to uphold it against all comers, and be resolute in supporting through thick and thin the Pact and all its members. This the United States omitted to do. Not only would it not join the Pact, but also its actions undermined the power and prestige of Britain, the principal Western member of the Pact, and exposed the rulers of Iraq to a radical ideological onslaught which in the end ruined them, and put paid to both Pact and policy.

The Baghdad Pact policy made sense if Iraq was to be supported, and the machinations of its rival, Egypt, opposed and counteracted. It was therefore logical that the US should deny Nasser finance for the Aswan dam. What made no sense at all was for the US then to side with the Soviet Union and turn ferociously against its NATO allies, Britain and France, when they took up Nasser's challenge and sought to bring him down in the Suez expedition. The actions of the US in the autumn of 1956 ruined the British and French position in the Middle East, and left the US single-handedly to cope with a determined and activist Soviet Union in the region. The triumph which the US procured for Nasser made the appeal of his radicalism irresistible in the Arab world. This eventually led to the downfall of the monarchy in Iraq, and to a civil war in the Lebanon in which the US had to intervene by landing marines in Beirut.

By its uncompromising opposition to the Suez expedition, the US saved Nasser from a disaster. But no profit was obtained from this action which, as the sequel showed, proved very costly to the friends and allies of the US and thus to the US itself. As Nasser's saviour and benefactor the US could have extracted from him a settlement of the conflict with Israel or at least insisted on conditions such as to make a renewal of hostilities very difficult. Sinai, for instance could have been demilitarized, and unhindered passage through the straits of Tiran the subject of a formal treaty. As it was, this issue was simply covered by a private US undertaking to Israel which, when put to the test in 1967, proved worthless. Again, Egyptian and Israeli armies were kept apart by a UN contingent, the presence of which depended strictly on Egyptian goodwill—though a unilateral attempt to qualify this unfettered discretion was made in a private memorandum by the tortuous and unreliable Hammarskjöld. This too proved worthless when the crunch came in 1967.

A constitutional government subject to the periodical verdict of the electorate will, of course, now and again introduce changes, and sometimes far-reaching ones, in the direction of foreign policy, and such changes may give rise in an onlooker to puzzlement or even bewilderment. But how much more bewildering is the hurly-burly of US Middle Eastern policy in the 1950s when the administration was in the hands of one political party, and foreign policy largely in the hands of one man, John Foster Dulles, and thus presumably enjoying the advantage of stability. The spectacle is alarming in its senselessness, the more so that such a lot for so many depends on the steadiness, sagacity and tough-mindedness of American statesmen.

The one consistent thread in US policy towards the Middle East has been an abstract and arid 'anti-imperialism', the benefits of which are problematic, not to say illusory, whether for the US itself or for the region. The considerable political and economic support given to Nasser is a case in point. So far as the Egyptians are concerned, such support helped Nasser to inflict on them 18 years of arbitrary government, a government which attempted to shackle and minutely control the activities of its subjects, and which engaged in expensive and catastrophic adventures abroad. One act for which John F. Kennedy's administration was responsible again exemplifies this ill-considered tendency. In September 1962, a *coup d'état* to which the Egyptians were not strangers toppled the monarchy in the Yemen. It was obvious from the beginning that the conspirators faced strong opposition within the country. In order to quell it Nasser promptly sent a strong expeditionary force which, however, in five years of fighting (during which they went so far as to use poison gas against pro-monarchical villages) proved unequal to the task of establishing his protégés securely in power. Nasser waged war in the Yemen not for the sake of the conspirators, but in order to gain a foothold in the Arabian Peninsula from which to threaten and eventually overwhelm the Saudis and lay his hands on their oil. It would not have been very difficult in 1962 to guess that this was indeed Nasser's object. Why then did the Kennedy administration hasten, as early as December 1962, to recognize the new regime? This act of recognition, taking place as it did when it was by no means clear that the conspirators were in control of the whole of the Yemen, inevitably looked like a gesture of support for them and for Nasser's military intervention in the Arabian Peninsula. As in the case of Suez in 1956 the advantages anticipated from such a policy remain utterly mysterious. Fortunately for US interests Nasser was finally unsuccessful in the Yemen. But, during the five years of Egyptian dominance the Yemen served as a base from which the British position in Aden and its hinterland was continually subverted and attacked. And this may have encouraged a Labour administration to give full rein to its traditional instincts and to abandon Aden as India and Palestine had been, abruptly and catastrophically, abandoned. The consequences for Western interests of this action were, as is well known, not long in manifesting themselves.

The British evacuation of Aden was followed shortly afterwards by that of the Persian Gulf; and by 1971 there were hardly any Western bases or *points d'appui* in the Red Sea, the Indian Ocean or the Persian Gulf. Furthermore, Aden was now a Soviet satellite from which the Soviet Union could extend its power and influence over neighbouring territories and, as the war in Oman showed, a base from which subversive and 'revolutionary' movements could be launched in the Arabian Peninsula. The acts of policy which led to such outcomes were manifest blunders, as any prudent calculation would have beforehand indicated. We however do not know whether US policy-makers viewed them as dangerous blunders, or attempted to persuade Mr. Wilson or Mr. Heath (who followed in Mr. Wilson's footsteps) of the impolicy of their actions. What is known however is that, following the departure of the British, Iran and Saudi Arabia came to be looked upon as the pillars of Western defense in the region. Enormous amounts of sophisticated arms and equipment were supplied to them, and, in the case of Saudi Arabia, they continue to be supplied. The consequences of such a policy do not seem to have been seriously considered. Iran and Saudi Arabia could by no stretch of the imagination be thought capable of effectively using these arms or acting as the proxy of the US and its allies in facing the Soviet Union. Furthermore, the fact that these arms were supplied and go on being supplied in order to pay for oil compound the miscalculations and increase the dangers. Arms supplied in order to cover a deficit in the balance of payments are not the same as arms supplied in support of a policy or a strategy. Arms supplied to pay for oil become a commodity like any other—the more sold, the better; and the use made of them cannot be controlled in the same way as when arms are supplied in pursuance to a political objective. Nor is there a prospect of the effective demand for arms being exhausted since its purchasers are free to increase at will the price they charge for oil, and thus to increase the burden of the tribute which they exact from consumers.

This state of affairs, i.e. the steady erosion of the US and Western position in the Eastern Mediterranean, the Red Sea and the Persian Gulf, the ability of the oil producers to exact from their customers whatever price they please, and the accumulation of powerful weapons in the hands of unstable and unreliable governments over whose actions little or no control is possible are of the essence of the Middle Eastern problem as it confronts the US. These conditions form the context of the Arab-Israeli conflict—a conflict which, from the vantage point of the outside powers involved, is decidedly less significant than its context. In his *Decade of Decisions: American Policy Toward the Arab-Israeli Conflict 1967-1976* Professor William B. Quandt recognizes the importance of these issues for his subject, but the recognition remains formal and perfunctory. The reader gets little sense of the course of policy-making, of the way in which the larger, strategic considerations mesh with the daily concerns arising out of sudden emergencies, or from the ebb and flow of bargaining and negotiation. Quandt's account is then somewhat arid and sketchy. The reason is not far to seek: the vigour and liveliness of a diplomatic and political narrative lies in its detail—the debate over alternatives, the unexpected somersaults in policy, the hedging and the trimming, the cut-and-thrust of negotiation, the influence of personality and the compulsion of circumstances. It is not Quandt's fault if the evidence on which a detailed narrative can be based is not yet available. But because of this lack we come to feel that even though all that Quandt says about the 'decade of decisions' may be true he is not in a position to show us that it is true and, more important, in what manner exactly what he states to have taken place did take place.

For instance, the book includes a chapter on the crisis of September 1970 in Jordan, when Jordanian forces clashed with and defeated the PLO, and when in an attempt to avert this defeat the Syrians moved troops across the Syrian-Jordanian border and actually occupied the town of Irbid. Husayn appealed for help and the US, fearing the consequences of his overthrow, decided on a show of force, and was even prepared to have Israel intervene against the Syrian forces in Jordan with air strikes and, if need be, with ground troops as well. The Syrians then retreated behind their border and the crisis came to an end.

So far so good. But Quandt has criticisms to make of US policy. We are told that 'they misinterpreted the Syrian invasion, overemphasizing the Soviet role and minimizing the degree to which it grew out of internal Syrian politics'. We are also told that Nixon and Kissinger were caught 'in a perceptual trap of their own making' which led them to ignore 'regional trends' and to misjudge 'the very forces that would lead within three years to a much more dangerous outbreak of war in October 1973'. These are self-assured statements about matters concerning which we know very little indeed. For in the absence of evidence—which Quandt does not supply—who can say with any certainty what exactly the motives and actions were of such secretive autocracies as the Syrian Ba'thist regime and the Soviet Union? Furthermore, even granting that the invasion of Jordanian territory 'grew out of internal Syrian politics', does this make the threat to the Jordanian regime any less serious, or the Soviets deriving advantage from its collapse any less of a possibility? And before deciding that Nixon and Kissinger were the unwitting and maladroit victims of a self-devised 'perceptual trap', ought we not to know what evidence they had at their disposal, how they interpreted it and what their calculations were? What may not be gainsaid is that the US succeeded in 1970 in checkmating the Syrians. But, says Quandt, this success laid the foundations of failure in October 1973. A conclusion of this kind is either historical or it is nothing. An historical conclusion has, however, to be the outcome of a complex of evidence and inference that would establish how, from September 1970 to

October 1973, the events that happened and the decisions that were taken 'culminated' in the Yom Kippur war. The book provides neither evidence nor inference. It may be, of course, that Quandt's judgment is correct, but for the reader its correctness is accidental—no more than an informed or perhaps merely plausible guess, or a speculative hunch. But one can imagine speculations equally plausible leading to quite different conclusions: as, for instance, that a different policy towards the Syrian-Jordanian conflict in 1970 would still not have prevented a general Arab-Israeli war and might even have hastened it; or that the October 1973 war might not have taken place but for a failure of judgment in Israel and the US about Egypto-Syrian intentions in the days immediately preceding its outbreak.

Quandt is equally critical of US policy in the aftermath of the October war. Kissinger's step-by-step diplomacy 'rates high as a tactic but fails to convey any sense of long-term purpose'; he 'knew what he wanted to avoid better than he knew what positive goals he might be able to achieve'; he had 'a blind spot toward the Palestinian issue', and 'geared much of his diplomacy to trying to circumvent this crucial issue, to putting off the moment of truth, to weakening the appeal of the Palestinian movement, all the while hoping that some alternative would appear'. Here too, in the absence of detailed evidence about Kissinger's calculations and actions, and their day-to-day political and diplomatic context, we are quite at a loss to judge the truth of these seemingly historical assertions. Taken, however, not as historical judgments, but as prescriptions for future policy, these assertions are open to all kinds of objections. It is by no means obvious that 'the Palestinian dimension' is the 'heart' of the Arab-Israeli conflict; it could, on the contrary, be argued to be the least important part of it. Again, it is by no means obvious that a 'step-by-step diplomacy' is either inferior to the pursuit of a grand and comprehensive scheme, or indeed that it precludes such a scheme. It is also not easy to see that the search for 'positive goals' is manifestly superior to the avoidance of undesirable outcomes: sufficient unto the day, a statesman might with justice say, is the evil thereof. The maxims of policy which Quandt recommends are thus on a perfect equality with their opposites. They are as likely to be untrue and unhelpful as to be true and helpful. Their purpose in his book is, however, clear. It is to recommend and support a particular policy for dealing with the Arab-Israeli conflict, the policy associated with the so-called Brookings Report which Quandt had helped in drawing up. But if there has been movement in the Arab-Israeli conflict, it has come from a direction not looked for in the Brookings Report with its hankering after a 'comprehensive' settlement, and unexpected by the administration which began by adopting its recipes. In the closing pages of his work Quandt has pointed up and made more specific the Brookings recommendations. He looks, for instance, to a coalition of Arab regimes including Egypt, Syria and Saudi Arabia, perhaps together with Jordan, the Palestinians, and—for good measure—'perhaps even Algeria' to make peace with Israel. Long experience has shown such a coalition for such a purpose to be unobtainable. To have any hope of success, statesmanship must move with and not against the grain. A suggestion of this kind, in seeking the unattainable, in moving against the grain of Middle Eastern conditions, shows itself to inhabit the same arid region of abstraction and fancy into which US foreign policy has been all too prone, at times, to seek refuge.

15

COLONEL LAWRENCE AND HIS BIOGRAPHERS

During his lifetime, and even more so after his death, Colonel T. E. Lawrence, 'Lawrence of Arabia', was the subject of a great deal of curiosity and speculation. The literature about him is voluminous and varied, ranging from accounts of his military career during World War I and his political activities afterward to investigations of his private life and explanations— sometimes involved and far-fetched and sometimes downright sensational —of his personality and behavior.

The Lawrence corpus—as we may call it—began to be formed almost immediately after the end of the war. It can be said to begin with the popular show which Lowell Thomas put on in 1919 at the Royal Opera House, Covent Garden, and which he called 'With Allenby in Palestine and Lawrence in Arabia'. Five years later, in 1924, Thomas published *With Lawrence in Arabia*, which also proved to be highly popular, and which made Lawrence a familiar name and a thrilling legend to many more than could have seen the Covent Garden spectacle. Though this was not known at the time, it appears that Lawrence helped Thomas both with his show and his book. Two other works published before World War II were, in their turn, heavily indebted to Lawrence's help and inspiration. They spread the story of his wartime activities in a version which he approved, magnifying the significance of his adventures in the war against the Ottomans and extolling the originality of his military tactics and doctrine. These books were *Lawrence and the Arabs* by Robert Graves, which came out in 1927, and *'T. E. Lawrence': In Arabia and After* by B. H. Liddell Hart. These two books, written, in the one case by a poet and man of letters and in the other by a notable and influential writer on military topics, would be respectfully received in circles where Lowell Thomas's productions may not have impressed. Again, after his death, Lawrence's brother, Arnold, edited a symposium, *T. E. Lawrence and his Friends* (1937), in which contributors drawn from various walks of life combined to present an impressive picture of a many-sided, indeed a universal, genius.

But, of course, the most powerful by far of all the accounts which served to establish the received version of Lawrence's life and activities were his own writings: *Revolt in the Desert,* an abridgement of *Seven Pillars of Wisdom*, published in 1927; and *Seven Pillars* itself, which was first issued in a small 'subscribers' edition in 1926, and in a trade edition in 1935, immediately after his death. Both works were instant bestsellers in English and other languages, and *Seven Pillars* indeed continues to sell steadily, judging by the frequency of its reprints. To these two works we may add Lawrence's *Letters*, published in 1938, which were selected and edited by the well-known writer, David Garnett. Together with *Seven Pillars*, the *Letters* served firmly to establish in the public mind Lawrence's *persona* very much as he himself wished to have it established: a brave and heroic spirit who had championed a downtrodden nationality, and led it brilliantly and victoriously against its oppressors, only to be let down and double-crossed by his own government—a government which, out of greed and cowardice, defaulted on promises solemnly given to the Arabs. This tormented spirit, therefore, out of shame and remorse, gave up a brilliant career, enlisted as a private in the Royal Air Force, and spent the rest of his life in menial and humdrum obscurity, managing, nonetheless, to produce a literary and historical masterpiece.

This, we might say, was Lawrence by Lawrence and his friends. The veracity of all this literature in depicting Lawrence's character, activities and significance was generally, not to say universally, accepted. This remained the case until the appearance in 1955 of Richard Aldington's *Lawrence of Arabia: A Biographical Enquiry*. The most important, indeed practically the only, new source which Aldington had at his disposal consisted of a number of letters which Lawrence had addressed to Mrs. Bernard Shaw that had become available at the British Museum, in which he disclosed that he had been born out of wedlock, and described the devastating effect that the discovery of this fact had had on his life. Aldington put a great deal of weight on Lawrence's illegitimacy (which, though it had been mentioned in print in one or two places, was not then generally known) and on Lawrence's reaction to it, in order to account for Lawrence's public and private conduct.

Such an explanation of Lawrence and his activities was also favoured by Anthony Nutting, who served as principal adviser to Sam Spiegel during the production of the film *Lawrence of Arabia*. In his *Lawrence of Arabia: The Man and the Motive* published in 1961, Nutting took the line that Lawrence's bastardy gave him an assertive personality, and made him want to prove that he was as good as, if not better than, those born in wedlock—hence his vision of himself as a messiah destined to lead the Arabs to salvation. To this psychohistory (as we may now call it) Nutting added another ingredient. In November 1917, Lawrence—according to his own account—was arrested while on a reconnaissance mission in

Deraa, then under Ottoman control, and taken to the Ottoman commander. What exactly happened before he was set free the following morning Lawrence left somewhat vague, but he hinted that apart from being savagely beaten, he was also sexually assaulted by, or on the orders of, the commander. This incident left Lawrence—so Nutting argued—a 'rabid masochist'. His sense of mission was lost 'and his motors were henceforth driven by an unvarnished ambition and lust for power'.

The explanations which Aldington and Nutting put before us are highly speculative. They depend entirely, in the first place, on Lawrence's own unsubstantiated assertions; but even if we knew, beyond any reasonable doubt, that Lawrence's reactions to his illegitimacy were as he described them, and that he was really arrested, beaten and sexually assaulted in Deraa, it would still be impossible for us to link these occurrences to his military and political activities. To do so we would require specific evidence showing, for example, that the events of Deraa governed Lawrence's decisions in the conduct of a particular battle, or that the shame of his illegitimacy led him to adopt a particular line in a political negotiation. And such evidence is, of necessity, impossible to obtain. But it is not only Nutting's and Aldington's accounts which these considerations render doubtful and shaky, it is the whole enterprise of psychohistory.

Though Aldington relied heavily on the facts of Lawrence's birth, and on Lawrence's supposed reaction to these facts, his book is by no means concerned only with this issue. Aldington also casts a cold and critical glance over the public events in which Lawrence was involved; and though he did not have at his disposal the documents which have become available with the opening of the archives in the 1960s, he was yet able to throw legitimate doubt on a great many of the incidents connected with the Arab revolt and its aftermath as Lawrence and his friends had depicted them. His book was received with great animosity and indignation. It is said that efforts were made to persuade the publishers to suppress it, and that one of Lawrence's friends wanted to give Aldington a public thrashing. Sir Ronald Storrs, whose voice in the chorus was particularly noticeable, denounced Aldington in a BBC broadcast as a mean and contemptible cad, traducing and maligning a hero who was 'a touchstone and a standard of reality'. Storrs—and others—also took great exception to Aldington's revealing to the world at large the fact of Lawrence's illegitimate birth, particularly when his mother was still alive.

It is undoubtedly very praiseworthy to preserve and defend the privacy of public figures—and it was, of course, entirely because of his public activities that Lawrence attracted so much attention. But it must be said that Lawrence himself was the first to tincture public affairs with his own private passions, thus inaugurating the dangerous and pernicious fashion which so many of his biographers—and detractors—were to follow.

In the course of expatiating over Aldington's unspeakable malice,

Storrs, with haughty contempt, remarked: 'To what purpose has this been done? . . . What can be the gratification in attempting to destroy a famous name—an inspiration to youth all over the free world?' Storrs' exalted language in referring to Lawrence as 'an inspiration to youth all over the free world' is by no means exceptional. Lawrence seems to have attracted, from the time when his career became generally—albeit inaccurately—known, this kind of extravagant hyperbole. Perhaps the best example of this exaggeration occurs in a sermon preached by the Reverend L. B. Cross, Chaplain of Jesus College, Oxford (Lawrence's own college), at a memorial service held shortly after his death. The sermon drew parallels between Lawrence and Jesus. In both cases, the preacher declared, the period of preparation for their life's work lasted three years; both, again, received similar treatment from society; both were ascetic; and both felt the need to humble themselves before others.

Some 13 years after the appearance of Aldington's book, such solemn and high-flown sentiments as those expressed by Storrs and Cross came to be viewed in an ironical light as a result of revelations which first appeared in 1968 in the London *Sunday Times* and which were then substantially incorporated in a book published in 1969 and written by Phillip Knightley and Colin Simpson (the original authors of the articles), *The Secret Lives of Lawrence of Arabia.* According to these revelations, for 12 years, from 1923 to 1935, Lawrence induced a young Scotsman, John Bruce, to give him periodic beatings. These beatings were administered at the orders of a nonexistent uncle, conveyed in letters which Lawrence gave to Bruce— letters which in reality he himself had written. But Bruce, it would seem, was not the only one whom Lawrence persuaded to give him beatings. At least two others were also involved, while a third, 'a service companion' (as John E. Mack calls him in his recent biography, of which more below), was asked by Lawrence to witness the beatings, at the request of the mythical uncle, in order that he might report to him on Lawrence's reactions. According to this observer the beatings were administered with a metal whip on the bare buttocks, and Lawrence required the beatings to be 'severe enough to produce a seminal emission'.

These beatings and the bizarre arrangements associated with them had become known to Lawrence's family and friends immediately after his death. We learn from *The Secret Lives* that Mrs. Bernard Shaw interviewed Bruce in 1935 in a solicitor's office and asked him to refrain from publishing what he knew. As in the case of the facts relating to his birth, this attempt to protect Lawrence's privacy is natural and entirely laudable. On such matters the only seemly thing for those involved is absolute silence. But some might find surprising that his brother and literary executor, Professor Arnold Lawrence, should describe Lawrence's practices in a manner such that uninstructed readers—already fed on Thomas, Graves, Liddell Hart, and *Seven Pillars*—would inevitably be persuaded that Colonel Lawrence was indeed a superhuman being. In a piece published in 1937, Professor Lawrence referred in cryptic words to his brother's craving for flagellation, declaring that his 'subjection of the body was achieved by methods advocated by the saints whose lives he had read'.

The Secret Lives of Lawrence of Arabia originated in John Bruce's story which the *Sunday Times* purchased from him, but the authors' aim was decidedly more ambitious than the investigation of possibly scabrous revelations. Two years before Bruce's story appeared, British official records relating to World War I were opened to the public, and Knightley and Simpson thought to take advantage of this to examine Lawrence's role in war and politics. It cannot be said that this part of their book is a success. The British records are extremely voluminous and scattered, generated as they had been in a great many departments and agencies, and it is clear from *The Secret Lives* that the authors did not examine them with the necessary meticulousness—or perhaps did not have the time or leisure to examine, ponder and make sense of this difficult material. Their account, therefore, of Lawrence's public career—which, after all, is the only reason for any interest in him—is uncritical and unsatisfactory. Here, the authors take for granted certain received ideas about British policies during and after the war; they are too ready to assume that the British broke promises and behaved shabbily toward the Arabs; and they have a tendency to pounce on a document and wrench it out of context simply because it seems to make a sensational revelation. Knightley and Simpson were privileged to have access to one source, namely, the collection of Lawrence's letters and papers at the Bodleian Library, Oxford, which is closed to the public until the year 2000. The conditions of their access to the collection are not clear, but the authors do say that apart from giving permission to quote letters, and some amendment of material which originally appeared in the *Sunday Times,* Professor Arnold Lawrence gave no assistance in the writing of the book. This would seem to imply that Professor Lawrence wished to keep his distance from *The Secret Lives of Lawrence of Arabia.*

This manifestly is not the case with the longest and most comprehensive biography of Lawrence to appear so far, *A Prince of Our Disorder*, which came out in 1976. Its author, John E. Mack, refers to and often quotes copiously from the Bodleian Library material and acknowledges Professor Lawrence's help at many points in his narrative. But this is not to say that Mack's work is the official or authorized biography. Such a work is now in preparation and has been entrusted to J. M. Wilson. Mack is by profession a psychiatrist, but his biography of Lawrence is by no means a psychohistory, though he does on occasion have recourse to a psychoanalytical explanation of his hero's character and some of his activities. These explanations are not very convincing, but it is not by them that his work has to be judged. Like any other biography, its merits depend on the author's ability to show that he has used all the available evidence, and that he has made use of this evidence persuasively and cogently—that, in short, he has painted a lifelike picture.

Mack's book is very long—over 500 pages of text and footnotes. And, in keeping perhaps with its length, it bears a grandiose title: a prince Mack proclaims Lawrence to be, a prince of our disorder. The appellation Mack takes from an essay on Lawrence by Irving Howe which purports to investigate the 'problem of heroism'. The portentous metaphor is no doubt meant to indicate that Lawrence's life and doings are emblems and exemplars of the human condition. This seems to be Mack's belief, for he tells us that Lawrence's case is particularly important to the 'psychologically minded biographer', because 'to a varying degree we all share some of his characteristics'. Compared to the magniloquence of the title, the cautious and elastic qualifications at first sight disappoint, let down. But in truth it was prudent of Mack to retreat from the wide claim made by his title, for after all it is not true that Lawrence's 'disorder' afflicts all of humanity; we do not all, as adults, feel ourselves to be deceivers because we were deceived as children—if indeed this is what happened to Lawrence, as Mack obscurely claims; we are not all flagellants; nor are we all compelled, as again Mack says Lawrence was compelled, to live out the demands of our inner life in the public domain.

Mack is not the only writer to endow Lawrence and his misadventures with a universal, a cosmic, significance. A recent work, *Lawrence of Arabia: The Literary Impulse* by Stanley and Rodelle Weintraub (1975), claims that to dismiss Lawrence (as Herbert Read had done) as 'an uneasy adventurer', 'an Oxford graduate with a civilian and supercilious lack of discipline', 'a mind not great with thought, but tortured by some restless spirit that drives it out into the desert, to physical folly and self-immolation', is to dismiss not so much Lawrence as the 20th century. To identify the 20th century—such as it is—with these particular characteristics smacks of the extravagance to which so many writers on the subject of Lawrence are driven.

In keeping with his view of Lawrence as an exemplar and an archetype, Mack adopts toward his hero a solemn and reverential tone. With meticulous detail he chronicles the events of Lawrence's infancy and childhood: how he was breast-fed for at least a year; how early in his second year he had to be rescued from a high window ledge which he had reached by climbing over a sewing machine; how as a child he ate chiefly porridge and bananas, while as an undergraduate he liked cakes and fruits; and how on a walking tour in Brittany he carried two pairs of socks and wore one pair. Mack goes to great trouble in order to guide us through the adventures of the boy Lawrence, dressed in his blue-and-white striped jerseys, expatiating on the excitement, humour and sense of delightful mischief which he inspired in his playmates; he has even tracked down and recorded the testimony of 'the only girl to my knowledge to pass under the city of Oxford in a punt with

Lawrence'. This hagiographical style—as it may fairly be called—is the outcome of Mack's clear conviction that by 1914 (when Lawrence was 26 years old) his subject had proved himself to be an 'unusual, versatile and reasonably well-balanced genius'. It has to be said that, unless it is seen with the eyes of faith, the material which Mack puts before us warrants no such judgment. At 26 Lawrence had shown himself to be a lively, spirited and intelligent young archeologist—but one who, whatever his promise, had yet to make his mark. And he was assuredly not the only young man of promise in his generation, nor the only such young man subsequently to make his mark.

As it happened, he made his mark not in archeology but in war and politics and, as has been said earlier, it is what he did in this sphere which entitles him to our notice. This Mack in part explicitly recognizes when he says that the years 1917-18—the two years of Lawrence's participation in the Arab revolt in the Hijaz, led by Sharif Hussein, against the Ottoman Turks—were the most critical of Lawrence's life, and the 200 pages and more which the book devotes to the period 1914-22 also constitute an implicit acknowledgment of this. But these pages, which are the core of the book, are also what is least satisfactory in it. For extensive as are the sources which Mack has used, they are not nearly extensive enough. Between 1916 and 1922 Lawrence was involved in a complex web of war, politics and diplomacy. For a biographer to give an accurate and intelligible account of his role, he would have to place this role in its proper historical context—and this requires studying and digesting and working into his own narrative the evidence disclosed by the voluminous records which the Sharifian revolt and its aftermath generated in British—and to a lesser extent, in French—archives. No biographer of Lawrence could have done this before 1966, simply because the records were not then available. Knightley and Simpson were the first to explore the new material, but theirs was a hurried and perfunctory foray. It cannot be said that Mack has improved on them to any extent. His footnotes, it is true, do refer here and there to various volumes of Foreign Office and Cabinet documents, but those who know how rich and extensive the public archives of this period are will also know that Mack has, regrettably, done no more than scratch their surface.

This failure to consult and take into account the available evidence, and the reliance on authors who either did not have access to this evidence or who, like George Antonius, are so suspect as to be worthless, have made Mack's historical judgment uncritical and unreliable. If he had attended to the evidence he would, for instance, not have unquestioningly accepted Lawrence's false assertion that the British authorities in Cairo heard of the Sykes-Picot agreement—which embodied Anglo-French arrangements about the post-war fate of Ottoman territories—only in 1917. The truth is that these authorities knew of the provisions of the agreement as soon as it was signed, and furthermore had been kept regularly informed of the progress of the negotiations. Again, Mack uncritically accepts Lawrence's version of the Sharifian revolt and its achievements, saying, for example, that the capture of Aqaba in July 1917—in which Lawrence played a major role—ended the war in Hijaz, made Sinai secure for the British, and provided them with 'a vital seaport'. The truth is that the capture of Aqaba did not end the war in the Hijaz, where Medina remained under Ottoman occupation until January 1919 and where hostilities between Sharif Hussein and Ibn Sa'ud were continually threatening; that Sinai had ceased to be threatened by the Ottomans quite a while before the Sharifian revolt (and that if it had been under Ottoman threat, it was not the Sharifian occupation of Aqaba that would have removed this threat); and that Aqaba, an insignificant hamlet on the Red Sea, neither was (nor could have been) a vital seaport for the provisioning of British armies advancing to attack the Ottomans up the Mediterranean coast.

Mack also entertains the bizarre idea that half of General Townshend's force (which the Ottomans besieged and forced to surrender at Kut in Mesopotamia in April 1916) was Arab; however, it is well known that if Arabs fought at all in Mesopotamia they did so on the side of the Ottomans, or simply to harass and despoil British troops. On this elementary mistake Mack erects a heavy structure of sententious disapproval. The war in Mesopotamia, he tells us, shows 'the futility, and ultimately the terrible danger, for *all* the population involved, of a Western power's pursuing its national policies on foreign soil with utter disregard for the nature and political aspirations of the local population'. Even if the events which have elicited this comment did actually take place, the comment itself remains eccentric and highly strung. For, after all, war is not a monopoly of the West. Again, absolutely no warrant exists for the belief that 'a local population' pursuing its own 'political aspirations' will not suffer disaster; likewise, no warrant exists for denying that 'a local population' may derive great benefits from rule by a foreign power—even though such a power is, of course, primarily intent on securing its own interests. It is because such conjunctions are continually arising that Clio may be called an ironic muse; history is not a morality tale in which elevated motives always lead to good results and low motives to bad results.

Mack seems a stranger to this, the oldest and most common worldly wisdom. Hence his ready acceptance of the slick and simplistic cant of the age, and his unconcealed and ready admiration for holy humbugs like Gandhi and Dag Hammarskjöld, to liken Lawrence to whom (he must believe) will elevate his hero in our estimation. The conjunction of these various influences—namely, the neglect of the evidence from the official archives, reliance on the conclusions of indifferent writers, uncritical acceptance of modish slogans and shibboleths—means that situations and episodes which must be at the center of any study of Lawrence are treated inadequately and unsatisfactorily. Thus, for instance, chapter 10 deals with the Hijaz under the Ottomans before and after the outbreak of war, and with the secret Sharifian negotiations with the British; it presents us with a simple story of Arabs yearning for national independence having to contend with Turkish oppression on the one hand and European 'colonialist' greed on the other. This simple story is in its simplicity quite deceptive. For the relations between the Ottoman state and its Arabic-speaking subjects cannot be described merely as those between oppressor and oppressed. The Ottoman state was an Islamic state, and Islamic loyalty was a strong bond between rulers and ruled. Apart from the Sharif in the Hijaz (and the small number of Ottoman Arab officers who joined him), the Arabic-speaking provinces remained, in spite of the great wartime hardships, faithful to the empire until the end.

The Sharif, it is true, claimed to be the standard-bearer of Arabism, but this was a mere claim *pro domo*, unwise for the historian to accept as the reality. The reality, rather, was that the Sharif, like many of his predecessors in this post, was tempted to play the overmighty subject, and to exploit the remoteness of the Ottoman state from the Hijaz and the emergency of war. He was, in fact, one power among many in the Arabian Peninsula, the rival and sometimes bitter enemy of fellow Arab rulers. The affair of the deserting Ottoman officers who joined the Sharif is scarcely less complicated. These officers, moved by ideological passions, were the counterpart of the Young Turk officers, the authors of the *coup d'état* of July 1908 against the Ottoman Sultan. Together with the Young Turks, they may be considered an ominous manifestation of a new style of Middle Eastern politics which has since become quite familiar.

Mack's pages are innocent of these and similar complexities; nor do they convey to us a sense of the international context in which the Sharifian rebellion took place—of the traditional Great-Power connections and rivalries in the Middle East, or of the need of the Powers (entirely as legitimate as that of the Sharif) to secure and preserve for themselves a strong position in the area. And what has been said about the deficiencies of Mack's account of the background of the Sharifian rebellion holds equally true of his perfunctory chapters dealing with the Paris Peace Conference and with Lawrence at the Colonial Office. The Peace Conference was a negotiation. The duty of the historian is to set out the interests of the various parties and describe how the bargaining proceeded, not to make question-begging and sentimental assertions such as that 'Lawrence was one of the few voices of conscience' in Paris—as though the Sharifian interest had some transcendental merit denied to other interests, and as though the upholders of these other interests were conscienceless, rapacious sharks. Similarly, the policy which Lawrence supported and applied at the Colonial Office was, like any other policy, based on a medley of calculations and miscalculations; it is far from clear that its consequences were so excellent that his biographers must complacently endorse Lawrence's view that his part of 'the Middle East job' was 'on the whole, well done'.

There is, of course, one other aspect of Lawrence's public life which a biographer must take into account, namely his military activities in Hijaz and Transjordan. For it is these which became the foundations of his renown, not to say his legend. That he was resourceful and imaginative in leading Bedouin guerrillas, that he showed endurance and bravery in this activity, cannot be gainsaid. But the claims which he, and others on his behalf, made go much further than this. Liddell Hart, and now Mack, speak as though it were Lawrence who had invented the technique of guerrilla warfare. Mack, for instance, claims that Lawrence was 'decades ahead of his time and his government' in understanding the actualities of guerrilla warfare. This is an absurd exaggeration since, as is well known and as has been extensively documented anew in Walter Laqueur's recent book on the subject, both the practice and the theory of guerrilla warfare are appreciably older than Lawrence. Lawrence himself spoke as though he had invented a bloodless way of winning battles. In the introductory chapter to *Seven Pillars*, he boldly affirms that the defeat of the Ottoman empire 'was at last done in the wisdom of Allenby with less than four hundred killed, by turning to our uses the hands of the oppressed in Turkey'. This exorbitant gasconade, worthy of Tartarin or Falstaff, is particularly piquant coming from someone who so much disliked professional soldiers.

This estimate of the efficiency of guerrilla warfare—which the long and difficult war between the Allies and the Ottomans serves to show up for the empty boast that it is—was combined with a doctrine which Lawrence held, at any rate in his early days in the Hijaz. He seems to have believed that what was going on in the Hijaz was much more than a *fronde* among often dissident tribesmen—a *fronde* being shrewdly made use of by an ambitious magnate. In a despatch from the Hijaz of October 1916, Lawrence wrote:

> The Bedouin of the Hijaz is not, outwardly, a vehicle for abstract or altruistic ideas. Yet again and again I have heard from them about acts of the early Arabs or things that the Sharif and his sons have said, which contain nearly all that the exalted Arab patriot would wish. They intend to restore the Sheria, to revive the Arabic language, and to rebuild the prosperity of the country. They believe that by liberating the Hijaz they are vindicating the rights of all Arabs to a national political existence. . . .

The sequel was to show that these were far-fetched ideas, that the Bedouins remained what they ever had been—simply nomads who lived, whenever they could, by exaction and plunder. Lawrence's doctrine about them justifies us in calling him the Che Guevara of the Arab revolt, but fortunately for him, he did not have to pay the price which Guevara paid for his fancies about the Bolivian peasants.

The doctrine also indicates that Lawrence in Arabia held simple and uncritical views on politics, views commonly described as 'radical', or 'anti-imperialist'. Thus, in the introductory chapter of *Seven Pillars*, he declares that British soldiers, 'young, clean, delightful fellows' were sent 'to the worst of deaths, not to win the war, but that the corn and rice and oil of Mesopotamia might be ours'. This is no more than the Hobsonian-Leninist notion that it is 'capitalism' which causes war. These 'anti-imperialist' sentiments remained with Lawrence after he enlisted as a private in the Royal Air Force. While serving in India, he informed Mrs. Shaw that 'no native troops are loyal to their foreign masters: or rather, only those who had no self-respect would be loyal'. This harsh verdict on the rank-and-file of the Indian army was an ideologue's verdict, both presumptuous and unjust; the Indian army under its British officers remained to the end in its overwhelming majority faithful to the British crown, and its men, whose lives were molded and given significance by loyalty to their regiments, are not to be dismissed, with injurious ignorance, as shifty and despicable traitors.

But whatever Lawrence's activities in the war and its aftermath, their actual import and significance is dwarfed by the retrospective account of his doings which he provided in *Seven Pillars*, and by the immense influence which this writing has exercised. For many years, Lawrence's friends and admirers pitched the merits of his writings very high indeed. To take one example, the *Times Literary Supplement* has recently revealed that it was Lawrence's patron and friend, D. G. Hogarth, who anonymously reviewed in its pages *Revolt in the Desert* when it appeared in 1927. Hogarth, we find, ends his review by affirming that 'the book leaves from first to last an impression of absolute truth'. Hogarth, who was as deeply involved in the Arab revolt as Lawrence himself, should have known better. It was this kind of glorification, repeated over the years *ad nauseam*, which no doubt led Aldington to speak somewhat unkindly of what he called the Lawrence Bureau.

Lawrence's most recent admirers have been more circumspect, less sweeping and categorical, in their praises. In their book mentioned above, the Weintraubs explain that though Lawrence 'exaggerated and even invented some of the details in his narrative,' this only serves to establish 'his flair as a writer'. Lawrence, they tell us, was simply engaged in 'transmuting autobiographical chronicle into legend'; and, 'despite its confessed inexactitude and subjectivity, it *is*,' they insist, 'a work of history—a work which has the poetry of history'. Mack, for his part, advances a number of explanations for what he describes as 'distortions and partial truths' in *Seven Pillars*. He tells us in one place that their purpose is either embellishment 'for dramatic purposes', or the protection of other people. In another place he claims that 'the distortions and inaccuracies result from Lawrence's need to elevate the tale to epic proportions and to make himself a contemporary legendary figure'. Again, he explains that Lawrence's 'tendency to fictionalize his experiences, to turn his life into a legend, was most prominent when Lawrence was feeling particularly troubled in his self-regard. 'At these times,' Mack's diagnosis runs, 'he would give way to an unconscious need to create a fictional self, drawn on lines of childish hero-ism, to replace the troubled self he was experiencing'. In yet another pas-sage, Mack invites us to consider Lawrence's literary labours as so many attempts to overcome the 'continuing effects of traumatic experiences'. Since these writings were meant to reach the public, Mack also invites us to look upon Lawrence as a benefactor—albeit an unwitting one—of the cause of mental health: 'He would be glad, I am sure,' Mack solemnly opines, 'if his public self-exposure could contribute to human understanding and to the relief of suffering. He would, I am quite certain, want others to benefit from any knowledge or insights gained from studying and analyzing the struggles he could not resolve altogether for himself.'

On the face of it, *Seven Pillars* is simply the account of a war-time episode. It requires some ingenuity to turn it into a myth, or a neurotic's confession requiring the analyst's transformative logic to unlock its esoteric meaning and unveil its hidden significance. But whatever the analyst's skill, it is difficult to see *Seven Pillars* as a myth, like Gilgamesh or Prometheus or Oedipus. And if the book is a piece of self-exposure, the maunderings of a neurotic on his psychoanalyst's couch, it is not clear why it should benefit humanity at large: at the most the benefit will accrue to the patient himself and to his doctor. All this laborious huffing and puffing, in short, sounds uncommonly like apologetics—which are necessary, since the fact cannot be gotten over that at certain points, some of them crucial, *Seven Pillars* is knowingly and deliberately untruthful. Lawrence, for instance, knew that Faysal, third son of the Sharif of Mecca, whose champion he became, was a timid, perhaps even a cowardly, man in battle, and lacking in judgment, and yet he portrayed him in *Seven Pillars* as a heroic figure, 'the leader who would bring the Arab revolt to full glory'. He chose to disguise the truth because—as he later told Liddell Hart—it was 'the only way to get the British to support the Arabs—physical courage is an essential demand of the typical British officer'. This may have been a necessary—albeit question-able—proceeding when Lawrence was acting as Faysal's champion. To perpetuate the deception in a work later composed at leisure is to take advantage of the reader's good faith. But perhaps the most flagrant example of this abuse is Lawrence's account of the fall of Damascus. The reader of *Seven Pillars* is led to believe that the city was captured by Faysal's forces, when the truth was— as Lawrence well knew—that on Allenby's orders all Allied forces were forbidden to enter Damascus, only Faysal's being allowed to do so, and thus—falsely—to claim its capture.

Lawrence's book, we may then fairly say, is a corrupt work, which deliberately sets out to induce in its readers—by means of falsehoods—feelings of admiration, pity, indignation and guilt, in respect of events which in reality do not possess that tragic quality for which such emotions are appropriate. The political and military events in which Lawrence was mixed up, and which in his fashion he later recounted, involved conflicting interests and ambitions, no single one of which was, however, particularly righteous or signally elevated. *Seven Pillars* pretends to the contrary, and by transforming the mediocre and the shady into noble and exalted beings, the book is not only corrupt but also corrupting—corrupting in a manner particularly familiar to the modern age, when political causes have come to be endowed with transcendental significance, to warrant the greatest sacrifices and justify the most heinous crimes. This kind of corruption may properly be called romantic, since it rests on yearning for a harmonious or paradisaical existence to be established or regained by means of political action.

Evidence of such romanticism is abundant in Lawrence's writings. Consider, for instance, the dedicatory poem which stands at the beginning of *Seven Pillars*. It is not known for sure to whom the poem is dedicated, but such evidence as exists points to Dahoum, a donkey boy who was employed on the diggings at Jerablus, and with whom Lawrence established a close relationship. But whatever the identity of the person to whom the poem (and the book) is dedicated, the poem itself is clearly erotic. It begins: 'I loved you', and its third stanza constitutes a typically romantic amalgam in which love and death are simultaneously and nostalgically evoked:

> *Love, the way-weary, groped to your body, our*
> *brief wage ours for the moment*
> *Before earth's soft hand explored your shape,*
> *and blind worms grew fat upon*
> *Your substance.*

Not only is this love poem—memorial of a private relationship—made to stand at the head of a book dealing with public events, but it is also itself made to affirm that the writer's actions in war and politics were motivated by a desire to give pleasure to the loved one. The first stanza reads:

> *I loved you, so I drew these tides of men into*
> *my hands*
> *and wrote my will across the sky in stars*
> *To earn you Freedom, the seven-pillared worthy*
> *house,*
> *that your eyes might be shining for me*
> *When we came.*

We may add that the poem, as it figures in *Seven Pillars*, was amended and toned down by Robert Graves, and that Lawrence's original version—as

Knightley and Simpson show in their book—was palpably more explicit. It is all very peculiar.

Equally peculiar is the fact that while Lawrence's biographers have speculated a great deal on the identity of the person to whom it is dedicated, they have seldom paused to consider the significance of what the bare text of the poem so revealingly discloses about Lawrence's attitude to politics and public affairs. The poem, and other statements by Lawrence, indicate that he was perhaps homosexually inclined. Mack quotes a passage from some unpublished notes made for a projected autobiography in which Lawrence declares: 'I take no pleasure in women. I have never thought twice or even once of the shape of a woman: but men's bodies, in repose or in movement—especially the former, appeal to me directly and very generally.' Side by side with this disgust for the female sex went hatred for generation and childbirth which, he told Mrs. Bernard Shaw, was 'so sorry and squalid an accident . . . if fathers and mothers took thought before bringing children into this misery of a world, only the monsters among them would dare to go through with it'. Such an outlook, so much at variance with the common experience of mankind, has for its corollary a view of politics in which are entirely absent those aims usually held to justify political activity—namely, the preservation and perpetuation of a human group. Hence perhaps Lawrence's occasionally wild and nihilistic outbursts, such as this one which occurs toward the end of *Seven Pillars:* 'To the clear-sighted, failure was the only goal. We must believe, through and through, that there was no victory except to go down in death fighting and crying for failure itself.'

In the dedicatory poem which inaugurates *Seven Pillars*, Lawrence boasts that 'I drew these tides of men into my hands and wrote my will across the sky in stars'. Here the self, by a sheer exercise of will, claims to master the world. In *The Mint*, which consists of sketches describing his life as an enlisted man in the Royal Air Force, Lawrence's attitude is the very opposite. The self is now wholly mastered by the world, governed by abject fear which, however, is perhaps as pleasurable as absolute domination: *les extrêmes se touchent.* He writes: 'The root-trouble is fear: fear of failing, fear of breaking down.' And: 'My soul, always looking for some fear to salt its existence, was wondering what seven whole years of servitude would do against the hasty stubbornness which had hitherto buttressed my values.' Having, in his search for a superhuman harmony, attempted (and failed) to soar to the heights, he would now seek the ineffable by immersing himself in a bovine existence where 'unquestioned life is a harmony': 'here are men so healthy that they don't chop up their meat into mince for easy digestion by the mind: and who are thereby intact as we are thereby diseased.' Therefore, deliberately, now preferring his world 'backwards in the mirror', Lawrence abandoned himself to the 'urge downwards, in pursuit of the safety which can't fall further'. It did not work: *qui veut faire l'ange,* as Pascal said, *fait la bête;* but not vice versa.

Lawrence's record, then, shows bravery in war, a great capacity for physical endurance, ingenuity as a guerrilla leader, and later some literary talent. But it also shows that he was self-centered, mercurial and violently unstable. In his concluding chapter Mack notes that Lawrence 'sought *new possibilities* for the self'. But this cannot redound to his praise, as Mack evidently means it to do. For these possibilities and the quest for them can be mischievous and even catastrophic. So in Lawrence's case they have proved to be—not only in his own restless and unhappy life, but also in the example which he set, and which his legend (which he took such care to put together and to promote) made immensely popular. Mack's further verdict, that Lawrence was a civilizing force, cannot therefore stand. The cause of Arab nationalism which he embraced (and which he falsely claimed to have been double-crossed and betrayed by his country) was not more virtuous or worthy than any similar cause. Why a foreigner should so fervently embrace it, and what it has contributed to civilization, are both quite obscure. Lawrence, on the other hand, promoted a pernicious confusion between public and private, he looked to politics for a spiritual satisfaction which it cannot possibly provide, and he invested it with an impossibly transcendental significance. In doing so, he pandered to some of the most dangerous elements to be found in the modern Western mentality. His influence and his cult, here at their most extensive and enduring, we may judge to be not civilizing, but destructive.

16

THE SURRENDER OF MEDINA, JANUARY 1919

According to clause 16 of the armistice of Mudros, signed on 30 October 1918, all Ottoman garrisons in the Hijaz, Asir, Yemen, Syria and Mesopotamia were, on the coming into force of the armistice, to surrender 'to the nearest Allied Commander'.[1] But, as is commonly known, this stipulation was not carried out in the case of Medina, the Ottoman garrison which had succeeded in holding their own against Sharifian hostility from June 1916 onwards. In fact it was not until 10 January 1919 that the Ottoman commander, Fakhri Pasha, surrendered and the city was entered by the Sharifians. The official version of these events is enshrined in an official communiqué composed in the Cairo residency and published on 16 January. This document explained that the sacred character of the city 'rendered it incumbent on King Hussein to secure its capitulation by arrangement and not by assault'. Assault, it was explained, was rendered out of the question by the fact that the Ottoman forces were using the Great Mosque as an ammunition depot. Hence, 'not a single shell could have been thrown into the position without grave risk of the destruction of the Prophet's tomb'.[2]

Some such version was also put about by Colonel T. E. Lawrence in an anonymous article on 'The Arab Campaign' published in *The Times* of 26 November 1918, i.e. before the surrender of Medina. 'It is', he explained, 'a Holy City, so that the Arabs have never fired, and will never fire, a shot against it (ideal conditions for a besieged army)'.[3] This story, or a variant of it, seems to have established itself as the truth, for we find, over half a century after the event, a writer in *The Economist* categorically declaring that 'the physical reason why, after the armistice, Ali's [i.e. the Sharifian] troops could not storm Medina and force the surrender of the Ottoman garrison was that the Ottoman commander had threatened to blow up the Prophet's tomb if attacked'.[4]

But what the writer in *The Economist* has asserted with the anonym's bold assurance has little or no relation to the facts of the case. This emerges from the evidence yielded by documents which, since 1966, have been in the public domain. Medina was one of the objects of the Sharif's anti-Ottoman conspiracy in 1915-16. Early in 1916 he had sent his eldest son Ali there to organize a rising of tribes and occupy Medina at the right moment. But the moment never came. The Ottomans became suspicious, and sent Fakhri Pasha, Jemal Pasha's deputy, with reinforcements from Syria. When the Sharif, fearing to delay further, proclaimed his rebellion in June, Ali failed to oust the Ottomans from the city, and his younger brother Faysal tried to come to the rescue, but failed equally. In a report dated 30 October Lawrence, who had by then established friendly relations with Faysal and heard his account of these events, wrote that he did not think the Sharifians had ever been near taking Medina, 'as Feisal's forces are only a mob of active and independent snipers' who were frightened and demoralized by the Ottoman artillery.[5]

The initial *coup* having failed, the Sharifians had to try and cut the railway linking Medina to Ottoman-controlled territory in the north, and to lay siege to the city itself. In the autumn of 1916 Fakhri Pasha disposed of— in Medina and its protecting posts of Bir Darwish, El Ghayir and Bir el Mashi—approximately 9,500 men, two field guns and three mountain guns.[6] It is against these forces that Ali, Abdullah and, to start with, Faysal had to lead their Bedouin levies fortified by contingents of regular Egyptian troops which were sent to the Hijaz immediately after the outbreak of the Sharif's rebellion, in order to guard against the by-no-means negligible risk that Fakhri might succeed in recapturing Mecca.[7]

What strategy was it advisable for the Sharifians to adopt towards the Ottomans in Medina? Lawrence's well-known view was that it was an advantage for the Ottomans to have their troops tied down in guarding the city and the lines of communication, and that the Sharifians should therefore content themselves with harassing and steadily weakening their enemy. An expression of such a view occurs, for instance, in an *Arab Bulletin* report, 'Situation of the Sherifian Revolt', which appeared in October 1917. 'On the whole', this appreciation said, 'seeing what the retention of Medina and of the long L[ines] of C[ommunication] is entailing on the Ottoman General Staff, we may look with equanimity on a prolongation of the present situation'.[8] But different objectives and changes in the situation in the Hijaz entailed other strategies. Thus, Abdullah, as always looking forward to the conquest of Syria, considered that this had to follow the fall of Medina.[9] Faysal also, jealous of his brother Abdullah who had acquired glory by occupying Taif, and not yet established in Akaba, wanted to be the one who would take Medina.[10] But much more important than the dreams and wishes of the sons of the Sharif, the British authorities in Cairo were not always sure that it was so very safe to leave Medina unsubdued. Thus the French military attaché in Cairo, who was generally well informed, wrote at the beginning of November 1917 that he had gathered from Brigadier Clayton that 'the Arab Bureau, long indifferent to the fall of Medina must now bring it about before the end of the year. It considers this the only way to guard against the serious danger represented by the increasing disaffection of the Southern tribes towards the Grand Sharif. In addition, it thinks this will enable it to confine the Mecca regime within the confines of the Hijaz, and ensure for the Emir Faisal independence vis-à-vis his father. This autonomy of Faisal's, who would be under the Allies' exclusive control, will become necessary when communications between the British Army in Palestine and the Northern Sharifian forces become easier'.[11]

Thus, at various times and for various reasons—whether to isolate the Medina garrison, or to prevent the city's serving as a focal point for anti-Sharifian or pro-Saudi tribes or to enhance the Sharif's position in the Hijaz or (however improbably) to use it as a jumping-point for a Sharifian conquest of Syria—it was thought desirable that the Sharifian troops should adopt an active and aggressive posture towards the Ottomans in Medina and its outposts. But, as it turned out, successive plans for occupying Medina or inflicting a defeat on Fakhri in the end came to naught. In his first despatch on military operations in the Hijaz, dated 25 June 1917, Wingate expressed the hope that continual pressure on the railways and lines of communications 'now being followed' would in the end 'result in wearing down the enemy and securing the capture of Medina, retaining meanwhile in the Hedjaz a considerable Turkish garrison and cutting off from all communication with Headquarters the enemy units in Asir and Yemen'. In his next despatch, dated 15 June 1918, Wingate had to record the disappointment of these hopes. The plan had been for Faysal, Abdullah and Ali to attack Medina separately from different directions. 'Owing, however, to the various causes of delay inseparable from Arab combinations', by the time preparations were completed serious difficulties had arisen with regard to the water supply and the prospect was abandoned. Wingate however affirmed that raiding operations, rigorously carried out, had inflicted heavy casualties, and succeeded in severing the railway communications in a manner such that 'the effective isolation of Medina . . . may at last be regarded as accomplished'. In the same despatch, Wingate expressed the belief that the reaction of his brothers to Faysal's success in Akaba 'has produced, in emulation, a degree of activity in the southern theatre never hitherto attained, and a determination on their part to undertake the long-deferred combined offensive north of Medina, with a view to securing the close and permanent investment of that fortress'. The third and last despatch on the Hijaz operations, dated 27 December 1918, recorded the failure of these hopes. Abdullah attacked some positions at the end of May 1918; at the first assault some outlying advanced posts were captured, but the attack failed to develop. A week later, another attack in co-operation with Ali was undertaken, 'but, again, little more than demonstration was effected'. An attack by Abdullah in June did result in the destruction of 1200 rails, a bridge, three large culverts, and of a water train and its locomotive; Ottoman losses were said to be heavy and prisoners were taken. At the end of July, Ali attempted another offensive against an Ottoman position, but the offensive failed. Early in August a mobile force of camel-mounted infantry and artillery began to be formed at Wejh with a view to an autumn offensive, but plague broke out in September and spread to the troops; preparation for the operations in prospect were therefore 'indefinitely postponed'.[12] There matters stood when the Ottoman troops suffered in September a debacle in Syria, and when the Ottoman government decided in October to seek a general armistice.

The formal, measured and discreet prose of a public despatch is not, of course, meant to expose the inner history of the long campaign against Medina. It does, however, establish that it was far from brilliant or successful and, more important, that, contrary to Lawrence's assertions in *The Times* and to those of the official communiqué issued on the surrender of Medina, if the city did not fall, it was hardly because the Sharifians had refrained from attacking it. But other evidence is available to fill out the sketchy picture which Wingate's despatches provide. Thus we see the *Arab Bulletin* of 23 May 1917 reporting that Captain Lawrence, in the course of a stay in Abdullah's camp, trying to prod him into activity. Abdullah, Lawrence reported, was 'too fond of pleasure and, in a sense, evidently too civilized for his present wild work'. But Lawrence, it seems, 'got him to do a great deal'—to pay some tribes their allowances which were in arrears, 'to take an interest in his guns and machine-guns, to send out his dynamite parties, and to begin to prepare for a general move towards the railway.'[13] Lawrence's prodding does not seem to have produced results since we find Colonel C. E. Wilson, the British representative at Jeddah, pressing Husayn and his sons Ali, Abdullah and Zayd 'to try to get a move on against Medina' and writing to the Arab Bureau that he was 'constantly rubbing it in to them but without much success up to date I fear'.[14]

Sharifian inaction had many reasons. His brother Faysal offered an apologia for Abdullah's quiescence on the Medina front in a conversation with Lawrence which took place at the beginning of December 1917. 'It is not fair', Faysal said, 'to condemn my brother Abdullah without reserve. He is taking no part in the war against the Turks, because his whole heart, his head, and all his resources are engaged in the problems of Nejd'. What was important was to unite all the Arabs of the Peninsula under the Sharifian flag and 'strangle' the Wahabi creed. 'If we fail', Faysal claimed, 'all our efforts and victories over the Turks will be wasted. Great Britain will not profit by the Arab revival, if the tomb at Medina and the Haram at Mecca are destroyed, and the pilgrimage is prevented. Abdullah is fighting all our battles, and if he had no leisure to campaign against the railway meanwhile, he should not be judged too harshly.'[15] Faysal's reasoning, if taken seriously, meant that the British should help to levy war against Ibn Sa'ud. It was an unexpected outcome to McMahon's negotiation of 1915-16 from which so much had been hoped in the the war against the Ottomans. Whether the British authorities in Cairo grasped the irony of this we do not know, but it seems that they were either unwilling or unable to prevent Abdullah from using their subventions for anti-Saudi, rather than for anti-Ottoman, purposes.[16]

A report on the 'Situation of the Sherifian Revolt' appearing in the *Arab Bulletin* of 26 February 1918 recorded the disappointing performance of Ali's and Abdullah's forces. Ali's contingent had done 'practically nothing' except to 'effect some minor demolitions and capture of small enemy posts. The rest of this force has been content with watching the outposts of Medina on west and southwest and with occasional, and rather futile, artillery practice'. As for Abdullah, he had effected—over a stretch of 112 miles—'a desultory series of demolitions, which latterly have been on a larger scale than formerly, and appear to have taxed severely, if not the enemy's supply of spare rails, at least that of bolts, nuts, etc.' Of both Ali's and Abdullah's forces the *Arab Bulletin* declares that the improvement in their situation 'consists more in the relative decline of enemy strength' opposed to them, in the 'serious losses' sustained by the Ottomans in both men and rolling stock, and in the successful blockade which had for a month or two stopped the supply of fresh meat. These were optimistic appreciations, even though the report did admit that the enemy's long line of communication had not been cut definitely. But the optimism does not seem to have been well founded. When Medina was surrendered Fakhri Pasha told Captain H. Garland that he could have held Medina for many months more—he had enough to see him adequately through for a period of three months. As for the blockade, it does not seem to have been as watertight as the report in the *Arab Bulletin* claimed, for in the same conversation with Garland Fakhri remarked that he 'had often felt grateful to [the British] for issuing supplies so freely to the Bedouin'.[17]

The *Arab Bulletin* report of February 1918 had something to say about the quality of the Sharifian forces which may serve to explain their mediocre performance:

Abdullah's army [the report explained] is largely drawn from fluctuating contingents of Bedouins of inferior fighting quality, whose spirit has been impaired by various causes—by the winter cold (the Bedouin campaigning season is summer), by protracted failure of supplies due to certain maneuvres of those responsible for transport from Yanbo, by enemy propaganda, and, most of all, by the slow payment of promised subsidies. The last cause has particularly affected the Harb in both Abdullah's force and Ali's. On the other hand, the Juheinah, for what they are worth, have kept loyal, and the Ateibah contingent, though worth even less, has been favoured at the others' expense, while a new and energetic auxiliary has been found in Ferhan el-Aida and his Anazeh. To the latter and to the co-operation of a French Algerian detachment, Abdullah has chiefly owed such enhanced success as he claims in his raiding operations during the past five months.[18]

Ali's and Abdullah's difficulties clearly arose from the undisciplined and mercenary character of their forces. As it happens, there has survived a report by the editor of Husayn's Mecca newspaper, *al-Qibla*, which is quite invaluable in supplementing the hints and remarks offered by the *Arab Bulletin* report. Its author, Ahmed Shakir Karmi, was well placed to observe Sharifian politics and administration at close quarters, and he felt able, in a report destined for British authorities, to write frankly and without inhibition, and what he has to say not only is cogent and convincing in itself, but much of it can actually be confirmed from other sources. Karmi defines for us the relation in which the Bedouins, on whom the Sharif depended to carry on the anti-Ottoman rebellion, stood to Husayn:

> ... it is quite evident [he observes] that the tribes who have sub-mitted to him in this war have not done so out of fear or respect for his authority but from pure greed for the money which is lavished upon them regardlessly. Anyone who knows the character of the Bedouins of the Hijaz knows how true this is, for they are well known for their greed and their lack of any praiseworthy qualities, for they do not hesitate to kill pilgrims who come from far and near. It is [not?] strange that money which has been given them during the war has not inspired them with any respect for the King, for they realize that the Sharif pays nothing out of his own pocket and that he is paid just as they are, the money all being that of the English. As for the assistance rendered by the Bedouins, it has been given through sheer love of plunder, and they would not hesitate to help the Turks if it suited their purpose. The armies of the Amirs Ali and Abdullah were filled with Bedouin riff-raff, and they often deserted the regulars when they were in a tight corner, and the only heroism they ever showed was in a love of loot and a propensity to run away on the first appearance of danger.[19]

Karmi's observations chime in with what is known of the behaviour of the Bedouins in the Hijaz before and after the Sharifian uprising, and his judgments seem sounder and more accurate than the exalted picture pre-sented by Lawrence of men who were 'intensely national' and 'more sophisticated' than their appearance led one to expect. In the paper, dating from November 1916, where he expressed these judgments, Lawrence also pejoratively remarked that the 'towns are sighing for the contented obstructionist inactivity of the Ottoman Government, or for the ordered quiet of our own rule'.[20] The menace of Bedouin depradations was for townsmen in the Hijaz a constant threat—a threat which proved to be a reality as recently as the inception of the Sharif's rebellion when, as Karmi says, they 'plundered all the houses in Mecca . . . and every house in Taif when it surrendered', and when on the same occasion they similarly went on the rampage in Jedda.[21]

Karmi's report also gives us a glimpse of one reason why Ali's and Abdullah's forces could effect so little against Medina or the Hijaz railway. He recounts a story which the Director of Quarantine at Jedda, Dr. Muhammad al-Husayni, told him about the Bedouins' fighting methods. Husayni was present with the force which entered Medina upon its surrender. While there, a Bedouin shaykh asked him for tuition in the art of blowing up railways with dynamite. The shaykh explained that Husayn was paying his tribe half of what the Turks used to give 'as the price of peace', and blowing up railways would compel the King of the Hijaz to restore the subsidy to its customary level. Husayni then asked where the shaykh was able to obtain dynamite,

> and the Sheikh replied that he had enormous quantities of dynamite that he had collected from the Bedouins, for men sent by the Princes to blow up the railway used to throw away the dynamite they had with them two hours distance from the railway and then went back and told the Emirs that they had used up all their dynamite. The Bedouins then picked up this dynamite and so collected enormous quantities.

Both Ali and Abdullah had the benefit of military advice from European officers attached to their forces. With Ali was Captain Depui, a French officer who came with the French military mission led by General Brémond when the Sharif declared his rebellion. To Abdullah was attached Captain Garland of the Egyptian Army who was present in the Hijaz from the beginning of the rebellion, and who had begun by heading a training school in demolition work at Wejh. Both men were therefore experienced and knowledgeable in the ways of the Sharifian forces, and their reports are worth attending to. We find Depui reporting in March 1918 on the state of mind of the Arab officers with Ali's force, officers who had either deserted from the Ottoman Army or, having found themselves prisoners-of-war in British camps, had volunteered for service with the Sharif. Depui reported that Baghdadi officers had formed a committee of 'troublemakers' (*factieux*) and declared; 'These officers do not want to fight and, what is more serious, do not want that there should be fighting' (*'Ces officiers ne veulent pas se battre et ce qui est plus grave, ne veulent pas qu'on se batte'*). They attempted to subvert North African officers who had been sent by the French to reinforce the Sharif by asking them whether they really intended to make use of their weapons against their 'Muslim brethren'; while one officer used, in his reports, the term *shahid* (martyr) in referring to Turks who had been killed in engagements with the Sharifians.[22]

Captain Garland also reported about the operations of Abdullah's force and the conditions in his camp, but, more striking and informative than a formal report, there has survived a sketch which he wrote sometime between the Armistice and the surrender of Medina, entitled 'A Day at El Jafr'. It conveys vividly the atmosphere which reigned in Abdullah's camp, relaxed, unmilitary and *fainéant*, its inmates being above all pre-occupied with burning issues of pay and post-war politics. The sketch, by someone who had served with the Sharifian forces from the inception of the rebellion, is in refreshing contrast to Lawrence's exalted and overheated productions and, to judge by what we know from other evidence, sensibly more faithful to the reality. It is reproduced in an appendix.

In his final despatch on operations in the Hijaz, Wingate stated that 'From the beginning of August until the Turkish debacle in Syria in the last week of September no operations worthy of separate mention were carried out by the forces of Emirs Ali or Abdullah'.[23] What Wingate does not reveal is that in August he sent Fakhri a summons to surrender to which he received a scathing and contemptuous rejoinder. Fakhri's curt reply, dated 4 September, was addressed 'To Him who broke the power of Islam and caused bloodshed among Moslems and placed the Caliphate of the Emir, who was God's representative, in bondage and under the domination of the British', and informed Husayn that 'As I am now under the protection of the Prophet and most high commander, I am busying myself with strengthening the defences and the building of roads and squares in Medina. I beg you not to trouble me with useless requests.'[24]

In his final despatch Wingate is also silent on another episode relating to Medina which took place in October, before the signing of the armistice of Mudros. The Foreign Office informed Wingate on 16 October that the French high commissioner in Arabia was suggesting that his government should supply 25 mm. guns to enable the Sharifians to take Medina. This seemed to alarm the British authorities in London. The Director of Military Intelligence at the War Office urged that the use of guns would entail considerable damage to the city, and that it could be peaceably secured under the terms of the armistice which then seemed impending. Sykes at the Foreign Office, however, was of another opinion, in which he was supported by Sir Eyre Crowe and Lord Robert Cecil. 'Political considerations', the Foreign Office told Wingate, had to be taken into account: it was in the 'Interest both of ourselves and of Arabs that Medina should be taken by force of arms than as the result of an armistice; and this, if operations are to remain under Arab control, would point to their being urged to act with all possible speed and determination'. Wingate agreed with this view. He answered on the following day that Abdullah was undertaking a 'more vigorous prosecution of siege' and that the Sharifians 'appear to realize importance of capture of town and are showing increased energy'. He followed up this information—which there was no evidence to justify—by another telegram on 18 October in which he insisted that the Sharifians did not need French guns since they 'have been sufficiently gunned by us and use of artillery against Holy City has to be restricted on political grounds'. He himself had urged on Husayn and his sons the 'importance of their obtaining early capture of Medina' and this advice coupled with news of victories in Syria seems to have decided them to take energetic action. But Wingate clearly did not expect much result from his urgings, since he ended his telegram by expressing the hope that the military situation would compel Fakhri to surrender, even though the Hijaz Arabs 'are not disposed to attack a fortress'.[25] The events of the next few months were to show that Wingate's judgment in this respect was entirely correct and that the conclusion of his final despatch—namely that the Sharifian forces were preparing in October, by an 'early and vigorous effort to secure the capitulation of Medina', but that these preparations were 'rendered abortive by the Armistice with Turkey'—merely drew a decent veil of decorous reticence over the real course of events.

The Allied armistice proposals included a clause which stipulated the surrender of all garrisons in the Hijaz, Asir and the Yemen 'to the nearest Allied Commander or Arab representative', but the Ottoman negotiators feared for the fate of their troops if they were to surrender to an 'Arab representative', and succeeded in deleting this condition from the final text which, as has been said, was signed at Mudros on 30 October 1918.[26] The armistice terms were, immediately afterwards, transmitted by the Ottoman government to its commanders in the field, including Fakhri at Medina. But it soon appeared that Fakhri was absolutely unwilling to surrender Medina. He did not recognize Ali or Abdullah as an 'Allied Commander', neither would he concede that Captain Garland, for instance, had such a status. The Ottoman government repeated, in cypher, the instructions to surrender which had at first been sent *en clair*. Fakhri again refused to surrender, declaring, first, that he would surrender only 'on written order duly certified' from his government, and then that he would endeavour to hold Medina 'until a decree from the Khalif was communicated to him'. These exchanges took up the whole of November. Wingate reported on 22 November that the delay was 'exasperating Arabs who threaten attack and reprisal'. In reply, on 3 December the Foreign Office instructed him, at the suggestion of the War Office, to fix a date by which Medina was to be surrendered, and that unless it was surrendered by then 'we shall take no further measures to restrain Arabs'. Wingate replied on 6 December that he was informing Fakhri that Medina had to be surrendered by noon on 15 December.[27] The 15th of December came and went but Fakhri did not surrender. Some two months later Wingate told General Lynden-Bell that Fakhri's response to his ultimatum had been: 'I am a Mohammedan. I am an Osmanli. I am the son of Bayer Bay. I am a soldier'.[28]

In spite of their 'exasperation' as reported by Wingate, the ultimatum by no means pleased the Sharifians. When he read it, Abdullah's 'high spirits', Garland wrote, 'deserted him, and the prospect of war did not seem to give him the satisfaction his previous declarations had led me to expect at times when he was grumbling at the delay. Moreover', Garland significantly added, 'a resumption of hostilities here would interfere with all his plans against Ibn Sa'ud.' Garland explained that the fall of Medina to Sharifian arms would possess two unusual features in that the investing regular force was much weaker than the besieged force, and the greater part of the besiegers, namely the Bedouins, would be likely to require more control than the army to be evacuated. Garland expressed the opinion that it was necessary to keep constantly in mind the necessity for effectively preventing the Bedouins from entering the city before the regular army for fear of plunder. If—as later events were to show—Garland went wrong in his estimate, this was in thinking that the Sharifian regulars would behave better than the Bedouins. When the hope that Fakhri would surrender faded, Wingate ordered hostilities to be resumed on 20 December, but Garland did not believe that the renewed hostilities would bring about the fall of Medina. He did not anticipate more than desultory Bedouin raids 'as they are evidently waiting for the Allies to send troops to their assistance'. In Garland's view, to attack the strong defensive positions around Medina and to capture the city was an operation that required a skilled military commander together with sufficient regular troops—and the Sharifians had neither.[29]

The armistice which was to expire on 15 December was not finally denounced until 20 December. The delay was allowed in the hope that an Ottoman officer who had been sent from Constantinople with written instructions from the government would succeed in persuading Fakhri to surrender. In this the officer, Zia Bey, was completely unsuccessful. He spent some days in Medina and then returned to the Sharifian headquarters, which he reached on 24 December. He reported that as the officer responsible for the Prophet's Tomb, Fakhri considered that he could be relieved of his responsibility only by a personal order from the Sultan, and not by a letter from the government such as Zia was carrying. In this attitude Zia believed Fakhri to be 'implacable'.[30] In a conversation with Captain Wiggin of the Arab Bureau after the surrender of Medina Zia explained Fakhri's attitude. Fakhri, he said

> felt it an outrage to his dignity to surrender to the Arabs, who were rebels and had shown themselves inferior to his own men in every respect. With their superiority in numbers they could have carried Medina by assault at any time had they been troops of any fighting value whatsoever.

Again, and significantly,

> he was securely installed where he was and had a fairly good supply of food, chiefly rice and dates. Further, as a rule, no Arab Forces were to be met with for many miles from Medina and trains ran freely out of the town while he was there; the state of affairs could, in fact, hardly be called a siege, so that, by comparison, surrender to an enemy who could not for a moment be trusted to observe the laws of war was much the worse alternative.

Wiggin asked Zia whether Fakhri was a religious fanatic. Zia replied that

> Fakhri was intensely religious, but he had at the same time too strong a vein of practical shrewdness in him to allow him, for instance, to commit suicide in the Haram purely from religious sentiment. His insistence on his duty of protecting the Prophet's Tomb was due chiefly to the fact that religion was his chief instrument of discipline. Captain Zia illustrated his meaning by saying that Fakhri would probably have resisted indefinitely and died in the Haram if his troops had stood by him, and if there had been any chance that such resistance would be of any practical value to his country.[31]

This picture of Fakhri, a stout-hearted and resourceful military leader, full of stamina and jealous of his honour, stands in marked contrast to that of the passive and supine Abdullah who, when Garland informed him of Wingate's ultimatum to Fakhri—mentioned above—countered by citing a telegram from his father advising him not to worry, and not to embark on hostility since an Ottoman envoy, i.e. Zia, was coming 'by a special ship' with a letter from the Ottoman government which would secure Fakhri's surrender.[32] Our impression of Fakhri's character is confirmed and enhanced by the language which he himself held while a prisoner-of-war. He told Captain Bassett—Wilson's deputy in Jedda—that

> In his eyes the Arabs were insurgents, and in subsequent negotiations with Captain Garland he, as a General of Division and the Commander of a fortress which was further one of the Holy Cities of Islam, could not regard a Captain who signed 'for British Representative in the Hedjaz' as an 'Allied Commander' under the terms of the Armistice . . . He was [he continued] still up against what appeared to him to be a 'situation insupportable au point de [sic] militarisme'.
> Was he, 'Un General de Division et vieux soldat' to give his sword to a Captain holding apparently a political post? In battle, he said, a subaltern may take prisoner a Field Marshal but when it was a question of the surrender of an unbeaten garrison under the terms of an armistice such a position seemed to him impossible, quite apart

from the peculiar situation in which he was placed as regards the Holy City.[33]

Though the emissary from Istanbul was not able to induce Fakhri to surrender, yet his presence and the news from the outside world which he brought with him seem to have had an unsettling and demoralizing effect on some of Fakhri's officers. One of them, Emin Bey, organized a secret society among some officers and circulated on 28 December 1918 a manifesto attacking the general's policies. Fakhri sent for this officer, who took fright, decamped and surrendered to the Sharifians. But Fakhri was not able to destroy the secret society, the members of which decided to arrest Fakhri and appoint another officer, Ali Negib, to command in his place. Fakhri was enticed outside the Haram where he had retired with a few officers and soldiers, arrested by his mutinous officers and handed over to the Sharifians. The conspirators signed a surrender agreement which was described as 'Drawn up between Captain Garland and the Arabs with Negib Bey independently of Fakhry'.[34]

In conversation with Garland Fakhri expressed his belief that the two ringleaders of the conspiracy, Emin Bey and a Baghdadi officer called Sabry, had, as Arabs, intrigued with 'persons in Arab Camp' to bring about his arrest and supersession.[35] This, then, was the manner in which Medina fell to the Sharifians. In June 1920, the British representative in the Hijaz, Colonel C. E. Vickery, reported Abdullah as 'frequently' saying to him that the great leaders in the late war were Foch, Haig, Allenby and himself, adding that

> history will probably give me the first place because I have personally been engaged in so many more battles than they. I have fought in 128 actions![36]

The Sharifian entry into Medina realized the fears which Garland had expressed only a few days before. The events which took place in Medina after its surrender would probably never have been known but for the presence of two experienced Muslim observers who were not Sharifian dependents, and who deemed it their duty to report to their own authorities what their eyes had seen and ears heard. One was an Egyptian officer with Abdullah's forces, Miralai (Colonel) Sadik bey Yahya, DSO; the other was the French Muslim Captain Depui, who was with Ali's forces. Both of them witnessed the events in Medina and its environs and compiled their record while they were still in the city. The reports were entrusted to camel messengers for despatch to Jeddah but they never reached their destination. Miralai Sadik Yahya returned to Jeddah in May 1919, and it was only then that the British representative heard about his missing report, 'and there is reason to believe', wrote Bassett to the Arab Bureau, 'it was purposely held up by order of H. H. Emir Ali'. Depui's report was presumably suppressed on the same orders.[37] But Miralai Sadik Yahya had with him a copy of the report, minus some appendices that had been attached to the original, and he handed it over to Bassett. And, while Depui's report never came to light subsequently, some of the matter it contained we may reasonably assume to have been incorporated in the monthly report on the Hijaz for February 1919 sent to Paris by the French military mission in Egypt, and which Depui himself wrote.[38] In due course, Sadik Yahya's report was sent by the Cairo residency to London, but in a somewhat shortened—and bowdlerized—version.[39]

In view of the allegations made at the time, and still being retailed 56 years after the event by the anonym of *The Economist*, it is interesting to note that Colonel Sadik Yahya (who knew Medina from a previous visit in 1909) reported that 'Not a single Maxim or any other gun was put in or on the Haram as we had heard before'. Fakhri did use three mosques to store ammunition, but this was on the calculation that should an airplane attack Medina, it would not bomb such places. The report goes into great—not to say minute—detail about Fakhri's administration, the result, clearly, of extensive enquiries among the inhabitants who had experienced for over two years stringencies and shortages. The picture that emerges is one of orderly and equitable rule in which property rights were respected, food supplies assured and morale maintained. To increase food supplies, Fakhri took particular pains to foster agriculture. A month before the surrender he bought 6,000 kgs. of wheat, which he had planted in land on the outskirts of Medina: 'The crop grew splendidly until the blades were about 10 inches high just before the arrival of the Arab Armies at Medina. The Arab troops soon after their arrival at Medina went directly with their camels, horses, mules, etc. to the cultivated area to graze their animals and in seven days there was not a single blade to be seen'. Particularly interesting in view of the siege which the Sharifians were supposed to be enforcing against Medina is Colonel Sadik Yahya's observation that 'Goods used to come to Medina from different parts of Arabia, Hail, etc., until 5 months before the surrender of Medina. During the last 5 months everything that came was from Wejh and Rabegh [in Sharifian territory]'. The Colonel also reported that all the forts, towers, outer defenses and posts around Medina were strongly fortified 'and were very carefully controlled and well arranged', thus confirming Garland's view that the taking of Medina would have required a regular force led by an experienced commander.

Fakhri was taken prisoner on 10 January 1919; Abdullah entered Medina on 13 January with some of his Bedouins; on 15 January the officer commanding Ali's regular troops, Nuri el-Kueri, arrived in Medina (of which he was to be the governor on behalf of Ali, to whom the city was apparently to be handed over). It was on the same day that Colonel Sadik Yahya arrived in the city.

I regret to say [he declared in his report] that when I entered
Medina on the 15/1/1919 I found all the houses which number
about 4850 and which were locked and sealed by the Turkish
Government had been broken open by the Arabs who looted the
furniture which they sold at a very cheap price in the Suk because
they were ignorant of their value. The Ashraf and others who
entered Medina with the Emir Abdullah used to go from house to
house and take what they liked and they used to live in the houses as
they pleased and this went on for 12 days and even the houses
whose owners were at Medina were looted. I myself have seen the
Bedouin boys carrying pieces of good and valuable furniture in the
town and selling them cheap . . . There were no guards at Medina
for 20 days after the entrance of the Emir. It was not only the
Bedouin who practised looting but 80 percent of the Baghdadi and
Syrian officers took part in the game by means of their regular and
Bedouin troops. Only one-eighth of the houses were saved from
being looted.

Sadik Yahya also recounted how his own Somali cook, while on his way one
afternoon to the Prophet's mosque, was attacked and beaten by Bedouins
who took his money and his revolver. Sadik Yahya complained to Abdullah,
who said that the Bedouins were denying the whole thing. When Sadik
Yahya insisted that the incident be properly investigated, Abdullah said that

he had issued an order to bring the mulahhas (It is customary
amongst the Bedouin when one steals anything and denies it they
bring a man whom they call mulahhas who puts a thin rod of iron in
the fire until it becomes red hot and then passes it over the tongue of
the suspected one and if the tongue is burnt, i.e. swollen, then the
suspected one will be considered as the real thief, if not he will be
considered as innocent). I told the Emir that it is not wise to
substitute the mulahhas for the proper judgments of the well
organised courts and mehkemeh sharia — the word mulahhas is
derived from the verb lahasa which means the one who makes
another lick something—especially in a place like Medina.
Nothing was done by the Emir and the cook did not get his money
back nor were the culprits ever punished.

It was Sadik Yahya's judgment that the people of Medina lost more in the
days following the Sharifian occupation than they had during the two years
of Fakhri's rule.

Sadik Yahya and Depui concurred in the view that Medina suffered
these disorders because Abdullah was unwilling to curb his troops—
whether regular officers or Bedouins. Depui attributes this attitude of
Abdullah's to the bad relations between him and his brother Ali owing to

jealousy over the succession to their father's throne. The two brothers, outwardly friendly, remarked Depui, 'were constantly seeking to harm one
another. This hatred', Depui added, 'is much more marked in Abdullah's
case'.

It may have been their antagonism which led to the dismissal from
his post of Ali's chief of staff, Kueri, who (as has been seen) had been
appointed commandant of the city and who, according to Depui, tried to
suppress the looting and the disorder. It does not seem, however, that
Medina fared any better under the regime of Ali, who entered the city on 2
February.[40] Disorders and pillage in Medina continued to be reported
months later. For example, a report from Medina by a North African
Muslim, written in June 1919, speaks of Ali's grudge against the Medinese
who had stayed in the city during Fakhri's rule, and how he allowed his
deputy Sharif Shahhat to make free of their goods and persons.[41] Again, in a
survey of conditions in the Hijaz dated 1 March 1920, Catroux reports that
Bedouins were blockading the roads to Medina and preventing food from
reaching the inhabitants. The military governor, Shukri al-Ayyubi, and the
civil governor Sharif Shahhat

> se partagent une autorité aux attributions confuses dont ils
> n'usent guère que pour se créer mutuellement des embarras.
> Les Administrés sont les victimes de ces rivalités. Au scandale
> de ces méthodes de gouvernement [Shahhat] ajoute la honte de sa
> conduite privée, l'ivrognerie et la débauche. On comprend que
> l'écoeurement ait gagné les Médinois, qu'ils regrettent le
> régime ottoman, qu'ils fassent des voeux secrets pour le rattache-
> ment de leur ville à la Syrie et que pour sauvegarder leurs biens et
> leurs personnes, ils se placent sous la protection de Cheikhs
> Bedouins auxquels ils paient en retour une redevance.[42]

It remains to record that when those extracts from Sadik Yahya's
report which Cairo considered fit for the eyes of the authorities in London
reached the Foreign Office, a member of its Eastern Department, Captain
W. H. Young, minuted the despatch as follows:

> The scenes which took place on the occupation of Medina by the
> Arab Army were reproduced at Deraa, Damascus and Aleppo, and
> the apprehensions of the educated townsmen were fully shared at
> these three places. Arab civilization is a distinct putting back of the
> clock when compared to the Turkish.[43]

Young, it is well known, did a great deal to establish a Sharifian regime in
Mesopotamia. We may deprecate the sweeping (and unjustified) judgment
by this staunch Arabophile on the merits of Arab civilization; but the minute
as a whole is reassuring evidence that, though in his published memoirs
(engagingly entitled The Independent Arab) Young chose to be discreet

about the scenes which he witnessed on the fall of Dar'a and Damascus, this liberal and high-minded official, in doing what he did over Mesopotamia, was not (be it said to his credit) acting in, or out of, ignorance.

APPENDIX

(F.O.882-7, folios 385-390)

PRIVATE

A Day at EL JAFR

As I finish my breakfast in my tent about 7:30 a.m. GAMAL BEY ALI enters: the 'Bey' is intrusive, and I know not want rank he held in the Turkish Army, but he is now a Bimbashi in the Hedjaz forces. Will I do him a favour? I reply 'yes, if possible'. His family is at MECCA and he wants leave to bring it to YANBO.

'How do you, a Baghdadi, come to have your family at MECCA?' I ask.

'I brought it from MESOPOTAMIA when I joined the Hejaz Army.' I promise to write a letter to Jeddah asking that facilities for travel be given if Hedjaz authorities approve the move. He goes out amidst a reiteration of profound thanks, and in his place enters Monsieur Lieut. Claude PROST of the French Army.

'Bon jour, monsieur Garland'.

After a lot of unnecessary enquiries as to the state of my health, he proceeds to divulge his latest piece of intelligence. 'There is', he says, 'a cinematograph in MEDINA, with 4000 films.'

French intelligence always deals in units of thousands.

After a protracted stay, during which he has smoked about half a dozen of my cigarettes, and pumped me for all he is worth to make me exude, reciprocally, any similar momentous intelligence I may have, he takes his leave and I apply myself to my correspondence.

But not for long. I am interrupted by the boisterous pigeon-English 'Good morning' of Said Bey Hamid, Inspector of Artillery and assistant chief Bandit of Sherif Abdullah's force.

'Any news?' he asks.

'Mafeesh' I reply.

'Do you know', he breaks out after a silence which I have endeavoured to render very suggestive, 'I believe the king is not going to give us officers any gratuity when we leave.'

'Indeed' I reply, half hoping His Majesty has that intention. 'But what more do you want? You've been getting good pay.'

'But all Governments give their soldiers a gratuity after a war.'

I say that I do not know the arrangements of the Sherifian Army, and he replies that if the Sherifian Government fails to do its obvious duty in this manner, the British Government, which was responsible for bringing

Syrian, Baghdadian and other soldiers to fight the Turk, should give the gratuities.

My efforts to change the subject of conversation are unavailing and SAID Bey proceeds to detail the circumstances under which he and his brother officers were induced to take arms against the Turks.

As I happen to know that SAID Bey Hamid is about as undeserving of a gratuity as anyone possibly could be, I feel I cannot take much interest in his arguments, and he accepts the dismissal I infer by continuing my correspondence.

It is now 11 a.m. and a post from Yambo arrives. I am in the midst of reading it through when Doctor Issa walks in. Dr. Issa is a stayer and very fond of cigars. I have not had time to hide the box containing my last five, consequently he helps himself and proceeds to ask:

'Are the Allies going to give Syria to the King of the Hedjaz?'

'I don't know'.

'Surely they are not going to put an intellectual people under the King of a country like this?'

'I don't know'.

'Do you think the French will get Syria?'

'I don't know'.

'Do you know the Syrians want independence?'

'I know nothing except that I recently read in a paper that Syria is to select its own Government'.

'Oh yes', replied Dr. Issa, 'Some few people who have received French gold in the past will vote for France, but they are not representative.'

Dr. ISSA then enters into a lengthy discussion in the course of which he describes the awful results that will ensue if either the French Government or the King of the Hedjaz takes over Syria, or if the King retains Damascus.

I have nothing to say. Being at present a soldier, I am prevented from stating any personal opinions.

Having finished his cigar, Dr. Issa takes another, and departs. In a few moments Sherif Abdullah pops in and after seating himself, breaks out 'Ya Major Garland', (he always insists on the 'Major'). 'What is going to happen to Mesopotamia and Syria?'

Mentally I feel round for my bump of diplomacy, but cannot think of a better answer than the one I gave to Dr. Issa, 'I don't know'. Then he expounds, 'When we entered the war, we had an agreement with the British Government that the Arab Countries, except those already under British Protection, should be ours.'

'The British Government', I reply, 'as you no doubt know, makes a point of standing by its agreements: but the map of the world is going to be decided now, not by the British Government, but by a conference of all the Powers that have been associated against Germany and her Allies. I feel sure that the decisions they make will not be unfair.'

Sherif Abdullah does not appear to be too pleased with this reply but it was my best effort on the spur of the moment.

After asking me what whisky is made from, the Emir leaves for his mid-day prayer, I begin to feel tired of visitors, but there is no relief, for Rashid Bey comes into the tent full of 'good mornings' which he follows with the question: 'Is it true Mesopotamia is getting independence?'

'I don't know'.

'The British will have a lot of trouble if they try to govern Mesopotamia,' he states frankly.

I reply that although I don't know whether the British Government wants MESOPOTAMIA or not, I do know that *I* don't.

Rashid Bey has got a comfortable bank account and thinks of nothing else but getting back to BAGHDAD to invest his money there. He is the very picture of exquisite misery.

But he eventually says 'adieu', and I settle down again to my letters.

In a few moments, a slave of the Emirs comes to tell me that lunch is ready.

We lunch off very palatable food, though one could wish the servants who serve it would cleanse their garments more frequently. Sherif Abdullah is always very amiable at mealtimes and monopolises the conversation.

When coffee and tea is served, we sit in a circle and the Emir suddenly breaks the silence with 'Ya Major Garland, in your country do the girls on their bridal nights cry and refuse their husbands?'

Abdullah has an awful bad habit of breaking a splendid silence with an astounding question of that sort.

I do not propose to record my reply, but the Sherif said that Arab wives usually do, and that they put up a tremendous barrage of tears; which gave Sherif Nasir the chance of epigrammatically adding 'the greater the fortification, the more satisfaction in reducing it.'

Then I was regaled with tales of Arab marriages and took my leave about 3 p.m.

Shortly afterwards a Turkish prisoner appeared at my tent complaining that he had no blanket and the weather is very cold. I gave him a note to the Commandant asking that a blanket be issued and he went away feeling that the British are THE people.

I felt that I was now justified in taking a little rest, but hardly had I settled on my bed before ISSET Eff. came into the tent and said he would like to send some money to his family at BAGHDAD. I couldn't help feeling sorry he had a family, but took his money and agreed to despatch it in due course. He seemed inclined to make a protracted stay but left when I took off my coat and returned to my bed.

Shortly after, my servant came in and said an Egyptian wanted to see me. Now, after mixing with BAGHDADIS and BEDUIN it is a real treat to see an Egyptian and I felt compelled to listen to his grievance. He said he was a civilian but had been in the E.A. He had lost his Army discharge certificate. I told him not to worry and that I would give him a certificate swearing . . . . 1918 he had come to me and had stated that he had just lost his discharge certificate. He went away quite content. Five o'clock had come round and with it came Sherif Abdul Kerim el Bedawi. Abdul Kerim had a terrible lot of salaams to get through because he had not seen me for a long time, to wit, one month.

Abdul Kerim is distressingly important in demeanour, almost regal, and considers himself the last word in correct conduct. We are old friends, or at least I should say he considers I am an old friend of his. I know Abdul Kerim through and through, but I must keep in with him now, because the Turkish prisoners have shortly to pass through his country.

'Mafeesh mowash', he exclaims.

'Ya salaam', I reply.

'No', he continues, 'now eleven months without pay, and the Bedu will not stand such treatment.'

'No doubt the Emir will give you a nice sum out of the next consignment,' I answer.

'Inshallah'.

Abdul Karim helps himself to half a dozen cigarettes and leaves.

Enter a very black person whom I do not recognize in the darkness. He attempts to kiss my hand and turns out to be one of Abdullah's slaves.

From his enquiries and those that have preceded them during the day, one would think my state of health was one of the most momentous questions of the day. I satisfy his anxiety and, seating himself, he tells me how, about a year before the war, he took a voyage from Port Sudan in a sambuk and on arrival at Jeddah was taken by BEDUIN as a slave, the price paid being 7 Reals; how he was ultimately sold for £32 somewhere near Rabegh. But he has not come to ask for freedom from slavery, for he proceeds:

'No pay for four months now'.

'Really'

'No, and we are all hard up'.

'Really!'

Another silence ensues, but he spoils it with a request that I should lend him four pounds.

'Four pounds! Do you think I am a bank?' I ask.

'It is very necessary for me', he responds.

'I'm sorry, but it can't be done.'

I hand him PT.50 to cover immediate demands and he departs without much external indication of gratitude.

Dinner time has come round and I go to dine with SAID HILMI

and his senior officers. The topic of conversation is WADI KHURMA. Sherif Abdullah has told them during the day of the Army's forthcoming move to that district and the officers, in turn, explain for my benefit how they were brought from India and elsewhere under the auspices of the British Government, and that they agreed to fight, not under any special flag, but solely to drive away the Turk. They explain that when the Turks have evacuated Arabia their duty will be finished, and they have no intention of joining in any combat of Arab versus Arab.

And how hard they try to draw from me some statement of opinion on the matter! But my ignorance is again colossal and I can only reply that, if, as they assert, they are now citizens of independent countries, viz Syria and Mesopotamia, no doubt they will be able to claim all the privileges of such citizenship in due course.

And with that I retire feeling that my camp bed is a relief from the hot-bed of Arab politics in which at present I have my being.

signed: H. Garland
Captain

Copies to:—Colonel Wilson, C. M. G., D. S. O.
          Major Cornwallis, D. S. O.

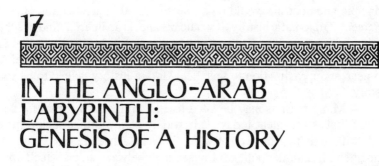

IN THE ANGLO-ARAB LABYRINTH: GENESIS OF A HISTORY

In *the Anglo-Arab Labyrinth,* published in 1976 would, I suppose, be classified by librarians and bibliographers as a work of diplomatic history. This would no doubt be appropriate, for, as its subtitle indicates, the work deals with the letters which were exchanged in 1915-16 between the British High Commissioner in Egypt and the Sharif of Mecca, and which prepared the way for what is known as The Arab Revolt.

But what does this classificatory label, diplomatic history, signify? At the beginning of the book I quote, as an epigraph, a sentence which occurs in G.M. Young's *Victorian England.* This is to the effect that diplomatic history is no more than 'the record of what one clerk said to another clerk'. My intent in putting these words at the head of my book was ironical: it was to dismiss Young's own dismissive attitude towards diplomatic history, in the belief that what 'one clerk said to another clerk' is quite as worthy of historical investigation as any other human activity.

But why was Young so dismissive of this kind of history? We do know that his tastes and talents as an historian lay elsewhere; in history, he believed, what was important was 'not what happened, but what people felt about it when it was happening'. This distinction, we may feel, is in the end unsatisfactory and untenable, the erection into a dogma of what can be a matter only of sentiment and inclination. Young's own work, in its strengths and weaknesses, confirms this view. His masterpiece, *Victorian England, Portrait of an Age* is a marvellous and unmatched account of what English people felt about the Victorian age 'when it was happening'; whereas his biography of Stanley Baldwin—concerned, as such a work would have to be, with 'what happened'—is by common consent a failure. But who can doubt that the one is as fully legitimate an historical enterprise as the other,

I have to thank Professor J. C. Hurewitz of Columbia University for asking me to give a talk to his seminar on the writing of *In the Anglo-Arab Labyrinth*, and thus setting me thinking about its genesis.

or that political biography in the hands of a master can be as accomplished as *Victorian England*?

A great many historians would now agree with Young in his low estimate of diplomatic history, but the reason is unlikely to be the same. Principle and doctrine would today be advanced in justification of such a judgment. Diplomatic history, it would be said, is an inferior kind of subject dealing with the surface of things, and by no means able to give us that total picture of a society which the historian should ideally aim to provide. And the nearest approximation to this ideal kind of history is held to be social history.

Many reasons may be cited to explain the high regard for social history that is prevalent today. It is widely believed that such a history deals with activities and events which in some sense are more real, more fundamental, than the political transactions between states which are the usual concern of diplomatic historians. This belief in the primacy of social history is no doubt one outcome of Marxist ideas and of their wide dissemination. For if it is assumed that the particular mode of production prevalent in a society determines the character of all its other activities, then social history, or a variant thereof, must assume a commanding position. As is well known, the so-called *Annales* school has done a great deal to endow social history with its newly found prestige, and as it happens, one reason why two of the principal founders of the school, Marc Bloch and Lucien Febvre, became attracted to social and economic history was their belief that the real history of a society must begin with and be based upon the history of its economic activity. The rest was dismissed and damned as mere *histoire événementielle*, i.e. as so much frothy gossip about Cleopatra's nose, the Ems telegrams and sealed wagons speeding towards the Finland Station.

Another feature of what may be called *Annales* doctrine leads in the same direction. In this doctrine *histoire événementielle* is contrasted to the *longue durée*, by which is meant those features of a society which are believed to persist through generations and centuries, to be almost permanent if not eternal. These features, it is said, yield the key to reality, the real reality. This prejudice in favour of that which is believed to change very slowly or not at all ends in paradox, by diverting the historian from what is, after all, the *raison d'être* of his activity: to exhibit change (whether it is slow or rapid) and account for it. The historian, stopping his ear to the din made by events tiresomely following one another in quick succession becomes the servant and priest of this majestic and immutable *longue durée* and, in Febvre's words, devotes himself to the 'static study of the facts of history'. Whoever says *longue durée* is on the brink of saying *structure*, and it is of course no surprise that the new fashion in history should be prevalent where Marxism, sociologism and structuralism (in its various senses) are fashionable. The whole of this movement is admirably encapsulated in a passage that occurs in the editorial which inaugurates the first number of *Review*, the Journal of the Fernand Braudel Center for the Study of Economics, Historical Systems and Civilizations at the State University of New York at Binghampton, which appeared in the summer of 1977. In this editorial entitled 'The Tasks of Historical Social Science', the editor, Immanuel Wallerstein, declares:

> *Annales* stood for the economic and social roots of history against the political and diplomatic façade, for the quantified trends against the chronological narrative, for the social sciences against historical uniqueness, for 'global man' against 'fractional man', for Braudel's *longue durée* against the *événementielle* [sic].

This is emphatically and categorically put, and such strict, uncompromising separation of sheep from goats is not without its heuristic uses. Is it so easy, we are moved to wonder, in the flow of historical events to say which is 'root' and which is 'façade'? Why is it that what one clerk writes to another clerk is not as real as technological change or a change in economic relations? By what criteria is one to decide that a diplomatic transaction or a battle is inherently less significant than a change in the quantity of money or in agricultural methods, or in techniques of manufacture? If consequences or the extent of change are the criteria, then Waterloo or the Nazi-Soviet Pact or the Final Solution are no less momentous than the enclosure of the commons, the steam engine or the industrial mode of production. No less, but also no more momentous. But to put it this way is to commit oneself exactly to nothing. Indeed on this point one can only say nothing, for how is one to establish that one criterion rather than another must have the historian's undivided allegiance? Equally with G. M. Young, then, the followers of the *Annales* school in practising their kind of history do no more than follow their bent—or perhaps the fashion. But to follow one's bent guarantees nothing. A social historian may be equally a genius or a mediocrity—and so may a diplomatic historian. Historians' choice of subject does not tell us whether their books are valuable or useless, dull or sparkling. The scribblings of clerks may indeed be unbearably tedious, but *longue durée*, too, can be a tremendous bore.

But diplomatic history, dominant for so long in the academy, has now fallen into some disrepute. It is widely taken to be in reality no more than a précis, more or less methodical, of diplomatic correspondence. If the idea of diplomatic history involves no more than this, then the disrepute would be well merited. But like all good history, good diplomatic history starts not with a heap of materials which it aspires to put into some kind of order, but with a sense of puzzlement. Puzzlement about an action or a statement which at first blush is obscure in its details or its significance, or perhaps not easy to reconcile with the surrounding circumstances or with the past behaviour of the agent. The history which an historian undertakes is an enquiry. An enquiry is a question, and the historian is an enquirer, an asker of questions. The diplomatic historian is, likewise, an asker of questions about transactions between those organized bodies politic which we now call states. His puzzlement may relate to one particular transaction, or to the character and *modus operandi* over a particular period of foreign ministries and their agents. He may ask questions about all these things or, starting from his original enquiry, he may come to be interested in a much wider range of issues. May come to be, because of course the initial enquiry does not and cannot itself specify what the answer will be, or through what unexpected meanderings and unlikely by-ways it may lead the enquirer.

All this can be illustrated from the history of my *In the Anglo-Arab Labyrinth*, a work which, as has been said, may be labelled as diplomatic history. So far as I can establish, its genesis occurred during a train journey from London to Oxford in May or June 1951. I had taken with me to read on the train Sir Ronald Storrs' well-known memoirs, *Orientations*, which had been published in 1937. Though I knew then little or nothing about the history of the Middle East, I had some personal experience of Middle Eastern society and politics. Judged by this experience, and by the tradition, which underpinned and interpreted it, Storrs' discourse rang false. The characters he described, their actions and reactions, seemed to belong to a political world more sophisticated and light-hearted, more benign and straightforward, than the crude corruption, brutality and ideological ranting which was what the political spectacle disclosed to a schoolboy growing up in Baghdad in the 1930s and '40s. Why exactly there was this discrepancy —if indeed there was a discrepancy—between Storrs' report and my own experience, I could not then possibly say. This discrepancy between the memorialist's reminiscences and what had been tested on the pulse of experience was the origin of the puzzlement that led me in ways then unforeseen to embark on the diplomatic history of the Middle East in the first world war. As I read on, the impression of falseness emanating from this book became gradually overwhelming. It was summed up for me, as I vividly remember, in the difference between two illustrations included in the book. One was a photograph of Storrs' taken while he was on a visit to the Sharif of Mecca in 1916, and the other was the reproduction of a drawing of the author executed by Eric Kennington for T. E. Lawrence's *Seven Pillars of Wisdom*. The contrast between Kennington's superior being and the rather ordinary shifty-looking character revealed by the camera seemed to me to symbolize and point up the dissonance which had struck me so forcibly.

As I have said, my knowledge of Middle Eastern history was then very small. Of the subjects we were required to read for the degree I had just taken—subjects which ranged from economics to British government—it was the history of European political thought which I found most attractive.

If I could be said to know any history then, my knowledge would have been found to lie in the general field of intellectual history, of the problems of which I had a more or less hazy idea. Diplomatic history was far from my thought. But if my knowledge of Middle Eastern history was minimal, I was certainly interested in a topic which had to do with the part of the world from which I came; hence my reading of such books as *Orientations*.

I found myself on a train to Oxford in 1951 because I was going there to be interviewed for a scholarship at St. Antony's College, which had just been founded. The upshot was that I spent two years at the College studying, and writing about Middle Eastern history. My first inclination had been to investigate the changing image that British writers had of the Middle East in the 19th and 20th centuries. This was a topic in intellectual history—the kind of history with which my undergraduate studies had made me most familiar—the kind of history, in fact, which (to recall and adapt Young's distinction) dealt not with what happened, but with what people thought about what was happening. But it was not very long before I came not so much to abandon the history of ideas as to feel the need for doing also another kind of history, namely, diplomatic history. Reading books like Storrs' memoirs made me increasingly feel that here were stories and episodes which, as recounted by the authors, left large areas obscure. There were these dissonances; things did not connect; there were large gaps in the narrative—gaps between what was said and what was done, between the description of a man's character and disposition and the report of his actions. It was no doubt possible to extract from a work like *Orientations* the image of the Middle East which its author had formed, but gradually such an enterprise began to seem unsatisfactory. Here it was not a simple matter of relating image to reality. The author of the image was himself engaged in changing the reality, and fully to understand the character of his image required one to understand his engagement with the reality. Knowledge of what did happen was necessary in order to understand how people—some people at any rate—felt about what happened.

The logic, or let us perhaps say the drift, of the original enquiry led me to an interest in political and diplomatic history. The circumstances that prevailed at St. Antony's and in the University of Oxford had their part to play in the redirection of my interests. At that time very few senior members of the University had any concern with the modern history of the Middle East, and since being in *statu pupillari* I had to be assigned to a supervisor, the Warden of St. Antony's, F. W. Deakin, agreed that John Wheeler-Bennett, then a Fellow of the College, could, as well as any other history don, serve as my supervisor. As is well known, Wheeler-Bennett's field was modern European history, and our contacts were infrequent. He gave me tea once a term and our conversations on these agreeable occasions ranged widely. I came away from these meetings with a picture of Central Europe and its political society which the Nazi ruffians had in part seduced and in part destroyed, a picture skillfully conveyed by this elegant, monocled scholar and man of the world. This of course had no direct bearing on my own concerns. But I was well content with this state of affairs since, if it did not forward my studies, it also did nothing to hinder them. This, however, is putting it too negatively, since my conversations with Wheeler-Bennett gave me, in some fashion, an insight into, a feel for, diplomatic history. But it was my fellow-students in the junior common room who were mainly responsible for my education as an historian. The junior common room at St. Antony's was, in those early days, quite small; it was composed overwhelmingly of historians, with a sprinkling of physicists. The historians were, as I recall, most of them Oxford men who for their undergraduate degree had had to read a great deal of political and diplomatic history. My education—as I can see in retrospect—was effected by means of casual conversations which sometimes turned into discussions about some problem or episode occurring in their work—work which related to the recent history of Central Europe, or to France, or Spain, or the British government of India. In these conversations or discussions I sometimes participated, but as often as not I was content to be the silent listener. The intellectual life of the junior common room, with its impromptu conversations and its informal discussions, worked on me, in diverse, indirect, unregarded and mysterious ways to elicit new questions concerning my own work, to open up hitherto unsuspected perspectives, and to stimulate a critical scrutiny of evidence, inference and narrative. What took place then is not without analogy to the obscure and silent movements of the mind underlying philosophical and poetic creativity which Valéry evokes in his poem 'Palme':

> Ces jours qui te semblent vides
> Et perdus pour l'univers
> Ont des racines avides
> Qui travaillent les déserts.

My work at St. Antony's resulted in a book which I finished writing in December 1953 and which was published in April 1956 under the title *England and the Middle East: the Destruction of the Ottoman Empire 1914–1921.* It was an enterprise of some temerity since it was by no means evident when the plan of the book took shape in my mind that I would have enough evidence at my disposal to enable me to produce a consecutive and coherent account which, if it could not be comprehensive—and it could not then possibly be—would at least show the reader where the gaps and the obscurities lay. Two things may be pleaded in palliation of my temerity. In the first place, accounts of Middle Eastern history in the first world war then extant were unsatisfactory. They were generally incurious and uncritical, and (what was worse) either plain (or disguised) political advocacy, or else unwittingly tainted with political *parti pris.* In the second place, though the evidence was not as abundant as it became when the British archives were opened after 1966, a close examination disclosed quite a respectable body of materials available for the historian's scrutiny. In the three decades or so after the end of the war a large literature of memoirs, eye-witness accounts and military histories in European languages had accumulated. Careful scrutiny of this literature, and the comparison of various accounts, statements and allegations proved very fruitful. A case in point here was T. E. Lawrence's *Seven Pillars of Wisdom:* treated not reverentially as the utterance of a genius, but coolly, for, as the apology of an interested party it could yield interesting, indeed revealing, evidence. In the second place, most opportunely a voluminous official selection from the British archives dealing with the Middle East in 1919 was published when I was in the middle of my research. Again there was, as I gradually and with difficulty discovered, an accumulation of Arabic chronicles and memoirs with a great deal of valuable documentation, of the existence of which practically no historian had hitherto shown himself aware. I was also lucky in locating a few small collections of archives of which the most important were Lord Milner's papers then in the Library at New College, Oxford, and those of William Yale who during the war acted as Special Agent in the Near East of the US Department of State and was subsequently attached to the King-Crane Commission, sent to investigate political conditions in the Levant in 1919. Like anyone concerned with studying British policy in the Middle East during the first world war, I had of necessity to consider the meaning and significance of the McMahon-Husayn correspondence. And here, one document which I came upon in the Yale Papers I found of great use. As it figured in the Yale Papers, the document was anonymous, and I had no means of guessing its provenance or authorship. This long typescript, entitled 'British Commitments to King Hussein', seemed to be either a British official document or compiled from British official documents. Its value to me lay in the long and numerous extracts from letters and reports composed in 1914–16 which it included and which, taken together with the evidence from other sources, yielded a reasonably coherent picture of the course of the negotiations between the British and the Sharif of Mecca. What further struck me about the document was that some of the judgments its author made did not seem to be supported by the evidence he was quoting. But, knowing nothing about the provenance or purpose of the document, I was not in a position to say whether perhaps its author was relying for his conclusions on further evidence which he knew but was not quoting.

Taking, however, the evidence yielded by this paper (such as it was), and putting it side by side with that gleaned from my other sources, it became possible to make for myself a coherent and credible picture of the Anglo-Sharifian negotiations. While attending to these fragments of evidence, turning them over in my mind and deliberating upon them, I happened upon a passage written by D. G. Hogarth, who had been intimately involved in Anglo–Sharifian affairs during the last two years of the war. This passage figured in a chapter which Hogarth contributed to a work edited by the historian Temperley, *History of the Peace Conference*, which appeared in 1924. In this passage Hogarth summed up, within the compass of a single sentence, McMahon's commitments. He wrote:

> While [McMahon's letter of 24 October 1915] explicitly ruled out of the negotiations all the Turkish speaking districts which Hussein had claimed as Arab, and all Arab societies with whose chiefs we already had treaties—while further, it reserved to French discretion any assurance about the independence of the Syrian littoral, or the freedom from tutelage of the interior, i.e. the districts of the four towns, Damascus, Homs, Hama and Aleppo—while by reserving other Arab regions in which France might have peculiar interests, it left the Mosul district and even, perhaps, Palestine, in doubt—while, finally, it stated expressly that no guarantee for the unconditional delivery of either Lower or Upper Iraq to the Arabs could be given by us—in spite of all those reservations it recognised an Arab title to almost all the vast territories which Hussein had claimed, including Mesopotamia, subject only to limiting, but not annulling conditions.

This marvellously intricate sentence confidently driving with an easy rein its elaborate equipage of subordinate clauses, negotiating detail after detail in its leisurely progress and dexterously bringing the reader through at last to the ironical conclusion—this sentence acted as a catalyst for my thoughts. It was one of those rare passages which, as one reads them, immediately and irrevocably make a difference to one's mental landscape, such that things will never seem quite the same again. I felt somehow that Hogarth's words encapsulated the truth about this transaction the full details of which I did not, at that point, possess. The passage made sense, as no other statement had done, of the evidence I had collected. The feeling was to be confirmed by the additional evidence that began to be available ten years after the publication of *England and the Middle East*. This evidence as set out in *In the Anglo-Arab Labyrinth* confirms that, as I wrote in the book, Hogarth's was a punctiliously accurate account of McMahon's promises.

McMahon's letter of 24 October 1915 has a reference to four Syrian towns: Damascus, Homs, Hama and Aleppo. McMahon declares that territory lying to the West of these 'districts' 'cannot be said to be purely Arab' and is thus to be excluded from the boundaries of the Arab state which the Sharif of Mecca had claimed. After the first world war this passage occasioned a great deal of controversy, in relation to an issue which had not in fact been specifically the subject of negotiation between McMahon and the Sharif. This issue was that of the territory known after the war as Palestine. The Arabs of Palestine claimed that Britain was not at liberty to make the promises embodied in the Balfour Declaration since McMahon's words about Damascus etc. meant that Palestine was to be included in the prospective Arab state. Not only was such a reading of McMahon's words not immediately obvious, but the more one looked at McMahon's statement, the more obscure and intriguing it became. The collection of towns enumerated in McMahon's letter seemed to be chosen at random, since they were not, administratively speaking, or in terms of population and economic importance, in the same category; it was not true, either, that territories to the West of them, were less (or for that matter, more) purely Arab than they were; and no one who thought in terms of the administrative geography of the Ottoman empire would have been likely to assume that these four towns were or ever had formed a distinct group, or had been a boundary line, or that they ever constituted the several centres of any identifiable province.

Why then did McMahon group together these four disparate place-names? The evidence I had when writing *England and the Middle East* did not afford an answer to this question. What at that stage could be established was that this peculiar formulation came not from the Arab, but from the British, side. All else was obscure, but here was one question which the opening of the archives, one hoped, would eventually settle. However, as it happened, before they were opened, unexpectedly, new light was thrown on the problem. In 1961, Emile Marmorstein published 'A Note on "Damascus, Homs, Hama and Aleppo" '. In this article he drew attention to the fact that the well-known Muslim chronicler, Ibn al-Athir (1160–1234), had stated that these four towns were all that remained to the Muslims following the Crusaders' invasion of Syria. The statement, as he went on to point out, through the intermediary of a French 18th-century Orientalist passed into Gibbon's *Decline and Fall*, where the historian declares (in chapter LVII) that 'the four cities of Hems, Hamah, Damascus and Aleppo were the only relics of the Mohammedan conquests in Syria' that remained following the Crusaders' onslaught. Marmorstein argued that here was the origin and explanation of the peculiar phraseology of McMahon's famous letter. He also thought that the real author of this passage was not McMahon himself, but Sir Mark Sykes, a Member of Parliament and an Eastern traveller and author, who was then serving as an assistant to Kitchener and advising him on Middle Eastern problems.

There was about Marmorstein's suggestion something immediately convincing, indeed obvious. For what else but such a literary source could account for this bizarre conjunction of the four towns—a conjunction hitherto known to no administrative usage or diplomatic negotiation? But of course, belief in the essential rightness of this explanation rested on no documentary evidence. And when the documents became available, voluminous as they were, they afforded, ironically enough, no conclusive proof one way or the other. The documents did establish that Mark Sykes, however inclined for sentimental reasons he might have been to confine the

Arabs to that part of Syria which the Crusaders did not invade, in fact had nothing to do with either the negotiations which led to the despatch of McMahon's letter, or with the drafting of its terms. Beyond this the documents are silent. But the records do provide some clues to the mystery. They do establish that it was the Oriental Secretary in Cairo, none other than Ronald Storrs, who mainly carried on the Sharifian negotiation, and that it was he who drafted other letters to the Sharif in the series now known as the McMahon-Husayn correspondence. It is also established that he considered the Sharif's territorial demands exorbitant. This son of an Anglican dean might also be thought to manifest a hint of bigotry mixed with an amused condescension towards the Muslims whom he, a servant of the British Empire, helped to administer and control. There was in him, again, a potent feeling of self-admiration—admiration of his own exquisite taste, of his cultivated sensibility, of his erudition. Of all those who were concerned, in Cairo, with Arabian affairs he was the one, it seemed to me, who would have thought it clever and amusing surreptitiously to introduce Gibbon into a diplomatic negotiation. Though, then, there was no evidence to prove its truth beyond peradventure, Marmorstein's inspired suggestion seemed to account best for what we know.

Yet another event between the publication of *England and the Middle East* in 1956 and the opening of the archives ten years later played its part in the genesis of *In the Anglo-Arab Labyrinth*. In 1964 the London *Times* published an article written by its foreign editor that purported to throw new light on the various promises which the British had made during the first world war. The article drew its inspiration from another article which shortly before had appeared in an Arabic magazine. The author of this latter article had had access to the Papers of Professor W. L. Westermann who had been a member of the US Delegation to the Paris Peace Conference in 1919, and which were now deposited in the Hoover Institution at Stanford University. Among those papers was a copy of the same report on 'British Commitments to King Hussein' which I had come upon in the Yale Papers when writing *England and the Middle East*. The Westermann copy (which I had examined myself in 1959), however, left absolutely no doubt that the report was an official British document. The author of the Arabic article drew from this the conclusion (in which he was followed by the foreign editor of the *Times*) that, given the remarks of its (still) anonymous author about British promises to the Sharif, here at last was official proof of a contention which British governments had been rather reluctant to accept, namely that Palestine had been included in these promises. Familiar as I was with the report, I wrote to the *Times* to draw attention to the discrepancy between the evidence marshalled in the report and the conclusions of its author: that the document was official did not *ipso facto* prove that what it asserted was true. The publication of my letter in turn moved Leonard Stein to write to me.

Stein, the author of the well-known *The Balfour Declaration* (1961), wrote to ask for some further details about the document in question. Though he had not himself seen it, he had, as he told me, heard of it. He had been told that its author was Arnold Toynbee, who had been in the Political Intelligence Department of the Foreign Office during the last months of the war. Stein had also heard that towards the beginning of the second world war Malcolm MacDonald, then Colonial Secretary, had called for a copy of Toynbee's report, and upon reading it had made marginal notes critical of Toynbee's conclusions. Stein's letter opened for me new vistas on the McMahon-Husayn correspondence. For if his information was correct, not only the correspondence and its immediately attendant circumstances fell to be investigated, the letters also had perhaps had a subsequent history of official commentary and interpretation which might also be worth examining. Stein's letter was thus for me, like the passage from Hogarth quoted earlier, again a kind of catalyst. It wakened the mind to possibilities which, when the opening of the archives two years later allowed the evidence to be examined, took shape as the organizing idea of the book and governed its structure. It may be said in passing that while Stein's information about Toynbee's authorship of the 'Commitments' report was correct, there is no evidence that MacDonald read the report, or annotated it. But the story possibly had a basis in an incident which took place in 1940 and which I describe in *In the Anglo-Arab Labyrinth*. It appears that in 1940 Toynbee told a colleague at Chatham House that he had written a memorandum in 1918 which showed that Palestine and Syria had been promised to the Sharif. Toynbee alleged that his conclusion had been accepted by the Foreign Office but that later, 'as the result of Jewish pressure', the British government changed their attitude and began to cast about for ways of showing that Palestine was not included in their promises. The colleague went with the story to MacDonald, who ordered an enquiry. The Colonial Office had no copy of Toynbee's memorandum. It asked the Foreign Office to investigate. There, the civil servant concerned, after investigation and to his chagrin, had to inform the Colonial Office that there was no evidence that Toynbee's conclusions had been suppressed in response to Jewish pressure.

When they were at last opened in 1966, the archives proved to be voluminous and scattered in different series somewhat difficult to piece together. The historian, of course, has no right to complain of such a state of affairs since archives are not collected or arranged for his benefit. But this characteristic of these particular archives had its bearing and influence on the conduct of policy. In a private letter of April 1916 to the Foreign Secretary, quoted in my book, McMahon confessed that in dealing with the Arab question 'I feel at times somewhat bewildered at the numerous agencies who have a hand in it'. Disorientation, as the evidence shows, generally marked the conduct of Sharifian negotiations on the British side.

There was, as I describe in the first part of my book, a failure at the highest level to think through the affair in its various bearings and implications, and a failure by the minister concerned, Sir Edward Grey, and by his immediate official advisers to exert proper control over the activities of their subordinates. It is this which led me to entitle the first part of my book (which deals with the Anglo-Sharifian negotiations between 1914 and the outbreak of the Sharif's rebellion in June 1916) 'The Quicksand'. This title I borrowed from a minute by Sir Edward Grey in which he sighed wearily that 'This Arab question is a regular quicksand'. The scattered and fragmentary nature of the voluminous archives would have had their role to play then and later in the muddle of Anglo-Arab relations.

The documents yield a picture of decisions taken in haste and in ignorance, and a Foreign Secretary clearly out of his depth and exhausted by the unremitting labour involved in conducting, under the stress and urgency of war, a world-wide foreign policy, and more often than not yielding to his forceful and impetuous colleague, Lord Kitchener; and of civil servants who, distracted by the same pressures, were incapable of remedying their master's shortcomings. But the evidence also reveals that this was not the case everywhere in Whitehall. The Secretary of State for India, Austen Chamberlain and his officials, Sir Thomas Holderness and Sir Arthur Hirtzel, showed a firm grasp of the issues and did not allow themselves to be bounced by eagerness or panic into ill-considered judgments. The evidence is at its most striking when it refers to the judgments and actions of the British officials in Egypt and the Sudan: McMahon, Storrs, G. F. Clayton, who was in charge of Intelligence, his colleague Kinahan Cornwallis, and Sir Reginald Wingate, the Governor-General of the Sudan. They are seen to be either incompetent and negligent, or frivolous, or injudicious, or over-eager and fanciful.

But if the archives do enable us to paint a rich, detailed picture of Anglo-Sharifian negotiations and of the context and ambience in which they took place, they do leave some crucial questions unanswered. It is likely that they will remain unanswered, unless a hitherto-unknown hoard of papers should be discovered. As has been said above, the papers do not disclose who originated the idea that the Arab state in Syria should comprise Damascus, Homs, Hama and Aleppo. What the documents show is that McMahon informed the Foreign Secretary that the Arabs would insist on 'boundaries . . . leaving in Arabia purely Arab districts of Aleppo, Damascus, Hama and Homs'. Grey agreed that an offer to the Sharif should be made in these terms. McMahon, however, without any authority or subsequent explanation departed from the terms he had suggested and which Grey had authorized. In his letter of 24 October 1915 he told the Sharif, instead, that he was excluding from the area of Arab independence, on the score that 'they cannot be said to be purely Arab', 'the portions of Syria lying to the West of Damascus, Homs, Hama and Aleppo'. That

McMahon had departed from his instructions was not known or suspected before. But though the archives disclose this change of phrasing—a change which was at the origin of the controversies for which the McMahon-Husayn correspondence became notorious—the file which might have shown who in Cairo suggested this change and for what reason, is missing, and our knowledge on this important point must remain—perhaps forever—incomplete.

As the full extent of the complication and muddle in Anglo-Sharifian negotiations gradually became clearer to me, the idea which Leonard Stein's letter had conjured in my mind began to have increasingly more point. It was no longer simply that the McMahon-Husayn correspondence had, perhaps, a history of subsequent interpretation which a student might want to elucidate. Rather, faced with a transaction which was in great part obscurity and equivocation, the student was irresistibly drawn to ask: What did the various interested parties make afterwards of these texts, and how did they understand their sibylline promises? It was, of course, well-known that the correspondence became involved after the war in the Palestine problem—a problem which did not exist when the letters were exchanged, and with which they did not set out to deal. But as I soon discovered when pursuing the fortunes of the correspondence following the Sharifian uprising and afterwards, the letters became a matter of controversy very soon after the last one in the series was despatched and received, and this in relation to a range of issues which had nothing to do with Palestine. And following the trail of the correspondence in the files between 1916 and 1939—when the letters were officially published—I was led to write the second part of my book, which in fact proved to be slightly longer than the first.

This second part I entitled 'The fly in the fly-bottle'. The expression I took from the philosopher Wittgenstein. In a well-known passage in his *Philosophical Investigations* he likened men caught in philosophical dilemmas to flies in a bottle from which they struggle in vain to escape until the philosopher shows them the way out—shows them that it is a pseudo-problem with which they are struggling. The analogy between such puzzlement and the muddles which ministers and officials got into in their various attempts to establish what had been agreed between McMahon and the Sharif seemed particularly apt. For between 1916 and 1939, as I discovered, one interpretation after another was suggested by various British officials in Cairo and London. All of these, except one, failed badly in putting together the evidence they had available in their own files, and in considering the meaning and implications of this evidence. The one—partial—exception was W. J. Childs of the Foreign Office, who in 1930 produced an extensive memorandum in an attempt to answer the question whether Palestine had or had not been included in the territories promised to the Sharif. Childs was diligent and intelligent and had some historical imagination. But even he failed to look at all the available evidence and failed to be critical enough in his scrutiny of it.

The second part of the book can thus be called an historiographical enquiry, in contrast to the first, which may be described as an historical one. And we are justified in speaking of the official historiography of the McMahon-Husayn correspondence since, as the evidence shows, almost all the officials who set out to explain the meaning of the correspondence did so in a genuinely historical spirit. They really wanted to discover what actually took place, not to make a political point or defend an established political position. This is all the more intelligible in that they were writing exclusively for the eyes of their colleagues and political masters. The only civil servant who can be said to have deliberately bent the evidence was the Foreign Office official who sported the name of Lacy Baggallay (and who in 1940 investigated Toynbee's claim that the Jews had suppressed his conclusions). During the so-called Palestine Round Table Conference of 1939 Baggallay was responsible for compiling a White Paper on 'Statements made on behalf of His Majesty's Government during the year 1918 in regard to the Future Status of certain parts of the Ottoman Empire'. By judicious cutting and re-arrangement Baggallay very skillfully made a report written by D. G. Hogarth in 1918 say the contrary of what its author had meant to say. Baggallay's activities here amounted to falsification. But it can be said that the fraud which he practised was in furtherance of a policy already adopted. This policy of cutting loose from the Zionist commitment was, however, adopted partly because he and other officials and political figures genuinely believed that the historical record indicated that Palestine had been promised to the Sharif. And this, in a way, is the more serious charge against Baggallay: that his duty as an official required him to have an accurate knowledge of the historical record, and that, out of incompetence, he failed in his duty and thus misled his superiors.

In the course of pursuing through the records the historiography of the correspondence, I of course once again came upon the 'Commitments' memorandum which I had first encountered when writing *England and the Middle East*. It was indeed by Toynbee, as Leonard Stein had told me. But the documents gave almost no indication of the sources on which he had relied, or of the stages by which his argument developed. The fact that, as he stated in an autobiographical passage published in 1967, he had to work in great haste in order to produce the memorandum together with a series of similar memoranda, meant perhaps that he had had little leisure properly to digest or even to track down all the relevant documents, scattered as they were in the files—files to which a card index, still in use at the Public Record Office, would have been a somewhat unreliable guide. In this memorandum he declares, without any doubt or qualification, that Palestine was included in the territories promised to the Sharif. We get a glimpse of his reasoning on the subject in a minute written at the same time in which he says that

Palestine was 'implicitly' included in the Sharif's original demands, and not 'explicitly' excluded by McMahon. This view of McMahon's promises depended on a particular interpretation of McMahon's words in that famous letter. McMahon, as we have seen, was authorized to offer boundaries 'leaving in Arabia purely Arab districts of Aleppo, Damascus, Hama and Homs'. But as we have seen he inexplicably disregarded his instructions, and excluded from his offer 'the portions of Syria lying to the West of Damascus, Homs, Hama and Aleppo'. Both formulations were somewhat vague, and certainly did not allow a boundary to be exactly delimited. To go with his memorandum, Toynbee prepared a map in which he joined the four towns by a line which he proceeded to prolong northwards and southwards in a manner such that McMahon's words were translated into a precise boundary; and further, the line was prolonged southwards in a manner such that the area later known as Palestine was included in the territories promised to the Sharif. What was Toynbee's warrant for doing so? Certainly not McMahon's words, still less the instructions which he should have followed, and which he disregarded. Toynbee, it would seem, had no warrant, but most likely he was relying on the authority of an earlier interpretation which perhaps in the press of urgent business, and working, as he later put it, 'desperately hard against time', he assumed without evidence to be a sound one.

This interpretation occurred in a memorandum produced in April 1916 by the newly established Arab Bureau in Cairo. The memorandum purported to set out and summarize negotiations with the Sharif and their outcome, and it offered the view that 'subject to undefined reservations' relating to French interests McMahon had offered the Sharif an area 'understood to be bounded N by about Lat. 37°, East by the Persian frontier, South by the Persian Gulf and Indian Ocean, West by the Red Sea and the Mediterranean up to about Lat. 33° and beyond by an indefinite line drawn inland West of Damascus, Homs, Hama and Aleppo'. None of this, needless to say, had been mentioned in McMahon's letter, which had deliberately fought shy of any precision, and which contained no mention of Latitude 37° or Latitude 33°. This latter is approximately that of Haifa, and the memorandum was therefore simply asserting on no evidence whatever that the whole of the area traditionally known in the West as Palestine was included in McMahon's offer. Between McMahon's original instructions and this document the gap had become unbridgeable. The memorandum was anonymous, and, again, no evidence in the voluminous archives exists to indicate who was its author, and he will probably remain forever unknown. Its significance is great since it inaugurated more than two decades of official historiography, which constituted a veritable labyrinth in which officials and ministers were hopelessly lost. Hence the title of my book, and the other epigraph which together with the passage by G. M. Young stands at its head. It is drawn from Plutarch's life of Theseus and is to the effect that the Cretans 'will not allow the Labyrinth to have been anything but a prison, which had no other inconvenience than this, that those who were confined there could not escape'. What the study has, in brief, suggested is that (apart from Childs, who had the genuine qualities of an historian, and Baggallay, whom political passion made slightly sinister and who showed some talent as a forger) the officials who had to enquire at various times into the correspondence were simply incompetent in their pursuit of knowledge—knowledge vital to the conduct of policy. Whether this had to do with their native abilities or the quality of their minds is an open question. But the fact is that they were officials—members, that is, of a hierarchical organization in which junior deferred to senior, and had many reasons for doing so; in which *idées reçues* had all the weight of precedent behind them; and in which therefore curiosity and inquisitiveness were discouraged—which, in brief, is not conducive to historiographical enquiry, however important for policy such inquiry might be.

I began by saying that *In the Anglo-Arab Labyrinth* is, according to the classifications of the bibliographers, a work of diplomatic history. But unquestionable as such tidy classifications may seem, they are in fact less cut-and-dried, more problematic and questionable, than they may at first sight appear. The book, it is true, may be considered as a contribution to the history of Anglo-Arab relations, but it is also an enquiry into the genesis of a bunch of letters and of the successive metamorphoses that their meaning underwent during a period of over two decades—metamorphoses such that what the correspondence was understood to signify in 1939 was far removed from what its authors had in mind in 1914-15. Viewed in this light, the first part of the book may be seen in some ways to fall into the same category as J. L. Lowes' *Road to Xanadu*, while its second part belongs to the same genre as C. S. Lewis' *Studies in Words* or Denys Hay's *Europe: The Emergence of an Idea*. It can, in other words, be in all appropriateness classified as an essay in the history of ideas—the kind of history that had been most familiar to me before I found myself writing political history in *England and the Middle East*.

So much for classifications. But for the author himself, the interest of the work was different. It did not primarily lie in its being a contribution, whether negligible or not, to the history of Anglo-Arab relations, or to the history of ideas. As I strove to puzzle out the hasty calculations and ambiguous transactions of agents lost in a murk of cross-purposes, misunderstandings and ulterior motives, I gradually came to see my enterprise as historical in a wider sense. If I were successful, I came to think, the work would speak not only to the amateurs of Anglo-Arab relations or the students of intellectual history. It would take its place—a modest one, assuredly—among those products of the historian's art—of which Maitland's writings, say, or Joseph Levenson's are a supreme example—that seek to restore, for whoever cares to read them, in all its singularity the meaning of thoughts and actions now dead and gone which once upon a time were the designs and choices of living men.

NOTES

Chapter 2

1. G.E. von Grunebaum, *Islam, Essays in the Nature and Growth of a Cultural Tradition*, London, 1955.

2. *Medieval Islam*, Chicago, 1946.

3. D.B. Macdonald, *Development of Muslim Theology, Jurisprudence and Constitutional Theory*, New York, 1903, p. 128.

4. Macdonald, p. 205.

5. D.S. Margoliouth, *Mohammedanism*, Home University Library, 1911, p. 92. The cool and astringent qualities of this book ought to ensure it against oblivion.

6. L. Gardet, *La Cité Musulmane, Vie Sociale et Politique*, Paris, 1954, p. 25.

7. The relevant passages from al-Ghazali are extensively translated by S.G. Haim, in her paper 'Islam and the Theory of Arab Nationalism', *Die Welt des Islams*, N.S., vol. IV, no. 2-3, 1955.

8. 'The Evolution of Government in Early Islam', *Studia Islamica*, vol. IV, 1955.

9. 'An Interpretation of Islamic History', *Cahiers d'Histoire Mondiale*, vol, I, 1953.

10. *Mohammedanism, An Historical Survey*, Home University Library, 1949.

11. Such a view is ably and cogently argued by Abd al-Rahman al-Bazzaz in his pamphlet 'Islam and Arab Nationalism' translated by S.G. Haim in *Die Welt des Islam*, N.S., vol. III, 1954. Gardet, in his book mentioned above seems to subscribe to such a view.

12. D.G. Hogarth, 'Arabs and Turks', printed in an appendix to my book, *England and the Middle East*, 1956.

13. Page 324.

14. To quote his own words: '*Sur bases volontaristes et uniquement positives, on se trouve rejoindre en fait un certain nombre de données susceptibles de fonder une notion démocratique d'autorité. Les textes coraniques qui les formulent ne suffiraient sans doute pas à en faire la dominante obligatoire de la cité souvent livrée dans le passé à l'autocratie et à l'arbitraire des chefs. Mais si des influences nouvelles offrent à ces données comme un dépassement d'elles-mêmes?*' (p. 45).

15. See n. 7 above.

16. Chicago, 1947.

17. Ann K.S. Lambton, *Islamic Society in Persia*, 1954.

Chapter 3

1. Some of Khomeini's speeches and declarations on current issues have been translated into English. The United States Joint Publications Research Service, Arlington, Virginia, has published two selections in translation: #1902, dated 29 January 1979, 'Collection of Speeches, Position Statements by Ayatollah Ruhollah Khomeyni', and #1920, dated 8 March 1979, 'Imam Khomeyni versus Imperialism, Zionism, Reactionism'. The Service has also translated the lectures *Islamic Government* mentioned above, #1897, dated 19 January 1979. This translation is, on the whole, unsatisfactory. A French translation of *Islamic*

Government has also been published recently. See also *Iran Erupts,* ed. Ali-Reza Nobari, published by the Iran-America Documentation Group, Stanford, California, December 1978. This work contains statements by Khomeini and one of his most prominent supporters, Abol Hasan Bani-Sadr, as well as other relevant documents.

2. Two recent noteworthy studies of Shi'ite thought to which I am much indebted are J. Eliash's 'Misconceptions Regarding the Juridicial Status of the Iranian Ulama' in *International Journal of Middle East Studies,* vol. 10, no. 1 (February 1979) and Said Amir Arjomand's 'Religion, Political Action and Legitimate Domination in Shi'ite Iran' in *European Journal of Sociology,* vol. 20, no. 1 (May 1979).

Chapter 7

1. *Archives du Ministère des Affaires Etrangères,* Paris, Série E. Levant, Syrie-Liban vol. 22, memorandum by de Caix, *'Note sur la politique de l'accord avec Feysal,'* January 26, 1920, in particular fos. 74–77.

2. Série E. Levant. Syrie-Liban vol. 31, *'Esquisse de l'organisation de la Syrie sous le Mandat français,'* fos. 44–45.

3. Serie E. Syrie-Liban, vol. 200. I am grateful to Mr. M. Zamir for drawing my attention to this report.

Chapter 8

1. C.O. 733/297, 75156 Pt. IV, folio 180. For a discussion of Wauchope's relations with the Mufti before 1936 see Y. Porath, *The Palestinian Arab National Movement 1929-1939,* 1977, pp. 112–118. In thinking that he could rely on the Mufti's goodwill Wauchope, as Porath shows, was clearly guilty of a misjudgment.

2. F.O. 371/20023, E 5434/94/31, Wauchope's despatch of 22 August 1936, printed in appendix to memorandum by Ormsby Gore, 26 August, circulated to the cabinet, C.P. 225 (36).

3. C.O. 733/311 75528/6, no. 62, contains the views of the Palestine police in the Mufti's involvement in the violence.

4. H.J. Simson, *British Rule, and Rebellion,* 1937, p. 196. Brigadier Simson was on the staff of General Dill, who assumed command of the troops in Palestine in the autumn of 1936. On the involvement of the Mufti, and the Supreme Muslim Council and the Arab Higher Committee (over both of which he presided) in the rebellion from its early stages, see Porath, op.cit.pp. 181, 186 and 193–199.

5. Wauchope's despatch of 3 June 1936, C.O. 733/297, 75156 part II, quoted in M. J. Cohen, *Policies and Politics in Palestine 1936-39,* unpublished Ph.D. dissertation, University of London, 1971.

6. C.O. 733/297, 75156, pt.V. Criticism by the British military authorities of Wauchope's policy and behaviour is discussed in Michael J. Cohen, 'Sir Arthur Wauchope, the Army, and the Rebellion in Palestine, 1936', *Middle Eastern Studies,* vol. 9 no. 1, (January 1973). See particularly pp. 26 and 28–30.

7. F.O. 371/20063, E2423/608/25, Ryan's despatch No. 28, Jedda, 1 May 1936.

8. Passages quoted in a letter from C. Weizmann to Lord Peel, Chairman of the Royal Commission on Palestine, Jerusalem, 19 Jan 1937 C.O. 733/342F. 75550/9A21 and reprinted in *The Letters and Papers* of Chaim Weizmann, vol. 18, series A, New Brunswick and Jerusalem, 1979, p. 5. Part of this passage is also

quoted from the Leo Kohn Papers in Michael J. Cohen, *Palestine: Retreat from the Mandate,* 1978, pp. 29–30.

9. The course of Anglo-Saudi exchanges in the summer of 1936 can be followed in C.O. 733/314, 75528/44 Pt. 1.

10. C.O. 733/297, 75156. Pt. 1V, Wauchope's letter to Parkinson, 21 August 1936; F.O. 371/20023, E 5434/94/31, copy of Wauchope's despatch of 22 August, with Peirse's recommendations included in Cabinet paper CP 225(36), quoted above.

11. The exchanges relating to Nuri's attempted mediation in August 1936 may be followed in two Cabinet Papers, C.P. 227 and C.P. 235 in Cab. 24/264.

12. Wauchope's telegram of 31 August, no. 8 in C.P. 235 cited immediately above, Cab. 24/264.

13. Cohen, *Policies and Politics*, pp. 86 ff. For a very abbreviated version see Ibid., *Retreat from the Mandate,* p. 25.

14. Cab. 23/85, 51(36)9, 52(36)5 and 56(36)8.

15. C.O. 733/314, 75528/44 Pt.II. See also Cohen, Policies and Politics..., pp. 101–2 and Porath, *op. cit.,* p. 212.

16. F.O. 371/20025, E 5779/94/31.

17. F.O. 371/20025, E5915/95/31, Cranborne's telegram 111 and 112 (L/N), Geneva, 19 September 1936.

18. F.O. 371/20026, E5985/94/31.

19. C.O. 733/314 75528/44, Pt.II, cited above.

20. F.O. 371/20026, E 6013/94/31 for record of meeting of Ministers on 22 September 1936.

21. F.O. 371/20026, E6010 and 6062/94/31.

22. F.O. 371/20026, E6010, 6196 and 6256/94/31, and F.O. 371/20027, E6296/94/31, for Rendel's minutes and exchanges with the Colonial Office, the Embassy in Baghdad and the Legation in Jedda, 25 September–10 October 1936. Text of published appeal in Porath, *op.cit.,* p. 214.

23. F.O. 371/20027, E6350 and E6415/94/31, for Rendel's fears lest martial law be declared and his negotiations with the Colonial and the War Office.

24. Simson, *op.cit.,* pp. 284–5, and Porath, *op.cit.,* p. 215.

25. Simson, *op.cit.,* pp. 289-90, and ch. XVIII passim.

26. Cab. 23/86, 60 (36) 5.

27. F.O. 371/20029, E7297/94/31.

28. C.O. 733/713, 75528/93, Ormsby Gore to Battershill (Officer Administering the Government of Palestine), 8 September 1937, quoted in Porath, *op.cit.* pp. 215-16.

29. F.O. 371/20811 E4597/22/31, telegram from Scott, Baghdad, 3 August 1937, Baggallay's minute, 9 August, and letter to the Colonial Office; *loc.cit.,* E4687, telegram from Scott, 11 August, F.O. 371/20812, E4782, letter from Downie, Colonial Office, 18 August, concerning the circumstances leading to Hall's declaration.

30. F.O. 371/20814, E5451/22/31.

31. C.O. 733/341, 75528/41, extract from Ormsby Gore's letter, 10 August 1937, to his Principal Private Secretary. The file has a minute by Downie, 13 August: 'I have again examined the rather ghastly files on the subject of the intervention of the Arab Kings'.

32. F.O. 371/20814, E5454/22/31. Memorandum by Rendel, 13 September 1937.

33. Sir George Rendel, *The Sword and the Olive,* 1957, p. 49.

34. F.O. 371/19983, E5815/3334/65, Rendel's memorandum of 14 Septem-

ber 1936, Vansittart's minute of 15 September and Eden's minute of 16 September.

35. F.O. 371/20804, E317/22/31, Rendel's minute of 14 January 1937.

36. F.O. 371/20804, E317 and E541/22/31.

37. Porath, *op.cit.,* p. 211, quoting a memorandum by Rendel of 1 September 1936.

38. F.O. 371/20805, E2012/22/31 for Rendel's memorandum of 12 April 1937, and F.O. 371/20806, E2202/22/31 for his letter to Downie of 28 April.

39. Cab. 51/3, for 49th meeting of the Standing Official Sub-Committee, 1 February 1937; Cab. 51/4, for 56th meeting, 8 February 1938; F.O. 371/21816, E1433/150/91, for Rendel's minute, 12 March 1938.

40. F.O. 371/20825, E1203/976/31, Colonial Office letter and enclosures, 25 February 1937, and minutes of 26 and 27 February.

41. F.O. 371/20825, E5644/976/31, Colonial Office letter, 27 September 1937, with enclosures, with minutes by Brenan and Rendel, 1 and 5 October.

42. F.O. 371/20818, E6320/22/31, letter from Colonial Office and enclosures, 27 October 1937, Rendel's minute, 3 November and reply to Colonial Office, 8 November, drafted by Rendel and approved by Vansittart. Shuckburgh's and Downie's minutes on the reply, 16 November, are in C.O. 732/79180.

43. F.O. 371/20817, E6063/22/31, Trott's despatch no. 152 Jedda, 28 September 1937.

44. F.O. 371/20812, E4921/22/31, Trott's despatch no. 134, Jedda, 3 August 1937.

45. F.O. 371/20817, E6063 cited above, despatch to Trott no. 421, 4 November 1937.

46. F.O. 371/20820, E6815/22/31, Trott's telegram no. 86, Jedda, 18 November 1937; minutes and Rendel's cancelled drafts, 25 November–1 December.

47. F.O. 371/20823, E7577/22/31.

48. F.O. 371/21869, E7624/1/31, Bullard's despatch no. 218, Jedda, 28 November 1938; Halifax's letter of appreciation, 19 January 1939.

49. F.O. 371/20804, E921/22/31.

50. See R. Melka, 'Nazi Germany and the Palestine Question', *Middle Eastern Studies*, vol. 5, no. 3 (October 1969). This article brings out the fact that Nazi anti-British propaganda directed towards the Arabs got into its stride and became most popular precisely when the British government seemed unsure of itself and open to pressure.

51. F.O. 371/21873, E788/10/31. The quotations from Cawthorn's memorandum of 9 February 1938 are at fos. 154, 162, 166 and 168. Baggallay's minute is of 21 March.

52. F.O. 371/20819, E6483/22/31, Rendel's minute of 4 November 1937 on a memorandum by him of the same date: 'Palestine: Further proposals for strong action.'

53. F.O. 371/20027, E6523/94/31; F.O. 371/20028, E6657 and E6743; and F.O. 371/20029, E7185.

54. F.O. 371/20818, E6317/22/31.

55. F.O. 371/20024, E5504/94/31, minute by Sterndale Bennett, 1 September 1936, recording Rendel's views.

56. F.O. 371/20027, E6367/94/31.

57. F.O. 371/20027, E6415/94/31.

58. F.O. 371/20025, Rendel's minute of 17 September 1936 on report of an interview between M. Shertok of the Jewish Agency and two Royal Air Force intelligence officers; F.O. 371/20804, E317/22/31, Rendel's minute of 14 January 1937.

59. F.O. 371/20818, E6312/22/31, Rendel's minute on Colonial Office letter of 26 October 1937; letter to Sir Eric Phipps, Paris, 9 November.

60. F.O. 371/21879, E4464/10/31, minute of 2 August 1938.

61. F.O. 371/20817, E6198/22/31.

62. F.O. 371/20818, E.6313/22/31.

63. F.O. 371/20819, E.6492/22/31, minute of 30 October 1937 initialled C.F.A.W.; see also minute by Rendel in ibid., E.6569 and in F.O. 371/20818, E.6318.

64. F.O. 371/20819, E.6635/22/31, Rendel's minute, 12 November 1937, on Rome telegram of the previous day; F.O. 371/20821, E.7019, Rendel's minute, 30 November 1937, on Rome telegram of 27 November. See also F.O. 371/20820, E. 6820, where his follower, Baggallay, adopts the same stance in regard to baseless rumours about a supposed ultimatum issued by Ibn Sa'ud: 'it may become the truth soon'.

65. F.O. 371/20823, E7537/22/31, minute of 29 December 1937.

66. F.O. 371/20819, E6557/22/31, Rendel's minute of 28 October 1937; F.O. 371/20822, E7230, annotation by Rendel on a minute of 10 December 1937 by Brenan; F.O. 371/20820, E6795, Rendel's minute of 13 November 1937; F.O. 371/21873, E724/10/31, Rendel's minute of 11 February 1938. In this respect, too, Rendel's views became the received doctrine in the Foreign Office. Commenting in July 1938 on a statement by MacDonald that the organization of the terror campaign in Palestine had its centre in the Mufti, Baxter wrote that while it was true that the Mufti took a leading part in the terror campaign in Palestine, 'we should not however allow ourselves to attach too much importance to his activities, which are more a symptom than the ultimate cause of the Palestine disorders'. See F.O. 371/21879, E4454/10/31, Baxter's minute of 26 July 1938.

67. F.O. 371/19980, E3039/381/85.

68. F.O. 371/20804, E275/22/31, MacKereth's letter to Rendel, 7 January 1937, Sterndale Bennett's and Rendel's minutes, 18 January. On the history and historiography of the McMahon-Husayn Correspondence see E. Kedourie, *In the Anglo-Arab-Labyrinth*, 1976; see, in particular pp. 261-3, for Rendel's belief that it was a 'fact' that Palestine had been the subject of 'contradictory promises'.

69. F.O. 371/20817, E5918/22/31.

70. F.O. 371/20816, E5875/22/31.

71. F.O. 371/20807, E3054/22/31. MacKereth's despatch was a response to a despatch from Lampson, Cairo, of 8 April previous (F.O. 371/20806, E2158) in which Lampson affirmed that Palestine remained 'the essential problem', and Britain was declared 'to be at the crossways leading either to Arab cooperation with us against Italy or to eventual Arab cooperation with Italy against us'.

72. F.O. 371/20808, E4052/22/91, MacKereth's despatch of 10 July 1937, and his letter to Rendel of the same date.

73. F.O. 371/20814, E5515/22/31, MacKereth's memorandum of 14 September 1937.

74. F.O. 371/20818, E6253/22/31, MacKereth's despatch, 18 October 1937, Rendel's minute, 26 October and draft despatch to MacKereth, sent on 28 October.

75. F.O. 371/20823, E7638/22/31, Rendel's minute, 29 December 1937, regarding request by Palestine government for MacKereth to be allowed to visit Jerusalem; F.O. 371/20818, E6402, minute by Rendel, 1 November, on MacKereth's telegram relating to the bandit leader Muhammad al-Ashmar. See also F.O. 371/20819, E6465 and 6486.

76. F.O. 371/20822, E7385/22/31, copy of MacKereth's letter to Cox, Amman, 28 November 1937.

77. F.O. 371/20818, E6313 cited above, Rendel's minute of 28 October 1937.

78. F.O. 371/20819, E6559/22/31 Rendel's minute of 12 and 13 November

1937 on MacKereth's despatch of 30 October.

79. F.O. 371/20818, E6291/22/31, Rendel's minute of 3 November 1937 where he declares that this was the scheme he had more than once put forward and would continue to press.

80. F.O. 371/20807, E3330/22/31, Rendel's minute, 18 June 1937; Oliphant's and Vansittart's, 21 June; and Eden's, 22 June.

81. F.O. 371/20810, E4297/22/31, Rendel's memorandum, 15 July 1937.

82. F.O. 371/20807, E3427/22/31, Rendel's memorandum of 23 June 1937.

83. F.O. 371/20808, E3613/22/31, Cabinet conclusions 30 June 1937; F.O. 371/20807, E3531, text of Ormsby Gore's Cabinet paper on proposed statement by government, 25 June, with Rendel's amendments in margin, and Rendel's minutes of 28 June and 3 July.

84. F.O. 371/20818, E6325/22/31, Rendel's and Oliphant's minutes, 28 October 1937; Rendel's draft, 9 November.

85. F.O. 371/20809, E4161/22/31, Rendel's memorandum, 9 July 1937.

86. F.O. 371/20814, E5501/22/31.

87. Porath, op. cit., pp. 229-30 and 235-6; F.O. 371/20810, E4444/22/31 for copy of Colonial Office draft telegram to Wauchope, 30 July 1937, suggesting cancellation of order to arrest Mufti.

88. F.O. 371/20808, E3919 and 3977/22/31, Clerk Kerr's telegrams from Baghdad, 10 and 13 July 1937, and telegram in reply, 16 July; F.O. 371/20809, E4068 draft telegram to Baghdad reporting interview between Eden and Iraqi Minister in London. The Minister said that Hikmat's statement was made for internal reasons, and that in his own view the principle of partition was the only solution to the problem. This latter statement was crossed out in blue ink [by Rendel?]. F.O. 371/20811, E4556, extracts from letter from Wauchope to Parkinson, Jerusalem, 14 July.

89. F.O. 371/20810, E4416/22/31.

90. F.O. 371/20810, E4390/22/31.

91. F.O. 371/20808, E3831/22/31.

92. F.O. 371/20808, E3854/22/31.

93. F.O. 371/20808, E3885 and 4034/22/31; Rendel's minute on Bullard's second telegram, 16 July 1937 in E4034.

94. F.O. 371/20809, E4063/22/31.

95. F.O. 371/20809, E4167/22/31. The Saudi Minister's similar démarches in the summer of 1937 are in F.O. 371/20813, E5390/22/31 and F.O. 371/20814, E5477/22/31.

96. F.O. 371/20818, E6322/22/31, Rendel's memorandum and minutes, 20 October 1937, followed by Oliphant's and Vansittart's 27 and 28 October; F.O. 371/21837, E476/476/65.

97. F.O. 371/20812, E4881 and 4898/22/31 communication from Saudi charge d'affaires 18 August, and memorandum of conversation with Hafez Wahba by Baggallay, 20 August 1937, with minutes; F.O. 371/20816, E5952, Rendel's, Oliphant's and Vansittart's minutes, 23-25 October; F.O. 371/20820, E6854, Baghdad despatch, 5 November 1937, enclosing Vyvyan Holt's memorandum.

98. F.O. 371/20811, E4556/22/31, cited above.

99. F.O. 371/21862, E 71/1/31.

100. F.O. 371/21876, E3123/10/31, copy of Bullard's despatch, Jedda, 1 May 1938, to MacMichael, Jerusalem; F.O. 371/21877, E3325/10/31, copy of telegram MacMichael, Jerusalem, 3 June 1938, to Colonial Office; F.O. 371/21878, E3791/10/31, Bullard's despatch, Jedda, 6 June 1938.

101. F.O. 371/20808, E4051/22/31, Lampson's telegram, 15 July 1937.

102. C.O. 733/312/75528/13, copy of Lampson's telegram of 8 July 1936, and Williams's minute, 27 July.

103. E. Kedourie, *The Chatham House Version* (1970), pp. 79-80, quoting Foreign Office telegram to Lampson, 16 November 1936.

104. F.O. 371/20810, E4320/22/31, Lampson's telegram, 25 July 1937, Rendel's and Vansittart's minutes, 27 July.

.105. F.O. 371/20819, E6568/22/31, Kelly's despatch, 27 October 1937; Rendel's minute, 12 November.

106. C.O. 733/354, 75730, Part I, Martin's minute of 19 November 1937, on Lampson's telegram of 16 November previous; Martin's undated minute on an anti-partition memorandum by the Foreign Office of 22 November.

107. F.O. 371/20821, E6900/22/31, minute by Rendel, 28 November 1937.

108. F.O. 371/20820, E6882/22/31, minute by Rendel, 9 November 1937.

109. F.O. 371/20807, E3121/22/31, minute by Rendel, 7 June 1937.

110. F.O. 371/20816, E5947/22/31, minute by Rendel, 15 October 1937.

111. Cab. 24/272, C.P. 269(37).

112. F.O. 371/20819, E6470/22/31, Rendel's memorandum, 3 November 1937, and Vansittart's minute, 5 November. F.O. 371/20820, E6801, Rendel's minute of 22 November.

113. F.O. 371/20816, E5964/22/31, Rendel's memorandum and minutes, 14 October 1937, Campbell's and Vansittart's minutes, 15 and 16 October.

114. F.O. 371/20820, E6836/22/31. Earlier drafts by Rendel, with corrections by Eden in E6750 and E6773.

115. F.O. 371/20821, E7096/22/31, Rendel's draft and Vansittart's shortened version, 7 December 1937.

116. F.O. 371/20816, E5964/22/31, cited above.

117. F.O. 371/20820, E6696/22/31.

118. Cab.24/273, CP.289(37), Ormsby Gore's Cabinet paper, 'Policy in Palestine,' 1 December 1937.

119. F.O. 371/21862, E559/1/31, copy of Ormsby Gore's letter to Neville Chamberlain, 9 January 1938 and minutes.

120. F.O. 371/20822, E7298/22/31, Cabinet conclusions 46(37)5. The Secretary of State for India read at this meeting Colonel Dickson's memorandum on Ibn Sa'ud's views about the Jews printed in chapter 5. F.O. 371/21862, E1653/1/31, text of Ormsby Gore's 'Secret and Personal' letter to Sir John Woodhead, Chairman of Partition Commission.

121. Rendel's campaign may be followed in F.O. 371/20822, E7297, 7315 and 7384/22/31 and in F.O. 371/20823, E7536/22/31.

122. F.O. 371/20823, E7537/22/31, Rendel's minute of 29 December 1937.

123. F.O. 371/21862, E1439 and 2254/1/31.

124. F.O. 371/21880, E5325/10/31, Baggallay's minute of 15 September 1938.

125. F.O. 371/21865, E6379/1/31.

Chapter 10

1. For one example see my *Arabic Political Memoirs, and other studies* (1974), pp. 195-6.

2. The most modern and fashionable economists of course enjoy the advantage denied to Hammarskjöld and Keynes, of combining in their persons the two separate attributes which this word denotes, the mathematical and the astrological.

3. Daniel P. Moynihan, 'The United States in Opposition', *Commentary* (March 1975).

Chapter 13

1. The Report was produced by a committee that included, among others, Professor Zbigniew Brzezinski and Professor William Quandt (who became in the Carter administration respectively, Assistant to the President for National Security Affairs, and Office Director for Middle East and North African Affairs at the National Security Council).

Chapter 16

1. Text of the Mudros armistice is reproduced in Gwynne Dyer, 'The Turkish Armistice of 1918: 2—A Lost Opportunity', *Middle Eastern Studies*, vol. 8, no. 3 (Oct. 1972), pp. 340–1.

2. Text of communiqué in F.O. 371/4166, 7853/740.

3. The article is reprinted in Stanley and Rodelle Weintraub, eds., *Evolution of a Revolt*, 1968. The quotation is at p. 35.

4. *The Economist*, May 1, 1976, p. 6, col. 3.

5. Lawrence's report, published in the *Arab Bulletin* of 18 Nov. 1916 is reprinted in his *Secret Despatches from Arabia*, 1939; the quotation is at p. 21. In the *Times* article mentioned above Lawrence also gave an account, presumably also derived from Faysal, of the unsuccessful attack on Medina; Weintraub, *op. cit.,* pp. 34–5.

6. Details in Sir Reginald Wingate's first despatch on military operations in the Hijaz, dated 25 June 1917. A proof of the three despatches on these operations which were eventually published in *The London Gazette* is conveniently filed in F.O. 371/4166, 86025/740.

7. See Wingate's first despatch, *loc. cit.,* and an interesting letter sent to him by Sultan Husayn Kamil, Cairo, 1916, copy in Grey Papers F.O. 800/48, folios 528-30. Lawrence's sarcasm at the expense of these troops (*Secret Despatches,* p. 24) seems misplaced.

8. F.O. 882/26, *Arab Bulletin*, no. 65, 1917, p. 397.

9. Service historique de l'Armée, Paris, Papers of the Mission militaire au Hedjaz, 17N498, Millet, Djedda, to Defrance, Cairo, tel. no. 66 (part I), 18 Feb. 1917.

10. *Loc. cit.* 17N498, Brémond, Djedda, to Defrance, tel. no. 81, 1 March 1917. Brémond describes here Sharifian views and ambitions at that juncture. In conversation, Abdullah said that the plan was for Husayn and his youngest son Zayd to reside in Medina, Ali would govern Mecca, Faysal would get Syria, and Abdullah himself Mesopotamia. Abdullah further said that there were only two great Muslim leaders remaining: his father and Imam Yahya of the Yemen.

11. *Loc. cit.,* 17N499, St. Quentin, Cairo, to Bercher, Djedda, tel. no. 205, 5 Nov. 1917.

12. F. O. 371/4166, 86025/740 cited above.

13. *Secret Despatches*, p. 111.

14. F. O. 882/7, C. E. Wilson, Jeddah, to Arab Bureau, 6 July 1917, enclosing copies of letters to Husayn and his sons on the subject of Medina.

15. *Secret Despatches* pp. 145–7, reproducing Lawrence's report published in the *Arab Bulletin*, 24 Dec. 1917.

16. Service historique de l'Armee 17N499, tel. from St. Quentin, Cairo, no. 21 to Commandant Cousse, Jeddah, 6 Mar. 1918. St. Quentin reported that at the Arab Bureau, *'on a l'impression qu'Abdalla consacre une bonne partie des subsides anglais à essayer de soudoyer la clientèle d'Ibn Saoud et néglige de payer régulièrement ses propres contingents donnant ainsi prise à la propagande turque'.*

17. F. O. 882/20, folios 180–84, Garland's interview with Fakhri on 6 April 1919. The report on Ali's and Abdullah's operations appeared in the *Arab Bulletin* no. 80, 26 Feb. 1918, pp. 57–60. F. O. 882/27.

18. F. O. 882/27, *Arab Bulletin* no. 80, *loc. cit.*

19. F. O. 882/22, folios 143–152, 'Translation of personal sketch of King Hussein and conditions in the Hejaz, written by the Editor of the "Qibla" (Ahmed Shakir Karmi)'. Undated, *circa* June 1919.

20. *Secret Despatches* p. 39, 'Nationalism among the Tribesmen' published in the *Arab Bulletin*, 26 Nov. 1916.

21. F. O. 882/22, *loc. cit.*, and report by Tewfik Aboucassem, the Syrian manager of the Ottoman Bank branch in Jedda enclosed with despatch no. 319 from Defrance, French Minister in Cairo, Archives du ministère des Affaires Etrangères, Paris, Guerre 1914–18, vol. 1684.

22. Service historique de l'Armée, 17N498, file 12/1, report no. 29 by Captain Depui, 24 Mar. 1918. On Depui, known also as 'Capitaine Ibrahim' see Georges Catroux, *Deux missions en Moyen-Orient*, Paris 1958, pp. 183–6.

23. F. O. 371/4166, 86025/740, despatch of 27 Dec. 1918.

24. F. O. 371/3393, 177593/7659, translation of Fakhri's letter enclosed with Wingate's despatch no. 232, Cairo, 30 Sept. 1918; translation of Husayn's earlier letter is enclosed with Wingate's despatch no. 202, 31 Aug., *ibid.*, 163511/7659.

25. F. O. 371/3393, 170870, 174125 and 175126/7659.

26. Dyer, *loc. cit.* p. 328.

27. F. O. 371/3416, file 187338, which contains the various telegrams summarized above.

28. F. O. 371/4166, 81504/740, copy of Wingate's letter of 20 Feb. 1919 to Lynden-Bell, War Office.

29. F. O. 882/7, Garland to Wilson, El Jafr, 29 Dec. 1918.

30. F. O. 371/3416, 213617/187338, Wingate's telegram no. 1985, Cairo, 30 Dec. 1918. See also the translation of Captain Mehmed Zia's report to the Ottoman Minister of War, Yanbo, 2 Jan. 1919, enclosed with Wingate's despatch no. 19, Cairo, 10 Jan. 1919, F.O. 371/4166, 12838/740.

31. F. O. 882/20 Captain A. F. Wiggin's report to Director, Arab Bureau, 18 Jan. 1919, sent to London with Cheetham's despatch no. 39, Cairo, 24 Jan. F. O. 371/4166, 21996/740.

32. F. O. 882/7, Garland's report from El Jafr, 29 Dec. 1918, cited above.

33. F. O. 882/20, Bassett to Wilson, Bir Darwish, 17 Jan. 1919.

34. F. O. 371/4208, 100945/17610; *Arab Bulletin*, no. 110, 30 April 1919, report on surrender of Medina; F. O. 371/4166, 12952/740, copy of telegram from Hijaz Operations Staff to War Office, 16 Jan. 1919; F. O. 882/20 folios 167–69 for translation of Medina surrender agreement.

35. F. O. 882/20, 'Interview with General Fakhri Eddin Pasha by Captain Garland', cited above.

36. F. O. 686/43, Vickery to Arab Bureau, Jeddah, 7 June 1920.

37. F. O. 882/23, Bassett to Arab Bureau, Jeddah, 27 May 1919, forwarding Sadik Yahya's report.

38. A. E., série E. Levant, Arabie, vol. 3, 'Rapport mensuel 31 Janvier–28

Février 1919', 2 Mar. 1919.

39. F. O. 371/4167, 101307/740, enclosed with Allenby's despatch no. 304, Cairo, 26 June 1919.

40. A. E., série E, Levant, Arabie, vol. 3, Picot's telegram no. 276, Beirut, 19 Feb. 1919.

41. *loc. cit.,* Arabie, vol. 5, extracts from letters dated 4 and 5 June 1919 from Benslimane, forwarded by Catroux from Jedda. Vol. 4 contains the Hijaz report for April 1919 written by Depui which declared that looting was still going on in Medina.

42. *loc. cit.,* Arabie, vol. 9.

43. F. O. 371/4167, 101307/740, cited above, Young's minute of 12 Aug. 1919. On the Armenian massacre in Aleppo in February 1919 see E. Kedourie, *England and the Middle East*, 1956, pp. 157–58. The incidents at Dar'a and Damascus are of course better known than the Aleppo massacre.

INDEX